Health Literacy in Context—Settings, Media, and Populations

Health Literacy in Context—Settings, Media, and Populations

Special Issue Editors

Don Nutbeam
Diane Levin-Zamir
Gill Rowlands

MDPI • Basel • Beijing • Wuhan • Barcelona • Belgrade

Special Issue Editors

Don Nutbeam
University of Sydney
Australia

Diane Levin-Zamir
University of Haifa School of Public Health
Israel

Gill Rowlands
Newcastle University
UK

Editorial Office
MDPI
St. Alban-Anlage 66
4052 Basel, Switzerland

This is a reprint of articles from the Special Issue published online in the open access journal *International Journal of Environmental Research and Public Health* (ISSN 1660-4601) from 2017 to 2018 (available at: https://www.mdpi.com/journal/ijerph/special_issues/health-literacy).

For citation purposes, cite each article independently as indicated on the article page online and as indicated below:

LastName, A.A.; LastName, B.B.; LastName, C.C. Article Title. *Journal Name* **Year**, *Article Number*, Page Range.

ISBN 978-3-03897-471-0 (Pbk)
ISBN 978-3-03897-472-7 (PDF)

© 2019 by the authors. Articles in this book are Open Access and distributed under the Creative Commons Attribution (CC BY) license, which allows users to download, copy and build upon published articles, as long as the author and publisher are properly credited, which ensures maximum dissemination and a wider impact of our publications.

The book as a whole is distributed by MDPI under the terms and conditions of the Creative Commons license CC BY-NC-ND.

Contents

About the Special Issue Editors ix

Don Nutbeam, Diane Levin-Zamir and Gill Rowlands
Health Literacy in Context
Reprinted from: *International Journal of Environmental Research and Public Health* **2018**, *15*, 2657, doi:10.3390/ijerph15122657 1

Jany Rademakers and Monique Heijmans
Beyond Reading and Understanding: Health Literacy as the Capacity to Act
Reprinted from: *International Journal of Environmental Research and Public Health* **2018**, *15*, 1676, doi:10.3390/ijerph15081676 4

Bas Geboers, Sijmen A. Reijneveld, Jaap A. R. Koot and Andrea F. de Winter
Moving towards a Comprehensive Approach for Health Literacy Interventions: The Development of a Health Literacy Intervention Model
Reprinted from: *International Journal of Environmental Research and Public Health* **2018**, *15*, 1268, doi:10.3390/ijerph15061268 16

Chiara Lorini, Francesca Ierardi, Letizia Bachini, Martina Donzellini, Fabrizio Gemmi and Guglielmo Bonaccorsi
The Antecedents and Consequences of Health Literacy in an Ecological Perspective: Results from an Experimental Analysis
Reprinted from: *International Journal of Environmental Research and Public Health* **2018**, *15*, 798, doi:10.3390/ijerph15040798 27

Emee Vida Estacio, Mike Oliver, Beth Downing, Judy Kurth and Joanne Protheroe
Effective Partnership in Community-Based Health Promotion: Lessons from the Health Literacy Partnership
Reprinted from: *International Journal of Environmental Research and Public Health* **2017**, *14*, 1550, doi:10.3390/ijerph14121550 41

Diane Levin-Zamir and Isabella Bertschi
Media Health Literacy, eHealth Literacy, and the Role of the Social Environment in Context
Reprinted from: *International Journal of Environmental Research and Public Health* **2018**, *15*, 1643, doi:10.3390/ijerph15081643 49

Anita Trezona, Gill Rowlands and Don Nutbeam
Progress in Implementing National Policies and Strategies for Health Literacy—What Have We Learned so Far?
Reprinted from: *International Journal of Environmental Research and Public Health* **2018**, *15*, 1554, doi:10.3390/ijerph15071554 61

Gill Rowlands, David Whitney and Graham Moon
Developing and Applying Geographical Synthetic Estimates of Health Literacy in GP Clinical Systems
Reprinted from: *International Journal of Environmental Research and Public Health* **2018**, *15*, 1709, doi:10.3390/ijerph15081709 78

Jonathan O'Hara, Crystal McPhee, Sarity Dodson, Annie Cooper, Carol Wildey,
Melanie Hawkins, Alexandra Fulton, Vicki Pridmore, Victoria Cuevas, Mathew Scanlon,
Patricia M. Livingston, Richard H. Osborne and Alison Beauchamp
Barriers to Breast Cancer Screening among Diverse Cultural Groups in Melbourne, Australia
Reprinted from: *International Journal of Environmental Research and Public Health* **2018**, *15*, 1677, doi:10.3390/ijerph15081677 . . . . **86**

Verna B. McKenna, Jane Sixsmith and Margaret M. Barry
A Qualitative Study of the Development of Health Literacy Capacities of Participants Attending a Community-Based Cardiovascular Health Programme
Reprinted from: *International Journal of Environmental Research and Public Health* **2018**, *15*, 1157, doi:10.3390/ijerph15061157 . . . . **99**

Linda Stein, Maud Bergdahl, Kjell Sverre Pettersen and Jan Bergdahl
Effects of the Conceptual Model of Health Literacy as a Risk: A Randomised Controlled Trial in a Clinical Dental Context
Reprinted from: *International Journal of Environmental Research and Public Health* **2018**, *15*, 1630, doi:10.3390/ijerph15081630 . . . . **118**

Luísa Campos, Pedro Dias, Ana Duarte, Elisa Veiga, Cláudia Camila Dias and Filipa Palha
Is It Possible to "Find Space for Mental Health" in Young People? Effectiveness of a School-Based Mental Health Literacy Promotion Program
Reprinted from: *International Journal of Environmental Research and Public Health* **2018**, *15*, 1426, doi:10.3390/ijerph15071426 . . . . **129**

Claudia König, Mette V. Skriver, Kim M. Iburg and Gillian Rowlands
Understanding Educational and Psychosocial Factors Associated with Alcohol Use among Adolescents in Denmark; Implications for Health Literacy Interventions
Reprinted from: *International Journal of Environmental Research and Public Health* **2018**, *15*, 1671, doi:10.3390/ijerph15081671 . . . . **141**

Suzanne D. Thomas, Sandra C. Mobley, Jodi L. Hudgins, Donald E. Sutherland,
Sandra B. Inglett and Brittany L. Ange
Conditions and Dynamics That Impact Maternal Health Literacy among High Risk Prenatal-Interconceptional Women
Reprinted from: *International Journal of Environmental Research and Public Health* **2018**, *15*, 1383, doi:10.3390/ijerph15071383 . . . . **153**

Stana Ubavić, Nataša Bogavac-Stanojević, Aleksandra Jović-Vraneš and Dušanka Krajnović
Understanding of Information about Medicines Use among Parents of Pre-School Children in Serbia: Parental Pharmacotherapy Literacy Questionnaire (PTHL-SR)
Reprinted from: *International Journal of Environmental Research and Public Health* **2018**, *15*, 977, doi:10.3390/ijerph15050977 . . . . **169**

Don Nutbeam, Diane Levin-Zamir and Gill Rowlands
Do Low Income Youth of Color See *"The Bigger Picture"* When Discussing Type 2 Diabetes: A Qualitative Evaluation of a Public Health Literacy Campaign
Reprinted from: *International Journal of Environmental Research and Public Health* **2018**, *15*, 840, doi:10.3390/ijerph15050840 . . . . **182**

Maricel G. Santos, Anu L. Gorukanti, Lina M. Jurkunas and Margaret A. Handley
The Health Literacy of U.S. Immigrant Adolescents: A Neglected Research Priority in a Changing World
Reprinted from: *International Journal of Environmental Research and Public Health* **2018**, *15*, 2108, doi:10.3390/ijerph15102108 196

Angela Chang and Peter J. Schulz
The Measurements and an Elaborated Understanding of Chinese eHealth Literacy (C-eHEALS) in Chronic Patients in China
Reprinted from: *International Journal of Environmental Research and Public Health* **2018**, *15*, 1553, doi:10.3390/ijerph15071553 214

Pedro Dias, Luísa Campos, Helena Almeida and Filipa Palha
Mental Health Literacy in Young Adults: Adaptation and Psychometric Properties of the Mental Health Literacy Questionnaire
Reprinted from: *International Journal of Environmental Research and Public Health* **2018**, *15*, 1318, doi:10.3390/ijerph15071318 226

About the Special Issue Editors

Don Nutbeam is a Professor of Public Health at the University of Sydney, and Principal Senior Advisor at the Sax Institute. His career has spanned positions in universities, government, health services and international organisations including WHO and the World Bank. He is a public health scientist with research interests in the social and behavioural determinants of health, and in the development and evaluation of public health interventions.

Diane Levin-Zamir, Associate Professor of Public Health and National Director of Health Education and Promotion, Clalit Health Services, Israel. She specializes in health promotion practice, policy and research with particular interest in community primary care, children, adolescents and elderly, people with chronic conditions, hospital and media settings, media/digital health literacy, measuring health literacy on the population level, immigrants and cultural appropriateness. She was one of the founders of the Israel Association of Health Promoters and Educators, is actively involved in international policy and research initiatives on health literacy of organizations including the WHO, and founded and co-chairs the IUHPE Global Working Group on Health Literacy. She has published extensively on various aspects of health literacy and health promotion, including co-editing books, published in a variety of languages.

Gillian Rowlands is a General Practitioner and a Professor in the Institute of Health and Society at Newcastle University. Her main research interests are in the area of health inequalities, particularly the role of health literacy in health, and the role of GPs in identifying and addressing the problems faced by patients with lower health literacy. She is committed to developing and implementing evidence-based policy and practice to promote equity and equality in health. She founded the Health Literacy Group UK and has authored, and co-authored, over 70 publications in peer-reviewed journals and co-edited a book 'Health Literacy in Context: International Perspectives'.

Editorial

Health Literacy in Context

Don Nutbeam [1,*], Diane Levin-Zamir [2,3] and Gill Rowlands [4]

1. School of Public Health, University of Sydney, Sydney 2006, Australia
2. Department of Health Education and Promotion, Clalit Health Services, Tel Aviv 62098, Israel; diamos@zahav.net.il
3. School of Public Health, University of Haifa, Haifa 31905, Israel
4. Institute of Health and Society, Newcastle University, Newcastle NE1 7RU, UK; Gill.Rowlands@newcastle.ac.uk
* Correspondence: don.nutbeam@sydney.edu.au

Received: 13 November 2018; Accepted: 21 November 2018; Published: 27 November 2018

Health literacy has been defined and conceptualized in multiple ways, but almost all definitions have similar core elements describing the personal skills that enable individuals to obtain, understand, and use information to make decisions and take actions that will have an impact on their health. These health literacy skills are not restricted in their application to personal behaviour, but can be applied to the full range of determinants of health (personal, social, and environmental).

To date, most published health literacy research has focused on assessing and improving personal skills and abilities. More recently, a better understanding has emerged of the extent to which these skills and abilities are mediated by environmental demands and situational complexities–the context in which health literacy is developed and applied. This has led to much greater attention being given to ways of reducing the situational demands and complexity in which an individual makes a health decision. A range of models and practical strategies are emerging to help create health literate organisations. These propose strategies to reduce the environmental demands on people engaging with those organisations and health professionals.

This Special Issue of the International Journal of Environmental Research and Public Health (IJERPH) was conceived with the aim of examining current progress in understanding health literacy in context, looking to attract papers that improve our understanding of the mutual impact of a range of social, economic, environmental, and organisational influences on health literacy.

We were especially interested in attracting submissions that reported on the relationships between physical and social environments and health literacy; interventions to reduce environmental demands and complexity, including, for example, interventions to reduce the organisational and administrative complexity of health services; health literacy interventions responsive to cultural preferences; and health literacy interventions that use the preferred media of disengaged populations.

Through the call for abstracts, we received a large number and wide range of potential submissions. This response is indicative of the high level of current interest in health literacy from a very wide range of country, sectoral, and cultural perspectives. The final group of papers selected and that completed the peer review process reflects this diversity. These papers also illustrate good progress in the evolution of research in the contexts in which health literacy is developed and applied, as well as signalling some areas in which more research would be useful.

The papers offer unique and original perspectives on the concept, distribution, and application of health literacy in very diverse populations. Several papers, including those by O'Hara et al. [1], König et al. [2], Schillinger et al. [3], Thomas et al. [4], and Lorini et al. [5], for example, offer cultural insights and a clear indication of the impact of social and environmental context on health literacy. Both individually and in combination, these findings have important implications for interventions designed to address the needs of different populations. Above all, they illustrate the need to routinely incorporate an understanding of "context" into the development of policies and programmes to improve health literacy in diverse populations.

The papers by Trezona [6] and Geboers [7], which examine differing national policy responses to health literacy and describe a comprehensive health literacy intervention model, respectively, illustrate how policy and practice can (and should) respond to this more complete but complex understanding of health literacy. The paper by Trezona and colleagues underlines the global interest in health literacy among policy-makers, but also highlights, in turn, the gap between this public commitment and the practical actions that can be systematically applied in diverse populations.

The papers by Levin-Zamir and Bertschi [8] on the application of new digital media and the creative harnessing of popular culture (as described by Schillinger et al.) offer great promise in extending the reach and customisation of communications. These contributions, along with the papers by Rademakers et al. [9], Thomas et al. [4], and Estacio et al. [10], also demonstrate that the content of communications as well as the medium is important.

The collection of papers published in this Special Edition includes some that focus on clinical issues (for example, McKenna et al. [11], and Stein et al. [12]), but we have also attracted a good range of papers that are community-based, give attention to the social context in which health decisions are made, and include communication content that improves our understanding of the wider social determinants of health. However, there remains a dearth of published papers that describe health literacy interventions. The great majority of published papers still focus on personal health behaviour and practices, most often in clinical settings [13].

Whilst the progress reflected in this journal is encouraging, it is evident that more discussion and research are needed to improve our understanding of health literacy in context, and how to reduce the situational demands and complexity in which an individual makes a health decision, including how organisations and social institutions can contribute.

It is our hope that this Special Issue will be a catalyst for further action and research on health literacy in context.

References

1. O'Hara, J.; McPhee, C.; Dodson, S.; Cooper, A.; Wildey, C.; Hawkins, M.; Fulton, A.; Pridmore, V.; Cuevas, V.; Scanlon, M.; et al. Barriers to breast cancer screening among diverse cultural groups in Melbourne, Australia. *Int. J. Environ. Res. Public Health* **2018**, *15*, 1677. [CrossRef] [PubMed]
2. Konig, C.; Skriver, M.V.; Iburg, K.M.; Rowlands, G. Understanding educational and psychosocial factors associated with alcohol use among adolescents in Denmark; implications for health literacy interventions. *Int. J. Environ. Res. Public Health* **2018**, *15*, 1671. [CrossRef] [PubMed]
3. Schillinger, D.; Tran, J.; Fine, S. Do low income youth of color see "the bigger picture" when discussing type 2 diabetes: A qualitative evaluation of a public health literacy campaign. *Int. J. Environ. Res. Public Health* **2018**, *15*, 840. [CrossRef] [PubMed]
4. Thomas, S.D.; Mobley, S.C.; Hudgins, J.L.; Sutherland, D.E.; Inglett, S.B.; Ange, B.L. Conditions and dynamics that impact maternal health literacy among high risk prenatal-interconceptional women. *Int. J. Environ. Res. Public Health* **2018**, *15*, 1383. [CrossRef] [PubMed]
5. Lorini, C.; Ierardi, F.; Bachini, L.; Donzellini, M.; Gemmi, F.; Bonaccorsi, G. The antecedents and consequences of health literacy in an ecological perspective: Results from an experimental analysis. *Int. J. Environ. Res. Public Health* **2018**, *15*, 798. [CrossRef] [PubMed]
6. Trezona, A.; Rowlands, G.; Nutbeam, D. Progress in implementing national policies and strategies for health literacy-what have we learned so far? *Int. J. Environ. Res. Public Health* **2018**, *15*, 1554. [CrossRef] [PubMed]
7. Geboers, B.; Reijneveld, S.A.; Koot, J.A.R.; de Winter, A.F. Moving towards a comprehensive approach for health literacy interventions: The development of a health literacy intervention model. *Int. J. Environ. Res. Public Health* **2018**, *15*, 1268. [CrossRef] [PubMed]
8. Levin-Zamir, D.; Bertschi, I. Media health literacy, ehealth literacy, and the role of the social environment in context. *Int. J. Environ. Res. Public Health* **2018**, *15*, 1643. [CrossRef] [PubMed]

9. Rademakers, J.; Heijmans, M. Beyond reading and understanding: Health literacy as the capacity to act. *Int. J. Environ. Res. Public Health* **2018**, *15*, 1676. [CrossRef] [PubMed]
10. Estacio, E.V.; Oliver, M.; Downing, B.; Kurth, J.; Protheroe, J. Effective partnership in community-based health promotion: Lessons from the health literacy partnership. *Int. J. Environ. Res. Public Health* **2017**, *14*, 1550. [CrossRef] [PubMed]
11. McKenna, V.B.; Sixsmith, J.; Barry, M.M. A qualitative study of the development of health literacy capacities of participants attending a community-based cardiovascular health programme. *Int. J. Environ. Res. Public Health* **2018**, *15*, 1157. [CrossRef] [PubMed]
12. Stein, L.; Bergdahl, M.; Pettersen, K.S.; Bergdahl, J. Effects of the conceptual model of health literacy as a risk: A randomised controlled trial in a clinical dental context. *Int. J. Environ. Res. Public Health* **2018**, *15*, 1630. [CrossRef] [PubMed]
13. Nutbeam, D.; McGill, B.; Premkumar, P. Improving health literacy in community populations: A review of progress. *Health Promot Int.* **2018**, *33*, 901–911. [CrossRef] [PubMed]

© 2018 by the authors. Licensee MDPI, Basel, Switzerland. This article is an open access article distributed under the terms and conditions of the Creative Commons Attribution (CC BY) license (http://creativecommons.org/licenses/by/4.0/).

Article

Beyond Reading and Understanding: Health Literacy as the Capacity to Act

Jany Rademakers [1,2,*] and Monique Heijmans [1]

1   Netherlands Institute for Health Services Research, 3500 BN Utrecht, The Netherlands; m.heijmans@nivel.nl
2   Department of Family Medicine, School for Public Health and Primary Care (CAPHRI),
    Maastricht University, 6200 MD Maastricht, The Netherlands
*   Correspondence: j.rademakers@nivel.nl; Tel.: +31-30-272-9847

Received: 9 May 2018; Accepted: 24 July 2018; Published: 7 August 2018

Abstract: Many health literacy interventions have a limited focus on functional/cognitive skills. In psychosocial models, the capacity to act however is seen as a major driver of behavioural change. This aspect is often lacking in health literacy concepts. In this study, we examine the impact of both aspects of health literacy (functional/cognitive and capacity to act) on specific healthcare outcomes (healthcare use, experiences with patient-centered care, shared-decision making, and self-management). In a sample of a national panel of people with a chronic disease (NPCD), questions about health literacy, patient activation, and outcomes were asked. The results indicated that 39.9% had limited HL levels and 36.9% had a low activation score. Combined, 22.7% of the sample scored low on both aspects, whereas 45.8% had adequate levels on both. Patients who score low on both use more healthcare and have less positive experiences with patient-centered care, shared decision making, and self-management. Patients who have adequate competency levels in both respects have the best outcomes. Both cognitive and non-cognitive aspects of health literacy are important, and they enhance each other. The capacity to act is especially important for the extent to which people feel able to self-manage.

Keywords: health literacy; health determinants; health competencies; health outcomes; patient-centered care; definitions; conceptual models

---

1. Introduction

Health literacy is regarded as an important prerequisite in order to take up a pro-active role with respect to one's health and lifestyle, and to be able to perform as an active partner in encounters with healthcare professionals and institutions. This is especially relevant for people with one or more chronic conditions, who have more frequent interactions with healthcare professionals and who are supposed to be active in the self-management of their disease.

In the past decennia, worldwide many definitions and conceptualizations of health literacy have emerged. At first, health literacy was defined as having basic reading and writing skills (which are essential e.g., to read consent forms, information leaflets and medicine labels). This is referred to as 'functional health literacy'. A more elaborate and much used model is the one proposed by Nutbeam in 2000 which distinguishes between functional, interactive and critical health literacy [1]. On top of the basic functional skills Nutbeam introduced interactive (also known as 'communicative') literacy: more advanced cognitive and literacy skills which, together with social skills, can be used to actively participate in everyday situations, extract health information and derive meaning from different forms of health communication, and to apply new information to changing circumstances. Critical health literacy refers to more advanced cognitive and social skills needed to critically assess health information and to use this information in one's personal situation [1]. In 2012, the Health Literacy Survey-Europe (HLS-EU) consortium developed a new conceptual model in which 12 dimensions of health literacy were discerned: four competency levels related to accessing, understanding, appraising, and applying health information in the three domains of healthcare, disease prevention, and health promotion [2]. Both the health literacy models of Nutbeam and the HLS-EU consortium address a broader range of competences compared to the original functional definition, such as communication and social skills and the ability to apply health information. Cognitive aspects and information processing, however, remain central elements in the models. A recent review (2017) on definitions and models of health literacy in childhood and youth discerned three different key dimensions of health literacy: (1) cognitive attributes (knowledge, functional health related skills, comprehension and understanding; appraisal and evaluation, critical thinking); (2) behavioural and operational attributes (seeking and accessing information; communication and interaction; application of information; other context specific skills; citizenship); and (3) affective and conative attributes (self-awareness and self-reflection; self-control and self-regulation; self-efficacy; interest and motivation) [3]. Definitions and models of health literacy have emerged that are more complex and comprehensive, including other elements than functional skills (literacy and numeracy), knowledge, cognitive abilities, and information processing. Especially behavioural, affective, and conative attributes have earned their place in some of the health literacy concepts and models. Furthermore, there is more attention for the context and domain in which people have to be health literate.

The development of health literacy measurement instruments, however, has not followed the movement toward a more comprehensive conceptualization of health literacy. Many of the questionnaires and tests focus on functional reading and numeracy skills (e.g., Rapid Estimate of Adult Literacy in Medicine (REALM), Test of Functional Health Literacy in Adults (TOFHLA), Set of Brief Screening Questions (SBSQ), Newest Vital Sign (NVS)) or predominantly on cognitive aspects (Short Assessment of Health Literacy (SAHL), Health Literacy Survey-Europe (HLS-EU)). There are only two instruments that employ a broader perspective: the Functional, Communicative, and Critical Health Literacy Scale (FCCHL), which measures functional, communicative, and critical health literacy [4], and the Health Literacy Questionnaire (HLQ), which includes nine different constructs including behavioural, affective, and conative elements [5]. Apart from the 'official' health literacy instruments, the Patient Activation Measure (PAM) also measures knowledge, skills, and self-confidence in dealing with one's own health, (chronic) illness, and healthcare [6]. The PAM is focused on the active role of individuals and discerns four stages: (1) believing that one's own (patient) role is important; (2) having the confidence and knowledge necessary to take action; (3) actually taking action to maintain and improve one's health; and (4) staying on course even under stress [6]. Even though there has been debate whether patient activation and health literacy cover the same concept [7–10], with a broader definition of health literacy, there is definitely overlap, especially in the non-cognitive domain. While it is true that the PAM measures different attributes and competencies compared to most traditional health literacy instruments that focus on functional skills and/or information processing, with a broader conceptualization of health literacy, the elements of the PAM become highly relevant and of added value as well.

As with the measurement instruments, many health literacy interventions have a limited focus on reading/numeracy skills, knowledge and (cognitive) understanding of health-related issues [11–14]. This is reflected in the measurement instruments they use and in the goals that are set for the intervention. In general, these interventions improve the understanding of health information [11,12]. Effects of health literacy interventions on other outcomes are mixed or limited [11,12]. This might be because of their narrow approach. In a recent international review, the conclusion was drawn that what discriminates more promising from less promising health literacy interventions is (a) whether they tailor their efforts to the needs of the patients or groups with inadequate health literacy—patient or citizen involvement in the process of intervention development is therefore crucial—and (b) whether they address interactive and/or critical skills and competencies (and not knowledge only) [13]. If the goal of the intervention is the capacity to better self-manage, or a more active contribution in the provider-patient encounter, literacy, knowledge, and understanding of information obviously will not be enough. In traditional psychosocial models, attitudes, perceived norms and perceived behavioural control determine the intention to display certain behaviour, whereas skills and abilities further determine whether the behaviour will actually occur [15]. Both intention and skills are thus major drivers of behavioural change. Recently, in the Netherlands, a report was published on the determinants of general life skills and self-reliance of people in the domains of health, finance and work [16]. On the basis of theory and empirical evidence, a behavioural model was proposed in which, on the one hand, cognitive elements were distinguished ('the capacity to think'), and on the other hand, non-cognitive elements ('the capacity to act') were distinguished. With the capacity to act, the authors refer to skills, such as goal-setting, making a plan, taking action, persevering and being able to deal with temptations and adverse events or stress. Part of these skills are determined by one's personality structure, but other aspects are learnable. The authors demonstrated the importance of both types of capacities in order to be in control and self-reliant. Since the non-cognitive aspects are often lacking in health literacy interventions, their mixed or limited effects on behaviour are not surprising.

In this study, we will look at the impact of both the cognitive and the non-cognitive aspects of health literacy and investigate their respective effects on specific healthcare behaviours and experiences (healthcare use, experiences with patient-centered care, shared decision making, and self-management). Since an active role is especially relevant for people with a chronic condition, we focus on this specific group. Our main research questions will be:

(1) How are cognitive and non-cognitive aspects of health literacy distributed in a sample of Dutch chronically ill patients and how does this compare to the general Dutch population?
(2) How are these types of attributes (cognitive vs. non-cognitive) related to patients' healthcare use, experiences with patient-centred care, shared decision making, and self-management?
(3) Which type of attributes (cognitive or non-cognitive) has most impact on these outcomes?

We expect that respondents who score high on both the cognitive and the non-cognitive aspects of health literacy will have the most favourable outcomes (less healthcare use, more positive experiences with patient-centred care, shared decision making, and self-management) but that the capacity to act will have a higher impact on outcomes in general than cognitive skills only.

2. Materials and Methods

2.1. Design and Data Collection

In 2017, the Dutch version of the HLS-EU questionnaire (16 items) as a measure for the functional/cognitive aspects of health literacy ('the capacity to think') and the Dutch Patient Activation Measure (PAM) (13 items) as a measure for 'the capacity to act' were included in a survey of the National Panel of the Chronically Ill and Disabled (NPCD) [17].

For this study data were used from a questionnaire sent in October 2017 to a sample of 2606 NPCD panel members who had at least one chronic disease diagnosed by a medical practitioner, and 2129 patients (81.7%) returned the questionnaire. As a reference, similar data—collected in the same period with the same instruments—from a sample of the Dutch Health Care Consumer Panel were used. This panel consists of almost 12,000 people aged 18 years and older [18]. The sample used for this study consisted of 668 people and was representative for the Dutch population regarding age and gender. Data in both panel studies are collected using online and/or paper and pen surveys.

Box 1. National Panel of the Chronically Ill and Disabled (NPCD).

The NPCD is a nationwide prospective panel-study on the consequences of chronic illness in the Netherlands. Panel members are recruited from the patient files of general practices (national random samples of general practices drawn from the Netherlands registration of General Practices. Patients are selected according to the following criteria: a diagnosis of a somatic chronic disease by a certified medical practitioner, an age > 15 years, being non institutionalized, being aware of the diagnosis, not being terminally ill (life expectancy > 6 months according to the General Practitioner (GP)), being mentally able to participate, and a sufficient mastery of the Dutch language. Patients who meet the selection criteria are invited by their GP to participate in the panel and asked to participate for a period of four years at a maximum. Patients who agree to participate fill in self-report questionnaires twice a year. NPCD is registered with the Dutch Data Protection Authority; all data were collected and handled according to the privacy protection guidelines of the Authority.

2.2. Materials

For this study, the HLS-EU 16 was used. The HLS-EU questionnaire is focused on cognitive aspects of health literacy and distinguishes four types of competences: the ability to access, understand, appraise, and apply health information [2]. In the 16-item version, 13 items refer to the first three types of competences (e.g., how easy/difficult would you say it is to (a) find information on treatments of illnesses that concern you; (b) understand what your doctor says to you; and (c) judge if the information on health risks in the media is reliable?). The three aspects that cover the application of information are mainly focused on decision making which is also a cognitive process: how easy/difficult would you say it is to (a) use information the doctor gives you to make decisions about your illness; (b) follow instructions from your doctor or pharmacist; and (c) decide how you can protect yourself from illness based on information in the media?). We used the version with five answering categories: a four-point Likert scale (very easy–very difficult) and a 'don't know' option. This last category was recoded as missing. Respondents had to answer at least 14 of the 16 items in order to be included in the analysis. Subsequently the answering categories were dichotomized (easy vs. difficult) and a sum score was calculated. For respondents with 14 or 15 answers, a weighted sum score was computed by dividing the total score by the number of answered items. The final sum score varied between 0 and 16. We used the following cut off points: 0–8 is inadequate health literacy, 9–12 is limited, and 13–16 is sufficient health literacy. For more information on the HLS-EU 16 and the method of data management we used see Vandenbosch et al. [19]. In this study, we divided the respondents in two groups: inadequate/limited health literacy (HL low) and sufficient health literacy (HL high). The reason to do so is because both the people with inadequate and with limited health literacy encounter problems in healthcare and therefore require extra attention. Reliability of the HLS-EU in this study was good: Cronbach's α was 0.87.

The PAM focuses on people's self-perceived ability to deal with one's own health, (chronic) illness and healthcare. The 13 items are (1) When all is said and done, I am the person who is responsible for taking care of my health; (2) Taking an active role in my own healthcare is the most important thing that affects my health; (3) I am confident I can help prevent or reduce problems associated with my health; (4) I know what each of my prescribed medications do; (5) I am confident that I can tell whether I need to go to the doctor or whether I can take care of a health problem myself; (6) I am confident that I can tell a doctor concerns I have even when he or she does not ask; (7) I am confident that I can follow through on medical treatments I may need to do at home; (8) I understand my health problems and what causes them; (9) I know what treatments are available for my health problems; (10) I have been able to maintain (keep up with) lifestyle changes, like eating right or exercising; (11) I know how to prevent problems with my health; (12) I am confident I can figure out solutions when new problems arise with my health; (13) I am confident that I can maintain lifestyle changes, like eating right and exercising, even during times of stress. It consists of 13 items, which have five answering options: a four-point Likert scale (disagree strongly–agree strongly) and a 'not applicable' option. For calculating patients' activation scores, we followed the guidelines of Insignia Health [20]. According to these instructions, participants who answered less than seven questions or answered all items with 'disagree strongly' or 'agree strongly' were excluded. The mean score was calculated leaving out items that were deemed not applicable by the respondents and then transformed into a standardized activation score ranging from 0 to 100. Higher scores indicate that patients are more activated. On the basis of their mean score, patients were assigned to one of the four groups described above. The cut-off points of these groups are described in the manual of Insignia Health [21]. For this study, the two lowest groups (1 and 2) and the two highest groups (3 and 4) are taken together (respective PAM low and PAM high). On the basis of a combination of the scores on the HLS-EU 16 and the PAM, four groups were distinguished (1) HL low/PAM low; (2) HL high/PAM low; (3) HL low/PAM high; (4) HL high/PAM high. Reliability of the PAM in this study was good: Cronbach's α was 0.78.

Outcome measures with regard to healthcare behaviours and experiences were: number of visits to GP, questions concerning patient-centered care, shared-decision making and self-management. Items to measure the latter three came from the Person-Centred Coordinated Care Experiences Questionnaire (P3C_EQ) [21]. Age, gender, education level (low i.e., no, primary school, or vocational training, middle: secondary or vocational education or high: professional higher education or university), ethnicity (Dutch, western immigrant, non-western immigrant), and self-reported health (VAS scale from the EQ 5D [22]) were included as background variables.

2.3. Statistical Analyses

Descriptive statistics were conducted to provide information on the characteristics of the total study sample t-tests ANOVA's were used to test differences between the four groups in main outcome measures. We performed stepwise multiple regression analyses to establish which aspects of health literacy (cognitive or non-cognitive) has most impact on specific outcomes. In step 1, demographic variables were included, in step 2, the HLS-EU score (cognitive aspects) only, in step 3, the PAM score (non-cognitive aspects) only, and in step 4, both the HLS-EU and the PAM scores.

3. Results

3.1. Participants

Of the NPCD sample (n = 2.129), 1416 (67%) had a valid score on the HLS-EU questionnaire, and 1956 (91.9%) had a valid score on the PAM. For this study, we further selected those respondents that had a valid score on both the HLS-EU and the PAM, resulting in a sample of 1341 people with at least one chronic disease from NPCD. In Table 1, the NPCD sample is described.

Table 1. Characteristics of the samples.

Characteristics	People with Chronic Disease (n = 1.341)	
	n	%
Female	736	54.9
Age		
≤39 years	70	5.2
40–64 years	534	39.8
65–74 years	434	32.4
≥75 years	303	22.6
Educational level		
Low	315	24.2
Middle	585	45.1
High	399	30.7
Ethnicity		
Dutch	1228	91.9
Western immigrant	95	7.1
Non-western immigrant	13	1

Table 1. Cont.

Characteristics	People with Chronic Disease (n = 1.341)	
	n	%
Disabilities		
None/light	768	60
Moderate/severe	411	40
Number of chronic conditions		
1	483	36
2	405	30.2
3	262	19.5
≥4	191	14.2
	n	M (Sd)
Self-rated health (0–100)	1.318	71.2 (17.3)
Health literacy	n	%
Inadequate	180	13.4
Limited	355	26.5
Sufficient	806	60.1
Activation level		
1	218	16.3
2	278	20.7
3	399	29.8
4	446	33.3
	n	M (Sd)
Activation score (0–100)	1.341	61.2 (15.2)

In Table 1, the distribution of cognitive and non-cognitive aspects of health literacy is also presented. Health literacy as measured by the HLS-EU represents the functional/cognitive aspects of health literacy ('the capacity to think'), whereas the PAM scores represent the non-cognitive aspects ('the capacity to act'). Among people with a chronic disease (n = 1.341), 39.9% had inadequate or limited HL levels, and 36.9% had a rather low activation score, i.e., activation level 1 or 2. People in these levels often lack the motivation, knowledge, and skills to take care for their own health and well-being and therefore may need support for prevention and (self-)management. In the reference sample of the Dutch Health Care Consumer Panel, 36.4% had inadequate or limited HL levels [23], and in total, 31.6% had an activation score in level 1 (14.3%) or 2 (17.3%) (M = 63.7 (SD = 16.1)). Both the HL and the activation scores in the general population were somewhat higher, presumably as a result of differences in age and education level. Participants in the NPCD are generally older and lower educated compared to the participants in the Health Care Consumer Panel.

3.2. Relation of Cognitive and Non-Cognitive Aspects and Healthcare Use

One of our aims is to investigate the relationship between cognitive and non-cognitive aspects of health literacy on one hand and healthcare use on the other hand. To this purpose, we selected the sample of people with a chronic disease and divided them into four groups (see Table 2):

- Group 1: HL low, PAM low
- Group 2: HL high, PAM low
- Group 3: HL low, PAM high
- Group 4: HL high, PAM high

Related to healthcare use, there were significant differences between the four groups regarding their visits to general practitioners (% patients who had contact and number of contacts), primary care practice nurses (number of contacts), medical specialists (% patients who had contact), and use of informal care (Table 3). There were no significant differences with respect to the percentage of patients who visited the practice nurse or in the number of contacts with a medical specialist.

Table 2. Level of health literacy by patient activation level in people with a chronic disease ($n = 1.341$).

Groups	HL Low	HL High
	n (%)	n (%)
PAM low	304 (22.7%)—Group 1	192 (14.3%)—Group 2
PAM high	231 (17.2%)—Group 3	614 (45.8%)—Group 4

Table 3. Cognitive and non-cognitive aspects of Health Literacy in relation to healthcare use of people with a chronic disease ($n = 1.341$).

Aspects of Health Care Use	Group 1 $n = 304$	Group 2 $n = 192$	Group 3 $n = 231$	Group 4 $n = 614$	p
General practitioner (% contact during last year)	93.2	94.9	91.0	87.2	<0.01
General practitioner (number of contacts during last year)	6.65	5.26 *	4.48 *	4.35 *†#	<0.001
Practice nurse (% contact during last year)	61.3	62.2	57.8	58.6	ns
Practice nurse (number of contacts during last year)	3.31	3.81	3.06	2.69 *†#	<0.01
Medical specialist (% contact during last year)	82.4	74.5 *	76.5 *	66.3 *†#	<0.001
Medical specialist (number of contacts during last year)	5.04	5.45	4.50	4.36	ns
Use of informal care (%)	45.7	34.8 *	27.2 *†	29.8 *†#	<0.001

* significant difference with group 1 (HL low/PAM low); † significant difference from group 2 (HL high/PAM low); # significant difference from group 3 (HL low/PAM high).

Looking at the relative importance of cognitive aspects versus non-cognitive aspects of health literacy, it is clear that group 1, which scores low on both, visits the GP significantly more often than patients from the other groups, and a much larger percentage of this group (differences with other groups between 5.9% and 16.1%) visits a medical specialist as well. Furthermore, the use of informal care is much larger in this group (differences with other groups between 10.9% and 18.5%). Group 4, which scores high on both, uses less care, i.e., visits the GP and the practice nurse less often, fewer people of this group visit a specialist, and there is less use of informal care. Patients in group 2 and 3 hold an intermediate position between group 1 and 4. In general, they do no not differ significantly from each other, except with respect to the use of informal care, which is much higher in the group with low PAM scores.

3.3. Relation of Cognitive and Non-Cognitive Aspects and Patient-Centered Care and Self-Management

Furthermore, we wanted to examine the relationship of cognitive and non-cognitive aspects of health literacy with experiences of patient-centered care and self-management. In Table 4, the results of these analyses are shown. The groups differ significantly on all outcomes.

With respect to the relative importance of cognitive versus non-cognitive aspects, it is clear that group 1 (which scores low on both) reports significally less positive experiences, whereas group 4 (which scores high on both) reports significally better outcomes on all items compared to each of the other groups. Though group 2 and 3, again, hold an intermediate position between group 1 and 4, there is a slight trend that group 3 is more positive compared to group 2, especially on the items 'Patient feels that professional is interested his person as a whole' and 'Patient feels able to self-manage'. This suggests that for these items, the non-cognitive aspects of health literacy are more important compared to the cognitive aspects.

To further determine the impact of cognitive versus non-cognitive aspects of health literacy, we performed multiple regression analyses on the two outcome measures that both require an active role of the patient regarding their health and self-care. These two items were (a) shared-decision making—the extent to which the patient feels himself involved in decisions about their care (Table 5)—and (b) self-management—the extent to which the patient feels able to self-manage (Table 6).

Table 4. Cognitive and non-cognitive aspects of Health Literacy in relation to experiences with patient-centered care and self-management among chronic disease patients (n = 1.341).

Extent to Which Patient ...	Group 1 n = 304	Group 2 n = 192	Group 3 n = 231	Group 4 n = 614	p
Experiences patient-centered healthcare (1–4) [1]	2.14	2.28	2.28	2.55 *†#	<0.001
Feels himself involved in decisions about his care (1–4)	2.74	2.97 *	3.00 *	3.31 *†#	<0.001
Feels that the professional is interested in him as a whole person (not only the illness) (1–4)	2.42	2.59 *	2.65 *	2.99 *†#	<0.001
Feels that he gets enough support in caring for his health (1–4)	2.33	2.42	2.41	2.57 *#	<0.001
Gets useful and timely information (1–4)	2.91	3.19 *	3.16 *	3.40 *†#	<0.001
Feels able to self-manage (1–4)	2.71	2.91 *	3.16 *	3.37 *†#	<0.001

[1] scores range from 1 to 4 with higher scores being more positive; * significant difference with group 1 (HL low/PAM low); † significant difference from group 2 (HL high/PAM low); # significant difference from group 3 (HL low/PAM high).

Table 5. Extent to which patient feels involved in decisions about care (score 1–4)—stepwise multiple regression.

Variables	Model 1	Model 2	Model 3	Model 4
Constant	14.06 ***	9.38 ***	10.11 ***	7.79 ***
Female	0.01	0.01	0.3	0.02
Age	−0.9 ***	−0.05	−0.7 **	−0.05
Educational level	0.12 ***	0.10 ***	0.09 ***	0.08 ***
Immigrant	0.02	0.02	0.02	0.02
Moderate/severe disabilities	0.02	0.05	0.04	0.06
Perceived general health	0.06 *	0.01	−0.01	−0.03
HLS-EU score	–	0.25 ***	–	0.19 ***
PAM score	–	–	0.25 ***	0.19 ***
R^2	0.03 ***	0.09 ***	0.08 ***	0.11 ***
Change in R^2		0.06	0.05	0.08

Model 1: Background characteristics; Model 2: Background characteristics + health literacy (HLSEU-16 score); Model 3: Background characteristics + patient activation (PAM score); Model 4: Background characteristics + health literacy (HLSEU-16 score) + patient activation (PAM score); Dash indicates not applicable; * $p < 0.05$; ** $p < 0.01$; *** $p < 0.001$.

Table 6. Extent to which patient feels able to self-manage (score 1–4)—stepwise multiple regression.

Variables	Model 1	Model 2	Model 3	Model 4
Constant	15.44 ***	10.99 ***	10.23 ***	8.47 ***
Female	0.04	0.04	0.07 **	0.06 **
Age	−0.7 **	−0.04	−0.05	−0.03
Educational level	0.11 ***	0.09 ***	0.06 **	0.06 *
Immigrant	−0.01	−0.02	−0.01	−0.01
Moderate/severe disabilities	−0.10 ***	−0.08 ***	−0.07 **	−0.07 *
Perceived general health	0.35 ***	0.30 ***	0.25 ***	−0.24 ***
HLS-EU score	–	0.21 ***	–	0.11 ***
PAM score	–	–	0.35 ***	0.31 ***
R^2	0.19 ***	0.23 ***	0.30 ***	0.31 ***
Change in R^2		0.04	0.11	0.12

Model 1: Background characteristics; Model 2: Background characteristics + health literacy (HLSEU-16 score); Model 3: Background characteristics + patient activation (PAM score); Model 4: Background characteristics + health literacy (HLSEU-16 score) + patient activation (PAM score); Dash indicates not applicable.; * $p < 0.05$; ** $p < 0.01$; *** $p < 0.001$.

In this regression analysis, the total amount of explained variance in step 4 is 0.11, and the cognitive aspects (HLS-EU) are of equal importance as the non-cognitive aspects (PAM): both have a value of 0.19. As is shown in model 2 and 3, the relative contribution of the HLS-EU and the

PAM separate was similar. Furthermore, the educational level is an important factor throughout all three models.

With respect to the perceived ability to self-manage, we performed a second regression analysis.

The total amount of explained variance in step 4 was 0.31. Both the cognitive (HLS-EU) and the non-cognitive aspects (PAM) have a significant contribution in explaining the variance regarding the perceived ability to self-manage. The non-cognitive aspects (PAM), however, are contributing more to the R^2 than the cognitive aspects (HLS-EU), 0.31 and 0.11, respectively. Adding the PAM in model 3 led to a 0.30 change of the explained variance. Also, the perceived general health and, to a lesser extent, educational level and the severity of the disability are important factors in all three models.

4. Discussion

In this study, we have investigated the impact of both the cognitive and the non-cognitive aspects of health literacy on specific healthcare behaviours and experiences (healthcare use, experiences with patient-centred care, shared decision making, and self-management).

In general, four out of 10 Dutch men and women with a chronic disease have inadequate or limited functional/cognitive health literacy skills (compared to 36% of the general Dutch population), and 37% have a low patient activation score (compared to 32% in the Dutch population). This implies that either the capacity to think or the capacity to act pose problems for a vast minority of chronically ill people and the general population alike. When we combine the scores on both types of competencies, 23% of the people with a chronic illness score low on both (group 1), whereas almost half (46%) demonstrated adequate levels in both respects (group 4). Of the intermediate groups, 14% scored high on the cognitive aspects but had low activation scores (group 2), while for 17% this was the other way around (group 3).

The main differences regarding healthcare use were found between group 1 (who scored low on both aspects of health literacy) and the other three groups. People from this group visit the GP significantly more often, and a much larger percentage of this group visits a medical specialist as well. Furthermore, the use of informal care is much larger in this group. Group 4, as expected, uses the least professional and informal care. Patients in group 2 and 3 hold an intermediate position between group 1 and 4. In general, they do not differ significantly from each other, except with respect to the use of informal care. Obviously, people who lack the capacity to act need more help and support with their health issues and self-care from their family, friends and peers than people who lack functional and cognitive skills. Hibbard et al. have earlier suggested that activation could help to compensate for numeracy and literacy skill deficits [24]. But otherwise, both functional/cognitive and non-cognitive aspects seem to be equally important determinants of healthcare use. This finding differs from the study of van der Heide et al. [25] who demonstrated that only functional skills (compared to communicative and critical health literacy skills) were associated with more visits to the GP.

With regard to patient-centred care group 1 reports significantly less positive experiences. Group 4, as expected, reports the best experiences compared to each of the other groups. Group 2 and 3, again, hold an intermediate position, but now on some aspects group 3 is slightly more positive about the care than group 2. This suggests that for some aspects of patient-centred care, non-cognitive aspects of health literacy could be more important compared to cognitive aspects. Especially for the behaviours that require an active role of the patient, the capacity to act may be relatively more important than the capacity to think. Regression analyses confirmed this for the extent to which patients feel able to self-manage, but for the extent to which patient feels involved in decisions about care (shared decision making), both the cognitive and the non-cognitive aspects proved equally important.

We can conclude from our study that both the cognitive and the non-cognitive aspects of health literacy are important and that they enhance each other. In general, patients who score low on both have the least favourable outcomes (more healthcare use, less positive experiences with patient-centred care, shared decision making, and self-management). For patients who have adequate competency levels in both respects, the outcomes are the best. Our hypothesis that the capacity to act would generally have a higher impact on outcomes compared to cognitive skills only holds for the extent to which people feel able to self-manage. Neither on healthcare use nor on other experiences with patient-centred care the non-cognitive aspects have a significant higher impact. This is an interesting finding, since in earlier studies where (functional) health literacy and patient activation were compared, patient activation was a stronger predictor with respect to outcomes such as health information seeking and use [10,24], provider choice [26], and self-management [7]. This confirms the idea that the non-cognitive aspects that are measured by the PAM (knowledge, motivation, self-confidence) are predominantly important for outcomes that require an active role such as seeking and use of health information, choice of a healthcare provider, and self-care. For those behaviours, finding and understanding of health information is not enough.

The main strength of this study is that it contributes to the further conceptualization of health literacy by establishing the influence of specific aspects and competencies on different outcomes. Since both functional/cognitive and non-cognitive aspects of health literacy prove to be important, this study underscores the importance of including non-cognitive competencies in both health literacy measurement instruments and health interventions (e.g., through enhancing motivation, personal goal setting, and skills training). Hibbard and Mahoney describe the importance of taking small, realistic, steps in interventions that aim at activating more passive patients [27]. Realizing small successes can start an upward cycle toward positive affect and self-perception, just as failure produces the opposite. People with limited health literacy tend to be passive in the medical encounter and less effective self-managers. Interventions with more focus on the 'capacity to act' and tailored to the individual's health literacy and activation level will likely lead to more effective behaviour regarding health and healthcare.

A limitation of this study is that our sample is drawn from an existing panel (NPCD), in which people who are illiterate or have low literacy skills and non-Western immigrants are known to be underrepresented. The same holds for the people from our reference group. Since people with no or low literacy generally also have lower health literacy skills, this means that the percentages in our study regarding low/high health literacy are more positive than in reality. Especially group 1 will be larger than we found in this study, which is concerning given the fact that their outcomes were least favourable. Immigrants who are not able to speak or read the local language are faced with additional challenges.

Future research should use a more comprehensive conceptualization of health literacy in its design and develop and use health literacy measurement instruments that represent the multiple aspects of health literacy. A unilateral focus on functional (reading) and cognitive (understanding) competencies will neither lead to further insight into the process of how health literacy affects specific outcomes nor will it effectively guide the development of tailored interventions. It is important to get a better insight in the exact nature of the cognitive and behavioural aspects of health literacy and how they interrelate. In research as well as in development of interventions, people with low health literacy should be actively involved. That will entail new and different ways of collaboration and research. One consequence will be a lesser focus on quantitative, survey research and more attention for qualitative methods, e.g., interviews, focus groups and research material with visual cues.

5. Conclusions

Both the cognitive and the non-cognitive aspects of health literacy are important, and they enhance each other. Patients who score low on both use more healthcare and have less positive experiences with patient-centered care, shared decision making, and self-management. Patients who have adequate competency levels in both respects also have the best outcomes. Our hypothesis that the capacity to act would generally have a higher impact on outcomes compared to cognitive skills only holds for the extent to which people feel able to self-manage.

Author Contributions: J.R. and M.H. conceived and designed the study, M.H. was responsible for the data collection and performed the statistical analysis, J.R. wrote the paper.

Funding: For this study, data were used from the National Panel of people with Chronic illness or Disability (NPCD), which is financed by The Netherlands Ministry of Public Health, Welfare and Sports and the Netherlands Ministry of Social Affairs and employment.

Acknowledgments: Both the NPCD as the Dutch Health Care Consumer Panel are financed by the Dutch Ministry of Public Health, Welfare and Sports. NPCD is also financed by the Ministry for Social Affairs and Employment.

Conflicts of Interest: The authors declare no conflict of interest.

References

1. Nutbeam, D. Health literacy as a public health goal: A challenge for contemporary health education and communication strategies into the 21st century. *Health Promot. Int.* **2000**, *15*, 259–267. [CrossRef]
2. Sørensen, K.; Van den Broucke, S.; Fullham, J.; Doyle, G.; Pelikan, J.; Slonska, Z.; Brand, H. (HLS-EU) Consortium European Health Literacy Project. Health literacy and public health: A systematic review and integration of definitions and models. *BMC Public Health* **2012**, *12*, 80. [CrossRef]
3. Bröder, J.; Okan, O.; Bauer, U.; Bruland, D.; Schlupp, S.; Bollweg, T.M.; Saboga-Nunes, L.; Bond, E.; Sørensen, K.; Bitzer, E.M.; et al. Health literacy in childhood and youth: A systematic review of definitions and models. *BMC Public Health* **2017**, *17*, 361. [CrossRef]
4. Ishikawa, H.; Takeuchi, T.; Yano, E. Measuring functional, communicative, and critical health literacy. *Diabetes Care* **2008**, *31*, 874–879. [CrossRef] [PubMed]
5. Osborne, R.; Batterham, R.W.; Elsworth, G.R.; Hawkins, M.; Buchbinder, R. The grounded psychometric development and initial validation of the Health Literacy Questionnaire (HLQ). *BMC Public Health* **2013**, *13*, 658. [CrossRef] [PubMed]
6. Hibbard, J.; Stockard, J.; Mahoney, E.R.; Tusler, M. Development of the Patient Activation Measure (PAM): Conceptualizing and Measuring Activation in Patients and Consumers. *Health Serv. Res.* **2004**, *39*, 1005–1026. [CrossRef] [PubMed]
7. Greene, J.; Hibbard, J.; Tusler, M. How Much Do Health Literacy and Patient Activation Contribute to Older Adults' Ability to Manage Their Health? AARP Public Policy Institute Report. 2005. Available online: http://www.aarp.org/health/doctors-hospitals/info-06-2005/2005_05_literacy.html (accessed on 23 May 2018).
8. Lubetkin, E.; Lu, W.; Gold, M. Levels and correlates of patient activation in health center settings: Building strategies for improving health outcomes. *J. Health Care Poor Underserv.* **2010**, *21*, 796–808. [CrossRef] [PubMed]
9. Smith, S.; Curtis, L.; Wardle, J.; Wagner, C.; von Wolf, M. Skill Set or Mind Set? Associations between Health Literacy, Patient Activation and Health. *PLoS ONE* **2013**, *8*, e74373.
10. Nijman, J.; Hendriks, M.; Brabers, A.; de Jong, J.; Rademakers, J. Patient activation and health literacy as predictors of health information use in a general sample of Dutch health care consumers. *J. Health Commun. Int. Perspect.* **2014**, *19*, 955–969. [CrossRef] [PubMed]
11. Sheridan, S.L.; Halpern, D.J.; Viera, A.J.; Berkman, N.D.; Donahue, K.E.; Crotty, K. Interventions for Individuals with Low Health Literacy: A Systematic Review. *J. Health Commun. Int. Perspect.* **2011**, *16*, 30–54. [CrossRef] [PubMed]
12. Berkman, N.D. *Health Literacy Interventions and Outcomes: An Updated Systematic Review*; No. 11-E006; ARHQ Publication: Rockville, MD, USA, 2011.
13. Heijmans, M.; Uiters, E.; Rose, T.; Hofstede, J.; Devillé, W.; Heide, I.; van der Boshuisen, H.; Rademakers, J. *Study on Sound Evidence for a Better Understanding of Health Literacy in the European Union (HEALIT4EU)*; European Commission: Brussels, Belgium, 2015.
14. Dennis, S.; Williams, A.; Taggert, J.; Newall, A.; Denney-Wilson, E.; Zwar, N.; Shortus, T.; Harris, M.F. Which providers can bridge the health literacy gap in lifestyle risk factor modification education: A systematic review and narrative synthesis. *BMC Family Pract.* **2012**, *13*. [CrossRef] [PubMed]
15. Fishbein, M.; Ajzen, I. *Predicting and Changing Behavior*; Psychology Press: New York, NY, USA, 2010.
16. Wetenschappelijke Raad voor het Regeringsbeleid. *Weten Is Nog Geen Doen*; Wetenschappelijke Raad voor het Regeringsbeleid: Den Haag, The Netherlands, 2017. (In Dutch: Knowing is not yet doing)
17. Nivel. National Panel of the Chronically Ill and Disabled (NPCD). Available online: https://www.nivel.nl/en/national-panel-chronically-ill-and-disabled-npcd (accessed on 2 April 2018).

18. Nivel. Dutch Health Care Consumer Panel. Available online: https://www.nivel.nl/en/dutch-health-care-consumer-panel (accessed on 2 April 2018).
19. Vandenbosch, J.; Van den Broucke, S.; Vancorenland, S.; Avalosse, H.; Verniest, R.; Callens, M. Health literacy and the use of healthcare services in Belgium. *J. Epidemiol. Community Health* **2016**, *70*, 1032–1038. [CrossRef] [PubMed]
20. Insignia Health. *Patient Activation Measure (PAM) 13 License Materials*; Insignia Health: Portland, OR, USA, 2010.
21. Sugavanam, T.; Fosh, B.; Close, J.; Byng, R.; Horrel, J.; Lloyd, H. Codesigning a Measure of Person-Centred Coordinated Care to Capture the Experience of the Patient: The Development of the P3CEQ. *J. Pat. Exp.* **2018**. [CrossRef]
22. Herdman, M.; Gudex, C.; Lloyd, A.; Janssen, M.; Kind, P.; Parkin, D.; Bonsel, G.; Badia, X. Development and preliminary testing of the new five-level version of EQ-5D (EQ-5D-5L). *Qual. Life Res.* **2011**, *20*, 1727–1736. [CrossRef] [PubMed]
23. Heijmans, M.; Brabers, A.; Rademakers, J. *Gezondheidsvaardigheden*; Factsheet Utrecht; NIVEL: Utrecht, The Netherland, 2018. (In Dutch)
24. Hibbard, J.; Peters, E.; Dixon, A.; Tusler, M. Consumer Competencies and the Use of Comparative Quality Information; It Isn't Just about Literacy. *Med. Care Res. Rev.* **2007**, *64*, 379–394. [CrossRef] [PubMed]
25. Van der Heide, I.; Heijmans, M.; Schuit, A.J.; Uiters, E.; Rademakers, J. Functional, interactive and critical health literacy: Varying relationships with control over care and number of GP visits. *Pat. Educ. Couns.* **2015**, *98*, 998–1004. [CrossRef] [PubMed]
26. Rademakers, J.; Nijman, J.; Brabers, A.; de Jong, J.; Hendriks, M. The relative effect of health literacy and patient activation on provider choice in the Netherlands. *Health Policy* **2014**, *114*, 200–206. [CrossRef] [PubMed]
27. Hibbard, J.; Mahoney, E. Toward a theory of patient and consumer activation. *Pat. Educ. Couns.* **2010**, *78*, 377–381. [CrossRef] [PubMed]

© 2018 by the authors. Licensee MDPI, Basel, Switzerland. This article is an open access article distributed under the terms and conditions of the Creative Commons Attribution (CC BY) license (http://creativecommons.org/licenses/by/4.0/).

Article

Moving towards a Comprehensive Approach for Health Literacy Interventions: The Development of a Health Literacy Intervention Model

Bas Geboers *, Sijmen A. Reijneveld, Jaap A. R. Koot and Andrea F. de Winter

Department of Health Sciences, University Medical Center Groningen, University of Groningen, P.O. Box 30.001, FA10, 9700 RB Groningen, The Netherlands; s.a.reijneveld@umcg.nl (S.A.R.); j.a.r.koot@umcg.nl (J.A.R.K.); a.f.de.winter@umcg.nl (A.F.d.W.)
* Correspondence: b.j.m.geboers@umcg.nl; Tel.: +31-50-361-6967

Received: 30 April 2018; Accepted: 12 June 2018; Published: 15 June 2018

Abstract: Low health literacy (HL) is associated with many negative health outcomes, and is a major challenge in public health and healthcare. Interventions to improve outcomes associated with HL are needed. In this paper, we aim to develop a comprehensive HL intervention model. We used a multimethod approach, consisting of (1) a literature review of articles listed in MEDLINE, presenting HL intervention models, (2) online consultation of international HL experts, and (3) two consensus meetings with members (n = 36 and 27) of a consortium studying HL among older adults (50+) in Europe. In our literature review, we identified twenty-two HL models, only a few of which focused explicitly on interventions. Sixty-eight health literacy experts took part in the online survey. The results from all three methods came together in a comprehensive HL intervention model. This model conceptualized interventions as potentially targeting five factors affecting HL outcomes: (1) individuals' personal characteristics, (2) individuals' social context, (3) communication between individuals and health professionals, (4) health professionals' HL capacities, and (5) health systems. Our model is the first comprehensive HL model focused specifically on interventions. The model can support the further development of HL interventions to improve the health outcomes of people with low HL.

Keywords: health literacy; model; intervention; review; health system; health professional; community; context; health outcomes

---

1. Introduction

Many adults worldwide have low levels of health literacy, meaning that they are less able to access, understand, appraise, and communicate information to engage with the demands of different health contexts to promote and maintain health across the life-course [1]. Large-scale survey studies have found prevalences of low health literacy of 36% in the United States [2], and between 29% and 62% in various European countries [3]. As low health literacy is associated with various negative health outcomes, including self-rated health [4], quality of life [5], and all-cause mortality [6], it is considered a major health challenge of the 21st century.

A growing consensus suggests that health literacy research should focus less on descriptive studies, and more on the development and testing of interventions. This requires a health literacy intervention model to conceptualize how interventions can achieve better health outcomes among people with low health literacy. Such a model may lead to a more comprehensive approach to improve health literacy outcomes and support intervention research. In the last two decades, many studies on the causes and consequences of low health literacy have been published, resulting in the development of various health literacy models [7–9]. However, these models focus mainly on identifying associations between health literacy and its determinants and outcomes. Models focused on identifying targets for interventions are scarce, and those available are of limited comprehensiveness.

The authors conceptualized a provisional health literacy intervention model at the start of a European project entitled Intervention Research on Health Literacy among the Ageing Population (IROHLA; Figure 1). They developed this model based on their expertise and their experience with developing and implementing health promotion programs, as well as on existing literature on health literacy [3,8].

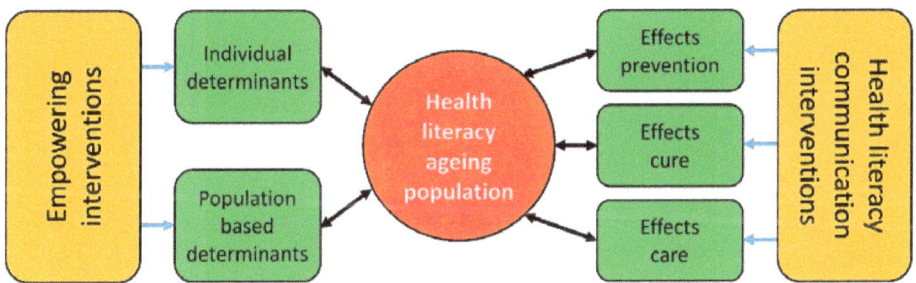

Figure 1. Provisional health literacy intervention model.

This provisional intervention model shows that health literacy levels are determined by both individual and population-based determinants, and by health systems. The model distinguishes between primary prevention (health promotion and protection), secondary prevention (detecting and treating health problems in an early stage), and tertiary prevention (softening the impact of existing health problems). The model includes two main types of interventions: (1) those aimed at empowering people by positively affecting individual or population-based determinants, and (2) those aimed at mitigating the negative consequences of low health literacy by improving the communication used in healthcare systems.

In this study, we aim to develop a comprehensive health literacy intervention model, using the provisional model as a starting point.

2. Materials and Methods

We used a multimethod approach to improve and build on the provisional health literacy intervention model. Three main methods were used:

1. A review of the literature on health literacy models.
2. Online consultation with health literacy experts.
3. Consensus meetings with members of the IROHLA consortium.

2.1. Setting

Part of the research activities for this study were conducted in the framework of the Intervention Research on Health Literacy among the Ageing Population (IROHLA) project. The IROHLA project (2012–2015) focused on improving health literacy for older adults above the age of 50 in Europe [10].

2.2. Literature Review

We conducted a search for articles presenting health literacy models by searching the MEDLINE electronic database from its inception through May 2013 (and updated in July 2017) for papers that included the term *health literacy* in their title and *framework(s), model(s), theory, theories, concept(s), pathway(s)* or *mechanism(s)* in their title or abstract. We defined a model as a graphical of textual representation of a concept, including its various aspects and/or its overlap or associations with other concepts.

The first author, BG, performed selection in three rounds: title screening, abstract screening, and full text screening. In the title screening round, BG was supported by research assistant JPMV. In case of doubts about inclusion, AFW acted as a second reviewer. This process was followed in the full text screening of five articles (7.1%). BG manually screened the reference lists of included articles for further articles meeting the inclusion criteria.

We included articles if they presented a model on health literacy: (1) based on evidence, a strong theoretical basis, or published literature, and (2) sufficiently generalizable to the broader adult population. We excluded articles if (1) the presented model was based on analyses of only a single dataset, (2) the model focused specifically on children or adolescents, (3) the type of health literacy addressed was insufficiently generalizable to health literacy in general, or (4) if no full text could be obtained. We imposed no restrictions with regard to article types (e.g., reviews, commentaries, empirical studies) or languages. However, other criteria led to the exclusion of all non-English articles before the full-text screening.

Data from the included articles were extracted by means of a form specifically developed for this review. Besides bibliographic information, the form captured the main aims and conclusions of the article, the theoretical basis for the model, the main focus and target group of the model, and its implications for interventions.

2.3. Online Consultation

We conducted an online survey among health literacy experts in the IROHLA consortium and among external health literacy experts. We identified the latter by searching the existing literature on health literacy and via recommendations by members of the IROHLA consortium.

The study encompassed two rounds consisting of closed and open-ended questions. We invited a total of 139 health literacy experts (34 members from the IROHLA consortium and 105 external experts) to participate in the first round (November 2012–February 2013). For the second round (May–August 2013), we invited 162 participants (60 from the IROHLA consortium and 102 external health literacy experts). The lower number of participants from the IROHLA consortium in the first round was because the formation of the consortium was still ongoing at that time.

In the first round, participants reflected on the concept of health literacy, and on its definition by Sørensen et al. (2012) [9]. Participants were also asked to list any constructs, theories, or existing best practices that they deemed relevant for developing health literacy interventions.

In the second round, participants again reflected on the concept of health literacy, but this time on its definition by Kwan (2006) [1]. Another definition of health literacy was chosen for the second round in order to get as much information as possible from the participants with regard to the elements they considered essential in a definition of health literacy. Participants were also asked to name the characteristics they considered most important in a health literacy intervention model and to reflect on an intermediate version of the model. Finally, the participants were shown a list of potentially modifiable determinants of health literacy, and asked to evaluate their relevance for health literacy interventions. The list of determinants was composed based on the results of the first round of the online survey.

2.4. Consensus Meetings

Consensus meetings were held in the Netherlands with members of the 21 organizations of the IROHLA consortium, in December 2012 in Groningen ($n = 36$), and in May 2013 in Amsterdam ($n = 27$). During these meetings, participants discussed intermediate versions of the health literacy intervention model. In an open discussion, all members present were invited to reflect on the model and provide suggestions for further improvements. Both consensus meetings took approximately one hour.

2.5. Analyses and Reporting

For each of the three main methods, we first describe the characteristics of the included participants. Next, per method, we report the findings regarding models on interventions aiming to improve the health outcomes of people with low health literacy. Finally, we amalgamate the findings of these three methods into the development of a final model.

3. Results

3.1. Literature Review

In our search, we identified a total of 822 articles, 16 of which were included after three rounds of screening. Reference mining led to the inclusion of six additional articles, resulting in a total of 22 articles. The full selection process is presented in Figure 2.

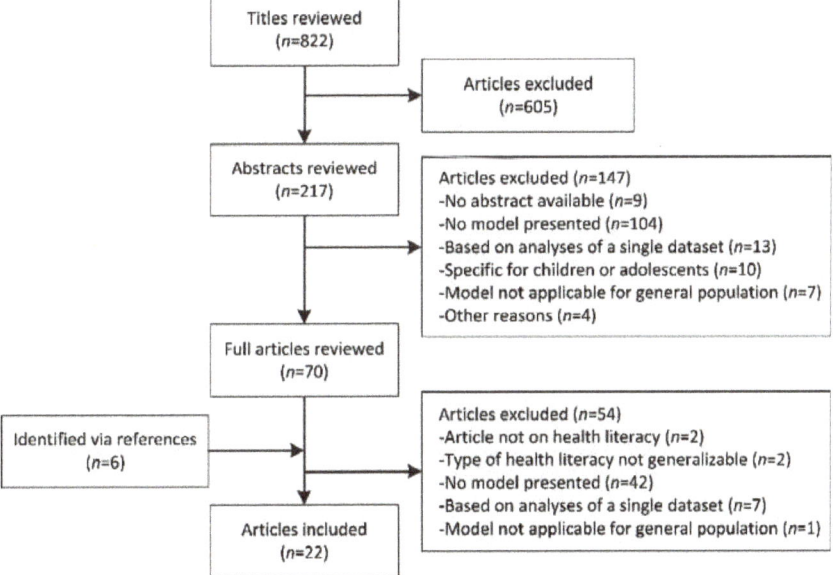

Figure 2. Flowchart of selection procedure.

The overall results of the literature review are shown in Table S1 in Supplemental Materials. For every article included in the review, this table contains the basis of the model as presented, a description of that model, and its implications for interventions, as stated by its authors.

Of the 22 models included in the literature review, most were based on existing literature on health literacy [7,9,11–21]. Others were primarily based on more general theories and concepts [8,22–25], concept mapping [26], practical experiences [27], or combinations of these sources [28,29].

Regarding the characteristics of the models, 16 primarily focused on associations of health literacy with determinants and outcomes [7–9,11–21,27,29], and of these, 15 included determinants of health literacy at the level of the individual (e.g., educational level, age, cognitive skills) [7–9,11–14,16–21,27,29]. Most of these models also included intermediate outcomes between health literacy and health outcomes (e.g., knowledge, health behaviors, self-care) [7–9,11–13,16,18–21,27,29]. Fifteen models included the role of health professionals and the health system [7,8,11–16,18,20,23,25,26,28,29]; this role was also the prime focus of four of these models [16,23,25,28]. One model specifically defined health literacy as the bridge between individual skills and abilities and the health system [15].

Most existing health literacy models do not focus explicitly on interventions. Many articles only briefly mention that their models are useful for the development of interventions, and only a few more specifically describe their models' implications for interventions [8,24,27,28]. Von Wagner et al. (2009) describe how their model can be used in three domains of health actions (i.e., access and use of health services, patient–provider interactions, and management of health and illness), by giving examples of interventions in these three domains [8]. McCormack et al. (2017) present five strategies to intervene in health literacy, based on the most important constructs of their model (i.e., health literacy, patient engagement, socioecological levels) [24]. Rootman and Ronson (2005) describe several specific intervention targets and strategies (i.e., health communication, education/training, community and organizational development, and policy development) [27]. Finally, Vellar, Mastroianni, and Lambert describe the design and development of their framework for implementation specifically in the context of the Illawarra Shoalhaven Local Health District in Australia, and the results of this implementation [28].

3.2. Anonymous Online Consultation

A total of 39 health literacy experts participated in the first round of the online survey (response rate: 29%). In the second round, we received responses from 49 health literacy experts (response rate: 30%). Of the 68 respondents who participated in at least one round of the survey, the largest group (63%, n = 43) were academia. Other participants (37%; n = 25) were healthcare professionals and policy makers. Respondents resided in Europe (n = 48; 71%), the United States (n = 10; 15%), Canada (n = 5; 7%), and other countries (n = 5; 7%). Results revealed a considerable disagreement between respondents regarding the nature of health literacy. Some experts perceived health literacy as the skills and abilities of individuals to access, understand, appraise, and communicate health information, while other experts perceived it as the interaction between individuals' skills and abilities and the demands of the health system.

Respondents considered the following characteristics most important for a health literacy intervention model:

1. The model should take into account that individuals' health literacy skills are influenced by their social context (e.g., family and peers).
2. The model should take into account that individuals' health literacy skills may change during the life course (e.g., health education, cognitive decline).
3. The model should take into account that individuals' health literacy skills are influenced by their personal characteristics.
4. The model should be flexible between different health contexts (e.g., differences in countries, types of care, etc.)
5. The model should be flexible in relation to various targets for interventions.

The modifiable determinants suggested by the respondents in the first round were split into four categories: (1) individual determinants (e.g., attitudes and skills to perform healthy behaviors or self-management), (2) contextual determinants (e.g., social cohesion, social support to enhance health behaviors), (3) determinants related to health professionals (e.g., skills to inform and educate people with low health literacy, skills to enable self-management), and (4) determinants related to the health system (e.g., cultural sensitivity, norms of professionals regarding health literacy). In the second round, respondents rated many of the modifiable determinants in all four categories as important for interventions on health literacy. Potentially modifiable determinants regarding professionals had the highest importance scores. Increasing awareness, knowledge, motivation, and skills of professionals were considered important aspects.

3.3. Consensus Meetings

Members of the IROHLA consortium present during the consensus meetings included staff members from universities, research institutes, international interest groups, non-governmental organizations, insurance companies, and ICT companies from nine countries in the European Union (a total of 21 organizations). Both consensus meetings were organized as parts of broader consortium meetings to discuss the progress of the IROHLA project.

In the consensus meetings, the nature of health literacy (i.e., skills and abilities of individuals vs. interaction between individuals' skills and abilities and the demands of the health system) was discussed extensively. However, all participants agreed that the model should make clear that health literacy outcomes are the result of both individuals' skills and abilities and the demands of the health system. Various participants also remarked that (1) the model should clearly show that health literacy affects health outcomes via intermediate outcomes, (2) that interventions to improve health literacy may also focus on individuals' social contexts, and (3) that interventions may address both individuals with low health literacy and health service providers.

3.4. Development of a Comprehensive Health Literacy Intervention Model

Based on the results of our three research methods, we developed a final version of the health literacy intervention model (Figure 3). This final version focuses on the individual and the health professional as the main actors that together determine health literacy outcomes. In the model, both actors are viewed as part of a broader context. For the individual, this encompasses the social context (e.g., family members, friends, peers); and for the health professional, it constitutes the health system.

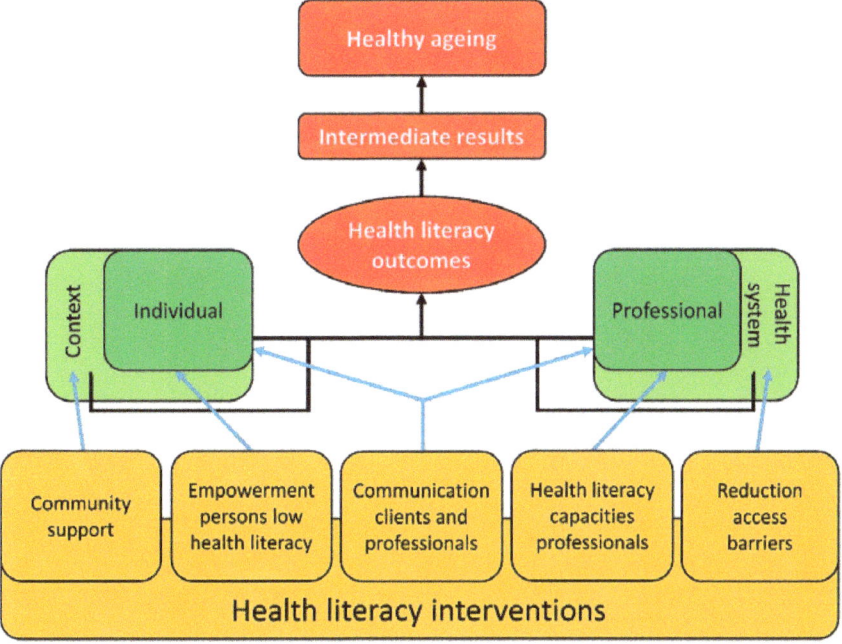

Figure 3. Final version of the health literacy intervention model.

The model shows that better health literacy outcomes can be achieved when interventions target (combinations of) the following five factors:

1. The context of the individual, via interventions that strengthen the social support systems (e.g., family, peers, caregivers, communities).
2. The individual with low health literacy, via empowering interventions (e.g., person-centered capacity building and self-management).
3. The interaction between individual characteristics and the demands of the health system, via interventions to improve communication between individuals and health professionals.
4. Health professionals, via interventions aimed at improving their health literacy capacities (e.g., recognizing health literacy related problems, communication skills).
5. Improving communication and accessibility of health systems, via interventions aimed at reducing barriers to access or policies to improve quality of care or patient safety.

The relations in the model show the interaction between characteristics of the actors and their contexts, and how this eventually affects health literacy outcomes. These include knowledge, understanding information, self-efficacy, making informed decisions, self-management skills, social engagement and patient–provider trust. The term health literacy outcomes (rather than health literacy) was chosen to make the model suitable, regardless of whether health literacy is perceived as a characteristic of individuals, or a result of the interaction between individual skills and the demands of the healthcare context. The model also shows that health literacy outcomes affect healthy ageing via a series of potential intermediate outcomes (e.g., health behaviors, adherence, access to care).

Unlike the provisional intervention model, the final model does not distinguish between empowering activities and communication activities. These two types of activities were merged into one element in the model, as the distinction between the two is not clear-cut. Interventions may often contain elements of both types of activities, and affect both individuals or their context, and health professionals or the health system.

4. Discussion

Using a multimethod approach, we developed a comprehensive health literacy intervention model. Our model constitutes a valuable addition to the existing health literacy models because (1) it is among the few models that focus specifically on interventions to improve health literacy outcomes; (2) it is comprehensive and promotes synergistic interventions that involve multiple actors and their contexts; and (3) it views health literacy as an asset, rather than as a risk. These three characteristics of our model are described in more detail below.

As confirmed by the results of our literature review, our model is among the first to focus explicitly on interventions to improve health literacy outcomes. Most existing models focus mainly on the determinants and outcomes of health literacy. Many of these models have led to important insights into the potential determinants of health literacy and the mediators between health literacy and health outcomes, but they provide limited guidance for the development of comprehensive interventions to improve these outcomes. The most relevant suggestions concerning health literacy interventions described in other models [8,14,19,23,27] have been included in the development of our model. Its comprehensive focus on interventions is a major strength of the proposed model, as it encourages developers of interventions to address multiple factors simultaneously (i.e., skills of people with low health literacy, social support, capacities of health professionals, health systems).

We found only few existing health literacy models that focused explicitly on interventions in any way. This is probably because, until recently, health literacy research generally focused on defining the concept, developing measurement instruments, and identifying associations between health literacy and its determinants and outcomes. Only very recently has health literacy research shifted its focus towards the development and testing of interventions, and the available models do not yet reflect this new trend in the research. Our comprehensive health literacy intervention model fits with these recent developments, and it may therefore be used to further advance the field of health literacy research.

By concretizing the necessary routes to be taken to improve health literacy outcomes, our model forms a bridge between existing health literacy models and actual practice.

Our comprehensive health literacy intervention model is supported by existing interventions on health literacy, and adequately captures the goals and targets of these interventions. In a recent study, the 15 most promising interventions aimed at improving the health literacy outcomes of older adults were selected and categorized by goals and target groups [30]. These interventions were found to address individuals at risk of having low health literacy, health professionals, or both these groups. Some interventions specifically addressed health professionals' capacities to communicate effectively with people with low health literacy. Finally, various interventions focused on improving contextual support or facilitating the involvement of individuals with low health literacy in health systems. Other results of the IROHLA project also support the fit of the health literacy intervention model with the goals and targets of existing interventions. These results are described in a policy brief [31].

The main goal of our model is to conceptualize various ways to achieve better health outcomes for individuals with low health literacy. The model also provides a conceptual framework for dynamic interactions between individuals with low health literacy and service providers, in which the context plays a role on both sides. When an intervention consists of multiple activities (e.g., capacity building of professionals in combination with empowering of persons with low health literacy) that take place simultaneously and in alignment, the activities are likely to reinforce each other, making them more effective than when used in isolation. Interventions that focus on more than one factor related to health literacy have, indeed, been suggested to be more effective than interventions focusing on only a single factor [32]. Further research on such synergistic effects in health literacy interventions is needed to improve our knowledge of how to optimize the beneficial effects of such interventions.

At the basis of our model is the view of health literacy as an asset that needs to grow, rather than a risk factor that needs to be managed [20]. In this view, persons with low health literacy and health service providers can together become agents of change, in interventions calling for peer education and support. Together they can create a momentum by which new capacities lead to confidence in decision-making, leading in turn to the development of critical health literacy [29].

4.1. Strengths and Limitations

The main strength of our study was the use of multiple, complementary methods. Our literature review allowed us to build on existing knowledge regarding health literacy, while our use of online consultations and consensus meetings provided us with more practice-oriented knowledge.

Our study also had a number of limitations. First, we cannot rule out the possibility that we missed a small number of articles presenting a health literacy model in our literature review, as we only searched for articles in MEDLINE. However, to minimize the risk of missing relevant articles, we adopted a broad and systematic search strategy. We also used a systematic procedure to select articles, and we checked the references of selected articles for further possible sources, also if they were not available via MEDLINE. Second, although 68 health literacy experts took part in the online consultation, providing valuable, diverse, and overlapping input, we cannot assume full saturation. However, to compensate for this, we additionally employed consensus meetings with health literacy experts. We expect that this broad approach enhanced the wider applicability of our results and of our intervention model. Third, the online consultation procedure and the consensus meetings were conducted in the framework of the IROHLA project, which focused specifically on older adults (50+) in Europe. As the model is also supported by the results of the literature review, which focused on the general population of adults worldwide, we expect that the model is applicable for other adult populations. However, this deserves further study.

4.2. Implications for Practice and Research

Our comprehensive intervention model has a number of implications for practice. First, developers of interventions should consider adopting a comprehensive approach and using different intervention strategies to promote positive health literacy outcomes. Cross-sectoral and intersectoral collaborations may be necessary to accomplish this. Second, our model can be used in health education to make (future) health professionals more aware about health literacy and the importance of using a comprehensive approach. Third, our model emphasizes a dynamic concept of health literacy, where interactions between actors can modify outcomes of interventions, where "demand" and "supply" play a role and where one can expect changes over lifetime. The model can support the longitudinal provision of prevention, treatment, and care to people with low health literacy.

Further research is needed to strengthen the evidence base of our intervention model. First, additional intervention research is needed to assess which combinations of interventions create the most synergistic effects and improve health literacy outcomes most effectively. Second, as the effectiveness of health literacy interventions can be expected to be context-dependent [33], further research should determine which combinations of actions are most useful in which context. Third, longitudinal research is needed to understand changes in health literacy skills and factors contributing to such changes during the life course. Studies on these topics may lead to refinements of our intervention model and accelerate progress in health literacy intervention research.

5. Conclusions

Based on expert opinions and the existing literature, we developed a comprehensive health literacy intervention model. Our model can contribute to the improvement of health outcomes among people with low health literacy by supporting the development of more effective health literacy interventions.

Supplementary Materials: The following are available online at http://www.mdpi.com/1660-4601/15/6/1268/s1, Table S1: Overview of health literacy models and frameworks.

Author Contributions: All authors were closely involved in the conceptualization and planning of the study. J.A.R.K. developed the provisional model. B.G. conducted the literature review and performed the selection procedures. A.F.d.W. acted as the second reviewer. A.F.d.W., J.A.R.K., and S.A.R. organized and monitored the online consultations and consensus meetings. B.G. drafted the manuscript and the table containing the results of the literature review. All authors contributed substantially to the interpretation of the results, the development of the final model, and the writing of the manuscript. All authors have read and approved the final version of the manuscript and accept full responsibility for its contents.

Funding: IROHLA was coordinated by the University Medical Center Groningen and has received funding from the European Union's Seventh Framework Programme (FP7/2007–2013) under grant agreement #305831.

Acknowledgments: The authors thank Johanna P.M. Vervoort for her contribution to the selection of literature for the literature review.

Conflicts of Interest: The authors declare no conflict of interest.

References

1. Kwan, B.; Frankish, J.; Rootman, I.; Zumbo, B.; Kelly, K.; Begoray, D.; Kazanjian, A.; Mullet, J.; Hayes, M. *The Development and Validation of Measures of "Health Literacy" in Different Populations*; University of British Columbia Institute of Health Promotion Research: Vancouver, BC, Canada; University of Victoria Centre for Community Health Promotion Research: Vancouver, BC, Canada, 2006.
2. Kutner, M.; Greenberg, E.; Jin, Y.; Paulsen, C. *The Health Literacy of America's Adults: Results from the 2003 National Assessment of Adult Literacy (NCES 2006–483)*; National Center for Education Statistics, US Department of Education: Washington, DC, USA, 2006.
3. HLS-EU Consortium. Comparative Report of Health Literacy in Eight EU Member States; The European Health Literacy Survey HLS-EU. 2012. Available online: http://ec.europa.eu/chafea/documents/news/Comparative_report_on_health_literacy_in_eight_EU_member_states.pdf (accessed on 5 February 2018).
4. Bennett, I.M.; Chen, J.; Soroui, J.S.; White, S. The contribution of health literacy to disparities in self-rated health status and preventive health behaviors in older adults. *Ann. Fam. Med.* **2009**, *7*, 204–211. [CrossRef] [PubMed]

5. Panagioti, M.; Skevington, S.M.; Hann, M.; Howells, K.; Blakemore, A.; Reeves, D.; Bower, P. Effect of health literacy on the quality of life of older patients with long-term conditions: A large cohort study in UK general practice. *Qual. Life Res.* **2018**, *27*, 1257–1268. [CrossRef] [PubMed]
6. Bostock, S.; Steptoe, A. Association between low functional health literacy and mortality in older adults: Longitudinal cohort study. *BMJ* **2012**, *344*, e1602. [CrossRef] [PubMed]
7. Paasche-Orlow, M.K.; Wolf, M.S. The causal pathways linking health literacy to health outcomes. *Am. J. Health Behav.* **2007**, *31* (Suppl. 1), S19–S26. [CrossRef] [PubMed]
8. Von Wagner, C.; Steptoe, A.; Wolf, M.S.; Wardle, J. Health literacy and health actions: A review and a framework from health psychology. *Health Educ. Behav.* **2009**, *36*, 860–877. [CrossRef] [PubMed]
9. Sørensen, K.; Van den Broucke, S.; Fullam, J.; Doyle, G.; Pelikan, J.; Slonska, Z.; Brand, H. Health literacy and public health: A systematic review and integration of definitions and models. *BMC Public Health* **2012**, *12*, 80. [CrossRef] [PubMed]
10. Health Literacy Center Europe. Available online: http://healthliteracycentre.eu/ (accessed on 13 July 2018).
11. Baker, D.W. The meaning and the measure of health literacy. *J. Gen. Intern. Med.* **2006**, *21*, 878–883. [CrossRef] [PubMed]
12. Devraj, R.; Gordon, E.J. Health literacy and kidney disease: Toward a new line of research. *Am. J. Kidney Dis.* **2009**, *53*, 884–889. [CrossRef] [PubMed]
13. Harrington, K.F.; Valerio, M.A. A conceptual model of verbal exchange health literacy. *Patient Educ. Couns.* **2014**, *94*, 403–410. [CrossRef] [PubMed]
14. Mancuso, L. Overcoming health literacy barriers: A model for action. *J. Cult. Divers.* **2011**, *18*, 60–65. [PubMed]
15. Nielsen-Bohlman, L.; Panzer, A.M.; Kindig, D.A. *Health Literacy: A Prescription to End Confusion*; National Academies Press: Washington, DC, USA, 2004.
16. Roter, D.L.; Erby, L.H.; Larson, S.; Ellington, L. Assessing oral literacy demand in genetic counseling dialogue: Preliminary test of a conceptual framework. *Soc. Sci. Med.* **2007**, *65*, 1442–1457. [CrossRef] [PubMed]
17. Shreffler-Grant, J.; Nichols, E.; Weinert, C.; Ide, B. The Montana State University conceptual model of complementary and alternative medicine health literacy. *J. Health Commun.* **2013**, *18*, 1193–1200. [CrossRef] [PubMed]
18. Squiers, L.; Peinado, S.; Berkman, N.; Boudewyns, V.; McCormack, L. The health literacy skills framework. *J. Health Commun.* **2012**, *17* (Suppl. 3), 30–54. [CrossRef] [PubMed]
19. Yip, M. A health literacy model for limited English speaking populations: Sources, context, process, and outcomes. *Contemp. Nurse* **2012**, *40*, 160–168. [CrossRef] [PubMed]
20. Nutbeam, D. The evolving concept of health literacy. *Soc. Sci. Med.* **2008**, *67*, 2072–2078. [CrossRef] [PubMed]
21. Lee, S.D.; Arozullah, A.M.; Cho, Y.I. Health literacy, social support, and health: A research agenda. *Soc. Sci. Med.* **2004**, *58*, 1309–1321. [CrossRef]
22. Dawkins-Moultin, L.; McDonald, A.; McKyer, L. Integrating the principles of socioecology and critical pedagogy for health promotion health literacy interventions. *J. Health Commun.* **2016**, *21*, 30–35. [CrossRef] [PubMed]
23. Koh, H.K.; Brach, C.; Harris, L.M.; Parchman, M.L. A proposed 'health literate care model' would constitute a systems approach to improving patients' engagement in care. *Health Aff.* **2013**, *32*, 357–367. [CrossRef] [PubMed]
24. McCormack, L.; Thomas, V.; Lewis, M.A.; Rudd, R. Improving low health literacy and patient engagement: A social ecological approach. *Patient Educ. Couns.* **2017**, *100*, 8–13. [CrossRef] [PubMed]
25. Yin, H.S.; Jay, M.; Maness, L.; Zabar, S.; Kalet, A. Health Literacy: An Educationally Sensitive Patient Outcome. *J. Gen. Intern. Med.* **2015**, *30*, 1363–1368. [CrossRef] [PubMed]
26. Yuen, E.Y.N.; Dodson, S.; Batterham, R.W.; Knight, T.; Chirgwin, J.; Livingston, P.M. Development of a conceptual model of cancer caregiver health literacy. *Eur. J. Cancer Care* **2016**, *25*, 294–306. [CrossRef] [PubMed]
27. Rootman, I.; Ronson, B. Literacy and health research in Canada: Where have we been and where should we go? *Can. J. Public Health* **2005**, *96* (Suppl. 2), S62–S77. [PubMed]
28. Vellar, L.; Mastroianni, F.; Lambert, K. Embedding health literacy into health systems: A case study of a regional health service. *Aust. Health Rev.* **2017**, *41*, 621–625. [CrossRef] [PubMed]
29. Nutbeam, D. Health literacy as a public health goal: A challenge for contemporary health education and communication strategies into the 21st century. *Health Promot. Int.* **2000**, *15*, 259–267. [CrossRef]

30. Brainard, J.; Loke, Y.; Salter, C.; Koós, T.; Csizmadia, P.; Makai, A.; Gács, B.; Szepes, M. Healthy ageing in Europe: Prioritizing interventions to improve health literacy. *BMC Res. Notes* **2016**, *9*, 270. [CrossRef] [PubMed]
31. IROHLA Consortium. *Health Literacy for Healthy Ageing*; Policy Brief for Health Organisations; IROHLA Consortium: Groningen, The Netherlands, 2015; Available online: http://healthliteracycentre.eu/wp-content/uploads/2015/11/Brochure_Organisations.pdf (accessed on 27 April 2018).
32. Cooper, L.A.; Roter, D.L.; Carson, K.A.; Bone, L.R.; Larson, S.M.; Miller, E.R., III; Barr, M.S.; Levine, D.M. A randomized trial to improve patient-centered care and hypertension control in underserved primary care patients. *J. Gen. Intern. Med.* **2011**, *26*, 1297–1304. [CrossRef] [PubMed]
33. Powers, B.J.; Olsen, M.K.; Oddone, E.Z.; Thorpe, C.T.; Bosworth, H.B. Literacy and blood pressure—Do healthcare systems influence this relationship? A cross-sectional study. *BMC Health Serv. Res.* **2008**, *8*, 219. [CrossRef] [PubMed]

© 2018 by the authors. Licensee MDPI, Basel, Switzerland. This article is an open access article distributed under the terms and conditions of the Creative Commons Attribution (CC BY) license (http://creativecommons.org/licenses/by/4.0/).

Article

The Antecedents and Consequences of Health Literacy in an Ecological Perspective: Results from an Experimental Analysis

Chiara Lorini [1,*], Francesca Ierardi [2], Letizia Bachini [2], Martina Donzellini [3], Fabrizio Gemmi [2] and Guglielmo Bonaccorsi [1]

1. Department of Health Science, University of Florence, Viale GB Morgagni 48, 50134 Firenze, Italy; guglielmo.bonaccorsi@unifi.it
2. Quality and Equity Unit, Regional Health Agency of Tuscany, 50141 Florence, Italy; francesca.ierardi@ars.toscana.it (F.I.); letizia.bachini@ars.toscana.it (L.B.); fabrizio.gemmi@ars.toscana.it (F.G.)
3. School of Specialization in Hygiene and Preventive Medicine, University of Florence, 50134 Florence, Italy; martinadonzellini@gmail.com
* Correspondence: chiara.lorini@unifi.it; Tel.: +39-055-275-1065; Fax: +39-055-275-1093 (ext. 50134)

Received: 13 March 2018; Accepted: 16 April 2018; Published: 19 April 2018

Abstract: This study analyses the relationship between the antecedents and consequences of health literacy (HL) at the ecological level among the nations involved in the European Health Literacy Survey (HLS-EU). The antecedents and consequences were investigated by means of proxy indicators. The HL was measured using the 47-item HLS-EU questionnaire (HLS-EUQ47) and the Newest Vital Sign (NVS). The two measures stood in significant correlation to the outcomes of the sub-discipline of the Euro Health Consumer Index (r = 0.790 for HLS-EUQ47; r = 0.789 for NVS). The HLS-EUQ47 also stood in correlation to the percentage of population with post-secondary education (r = 0.810), the reading performance for 15-year-old students (r = 0.905), the presence of a national screening program for breast (r = 0.732) or cervical cancer (r = 0.873). The NVS stood in correlation with the unemployment rate (r = −0.778), the Gross Domestic Product (r = 0.719), the Gini coefficient (r = −0.743), the rank of the Euro Patient Empowerment Index (r = −0.826), the expenditure on social protection (r = 0.814), the Consumer Empowerment Index (r = 0.898), the percentage of adults using the internet for seeking health information (r = 0.759), the prevalence of overweight individuals (r = −0.843), the health expenditure (r = 0.766), as well as the percentage of individuals using the internet for interacting with public authorities (r = 0.755). This study provides some preliminary considerations regarding alternative means by which to study HL and proposes new methods for experimentation. The methods and the results could offer a means by which the relationship between society and overall healthcare protection could be strengthened.

Keywords: health literacy; ecological study; antecedents; consequences; determinants of health

1. Introduction

Health literacy (HL) is a multifaceted concept that concerns the capacities of individuals to meet the complex demands of health in a modern society [1].

With regard to research and practice in terms of HL, two approaches have predominated during recent decades: the individual (clinical) level and the public health level. The first approach is the oldest: it focuses on an individual's capacity to obtain, process, and understand basic health information, including health services, needed to make appropriate health-related decisions. This approach highlights existing gaps within strategies of treatment, prevention, and health promotion as well as overall health behavior, including specific individual health-related outcomes [2]. The second approach incorporates knowledge as to the social determinants of health and relates to the definition of public health literacy, "the degree to which individuals and groups can obtain, process, understand, evaluate, and act upon information needed to make public health decisions that benefit the community" [3,4].

In terms of the public health perspective, Sørensen et al. [5] proposed a comprehensive model with an integrated definition: "Health literacy is linked to literacy and entails people's knowledge, motivation and competences to access, understand, appraise, and apply health information in order to make judgments and take decisions in everyday life concerning healthcare, disease prevention and health promotion to maintain or improve quality of life during the life course". The conceptual framework proposed by Sørensen identified four dimensions of HL (access, understand, process, and apply) which could be applied to three domains (health care, disease prevention, health promotion). The framework also took into consideration the proximal and distal factors (antecedents) which impact HL as well as its related outcomes (consequences). Within Sørensen's framework, antecedents specifically refer to societal and environmental factors (i.e., demographics, culture, language, political forces, societal systems) as distal factors whereas situational determinants (i.e., social support, family and peer influence, media use, physical environment) and personal determinants (i.e., age, gender, race, socioeconomic status, education, occupation, employment, income, literacy) are considered proximal factors. Consequences at both the individual and population level refer to health service use and health costs; health behaviour and health outcomes; participation and empowerment in health issues; equity and sustainability of public health issues. Such a framework suggests two levels of analysis and intervention, the subject level and the ecological level. Sørensen's model has been used as a basis for developing the multidimensional questionnaire used to measure and compare HL in the general population (the HLS-EU-Q) of eight European countries in the European Health Literacy Survey (HLS-EU) [6,7]. To date, it has been the first attempt to measure HL in different countries at the same time using the same measures.

Many studies have shown the correlation between antecedents and HL, as well as between consequences and HL [8–11]. The majority of such studies focused on only a few similar or correlating factors; this has led to a fragmentation of the results without an overall quantitative assessment of the relationship among all relevant factors.

To the best of our knowledge, no studies have been published regarding the ecological relationships between HL and its antecedents and consequences in terms of macro-level factors. Such information could guide policy makers in providing appropriate responses to the needs of citizens. As such, this study identifies a set of indicators, available using free data from international databases or from published documents, to test according to an ecological model. Accordingly, this paper provides a novel approach to the study of health literacy. This paper aims to advance our understanding of the relationship among nationally determined contextual characteristics within the countries included in the HLS-EU in terms of their role as HL antecedents or consequences.

2. Materials and Methods

The study objective was addressed using an ecological model in which the antecedents and consequences of HL were measured at country level. The design of the study was suitable to investigate macro-level properties, namely political, economic, demographic, and health contexts, through proxy indicators.

2.1. HL (Health Literac) Measurements

Data on HL were obtained through consultation of the published results of the first HLS-EU, conducted in 2011 in eight countries (Austria, Bulgaria, Germany, Greece, Ireland, the Netherlands, Poland, and Spain) [7,12,13]. In this survey, HL was measured by means of two tools: the HLS-EUQ47 and the Newest Vital Sign (NVS). The first consisted of 47 items comprising the core of the HL model, a twelve-cell matrix positing the key processes of accessing, understanding, appraising, and applying health-related information within three domains (healthcare, disease prevention, health promotion) [5,6]. According to Nutbeam's definition [14], it assessed functional, interactive, and critical HL (Table 1).

Table 1. Health literacy (HL) definition, according to Nutbeam [14].

Functional HL	Basic Reading, Writing, and Literacy Skills
Interactive HL	Communicative and social skills that can be used to derive meaning from different forms of communication, and to apply new information to changing circumstances
Critical HL	Cognitive and social skills required to critically analyse information, and to use this information to exert greater control over life events and situations through individual and collective action to address the social, economic and environmental determinants of health

For each item, respondents rated the perceived difficulty of a given task, resulting in a subjective assessment of HL. The answers were placed on a four-category Likert scale (from "very easy" to "very difficult") then converted into a score. Using the scores of the 47 items, the authors constructed a comprehensive general index of HL (total score ranging from 0 to 50) which was used to define the ranges for different levels of HL ("inadequate", "problematic", "sufficient", "excellent" general-HL).

The NVS is a rapid assessment instrument for measuring functional HL, including numeracy. It assesses the respondents' ability to read and apply information from a nutritional label for ice cream and constitutes an objective assessment of HL [15]. The UK version of the NVS [16], which was used in the HLS-EU, consisted of seven questions related to the nutritional label. According to the number of correct answers (from 0 to 6), a raw score was computed indicating the likelihood of a level of HL ("high likelihood of limited literacy", "possibility of limited literacy", "high likeliness of adequate literacy").

Literature data [7,13] report both the descriptive statistics of the total score and the levels of HLS-EU-Q47 and of NVS by country; however, for this study, only mean values of HLS-EU-Q47 and of NVS were considered.

2.2. Antecedents and Consequences of HL

The final set of antecedents and outcome indicators was identified following a three-stage approach. First, Sørensen review [5] was used to define antecedents and consequences by area. Then, a literature review was conducted to select a list of indicators related to antecedents and consequences according to the different areas. Finally, the availability of the listed indicators for the eight countries involved in the HLS-EU was verified via international databases and documents.

The literature review was conducted through a Pubmed search of ecological studies conducted at the national level, including studies which analysed any aspect of health. Moreover, web-available documents issued by international organizations focused on international comparisons describing health or health-related indicators at the national level were searched and reviewed. Selected documents were analyzed to identify all indicators used and a list of these indicators was compiled.

Subsequently, the availability of each of the listed indicators was checked. Aggregate country-level antecedent and consequence indicator data were extracted from several databases and/or documents which was available from the websites of Eurostat, European Health for All (HFA-DB), the Organisation for Economic Co-operation and Development (OECD), the Health Consumer Powerhouse (HCP), the World Health Organization, and the European Commission. To obtain the most reliable information for comparison with the HL average, data was considered adequate and included in analysis if it referred to the three-year period preceding the HLS-EU (2009–2011). When data were available which referred to more than one year within the three-year period, those relating to the year closest to the HLS-EU were included in the analysis. Finally, indicators were included in the analysis only when available for each of the eight countries included in the HLS-EU. If an area was over-represented in the final database (i.e., with more than five indicators), the less frequently used indicators for international comparison were omitted.

2.3. Statistical Analysis

Using each country as a unit of analysis, a correlation analysis was performed by means of Spearman rank correlation coefficients, which included the final set of indicators and the HL measures (HLS-EU-Q47 and NVS mean scores).

The analysis was conducted using STATA, release 12.1 (StataCorp LLC, College Station, TX, USA). Statistical significance was set at $p = 0.05$.

3. Results

3.1. The Selection of the List of Indicators

According to Sørensen's review, he antecedents and consequences by areas are listed in Table 2. Since health outcomes could be considered both antecedents and consequences of HL, this area was included in both sections.

Table 2. Conceptual models of the areas for antecedents (A) and consequences (B) of health literacy, developed from the results of Sørensen's review [5].

Levels	Areas	Sub-Areas
	A—Antecedents.	
Personal Determinants (Proximal Factors)	Demographic	Age Gender Race/ethnicity
	Competences	Literacy Education level Operational competences Interactive competences Autonomous competences Informational competences Contextual competences Cultural competences Media use Peer and parent influences Reading and arithmetical skills
	Socioeconomic	Occupation Employment status Income Income discrepancy
	Health	Disease severity Health status Health-related experience Personal competences such as vision, hearing, verbal ability, memory and reasoning Cognitive abilities Physical abilities
	Healthcare	Health coverage Health system Communication and assessment skills of people with whom individuals interact for health Complexity and difficulty of the printed and spoken messages in the healthcare environment
Situational Determinants (Distal Factors)	Policy	Health promotion actions (education, social mobilization, advocacy) Ability of the media, the marketplace, and governmental agencies to provide health information in an appropriate manner Social support Education system Social, environmental and political forces

Table 2. *Cont.*

B—Consequences.

Levels	Areas	Sub-Areas
Individual ↓ Community/Social	Health outcomes	Health status (also self-reported) Health outcome
	Health behavior	Health behaviors Prevention behaviors Health-promoting behaviors Screening behaviors Compliance Medical or medication treatment errors
	Empowerment	Attitudes Self-efficacy Capacity to act independently on knowledge Motivation and self-confidence Individual resilience Ability to apply information to novel situations Self-management skills/ability to care Health knowledge (risk, diseases and treatments) Improved capacity to influence social norms and interact with social groups Improved capacity to act on social and economic determinants of health
	Participation	Ability to participate in public and private dialogues about health, medicine, scientific knowledge and cultural beliefs Patients-provider interactions Screening behaviors
	Health services use	Hospitalization Emergency care Use of healthcare services Healthcare access
	Sustainability	Social injustice Healthcare costs
	Equity	Healthcare access Improved capacity to influence social norms and interact with social groups Improved capacity to act on social and economic determinants of health Social injustice

Literature review led to the selection of eight ecological studies [17–24] and 14 documents [25–38], generating a list of approximately 250 indicators (Table S1). As shown in Table 1, some areas were not represented by any indicator since they were not investigated in the selected studies. Most of the indicator data were not available in the consulted databases or documents for every county included in the HLS-EU in the period 2009–2011.

The final list of indicators ($N = 37$) included in the analysis as well as the data sources is reported in Table 3. Table S2 contains the final dataset.

3.2. The Correlation Analysis

The HLS-EUQ47 and the NVS mean scores are not significantly correlated ($r = 0.419$; $p = 0.301$). Table 4 reports the results of the correlation analysis. The HLS-EUQ47 and the NVS scores present different results. With regard to antecedents, the HLS-EUQ47 mean score stood in significant correlation to the percentage of population with post-secondary education ($r = 0.810$), reading performance for 15-year-old students ($r = 0.905$), the presence of a national breast cancer screening program ($r = 0.732$), and the presence of a national cervical cancer screening program ($r = 0.873$). Regarding consequences, the mean score stood in significant correlation to only the "outcomes" sub-discipline of the Euro Health Consumer Index ($r = 0.790$).

Table 3. Indicators included in the correlation analysis and data sources.

Sub-Area	Indicator	Data Source	Year
	Antecedents		
Gender	Women/100 men	Eurostat	2011
Age	Population aged 65+ (%)	Health for All	2011
Race/ethnicity	Foreign-born population (%)	Health for All	2011
Education level	Population with post-secondary education aged 25+ (%)	Health for All	2010
Education level	Lifelong learning-% persons aged 25 to 64 who stated that they received education or training in the four weeks preceding the survey	OECD	2011
Media use	Population that use the Internet at least ones a week (% of individuals)	Eurostat	2010
Reading and arithmetical skills	Reading achievement (average reading performance for 15-year-old students)	OECD	2009
Employment status	Unemployment rate (%)	Health for All	2011
Income	Gross Domestic Product (GDP), U.S.$ per capita	Health for All	2011
Income discrepancy	Gini coefficient	Health for All	2011
Health status	Prevalence of chronic depression (%)	OECD	2011
cognitive abilities	Prevalence of dementia (%)	OECD	2009
Health coverage	National breast cancer screening program (0 if not, 1 if yes)	European Commission	2011
Health coverage	National cervical cancer screening program (0 if not, 1 if yes)	European Commission	2011
Health systems	Hospitals per 100,000 abitants	Health for All	2011
Health systems	Euro Patient Empowerment Index-total score-rank	HCP	2009
Health promotion actions	Tobacco Control Scale Ranking	Joossens, 2013	2010
Social support	Expenditure on social protection (% of GDP)	Eurostat	2011
Social, environmental and political forces	Households with internet access (%)	Eurostat	2011

32

Table 3. *Cont.*

Sub-Area	Indicator	Data Source	Year
	Consequences		
Capacity to act independently on knowledge, Motivation and self-confidence, individual resilience, Ability to apply information to novel situations, Ability to participate in public and private dialogues about health, medicine, scientific knowledge and cultural beliefs, self-efficacy, attitudes	Consumer Empowerment Index score	Eurobarometer	2011
Health knowledge (risk, diseases and treatments)	Individuals (16–74) using the internet for seeking health information (%)	Eurostat	2011
Health behavior	Prevalence of overweight (%)	Health for All	2010
Health behavior	Pure alcohol consumption (litres per capita)	Health for All	2011
Health behavior	Adult population smoking daily (%)	OECD	2010
Health outcomes	Life expectancy at birth	Eurostat	2011
Health outcomes	Suicide and self-inflicted injury death rate per 100,000 abitants	Health for All	2011
Health status	Self-perceived health-% Bad	Eurostat	2011
Health outcomes	People having a long-standing illness or health problem by educational attainment level	Eurostat	2011
Health outcomes	Euro Health Consumer Index-Outcomes sub-discipline	HCP	2009
Hospitalization	Hospital discharges per 1000 inhabitants	OECD	2010
Healthcare costs	Total health expenditure (% of GDP)	Health for All	2011
Healthcare costs	Private expenditure on health as % of total expenditure on health	Health for All	2011
Healthcare access	Self-reported unmet need for medical examination or treatment	Eurostat	2011
Screening behaviors	Mammography screening, women aged 50-69 screened (%)	OECD	2010
Improved capacity to influence social norms and interact with social groups	Individuals using the internet for interacting with public authorities (last 12 months) (%)	Eurostat	2011
Social injustice	Crime, violence or vandalism in the area	Eurostat	2011
Social injustice	UNDP Human Development Index (HDI)	Health for All	2011

HCP: Health Consumer Powerhouse; OECD: Organisation for Economic Co-operation and Development; UNDP: United Nations Development Programme.

Table 4. Spearman's correlation between HL (mean value of HLS-EU-Q47 and NVS scores), its antecedents and its consequences in the eight European countries of the HL Survey.

	Indicators	HLS-EU-Q 47 Score Rho	HLS-EU-Q 47 Score p	NVS Score Rho	NVS Score p
	Women/100 men	−0.611	0.108	−0.614	0.105
	Population aged 65+ (%)	−0.405	0.320	0.168	0.691
	Foreign-born population (%)	0.262	0.531	0.275	0.509
	Population with post-secondary education aged 25+ (%)	0.810	0.015	0.635	0.091
	Lifelong learning: % persons aged 25 to 64 who stated that they received education or training in the four weeks preceding the survey	0.381	0.352	0.551	0.157
	Population that use the internet at least ones a week (% of individuals)	0.667	0.071	0.647	0.083
	Reading achievement (average reading performance for 15-year-old students)	0.905	0.002	0.299	0.471
	Unemployment rate (%)	−0.071	0.867	−0.778	0.023
Antecedents	GDP, U.S.$ per capita	0.667	0.071	0.719	0.045
	Gini coefficient	−0.524	0.183	−0.743	0.035
	Prevalence of chronic depression (%)	0.275	0.509	0.590	0.123
	Prevalence of dementia (%)	0.095	0.823	0.168	0.691
	National breast cancer screening program (0 if not, 1 if yes)	0.732	0.039	−0.113	0.789
	National cervical cancer screening program (0 if not, 1 if yes)	0.873	0.005	0.274	0.511
	Hospitals per 100,000	−0.595	0.120	0.000	1.000
	EPEI total score-rank	−0.595	0.120	−0.826	0.011
	Tobacco Control Scale Ranking	−0.518	0.188	0.248	0.553
	Expenditure on social protection (% of GDP)	0.381	0.352	0.814	0.014
	Households with internet access (%)	0.286	0.493	−0.036	0.933
	Consumer Empowerment Index	0.548	0.160	0.898	0.002
	Individuals (16–74) using the internet for seeking health information (%)	0.407	0.317	0.759	0.029
	Prevalence of overweight (%)	−0.024	0.955	−0.843	0.009
	Pure alcohol consumption, litres per capita	0.072	0.866	−0.548	0.159
	Adult population smoking daily	−0.476	0.233	−0.575	0.136
	Life expectancy at birth	0.238	0.570	0.228	0.588
	Suicide and self-inflicted injury (SDR) per 100,000	0.048	0.911	0.060	0.888
	Self-perceived health-% Bad	−0.595	0.120	−0.275	0.509
	People having a long-standing illness or health problem by educational attainment level	0.024	0.955	−0.530	0.177
Consequences	Euro Health Consumer Index-Outcomes sub-discipline	0.790	0.020	0.789	0.020
	Hospital discharges per 100) inhabitants	−0.524	0.183	0.228	0.588
	Total health expenditure (% of GDP)	0.095	0.823	0.766	0.027
	Private expenditure on health as % of total expenditure on health	−0.455	0.257	−0.602	0.114
	Self-reported unmet need for medical examination or treatment	0.371	0.365	0.566	0.143
	Mammography screening, women aged 50–69 screened (%)	0.381	0.352	0.419	0.301
	Individuals using the internet for interacting with public authorities (last 12 months) (%)	0.548	0.160	0.755	0.031
	Crime, violence or vandalism in the area	−0.286	0.493	0.323	0.435
	UNDP Human Development Index (HDI)	0.071	0.867	0.443	0.272

Note: UNDP: United Nations Development Programme.

In terms of the NVS mean score, significant correlations existed among the unemployment rate (r = −0.778), the Gross Domestic Product (GDP, r = 0.719), the Gini coefficient (r = −0.743), the rank of the Euro Patient Empowerment Index (EPEI) total score (r = −0.826), and the expenditure on social protection (r = 0.814) as antecedents. Moreover, the NVS mean score was also significantly associated with the Consumer Empowerment Index (r = 0.898), the percentage of adults using the internet for seeking health information (r = 0.759), the prevalence of overweight individuals (r = −0.843), the "outcomes" sub-discipline of the Euro Health Consumer Index (r = 0.789), the total health expenditure (r = 0.766), and the percentage of individuals using the internet for interacting with public authorities (r = 0.755) as consequences.

4. Discussion

This study investigates the ecological relationships between the antecedents and consequences of HL as related to macro-level factors. To the best of our knowledge, no previous ecological studies on HL have previously been published. Accordingly, comparisons with other studies are not possible. On the other hand, many studies have explored the relationships the antecedents and consequences of HL at the individual level.

According to other researchers [39–41], HL is not only an individual variable but also a social practice. It is a distributed resource (distributed HL) within an individual's social network, where health literate subjects share their HL skills to support other individuals as to how to manage their health, communicate with health professionals, and make overall decisions about their health. Batterham et al. [41] stressed the importance of a distributed HL both for individual empowerment (freedom of choices and participation in decision making) and adherence to professional medical advice. Accordingly, the study of HL as an ecological variable allows us to better understand the role of this determinant of health.

Ecological design is appropriate if researchers are interested in the effect of macro-level aspects. As such, this study could be a valid contribution in terms of the concept of HL, particularly on the level of national public health. However, this type of study is potentially susceptible to ecological fallacy which can encompass several potential biases: ecological confounding, model specification bias, and ecological bias. Nevertheless, many researchers are confident that this type of study can contribute to creating reliable causal relationships [42].

Sørensen's integrated conceptual model of HL describes its predominant antecedents and consequences, which resulted from reviewing existing HL concepts [5]. HLS-EU has contributed to a validation of the conceptual model, collecting individual data in eight countries using a comprehensive questionnaire that featured two measures of HL (HLS-EU-Q47 and NVS) and 39 items referring to antecedents and consequences outlined in the conceptual model [7]. Our research further contributes a validation of the conceptual model at the national level. In the HLS-EU-Q, the identification of the 39 items to be included in the questionnaire is the result of a literature review; in our study, the identification of the indicators to be included in the correlation analysis is the result of a literature review as well. As this is the first study which analysed HL at an ecological level, the list of indicators was selected those used in various ecological studies and were attributable to antecedents or consequences as outlined in the Sørensen conceptual model. Accordingly, this study could be described as an experiment to validate the Sørensen conceptual model of HL at an ecological level and an analysis of indicators that are applicable at the national scale. Unfortunately, data availability for the eight countries involved in the HLS-EU and which referred to the three years preceding the HLS-EU limited the possible number of indicators to be entered into the analysis.

No previous ecological studies have been published with either this level of focus on indicators or which have incorporated this many data sources. Indeed, the aim of this study was to identify novel sources of "ecological" data, combining information from international databases (Eurostat, Health for All, and OECD databases) and ad hoc surveys (HLS-EU, Eurobarometer, Eurostat, European Commission, and HCP surveys, Joossens' study).

Significant amounts of secondary data, already collected or produced by other researchers, are available for free online; this is an excellent opportunity for research, especially for emergent ecological studies. Information provided by databases associated with international organizations can usually be easily obtained via their websites; data from ad hoc surveys are usually described in the results of the studies or can be requested directly from the researchers. Nonetheless, the use of secondary data presents several limitations that could have influenced the quality of this study. Data are neither specific to the aims of this study (fitness for use), nor controlled for quality by the Authors of this study (the Authors are not responsible for primary data). The use of numerous data sources as well as the inclusion of eight nations could have reinforced these critical quality issues.

International databases are frequently compiled from various sources; they are validated and processed in a uniform way to improve the international comparability of statistics. Quality of data is a central issue in the production of health indicators for international organizations; they have quality management policies and they constantly review both their data sources and methodologies. Statistics are checked for consistency, coherence, and comparability [43–45]; however, their quality is primarily influenced by the quality of each respective nation's statistics. Additionally, for some indicators (e.g., migration statistics), a lack of international comparability is a well-known issue [46]. Moreover, the comparability and the accuracy of data reported in the international databases is limited in some cases, owing to a variety of factors including differences in definitions and/or time periods, incomplete registration, or other variations in national data recording and/or processing. Ad hoc surveys can help to overcome the limitations of internal consistency and comparability as a shared study protocol often can be generally applied across all research units. However, even these may present limitations on results due to differing sampling procedures which influence comparability across countries. Moreover, ad hoc studies are limited in time (i.e., data are not routinely collected). On the other hand, such studies usually are innovative and experimentally tentative. Occasionally, pilot exercises to describe macro-level aspects use novel indicators to compare the same phenomena in different countries. Our research may be comparable to such studies; a tentatively novel methodology to integrate significantly different sources of both routine and innovative indicators.

The results of our study are not exhaustive nor conclusive resulting from limitations in the selection of indicators (literature review not related to ecological studies on HL, lack of data availability, some areas outlined in the Sørensen model not represented in our study) as well as in the quality and comparability of some indicators. Moreover, the study design and the low number of countries involved (eight) limited the statistical analysis and the strength of the results. For example, correlation analysis is sensitive to outliers; although Spearman's correlation is less sensitive to outliers, the low number of observations may have influenced the results [47].

Despite these limitations, some tentative conclusions may be drawn from the results. This study provides some preliminary regarding the antecedents and consequences of HL which require additional analysis.

The HLS-EUQ47 and the NVS scores showed no significant correlation and presented different results in the correlation analysis. The data analysis of the HLS-EU, conducted at the individual level, showed a significantly positive but low correlation between the HLS-EU-Q47 and the NVS scores, with a coefficient equal to 0.25 [13]. The relationship between objective and subjective HL measures has received limited attention. Few studies using multiple instruments have been conducted to date [48]. At a conceptual level, these tools measure different constructs: the Sørensen definition of HL for the HLS-EUQ47 [5], that of the U.S. Department of Health and Human Services [49] for the NVS. The NVS provides a measure of individual HL, which is the consequence of both the individual skills and the complexity of the context within which people act [50]. In contrast, the HLS-EUQ47 is a measure of public HL [51]. Since they measure different aspects of HL in different ways, it is not surprising that they led to different results in this study; however, the two measurements provided a more complete picture of HL.

Without separating the results which emerged from the two different measurement tools, our data show that HL is related to the following antecedents on an ecological (national) level: the percentage of the population with post-secondary education (r = 0.810 with HLS-EUQ47 score), the reading achievement (r = 0.905 with HLS-EUQ47 score), the unemployment rate (r = −0.778 with NVS score), the GDP (r = 0.719 with NVS score), the Gini coefficient (r = − 0.743 with NVS score), the presence of a national breast cancer screening programme (r = 0.732 with HLS-EUQ47 score) or of a national cervical cancer screening programme (r = 0.873 with HLS-EUQ47 score), the national rank of the EPEI total score (r = −0.826 with NVS score), and the expenditure on social protection (r = 0.814 with NVS score). Surprisingly, demographic data (indicators related to gender, age, or ethnicity distribution) showed no correlation with HL. Moreover, HL stood in correlation to the following consequences: the Consumer Empowerment Index (r = 0.898 with NVS score); the percentage of adults using the Internet for seeking health information (r = 0.759 with NVS score); the prevalence of overweight (r = −0.843 with NVS score); the outcome sub-discipline of the Euro Health Consumer Index (r = 0.790 with HLS-EUQ47 score, r = 0.789 for NVS score); the total health expenditure, as percentage of GDP (r = 0.766 with NVS score); and the percentage of individuals using the Internet for interacting with public authorities (r = 0.755 with NVS score).

Accordingly, national policies devoted to promote and provide the prerequisites of health (specifically education, income, social justice, and equity), to increase health coverage (i.e., the introduction of national screening programmes), and to make healthcare systems more empowering for the patients should result in a widespread increase of HL among a nation's population. On the other hand, those policies (particularly those dedicated to increasing functional HL) should contribute to the following results: an increase in consumer empowerment, the decrease of the prevalence of overweight individuals, the increase of the health status of the population, and the increase of total health expenditure. It is important to highlight that the increase of consumer empowerment as well as the decrease of the prevalence of overweight individuals and general obesity are among the main objectives of the European Commission [52,53]. Moreover, the results suggest that, where the HL of the population is high, the Internet could be used effectively by policy makers and experts for the provision of information and services related to health and health services. It may also provide a means by which to interact with the population. In contrast, in countries where the HL of the population is low, such tactics may contribute to the digital divide [54], increasing overall inequality.

5. Conclusions

This study provides some preliminary considerations regarding different approaches to study HL including the potential of analyzing the ecological level of HL as well as other novel methods of analysis. It also provides a list of indicators by which one may validate the Sørensen conceptual model using secondary data. Both the methods and the results need to be analysed further; however, both will offer, when weaknesses and limits are reduced, a key method to strengthen the relationship between society and healthcare protection.

Supplementary Materials: The following are available online at http://www.mdpi.com/1660-4601/15/4/798/s1, Table S1: Conceptual model of HL and indicators reported in ecological studies/reports/documents by area. Table S2: Database.

Acknowledgments: None declared. This research did not receive any specific grant from funding agencies in the public, commercial, or not-for-profit sectors.

Author Contributions: C.L.: conception and design of the study; generation, collection, assembly, analysis and interpretation of data; drafting and revision of the manuscript. F.I.: conception and design of the study; generation, collection, assembly, analysis and interpretation of data; drafting and revision of the manuscript. L.B.: conception and design of the study; generation, collection, assembly, analysis and interpretation of data; revision of the manuscript. M.D.: conception and design of the study; generation, collection, assembly, analysis and interpretation of data; revision of the manuscript. F.G.: conception of the study; revision of the manuscript. G.B.: conception and design of the study; interpretation of data; drafting and revision of the manuscript.

Conflicts of Interest: The authors declare no conflict of interest.

References

1. Kickbusch, I.S. Health literacy: Addressing the health and education divide. *Health Promot. Int.* **2001**, *16*, 289–297. [CrossRef] [PubMed]
2. Institute of Medicine. *Health Literacy: A Prescription to End Confusion*; National Academy Press: Washington, DC, USA, 2004.
3. Freedman, D.A.; Bess, K.D.; Tucker, H.A.; Boyd, D.L.; Tuchman, A.M.; Wallston, K.A. Public health literacy defined. *Am. J. Prev. Med.* **2009**, *36*, 446–451. [CrossRef] [PubMed]
4. Guzys, D.; Kenny, A.; Dickson-Swift, V.; Threlkeld, G. A critical review of population health literacy assessment. *BMC Public Health* **2015**, *15*, 215. [CrossRef] [PubMed]
5. Sørensen, K.; Van den Broucke, S.; Fullam, J.; Doyle, G.; Pelikan, J.; Slonska, Z.; Brand, H.; (HLS-EU) Consortium Health Literacy Project European. Health literacy and public health: A systematic review and integration of definitions and models. *BMC Public Health* **2012**, *12*, 80. [CrossRef]
6. Sørensen, K.; Van den Broucke, S.; Pelikan, J.M.; Fullam, J.; Doyle, G.; Slonska, Z.; Kondilis, B.; Stoffels, V.; Osborne, R.H.; Brand, H.; et al. Measuring health literacy in populations: Illuminating the design and development process of the European Health Literacy Survey Questionnaire (HLS-EU-Q). *BMC Public Health* **2013**, *13*, 948. [CrossRef] [PubMed]
7. Sørensen, K.; Pelikan, J.M.; Röthlin, F.; Ganahl, K.; Slonska, Z.; Doyle, G.; Fullam, J.; Kondilis, B.; Agrafiotis, D.; Uiters, E.; et al. Health literacy in Europe: Comparative results of the European health literacy survey (HLS-EU). *Eur. J. Public Health* **2015**, *25*, 1053–1058. [CrossRef] [PubMed]
8. Bo, A.; Friis, K.; Osborne, R.H.; Maindal, H.T. National indicators of health literacy: Ability to understand health information and to engage actively with healthcare providers—A population-based survey among Danish adults. *BMC Public Health* **2014**, *14*, 1095. [CrossRef] [PubMed]
9. Mantwill, S.; Monestel-Umaña, S.; Schulz, P.J. The Relationship between Health Literacy and health disparities: A systematic review. *PLoS ONE* **2015**, *10*, e0145455. [CrossRef] [PubMed]
10. Rasu, R.S.; Bawa, W.A.; Suminski, R.; Snella, K.; Warady, B. Health Literacy impact on national healthcare utilization and expenditure. *Int. J. Health Policy Manag.* **2015**, *4*, 747–755. [CrossRef] [PubMed]
11. Van der Heide, I.; Wang, J.; Droomers, M.; Spreeuwenberg, P.; Rademakers, J.; Uiters, E. The relationship between health, education, and health literacy: Results from the Dutch Adult Literacy and Life Skills Survey. *J. Health Commun.* **2013**, *18* (Suppl. 1), 172–184. [CrossRef] [PubMed]
12. European Commission. *Study on Sound Evidence for a Better Understanding of Health Literacy in the European Union. RfS Chafea/2014/health/01 Contract No 20146201*; Publications Office of the European Union: Luxembourg, 2014.
13. HLS-EU Consortium. Comparative Report on Health Literacy in Eight EU Member States. Available online: http://ec.europa.eu/chafea/documents/news/Comparative_report_on_health_literacy_in_eight_EU_member_states.pdf (accessed on 12 March 2018).
14. Nutbeam, D. Health literacy as a public health goal: A challenge for contemporary health education and communication strategies into the 21st century. *Health Promot. Int.* **2000**, *15*, 259–267. [CrossRef]
15. Weiss, B.D.; Mays, M.Z.; Martz, W.; Castro, K.M.; DeWalt, D.A.; Pignone, M.P.; Mockbee, J.; Hale, F.A. Quick assessment of literacy in primary care: The newest vital sign. *Ann. Fam. Med.* **2005**, *3*, 514–522. [CrossRef] [PubMed]
16. Rowlands, G.; Khazaezadeh, N.; Oteng-Ntim, E.; Seed, P.; Barr, S.; Weiss, B.D. Development and validation of a measure of health literacy in the UK: The newest vital sign. *BMC Public Health* **2013**, *13*, 116. [CrossRef] [PubMed]
17. Davis, S.L.; Goedel, W.C.; Emerson, J.; Guven, B.S. Punitive laws, key population size estimates, and Global AIDS Response Progress Reports: An ecological study of 154 countries. *J. Int. AIDS Soc.* **2017**, *20*, 1–8. [CrossRef] [PubMed]
18. Fernández, E.; Lugo, A.; Clancy, L.; Matsuo, K.; La Vecchia, C.; Gallus, S. Smoking dependence in 18 European countries: Hard to maintain the hardening hypothesis. *Prev. Med.* **2015**, *81*, 314–319. [CrossRef] [PubMed]
19. Sun, L.; Lee, E.; Zahra, A.; Park, J. Risk Factors of Cardiovascular Disease and Their Related Socio-Economical, Environmental and Health Behavioral Factors: Focused on Low-Middle Income Countries—A Narrative Review Article. *Iran J. Public Health* **2015**, *44*, 435–444. [PubMed]

20. Wolf, A.; Gray, R.; Faze, S. Violence as a public health problem: An ecological study of 169 countries. *Soc. Sci. Med.* **2014**, *104*, 220–227. [CrossRef] [PubMed]
21. La Torre, G.; Mipatrini, D. Country-level correlates of e-cigarette use in the European Union. *Int. J. Public Health* **2016**, *61*, 269–275. [CrossRef] [PubMed]
22. Abela, A.G.; Fava, S. Association of incidence of type 1 diabetes with mortality from infectious disease and with antibiotic susceptibility at a country level. *Acta Diabetol.* **2013**, *50*, 859–865. [CrossRef] [PubMed]
23. The Development of a European Health Promotion Monitoring System (The EUHPID Project). Final Report to the European Commission, DG SANCO March 2004. Available online: http://ec.europa.eu/health/ph_projects/2001/monitoring/fp_monitoring_2001_frep_03_en.pdf (accessed on 12 March 2018).
24. Laut, K.G.; Gale, C.P.; Pedersen, A.B.; Fox, K.A.; Lash, T.L.; Kristensen, S.D. Persistent geographical disparities in the use of primary percutaneous coronary intervention in 120 European regions: Exploring the variation. *EuroIntervention* **2013**, *9*, 469–476. [CrossRef] [PubMed]
25. European Commission. *Health Inequalities in the EU. Final Report of a Consortium. Consortium Lead: Sir Michael Marmot*; European Commission Directorate-General for Health and Consumers: Brussels, Belgium, 2013.
26. European Commission. *Teaching Reading in Europe: Contexts, Policies and Practices*; Education, Audiovisual and Culture Executive Agency (EACEA P9 Eurydice): Brussels, Belgium, 2011.
27. TNS Opinion & Social. Standard Eurobarometer 76. Media Use in the European Union. European Commission—Directorate-General Communication, Report 2011. Available online: http://ec.europa.eu/commfrontoffice/publicopinion/archives/eb/eb76/eb76_media_en.pdf (accessed on 12 March 2018).
28. OECD Data. Forein-Born Population. Available online: Https://data.oecd.org/migration/foreign-born-population.htm (accessed on 12 March 2018).
29. Joossens, L.; Raw, M. *The Tobacco Control Scale 2013 in Europe*; Association of European Cancer Leagues: Brussels, Belgium, 2014.
30. Lefresne, F.; Fox, T. The diversity of European education systems. In *Education in Europe: Key Figures*; The French Ministry of National Education, Higher Education and Research Evaluation, Forward-planning and Performance Directorate: Paris, France, 2016.
31. European Commission—International Agency for Research on Cancer. *Against Cancer. Cancer Screening in the European Union*; Report on the Implementation of the Council Recommendation on Cancer Screening; European Commission: Lyon, France, 2017.
32. Health Consumer Powerhouse. *The Empowerment of the European Patient. Options and Implications*; HCP: Brussels, Belgium, 2009.
33. Nardo, M.; Loi, M.; Rosati, R.; Manca, A.R. *The Consumer Empowerment Index*; Publications Office of the European Union: Luxembourg, 2011.
34. OECD. *Adults, Computers and Problem Solving: What's the Problem?* OECD Publishing: Paris, France, 2015.
35. OECD. *Health at a Glance: Europe 2012*; OECD Publishing: Paris, France, 2012.
36. Eurostat. Internet Use in Households and by Individuals in 2011. Available online: http://www.ecdl.gr/el/presscenter/press/news/Documents/Digital_Agenda_survey.pdf (accessed on 12 March 2018).
37. United Nations Development Program. *Human Development Report 2016. Human Development for Everyone*; United Nations Development Programme: New York, NY, USA, 2016.
38. Cedefop. *On the Way to 2020: Data for Vocational Education and Training Policies. Country Statistical Overviews—2016 Update*; Cedefop Research Paper No 61; Publications Office of the European Union: Luxembourg, 2017.
39. Papen, U. Literacy, learning and health—A social practices view of health literacy. *Lit. Numer. Stud.* **2009**, *16*, 19–34. [CrossRef]
40. Edwards, M.; Wood, F.; Davies, M.; Edwards, A. "Distributed health literacy": Longitudinal qualitative analysis of the roles of health literacy mediators and social networks of people living with a long-term health condition. *Health Exp.* **2015**, *18*, 1180–1193. [CrossRef] [PubMed]
41. Batterham, R.W.; Hawkins, M.; Collins, P.A.; Buchbinder, R.; Osborne, R.H. Health literacy: Applying current concepts to improve health services and reduce health inequalities. *Public Health* **2016**, *132*, 3–12. [CrossRef] [PubMed]
42. Loney, T.; Nagelkerke, N.J. The individualistic fallacy, ecological studies and instrumental variables: A causal interpretation. *Emerg. Themes Epidemiol.* **2014**, *11*, 18. [CrossRef] [PubMed]

43. Eurostat, European Statistical System. European Statistics Code of Practice for the National and Community Statistical Authorities. Available online: http://ec.europa.eu/eurostat/documents/3859598/5921861/KS-32-11-955-EN.PDF/5fa1ebc6-90bb-43fa-888f-dde032471e15 (accessed on 8 April 2018).
44. World Health Organization. European Health for All Family Databases. Available online: http://www.euro.who.int/en/data-and-evidence/databases/european-health-for-all-family-of-databases-hfa-db (accessed on 8 April 2018).
45. Organization for Economic Co-Operation and Development. Quality Framework and Guidelines for OECD Statistical Activities. Available online: http://www.oecd.org/officialdocuments/publicdisplaydocumentpdf/?cote=std/qfs(2011)1&doclanguage=en (accessed on 8 April 2018).
46. Lemaitre, G. The Comparability of International Migration Statistics. OECD, 2005. Available online: https://www.oecd.org/migration/mig/36064929.pdf (accessed on 8 April 2018).
47. Hazra, A.; Gogtay, N. Biostatistics Series Module 6: Correlation and Linear Regression. *Indian J. Dermatol.* **2016**, *61*, 593–601. [CrossRef] [PubMed]
48. Kiechle, E.S.; Bailey, S.C.; Hedlund, L.A.; Viera, A.J.; Sheridan, S.L. Different Measures, Different Outcomes? A Systematic Review of Performance-Based versus Self-Reported Measures of Health Literacy and Numeracy. *J. Gen. Intern. Med.* **2015**, *30*, 1538–1546. [CrossRef] [PubMed]
49. U.S. Department of Health and Human Services. Health Communication. In *Healthy People 2010*, 2nd ed.; U.S. Government Printing Office: Washington, DC, USA, 2000.
50. Parker, R. Measuring health literacy: What? So what? Now what? In *Measures of Health Literacy: Workshop Summary, Roundtable on Health Literacy*; National Academies Press: Washington, DC, USA, 2009; pp. 91–98.
51. Pleasant, A.; Kuruvilla, S. A tales of two health literacy: public health and clinical approaches to health literacy. *Health Promot. Int.* **2008**, *23*, 152–159. [CrossRef] [PubMed]
52. European Commission. Health and Consumers. Empowerment. Available online: http://ec.europa.eu/consumers/consumer_empowerment/index_en.htm (accessed on 12 March 2018).
53. European Commission. Strategy on Nutrition, Overweight and Obesity-Related Health Issues. Available online: https://ec.europa.eu/health/nutrition_physical_activity/policy/strategy_en (accessed on 12 March 2018).
54. Bodie, G.D.; Dutta, M.J. Understanding health literacy for strategic health marketing: EHealth literacy, health disparities, and the digital divide. *Health Mark. Q.* **2008**, *25*, 175–203. [CrossRef] [PubMed]

© 2018 by the authors. Licensee MDPI, Basel, Switzerland. This article is an open access article distributed under the terms and conditions of the Creative Commons Attribution (CC BY) license (http://creativecommons.org/licenses/by/4.0/).

Article

Effective Partnership in Community-Based Health Promotion: Lessons from the Health Literacy Partnership

Emee Vida Estacio [1,*] , Mike Oliver [2], Beth Downing [2], Judy Kurth [3] and Joanne Protheroe [4]

1. School of Psychology, Keele University, Staffordshire ST5 5BG, UK
2. Stoke-on-Trent City Council, Public Health, Staffordshire ST4 1HH, UK; mike.oliver@stoke.gov.uk (M.O.); beth.downing@stoke.gov.uk (B.D.)
3. Centre for Health and Development (CHAD), Staffordshire University, Staffordshire ST4 2DF, UK; judy.kurth@staffs.ac.uk
4. Research Institute for Primary Care & Health Sciences, Keele University, Staffordshire ST5 5BG, UK; j.protheroe@keele.ac.uk
* Correspondence: e.v.g.estacio@keele.ac.uk; Tel.: +44-017-8273-3332

Received: 16 October 2017; Accepted: 30 November 2017; Published: 11 December 2017

Abstract: This paper aims to explore key elements needed to successfully develop healthy partnerships and collaborative working in community-based health promotion. It draws upon the lessons learned from a case study with the Health Literacy Partnership in Stoke-on-Trent, UK in developing the health literacy strategy in the area. The process was underpinned by respect for diverse yet complementary perspectives and skills from the grassroots up. This involved engagement with key stakeholders, development and support for community projects, and sharing of good practice with other national and local organizations. Stakeholders involved in developing the strategy also had a keen interest in health literacy and a strong commitment to promoting health and well-being in the area. Through patience, perseverance, and continuous open communication and learning, the health literacy strategy in Stoke-on-Trent, UK is beginning to have a ripple effect into local practice, and will potentially influence policy in the future.

Keywords: health literacy; effective partnerships; community-based health promotion; collaborative working

1. Introduction

Partnerships between academics, public, and voluntary sector organizations are widely reported in the health promotion literature [1–3]. Although tensions and conflicts may arise due to the blurring of relationship boundaries [4,5], it is important to recognize that working in partnership with multiple agencies is crucial to the successful implementation and maintenance of community-based work [6,7].

Health as a concept is complex and the promotion of health requires consideration of its wider social, economic, cultural, and environmental determinants. Inter-agency partnerships can provide a holistic approach towards improving health and reducing inequities. Understanding the role of partnerships on how health promotion initiatives are designed, delivered, and maintained can also provide useful insights for researchers, practitioners, and policy makers when funding, planning, and evaluating such programs [8].

This paper draws upon the lessons learned from a case study with the Health Literacy Partnership in Stoke-on-Trent, UK in developing the health literacy strategy in the area. These lessons are transferrable to other contexts and can provide insight into effective and collaborative working in community-based health promotion.

2. Context

Health literacy can be defined as the "personal characteristics and social resources needed for individuals and communities to access, understand, appraise, and use information and services to make decisions about health" [9]. The Health Literacy program described here was a Stoke-on-Trent City Council Public Health-led initiative which emerged from the UK Healthy Cities Network.

The health literacy partnership between academics at Keele University and Stoke-on-Trent City Council Public Health began in 2010 with a small exploratory project on health literacy and diabetes management [10]. This partnership grew and cascaded into more research projects, including an extensive (n = 1046) baseline survey of health literacy levels in the city and an assessment of the readability of health resources in the area. Findings suggest that 52% of the adult population in Stoke-on-Trent had less-than-adequate health literacy, and that it was associated with older age, poorer health, digital exclusion, and living in deprived areas [11]; whereas most patient information leaflets in General Practice (GP) surgeries were found to be too complex for 43% of the population [12].

These research findings have been influential in the development of the Stoke-on-Trent Health Literacy Strategy. They helped to define the problem and created a "sense of urgency" for change. They also helped to crystallize thinking from across a range of disciplines. Bringing different organizations together engendered a sense of hope that there is something that can be done to tackle the challenges of health literacy and that everyone has a role to play.

Research was used as a springboard for discussion in four large-scale annual community engagement events which raised the profile of health literacy in the city and generated ideas and commitment from local groups (see Table 1). The first workshop was designed specifically to create this sense of urgency and to rally support for creating change.

Table 1. Summary of key health literacy activities in Stoke-on-Trent.

Date	Location	Event	Purpose/Outcome
June 2014	Stoke-on-Trent Town Hall	Ideas Exchange	Raising awareness of the issue/challenge with local community groups and healthcare professionals. Capturing initial response and generating ideas
March 2015	The Bridge Centre, Stoke-on-Trent	From Ideas to Action	Building on the ideas and turning them into specific initiatives as part of a structured strategy
June 2016	Keele University	Update and Moving Forward	To hear progress on the projects and to stimulate debate on new ways of improving the health literacy environment in Stoke-on-Trent
June 2017	Hanley Library, Stoke-on-Trent	Is Stoke-on-Trent a health literacy friendly city?	To challenge ourselves—are we making progress? How can we empower people in addition to changing the health literacy environment?

By engaging multiple stakeholders in the process, insights from research and practice grew. These were used to inform local policy and future action plans. Good project management in maintaining this engagement and some seed corn funding also enabled people to put their ideas into practice which gave sufficient "quick wins" to keep the partnership interested. Several activities and grassroots initiatives were developed and supported as a result (see Table 2).

Table 2. Summary of key health literacy initiatives in Stoke-on-Trent (2015–2017).

Organization	Initiative	Those Supported by This	Intended Outcomes
Stoke Speaks Out	Using Early Years Story Boxes, Stoke Speaks Out works directly with childminders, children's centers, schools, nurseries, and parents to embed a range of early speech and communication strategies. Using play-based scenarios and a multi-sensory approach, the children are immersed in health-related vocabulary, which provides a foundation for later learning. So far, four health literacy Early Years Story Boxes have been created: (1) going to the dentist; (2) going to the hospital; (3) going to the doctors; (4) healthy eating	Early years children and their care providers	Increased familiarity and confidence with health scenarios and language
Open Network & Schools Sports Partnership	This partnership project within schools in the city adds value to the physical education and sport experience of primary-aged children in Stoke-on-Trent by embedding health literacy concepts into the way that School Sports Leaders (who are children themselves) encourage others to be more active and healthy	Children in primary and secondary schools	Easier to understand and act on information about healthy exercise and eating
Haywood Community Hospital	Based on health literacy best practice, the Centre is improving the well-being of people with arthritis and related conditions by (a) being thoughtful about how information is made available to people, (b) working in partnership with the local Public Health team to gain access to the latest health information, and (c) ensuring that volunteers working in the center receive training in health literacy	Inpatients and outpatients being supported by this hospital	Improved information sharing via the use of trained volunteers in the Patient Information Centre
University Hospital of North Midlands	University Hospital of North Midlands have launched the "It's OK to Ask!" initiative, which encourages patients to engage more fully with health care professionals by asking three questions: "What is my main problem?" "What do I need to do?" "Why is it important I do this?"	Outpatients	Increased confidence to engage with medical staff via the "It's OK to Ask!" initiative.
The Cultural Sisters	The Cultural Sisters is a participatory arts organization with a focus on Arts and Health, engaging with people using a creative processes to explore and learn about health and wellbeing issues. Health literacy concepts have been embedded into these arts projects, allowing people to engage more fully with the health messages being shared	Vulnerable groups in society	Increased esteem and confidence through participatory arts
Community Health and Learning Foundation	Health literacy training and awareness for a broad range of professions and service providers, including General Practitioners (GPs) and other GP practice personnel, pharmacists, dentists, school teachers and other educators, participatory art group leaders, social workers, local authority planners and commissioners, and fire service professionals. Training courses were also run alongside that equip other trainers and teachers to support service users, school children, and other people from Stoke-on-Trent with the confidence and knowledge to improve their own health literacy	GPs and other GP practice personnel, pharmacists, dentists, school teachers and other educators, participatory art group leaders, social workers, local authority planners and commissioners, and fire service professionals. 65 people trained, 3 courses delivered (Year 1); 92 people trained, 6 courses delivered (Year 2); 49 people trained, 3 courses delivered (Year 3)	Increased understanding of health and literacy and confidence in supporting service users to improve their own health literacy
Quality Improvement Framework	Quality Improvement Framework that includes health literacy as a key component and a health literacy video as part of the training.	GPs and other GP practice personnel, and the wider public	Increased understanding of health and literacy and confidence in supporting service users to improve their own health literacy

Starting from a small partnership involving a core group with less than a dozen members, the Health Literacy Partnership now involves a whole host of individuals and organizations with a common agenda to improve health in Stoke-on-Trent by promoting health literacy in the city. Members of the partnership now include researchers, healthcare professionals (e.g., GPs, nurses, pharmacists, hospital managers, dentists), public health professionals, social workers, home care visitors, teachers, community education workers, volunteer organizations, housing agencies, community advocates, librarians, city planners, patient groups, and The Fire Service. Overall, the partnership involves a network of around 245 people who have been involved in training and community events in health literacy in Stoke-on-Trent.

This flourishing partnership was recognized for good practice in national reports, including the Inquiry Report into NHS England's Five Year Forward View [13] and Public Health England's report on local action on health inequalities [14], and was commended by the Phase VI (2014–2018) of the WHO European Healthy Cities Network [15].

Building upon and working alongside Health Literacy UK pioneers, plans were also made to collectively influence policy at a national level. Members of the Health Literacy Partnership in Stoke-on-Trent are also members of Health Literacy UK (one of whom is the Chair, and a Health Literacy Clinical Advisor to NHS England), and are also members of the NHS England Health Literacy Collaborative.

While there have been discussions in the literature around some of the challenges in community-based health promotion and collaborative working [16], this paper will contribute to this area of health promotion practice by highlighting key factors that contributed to the success of this collaboration.

3. Shared Passion for Reducing Inequalities in Health

The literature suggests that partnerships are most successful when there is a clear goal for the partnership [17] and that partners are working towards a shared vision [18]. In this case study, while the promotion of health literacy was the key driver, members of the partnership shared the wider agenda of reducing health inequalities in the area. While Stoke-on-Trent can be proud of its rich cultural heritage, health and social outcomes in the area can still be improved. The success of this partnership is rooted in the shared passion and commitment from those involved to promote the health and well-being of residents in the city.

Regardless of their specialist area and background, members of the partnership were passionate about reducing health and social inequalities and improving the community's quality of life. The common agenda was to reduce health inequalities by improving patient experience, shared decision making, and self-management through health literacy. While improving the health literacy skills of patients was seen as important, members of this partnership also shared the same critical lens and recognized the importance of wider social and environmental factors that influence health.

From the original members of the steering group, to advocates joining in from the training and follow-up sessions, members of this partnership included a core group of committed enthusiasts who "get it" and "get on with it". They are catalysts for change.

4. Diversity Requires Respect and Trust

The adage *"the whole is greater than the sum of its parts"* fittingly applies in this case. The Health Literacy Partnership in Stoke-on-Trent achieved more by working together than individual organizations could achieve on their own [18]. Although these organizations shared the same vision, the background and expertise brought forward by individual members were quite diverse. This diversity contributed to the partnership's strength, since complementary knowledge, skills, and experiences were constantly being brought to the table.

For example, when collecting data to assess baseline health literacy levels in the city, academics in the team were able to advise on standardized measures that can be used for the project; city council partners were able to advise on potential barriers to recruitment; while grassroots leaders were able to advise on the best ways to engage community members.

Likewise, when developing and implementing health literacy programs, researchers were able to advise on robust methods to monitor and evaluate interventions, while service providers were able to advise on pragmatic ways to encourage uptake. Thus, maintaining a partnership that was equitable between community members and academics was vital in this process [19].

Strong public health leadership was also crucial in the early stages in engaging a wide range partners around a common set of community health promotion values and principles. This work built on the trust that had been established within the wide network of organizations that that the Healthy Communities team within the Public Health department has been working with as part of its remit. Equally important were the skills required to manage such a diverse network—particularly the project management skills from one of the core members of the partnership. Lack of awareness of the skill and capacity to manage this type of work often undermines it.

Involving multiple stakeholders from different backgrounds also required respect and trust to ensure that the partnership was sustainable and can achieve systemic transformations [20–22]. In this case, the growth and development of this collaboration was based on mutual trust from individual members and the understanding that the partners were contributing to the achievement of a common goal. There was also respect for the skills and expertise that members of the collaboration were contributing to the team.

Interactions in this partnership were often collegiate, and a great sense of respect and gratitude for the skills, expertise, and time offered by partners were often expressed. We believe that it is this spirit of co-operation that has led to the sustainability and on-going nature of this partnership. Strong partnerships are indeed created by our interactions with each other (i.e., our personal qualities) and the actions we take [5].

5. Learning, Networking, and Open Communication

Willingness to learn from one another is fundamental in establishing genuine partnerships such as this [21]. Considering the diversity of backgrounds in this partnership, it was inevitable that members would have different starting points in terms of knowledge and awareness of health literacy research, practice, and policy. Although some members were more familiar with the health literacy agenda than others, those who knew more were open to sharing, while those who knew less were open to learning.

Curiosity and eagerness to learn were matched by enthusiastic sharing of knowledge and ideas from research and practice. Meetings, events, and training opportunities were organized to cultivate learning and foster networking between members of the collaborative. Organizing these events also helped to encourage professional development and inter-disciplinary practice [23].

Clear and effective communication is another important feature of effective collaborations [24]. In this case, regular meetings were held, including an annual event to bring together the various organizations that were involved in this process. Regular email updates were also sent and workshops organized to foster further communication and learning.

6. Discussion

Partnership working in community-based health promotion can bring about fruitful and sustainable benefits for those involved. Although it takes some time to nurture relationships, when facilitated effectively, collaborative work can enable more systemic ways of working towards health promotion and community development.

As shown in the case study involving the Health Literacy Partnership in Stoke-on-Trent, committing to a shared vision, having mutual trust and respect for each other, and being open to share, learn, and communicate are vital elements that helped to make this partnership a success.

To maintain momentum, there is a need to sustain relationships and commitments. It is useful to continue to cultivate the knowledge and experience developed in this partnership so that other health promotion initiatives can also learn from this practice. The monitoring and evaluation of outcomes are particularly important, in order to ensure that efforts are recorded and recognized for their value to the community.

However, there are also threats to the sustainability of this partnership [25]. For example, availability of funding and the potential impact of staff and policy changes could be detrimental to the partnership's future. We could be disrupted by policy reform, as well as by internal and external political influences (individual and organizational).

Thus, there is a need for organizational level commitment to uphold the health literacy agenda in Stoke-on-Trent. For a start, the Health Literacy Partnership in Stoke-on-Trent is driving forward the Health Literacy Friendly Project, which aims to develop a partnership approach to help organizations improve their entire system and environment when it comes to health literacy (e.g., communications, signage, layout of physical buildings, and policies). As [8] states, "if organizations from diverse sectors can embed a vision for health that accounts for place, complex health promotion initiatives may be less vulnerable to broader system reforms, and health in all policy approaches more readily sustained."

Thus, embedding health literacy into the organizational culture in Stoke-on-Trent could buffer this threat by normalizing this as common practice, rather than it being something that only the health literacy aficionados do. One way to embed this into the organization might be to formalize this partnership as a specific work project with a specifically employed project manager. This would enable the practicalities of responsibilities for tasks; setting up of regular meetings and driving the agenda forward were taken on board. However, it is important not to neglect the diverse yet complimentary experience of the partnership, recognizing different strengths and different ways of working. One of the major benefits of this working partnership has been the space for both a shared vision, but also the flexibility that working together has led to, allowing accommodation of the visions and goals of individuals and different organizations involved.

7. Conclusions

As discussed in this paper, partnership working in community-based health promotion requires having a shared vision, mutual trust, respect, and openness to share and communicate. This involves engagement with key stakeholders, development and support for community projects, and sharing of good practice between organizations. As a result of the continuous support of the various members of this partnership, the health literacy strategy in Stoke-on-Trent is beginning to have a ripple effect into local practice that will potentially influence policy at local and national levels in the future.

Acknowledgments: We would like to acknowledge the support of all the individuals and organizations who are part of the Health Literacy partnership discussed in this paper.

Author Contributions: All of the authors have been actively involved in developing and facilitating the Health Literacy partnership discussed in this paper.

Conflicts of Interest: The authors declare no conflict of interest.

References

1. Caldwell, W.B.; Reyes, A.G.; Rowe, Z.; Weinert, J.; Israel, B.A. Community partner perspectives on benefits, challenges, facilitating factors, and lessons learned from community-based participatory research partnerships in detroit. *Prog. Community Health Partnersh. Res. Educ. Action* **2015**, *9*, 299–311. [CrossRef] [PubMed]
2. Davern, M.T.; Gunn, L.; Giles-Corti, B.; David, S. Best practice principles for community indicator systems and a case study analysis: How community indicators Victoria is creating impact and bridging policy, practice and research. *Soc. Indic. Res.* **2017**, *131*, 567–586. [CrossRef]

3. Littlecott, H.J.; Fox, K.R.; Stathi, A.; Thompson, J.L. Perceptions of success of a local UK public health collaborative. *Health Promot. Int.* **2017**, *32*, 102–112. [CrossRef] [PubMed]
4. Estacio, E.V. 'Playing with Fire and Getting Burned': The Case of the Naïve Action Researcher. *J. Community Appl. Soc. Psychol.* **2012**, *22*, 439–451. [CrossRef]
5. Mayan, M.J.; Daum, C.H. Worth the risk? Muddled relationships in community-based participatory research. *Qual. Health Res.* **2016**, *26*, 69–76. [CrossRef] [PubMed]
6. Dennis, S.; Hetherington, S.A.; Borodzicz, J.A.; Hermiz, O.; Zwar, N.A. Challenges to establishing successful partnerships in community health promotion programs: Local experiences from the national implementation of healthy eating activity and lifestyle (HEAL[TM]) program. *Health Promot. J. Aust.* **2015**, *26*, 45–51. [CrossRef] [PubMed]
7. Riggs, E.; Block, K.; Warr, D.; Gibbs, L. Working better together: New approaches for understanding the value and challenges of organizational partnerships. *Health Promot. Int.* **2014**, *29*, 780–793. [CrossRef] [PubMed]
8. Del Fabbro, L.; Rowe Minniss, F.; Ehrlich, C.; Kendall, E. Political challenges in complex place-based health promotion partnerships. *Int. Q. Community Health Educ.* **2016**, *37*, 51–60. [CrossRef] [PubMed]
9. Dodson, S.; Good, S.; Osborne, R.H. *Health Literacy Toolkit for Low and Middle-Income Countries: A Series of Information Sheets to Empower Communities and Strengthen Health Systems*; World Health Organization, Regional Office for South-East Asia: New Delhi, India, 2015.
10. Estacio, E.V.; McKinley, R.K.; Saidy-Khan, S.; Karic, T.; Clark, L.; Kurth, J. Health literacy: Why it matters to South Asian men with diabetes. *Prim. Health Care Res. Dev.* **2015**, *16*, 214–218. [CrossRef] [PubMed]
11. Protheroe, J.; Whittle, R.; Bartlam, B.; Estacio, E.V.; Clark, L.; Kurth, J. Health literacy, associated lifestyle and demographic factors in adult population of an English city: A cross-sectional survey. *Health Expectat.* **2017**, *20*, 112–119. [CrossRef] [PubMed]
12. Protheroe, J.; Estacio, E.V.; Saidy-Khan, S. Patient information materials in general practices and promotion of health literacy: An observational study of their effectiveness. *Br. J. Gen. Pract.* **2015**, *65*, e192–e197. [CrossRef] [PubMed]
13. All Party Parliamentary Group Primary Care and Public Health. Available online: https://www.pagb.co.uk/content/uploads/2016/06/5YFV_Behaviour_Change_Info_Signposting_15March16.pdf (accessed on 8 December 2017).
14. Public Health England. Available online: https://www.gov.uk/government/uploads/system/uploads/attachment_data/file/460709/4a_Health_Literacy-Full.pdf (accessed on 8 December 2017).
15. World Health Organization. Available online: http://www.euro.who.int/__data/assets/pdf_file/0017/244403/Phase-VI-20142018-of-the-WHO-European-Healthy-Cities-Network-goals-and-requirements-Eng.pdf (accessed on 8 December 2017).
16. Blumenthal, D.S.; DiClemente, R.J. (Eds.) *Community-Based Participatory Health Research: Issues, Methods, and Translation to Practice*; Springer: New York, NY, USA, 2013.
17. Cook, A. Partnership Working across UK Public Services Edinburgh: What Works Scotland. Available online: http://whatworksscotland.ac.uk/wp-content/uploads/2015/12/WWS-Evidence-Review-Partnership-03-Dec-2015-.pdf (accessed on 17 June 2017).
18. Wildridge, V.; Childs, S.; Cawthra, L.; Madge, B. How to create successful partnerships—A review of the literature. *Health Inf. Libr. J.* **2004**, *21*, 3–19. [CrossRef] [PubMed]
19. Langdon, S.E.; Golden, S.L.; Arnold, E.M.; Maynor, R.F.; Bryant, A.; Freeman, V.K.; Bell, R.A. Lessons learned from a community-based participatory research mental health promotion program for American Indian youth. *Health Promot. Pract.* **2016**, *17*, 457–463. [CrossRef] [PubMed]
20. Christopher, S.; Watts, V.; McCormick, A.K.H.G.; Young, S. Building and maintaining trust in a community-based participatory research partnership. *Am. J. Public Health* **2008**, *98*, 1398–1406. [CrossRef] [PubMed]
21. Eriksson, C.C.; Fredriksson, I.; Fröding, K.; Geidne, S.; Pettersson, C. Academic practice–policy partnerships for health promotion research: Experiences from three research programs. *Scand. J. Public Health* **2014**, *42*, 88–95. [CrossRef] [PubMed]

22. Jagosh, J.; Bush, P.L.; Salsberg, J.; Macaulay, A.C.; Greenhalgh, T.; Wong, G.; Pluye, P. A realist evaluation of community-based participatory research: Partnership synergy, trust building and related ripple effects. *BMC Public Health* **2015**, *15*, 725. [CrossRef] [PubMed]
23. Thompson, S.; Kent, J.; Lyons, C. Building partnerships for healthy environments: Research, leadership and education. *Health Promot. J. Aust.* **2014**, *25*, 202–208. [CrossRef] [PubMed]
24. Andrews, J.O.; Newman, S.D.; Meadows, O.; Cox, M.J.; Bunting, S. Partnership readiness for community-based participatory research. *Health Educ. Res.* **2010**, *27*, 555–571. [CrossRef] [PubMed]
25. Israel, B.A.; Krieger, J.; Vlahov, D.; Ciske, S.; Foley, M.; Fortin, P.; Tang, G. Challenges and facilitating factors in sustaining community-based participatory research partnerships: Lessons learned from the Detroit, New York city and Seattle urban research centers. *J. Urban Health Bull. N. Y. Acad. Med.* **2006**, *83*, 1022–1040. [CrossRef] [PubMed]

© 2017 by the authors. Licensee MDPI, Basel, Switzerland. This article is an open access article distributed under the terms and conditions of the Creative Commons Attribution (CC BY) license (http://creativecommons.org/licenses/by/4.0/).

Review

Media Health Literacy, eHealth Literacy, and the Role of the Social Environment in Context

Diane Levin-Zamir [1,2,*] and Isabella Bertschi [3]

1. Department of Health Education and Promotion, Clalit Health Services, Tel Aviv 62098, Israel
2. School of Public Health, University of Haifa, Haifa 31905, Israel
3. Department of Psychology, University of Zurich, Zürich 8050, Switzerland; isabella.bertschi@psychologie.uzh.ch
* Correspondence: diamos@zahav.net.il; Tel.: +972-50-626-3033

Received: 17 July 2018; Accepted: 30 July 2018; Published: 3 August 2018

Abstract: Health literacy describes skills and competencies that enable people to gain access to, understand and apply health information to positively influence their own health and the health of those in their social environments. In an increasingly media saturated and digitized world, these skill sets are necessary for accessing and navigating sources of health information and tools, such as television, the Internet, and mobile apps. The concepts of Media Health Literacy (MHL) and eHealth Literacy (eHL) describe the specific competencies such tasks require. This article introduces the two concepts, and then reviews findings on the associations of MHL and eHL with several contextual variables in the social environment such as socio-demographics, social support, and system complexity, as a structural variable. As eHL and MHL are crucial for empowering people to actively engage in their own health, there is a growing body of literature reporting on the potential and the effectiveness of intervention initiatives to positively influence these competencies. From an ethical standpoint, equity is emphasized, stressing the importance of accessible media environments for all—including those at risk of exclusion from (digital) media sources. Alignment of micro and macro contextual spheres will ultimately facilitate both non-digital and digital media to effectively support and promote public health.

Keywords: health literacy; Media Health Literacy; eHealth Literacy; social environment; health apps; social support; digital health; empowerment

1. Introduction

Several factors have led, and continue to lead, to the development of health systems that enable, but also partly expect their users to adopt a much more active role in their health management than was customary some decades ago. The empowerment of groups and individuals to engage in their own health, for example by shared decision-making with health professionals, or by adoption of health-promoting lifestyles, is an important goal of public health in the 21st century and a priority in the UN Sustainable Development Goals. Being able to actively manage one's health is very demanding of citizens. It is largely, although by no means entirely, dependent on the availability, accessibility, and appropriateness of health information. To reflect the skill set required to effectively manage health and navigate the health system from health care to disease prevention and health promotion, the concept of health literacy was developed. A wide variety of definitions exist, but in general Health literacy (HL) is conceptualized as skills and competences enabling people to obtain and interpret health information and apply their knowledge to inform health-related decision-making (for an overview of definitions see e.g., [1,2]).

In an increasingly media saturated and digital environment, a large proportion of health-related messages and information today is circulated and accessed through the media and digital sources. Thus, researchers together with health practitioners have developed two closely linked, but nonetheless distinct concepts related to HL: *Media Health Literacy* [3] and *eHealth Literacy* [4]. Media Health Literacy and eHealth Literacy have both proven to be associated with health information seeking and with health outcomes such as health behavior and health status across various population groups. Environmental factors linked to the social, organizational or economic context play an important role (a) in shaping individual, group or population MHL and eHL skills and (b) by posing specific demands on the situations in which such skills are required by the individual or group.

This article aims to introduce readers to the concepts of Media Health Literacy and eHealth Literacy, emphasizing their role in the social environment while demonstrating how context variables are relevant when applying the concepts in research and practice. We will critically discuss issues related to the two concepts and explore the ethical aspects of these concepts in research, practice, and policy.

2. The Concepts of Media Health Literacy and eHealth Literacy

Media Health Literacy (MHL) [3] is based on and builds on the synthesis of health literacy and media literacy [5]—two essential concepts for understanding the scope and significance of eHealth Literacy. The concept of Media Health Literacy is unique in that it takes into consideration not only information that has been communicated through the media to offer health guidance; but it also considers implicit and explicit mass media content commonly generated by commercial entities or health systems that can be either health-promoting or health-compromising. Based on the typology of the Nutbeam model of Health Literacy [6], Media Health Literacy is conceptualized as a continuum, ranging from (1) the ability to identify health-related content (explicit and/or implicit) in the various types of media; (2) recognize its influence on health behavior; (3) critically analyze the content (comparable to Critical Health Literacy), and (4) express intention to respond through action measured through personal health behavior or advocacy (comparable to Interactive Health Literacy). Thus, the validated measure of Media Health Literacy is comprised of these four categories and was shown to be highly correlated with health empowerment. As such, Media Health Literacy can be considered the precursor to eHealth literacy and is highly relevant for both non-digital (television, print, radio, etc.) and digital media (Internet, social media, and mobile tools).

While media in general has long since been recognized as the only social institution that accompanies the individual throughout the entire life course [7], over the past decade, digital media has received particular attention with regards to use for health purposes. The number of digital health offers has grown with impressive speed—an annual growth rate of about 25%. According to data from Research2Guidance, approximately 325,000 health apps were available in 2017, with 78,000 new mobile health applications being released between 2016 and 2017. Although it has been shown that only 7% of mHealth apps have more than 50,000 monthly active users, usage proportions are very likely to increase significantly in the near future [8]. The growing importance of digital media has led researchers, practitioners, and policy makers to reflect on the skills necessary for users, and the challenges they face to achieve effective outcomes, namely navigating the services, accessing relevant health information and adopting lifestyle changes. Well over a decade ago, Norman and Skinner [4] as pioneers in the field introduced the term eHealth Literacy (eHL) meaning "the ability to seek, find, understand, and appraise health information from electronic sources and apply the knowledge gained to addressing or solving a health problem" (p. 1). They also developed a measurement tool for eHealth Literacy that has been used in many different settings around the globe, the eHealth Literacy Scale (eHEALS) [9]. It consists of eight items for which respondents self-rate their ease and skills when navigating Internet sources for valid health information. The original English scale has been translated into many languages, including Japanese, Korean, German, Italian, Spanish, Greek, and Hebrew. Although widely used, the eHEALS' validity has been questioned, mainly due to the lack of correlation between eHEALS scores and actual task performance in online health information seeking [10,11], and because it does not sufficiently address critical and interactive health literacy skills [12,13]. Cameron Norman, the first author of the eHEALS, has also expressed some concern as to whether the scale is able to measure eHealth Literacy in its totality in a world that has witnessed the rise of Web 2.0, and that is generally characterized by the use of ever-changing technology: "The fundamental collection of skills that comprise eHealth Literacy have not likely changed, but the contexts in which they are expressed (...) have" [12] (p. 3). This illustrates the dynamic nature of the concept of eHealth Literacy, and thus also of Media Health Literacy, as both terms qualify skill sets that can only be understood and analyzed within the media environment in which they are applied.

3. Media Health Literacy and eHealth Literacy in Context

The media, and especially the realm of digital media, constitute a complex social environment to be navigated by consumers in order to promote and maintain health using the information available in this environment. Tasks related to Media and eHealth Literacy are thus by no means trivial. In order to understand how demanding they are, we illustrate the multi-faceted nature with a case study before focusing on context variables associated with Media Health Literacy and eHealth Literacy task performance.

Chan and Kaufman [14] used Cognitive Task Analysis to map consumers' performance during information-seeking and decision-making tasks involving eHealth tools. To disentangle knowledge, thought processes and skills necessary for task completion, they coded every reported step in a matrix involving facets of eHealth Literacy and levels of cognitive complexity. They drew on Norman and Skinner's [4] Lily model which postulates that eHealth Literacy combines six literacy domains: traditional literacy, information literacy, scientific literacy, media literacy, computer literacy, and health literacy. Any given eHealth Literacy task requires a certain degree of skills and knowledge in the said areas. In their study, detailed analyses of performance in a six-step task involving a consumer health webpage showed that any step required skills from at least two literacy domains, often more, with the cognitive complexity most often rated 4 or 5 out of 6 levels by experts. The most frequently identified barriers to task completion were encountered with steps requiring information and computer literacy. Surprisingly, the majority of challenges faced by participants fell within the lower ranges of cognitive demands.

This example demonstrates that eHealth Literacy, as mentioned, is by no means a trivial set of skills in a highly digitalized environment. On the contrary, it combines knowledge and skills from a wide variety of domains and is inherently relevant within the social contexts in which Health Literacy, Media Health Literacy, and eHealth Literacy are developed and applied by an individual or group. The following sections, as illustrated in Figure 1, will elaborate on what is known regarding how factors in an ecological model affect Media Health Literacy and eHealth Literacy. Growing academic attention has been given to system complexity, personal and socio-demographic factors such as age, gender, and education, social environment and context that together play a major role in shaping skills in performing health literacy related tasks in digital media environments.

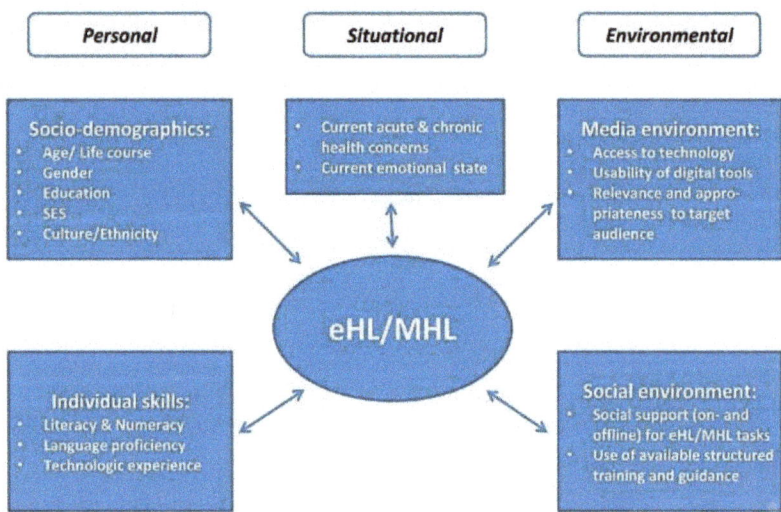

Figure 1. The complexity of eHealth Literacy (eHL) and Media Health Literacy (MHL) in context.

3.1. Complexity of Systems and Environments

In 2009, Parker [15] made an important statement that is occasionally forgotten in a discourse that focuses its attention predominantly on health literacy as an individual combination of skills: "One must align skills and abilities with the demands and complexities of the system" (p. 92). She illustrated this with a simple drawing of two arrows pointing toward each other, one representing "skills/abilities" and the other labelled "demands/complexity". Where the two arrows meet, she wrote, is where health literacy is expressed.

Digital media sources of health information have particular potential to reduce system complexity. Usability and accessibility are topics that receive specific attention from software developers and web designers. Several findings suggest that focusing on user experience and designing with the aim of reducing complexity are beneficial for digital health literacy. For example, disadvantage in written and spoken language skills can be barriers to accessing online health information [16]. Information should, therefore, be made increasingly available in more interactive formats that depend less on formal literacy and knowledge of the local language [17]. Meppelink and colleagues [18] provide empirical support for this claim. In an experimental study they show that recall and attitude change were significantly higher in low health literate participants when information was presented verbally and enriched with animations supporting the content compared to standard written text and illustrations. Content must be adapted to be relevant to the specific population, for example taking into consideration cultural eating habits when designing a smartphone app to support weight loss [19]. Thus, (digital) media solutions for health actually do have the potential to contribute to making health information more accessible and understandable for broad sections of the population, eventually fostering positive effects on health [20].

System complexity is also reduced when people become more experienced with health literacy tasks and with the technology that can be used to apply health literacy skills. Accordingly, eHealth Literacy scores are positively associated with frequency of use of the Internet [21,22] and with the number of Web searches for health information [23]. High eHealth Literacy levels are associated with the use of social media for the purpose of seeking health information, and with frequent use of electronic devices in general [24]. It can also be shown that eHealth Literacy scores are higher for students who had been actively involved in searching for health information online than for non-experienced peers [25]. Similarly, data suggest that parental online health information seeking is positively associated with adolescents' eHealth Literacy and engagement in online searches for health information [26]. These findings support the conclusion that eHealth Literacy skills are strongly shaped by exposure to technology, the Internet, and online health information sources in particular. It may therefore be deduced that the higher the usability of the underlying technology, i.e., reducing system complexity, the greater the exposure, and the greater the engagement of digital resources by the population.

3.2. The Role of Socio-Demographics

A number of socio-demographic variables are linked to Media Health Literacy, and specifically to online health information seeking and eHealth Literacy, measured at the individual level. Media Health Literacy, to date, measured mainly among adolescents, is highly associated with socioeconomic status (SES) and mothers' level of education [3]. Regarding digital sources of health information, people from different age groups, socioeconomic backgrounds, and from diverse ethnic groups refer to online sources when looking for information on health topics [27]. As early as 2006, 80 percent of adult American Internet users confirmed to have browsed the Web for health information [28]. Similar numbers of online health information seeking have more recently been shown in Eurobarometer data from 28 member states of the European Union [29]. American college students even seem to consider the Internet as their single most important source of health information [30]. Still, studies also identified some socioeconomic differences in online health information seeking. Low rates of online health information seeking were reported among older adults, among people with low educational attainment, and in men compared to women [31–34]. Regarding the use of eHealth tools among ethnic minorities, the data is inconclusive. According to recent studies, as opposed to previous ones, no significant differences between groups have been evidenced [35]. Yet, the cultural context of eHealth literacy including mobile health (mHealth) has been recognized [36].

According to Neter and Brainin [37], people with high eHealth Literacy are younger and better educated than people with low eHealth Literacy scores. These associations of eHealth Literacy with age and education are confirmed by data from various samples, e.g., financially disadvantaged US families [38] and immigrant communities in Canada [39]. These socio-demographic differences are consistent for mHealth use, health literacy, eHealth Literacy, and Media Health Literacy, particularly with regard to education and age, and secondarily with regard to gender and ethnic background. Cultural background has also been considered to significantly influence eHealth Literacy and Media Health Literacy such that researchers in South Korea [40] and Italy [41], conducted several validation studies for the eHEALS model to assure its relevancy to local culture.

3.3. Social Networks

Socio-demographics and experience with media and technology are factors on the individual level that influence eHealth Literacy and Media Health Literacy skill sets. Certainly, individual level variables contribute to shaping health literacy levels. However, caution is warranted as to "the individualistic premise of current literature (on health literacy) in which individuals are treated as isolated and passive actors" [42] (p. 1309). Several findings suggest that eHealth Literacy levels are shaped and can possibly be improved through guidance in online health information seeking activities by more experienced users as well as in structured learning environments. For example, Chang and colleagues [26] showed that active parental mediation of their adolescent children's Internet use predicted adolescents' eHealth Literacy. Participants in focus groups conducted among Spanish primary school students reported use of the Internet as a tool for learning about health topics and habits, but preferred their searches to be guided and supervised by their parents to promote their efficacy and confidence in dealing with online (health) content [43]. Similarly, in a sample of elderly living with chronic disease, participants reported the Internet as a useful information source on their condition. Still, they often relied on the help of relatives and friends when assessing the information [44]. A similar strategy has been observed for Hispanic breast cancer survivors in the United States; managing online health information in their case was a responsibility they consistently shared with their offline social networks [45]. Results from a nationally representative Israeli survey indicate that participants with low eHealth Literacy for whom finding someone (offline) to help them perform and analyze their online health information searches was easy, partly compensated for their lack of proficiency with digital health literacy through social support [46]. Caregivers' or significant others' guidance and support are thus vital in the development of abilities relevant to eHealth Literacy in context.

4. Improving Media Health Literacy and eHealth Literacy

Studies focused on the implementation and effectiveness of Media Health Literacy and eHealth literacy training programs, are relatively few. Regarding Media Health Literacy, as it inherently includes exercising critical thinking, and acknowledging that new channels of intervention need to be developed and applied for health promotion among adolescents, Wharf Higgins and Begoray [47] developed the concept of Critical Media Health Literacy. The concept focuses on attributes that include skill sets, empowerment, and competency of engaged citizenship. While the conceptual basis has been established, related intervention has been tested primarily on children and adolescents, focusing on media literacy related to health topics, e.g., alcohol [48]. Among adults, health literacy has been incorporated into media driven interventions, to learn of the differential effects of low and high health literacy. In order to influence the consumption of sugar sweetened beverages among the rural community in the US, a media driven intervention was developed and implemented while measuring the effects among various levels of health literacy. The program was found to be just as effective among participants with low health literacy as compared to high health literacy [49]. Media health literacy has also been given serious attention not only by public health entities, but also by media stakeholders, just as journalists, exemplified by the seriousness with which news media serves the public's health literacy needs while influencing public health policy as well [50]. Still, interventions aimed at improving Media Health Literacy across the lifespan, based on, and including critical health literacy, have yet to take a prominent place in intervention research.

Regarding eHealth literacy, a systematic review on eHealth Literacy among college students concluded that even this young, well-educated population has major shortcomings, the findings of which show that interventions to improve eHealth Literacy would not only benefit traditional at-risk groups [51]. While literature on interventions aiming to improve digital health literacy is scarce to date, some promising findings have been published. eHealth Literacy can be developed and improved by offering structured learning opportunities. For example, an intervention to improve eHealth Literacy among adolescents composed of three online training lessons yielded significant, though marginal improvements of digital health literacy levels among the participants. High identification with, and involvement in the intervention, i.e., feeling that improving eHealth Literacy was important and relevant, was one of the strongest predictors of changes in skill level, stressing the need to make eHealth Literacy personally relevant to potential intervention participants [52]. An intervention consisting of four two-hour sessions aimed at helping older adults perform online health information searches yielded significant improvements of eHealth Literacy from pre- to post-intervention. Participants also reported changes in health-related attitudes and behaviors following the intervention [53–55]. It should, however, be noted that a systematic review on eHealth Literacy intervention studies for older adults [56] concluded that many studies apply weak study designs and that some interventions lack a thorough theoretical base. Therefore, further research in the area is greatly needed. Likewise, it should be noted that the reported interventions are primarily skill-based interventions aimed at increasing individual competence. This type of intervention has its justification, however, coupling with interventions focusing more on empowerment and change in the environment where health literacy is applied, is of great importance in an increasingly digitized and media-saturated environment. Finally, as mentioned, reducing system complexity and improving the accessibility of new health technologies and media content ultimately benefit the general population, not only those with low levels of Media or eHealth Literacy.

5. Ethical Considerations in Media and eHealth Literacy Practice, Research, and Policy

The need for ethical considerations is just as pertinent and imminent in the areas of media and digital health literacy as in all areas of public health research. Ethical concerns need to be considered comprehensively—in practice, research, and policy.

5.1. Media and eHealth Literacy Ethics in Research

Regarding the ethical considerations of research on eHealth and digital/Media Health Literacy, two main aspects need to be considered for ethical scrutiny—namely sampling framework and generalizability of results. Increasingly, public health research relies on both samples that are drawn from big data, and self-reporting through digital systems. In normal research protocol, the use of personal data would require the consent of the participants. The use of big data systems for sampling should comply with the same standards even though the data is usually not identified [57]. Secondly, using digital technology (e.g., Smartwatches, fitness trackers) for data collection can seriously limit the extent to which data is collected from digitally excluded populations, often under-representing those whom have already been mentioned to tend to have low eHealth Literacy and Media Health Literacy. Thus, the results of such research cannot claim to be valid for all populations, nor is the principle of equity in research upheld.

5.2. Media and eHealth Literacy Ethics in Practice and Policy

As mentioned above, interventions with regard to MHL and eHealth literacy have two focal aspects: improving these areas of health literacy and/or adjusting interventions so that they are appropriate for the diversity of Media Health Literacy and eHealth Literacy skills. As such, ethical practice needs to be exercised as in any intervention, and applied to Media and eHealth Literacy practice. Intervention in the digital world requires that special attention be given to equity, allowing access according to need, guaranteeing cultural appropriateness, overcoming the digital divide, and taking into consideration various stages of digital development. Whether the intervention is through the digital media or in non-digital media, the characters, storyline, visuals, and content must be population appropriate. Finally, as the media and digital worlds attract commercial investors, public health practitioners must exercise scrupulous ethical standards in order to guarantee that no commercial vested interest is influencing any aspect of the intervention.

In light of all of the above, and in the interests of equity, it is essential that policies for health promotion, for improving health literacy of the individual, and for promoting organizational health literacy for the population, take into account the diversity of Media and eHealth Literacy skill levels.

6. Discussion

Media Health Literacy and eHealth Literacy are two concepts closely linked to health literacy which is defined as skills and competencies that enable people to obtain and interpret health information and empower them to maintain and improve their health and the health of the people around them. In Media and eHealth Literacy, the sources of the said health information and tools are specified to be the media, or in the case of eHealth Literacy more specifically digital media. Identifying, extracting, and understanding health information from media sources are by no means straightforward tasks, even less when the information is to be applied, leading to health decisions and adoption or change of health behavior. The complexity of processes underlying health literacy tasks explains why contextual and environmental variables play such an important role in shaping both the development and the actual use of the necessary skill sets.

Several research findings have indicated that health literacy levels vary by educational background e.g., [58,59], and similar findings have been summarized for eHealth Literacy and Media Health

Literacy e.g., [3], in earlier sections of this article. This may be the result of education acting as an SES proxy [35], as well as skill sets developed through educational settings in the lifespan. The latter is a standpoint supported by scholars who closely link the development of health literacy to school health education [6,60]. Still, caution needs to be exercised neither to interpret these findings as limitations of populations with low educational backgrounds, nor to conclude that formal education is the only key to improving general health literacy, Media Health Literacy and eHealth Literacy.

Beyond education, studies on general eHealth Literacy have repeatedly shown that the more often an individual engages in the search and interpretation of health information, the more confident they feel doing so. This has yet to be specifically measured for Media Health Literacy. A more overarching conclusion would thus be that self-efficacy [61], a strong predictor of health behavior adoption, is relevant for the eHL and MHL skills sets as well, supported by experience in the lifespan ("practice makes perfect"). It thus may be of secondary importance whether this practice is acquired in structured learning environments provided by formal education or elsewhere. As a third conclusion from findings summarized previously, it can be understood that social support is paramount for many, in executing tasks related to health information from media sources. Over a decade ago, Lee, Arozullah, and Cho [42] proposed a research agenda that would examine the associations of health literacy, social support, and health outcomes. Several studies have researched this assumption, with interesting results. For example, de Wit and colleagues [62] conducted a meta-analysis showing that social support and co-learning in communities were essential for critical health literacy based on qualitative evidence.

Furthermore, not only the social relevance of the practice of health literacy related tasks is of great importance, but also system complexity. Digital and non-digital media—and any other—environments where people encounter health-related information, vary greatly as to how difficult they are to interpret and navigate. Options exist to reduce complexity of content and presentation mode, as some examples introduced above can corroborate. It is the joint responsibility of public health researchers and practitioners, policy makers, and developers to apply what is known and to monitor whether necessary changes in system complexity are applied, leading to ease of access and usability for the actual end users. Thus, not only technical accessibility but also the content and modes of presentation of health information in the media are crucial. Specialists in health promotion, health technology, and health communication need to work together to create the tools that will empower patients to take responsibility for their health [63].

While an abundance of studies has been published in recent years on eHealth Literacy and Media Health Literacy, several limitations are noted, namely the lack of real-time surveys of usage, the response rates not reflecting the majority of users (30–35% response rates) and lack of research studying causal pathways (currently most studies are cross-sectional). In addition, comparative studies between Media and eHealth Literacy may be limited, as general Media Health Literacy includes media that are often not interactive, such as television, while specifically digital media is predominantly interactive.

Lastly, the media are unfortunately subjugated to vast commercial interests that in many cases conflict with the best health interest of consumers. As mentioned above, this leads to very pertinent ethical challenges in the realm of Media and eHealth Literacy research, further stressing the need for inter-sectorial cooperation and involvement of political stakeholders in the discourse on health literacy in media environments.

7. Conclusions

The influence of the social environment on public health is significant, as shown in a wealth of studies. As society and the social environment on the global level increasingly move towards use of digital and media tools for delivering health messages, offering health information, navigating health services, while also increasing the use of the Internet for commercial advertising, then eHealth literacy and Media Health Literacy skills will likewise play an increasingly essential role. eHealth Literacy has taken Media Health Literacy to a different level of meaning, as it enables and invites the public to actively interact, respond, and participate in creating, criticizing, and sharing health messages and information. Future research needs to be expanded to understand the symbiotic relationship between Media Health Literacy, eHealth Literacy, and the social and cultural environment. On the one hand, a clearer understanding is necessary to learn of how Media and eHealth Literacy can influence the social environment that promotes health, while also taking into consideration the influence of the social and cultural environment on all aspects of the involved skill sets. The pervasive and increasing access to mobile tools globally will ultimately transform what was once considered the "digital divide" into numerous degrees of "digital development". Continued concern must be exercised to enable and ensure access to media and digital tools for all, such that new technologies can fulfil their primary purpose: to promote health.

Author Contributions: Investigation, D.L-Z. and I.B.; Methodology, D.L-Z. and I.B.; Writing—original draft, D.L-Z. and I.B.; Writing—review and editing, D.L-Z. and I.B.

Funding: This research received no external funding.

Conflicts of Interest: The authors declare no conflict of interest.

References

1. Sørensen, K.; Van den Broucke, S.; Fullam, J.; Doyle, G.; Pelikan, J.; Slonska, Z.; Brand, H.; HLS-EU Consortium. Health literacy and public health: A systematic review and integration of definitions and models. *BMC Public Health* **2012**, *12*. [CrossRef]
2. Kickbusch, I.S. Health literacy: Addressing the health and education divide. *Health Promot. Int.* **2001**, *16*, 289–297. [CrossRef] [PubMed]
3. Levin-Zamir, D.; Lemish, D.; Gofin, R. Media Health Literacy (MHL): Development and measurement of the concept among adolescents. *Health Educ. Res.* **2011**, *26*, 323–335. [CrossRef] [PubMed]
4. Norman, C.D.; Skinner, H.A. eHealth Literacy: Essential skills for consumer health in a networked world. *J. Med. Internet Res.* **2006**, *8*, e9. [CrossRef] [PubMed]
5. Livingstone, S. Developing social media literacy: How children learn to interpret risky opportunities on social network sites. *Communications* **2014**, *39*, 283–303. [CrossRef
6. Nutbeam, D. Health literacy as a public health goal: A challenge for contemporary health education and communication strategies into the 21st century. *Health Promot. Int.* **2000**, *15*, 259–267. [CrossRef]
7. McGinnis, J.M.; Berwick, D.M.; Daschle, T.A.; Diaz, A.; Fineberg, H.V.; First, W.H.; Gawande, A.; Halfon, N.; Mourey, R. Systems strategies for better health throughout the life course. In *Vital Directions for Health & Health Care*; Dzau, V.J., McClellan, M.B., McGinnis, J.M., Finkelman, E.M., Eds.; National Academy of Medicine: Washington, DC, USA, 2017; pp. 43–69. ISBN 978-1-947-10300-9.
8. Research2Guidance. *mHealth App Economics 2017/2018. Current Status and Future Trends in Mobile Health*; Research2Guidance: Berlin, Germany, 2017.
9. Norman, C.D.; Skinner, H.A. eHEALS: The eHealth Literacy Scale. *J. Med. Internet Res.* **2006**, *8*, e27. [CrossRef] [PubMed]
10. Quinn, S.; Bond, R.; Nugent, C. Quantifying health literacy and eHealth literacy using existing instruments and browser-based software for tracking online health information seeking behavior. *Comput. Hum. Behav.* **2017**, *69*, 256–267. [CrossRef]
11. Van der Vaart, R.; van Deursen, A.J.; Drossaert, C.H.; Taal, E.; van Dijk, J.A.; van de Laar, M.A. Does the eHealth Literacy Scale (eHEALS) measure what it intends to measure? Validation of a Dutch version of the eHEALS in two adult populations. *J. Med. Internet Res.* **2011**, *13*, e86. [CrossRef] [PubMed]
12. Norman, C.D. eHealth literacy 2.0: Problems and opportunities with an evolving concept. *J. Med. Internet Res.* **2011**, *13*, e125. [CrossRef] [PubMed]
13. Van der Vaart, R.; Drossaert, C.H. Development of the digital health literacy instrument: Measuring a broad spectrum of health 1.0 and health 2.0 skills. *J. Med. Internet Res.* **2017**, *19*, e27. [CrossRef] [PubMed]
14. Chan, C.V.; Kaufman, D.R. A framework for characterizing eHealth literacy demands and barriers. *J. Med. Internet Res.* **2011**, *13*, e94. [CrossRef] [PubMed]

15. Parker, R. Measuring health literacy: What? So what? Now what? In *Measures of Health Literacy: Workshop Summary*; Hernandez, L.M., Ed.; National Academies Press: Washington, DC, USA, 2009; ISBN 978-0-309-13980-9.
16. Zanchetta, M.S.; Poureslami, I.M. Health literacy within the reality of immigrants' culture and language. *Can. J. Public Health* **2006**, *97* (Suppl. 2), S26–S30. [PubMed]
17. Bodie, G.D.; Dutta, M.J. Understanding health literacy for strategic health marketing: eHealth literacy, health disparities, and the digital divide. *Health Mark. Q.* **2008**, *25*, 175–203. [CrossRef] [PubMed]
18. Meppelink, C.S.; van Weert, J.C.M.; Haven, C.J.; Smit, E.G. The effectiveness of health animations in audiences with different health literacy levels: An experimental study. *J. Med. Internet Res.* **2015**, *17*, e11. [CrossRef] [PubMed]
19. Coughlin, S.S.; Hardy, D.; Caplan, L.S. The need for culturally-tailored smartphone applications for weight control. *J. Ga. Public Health Assoc.* **2016**, *5*, 228–232. [PubMed]
20. Vandenbosch, J.; Van den Broucke, S.; Schinckus, L.; Schwarz, P.; Doyle, G.; Pelikan, J.; Muller, I.; Levin-Zamir, D.; Schillinger, D.; Chang, P.; et al. The impact of health literacy on diabetes self-management education. *Health Educ. J.* **2018**, *77*, 349–362. [CrossRef]
21. Choi, N.G.; Dinitto, D.M. The digital divide among low-income homebound older adults: Internet use patterns, eHealth literacy, and attitudes toward computer/Internet use. *J. Med. Internet Res.* **2013**, *15*, e93. [CrossRef] [PubMed]
22. Richtering, S.S.; Hyun, K.; Neubeck, L.; Coorey, G.; Chalmers, J.; Usherwood, T.; Peiris, D.; Chow, C.K.; Redfern, J. eHealth Literacy: Predictors in a population with moderate-to-high cardiovascular risk. *JMIR Hum. Factors* **2017**, *4*, e4. [CrossRef] [PubMed]
23. Guendelman, S.; Broderick, A.; Mlo, H.; Gemmill, A.; Lindeman, D. Listening to communities: Mixed-method study of the engagement of disadvantaged mothers and pregnant women with digital health technologies. *J. Med. Internet Res.* **2017**, *19*, e240. [CrossRef] [PubMed]
24. Tennant, B.; Stellefson, M.; Dodd, V.; Chaney, B.; Chaney, D.; Paige, S.; Alber, J. eHealth literacy and Web 2.0 health information seeking behaviors among baby boomers and older adults. *J. Med. Internet Res.* **2015**, *17*, e70. [CrossRef] [PubMed]
25. Ghaddar, S.F.; Valerio, M.A.; Garcia, C.M.; Hansen, L. Adolescent health literacy: The importance of credible sources for online health information. *J. Sch. Health* **2012**, *82*, 28–36. [CrossRef] [PubMed]
26. Chang, F.-C.; Chiu, C.-H.; Chen, P.-H.; Miao, N.-F.; Lee, C.-M.; Chiang, J.-T.; Pan, Y.-C. Relationship between parental and adolescent eHealth Literacy and online health information seeking in Taiwan. *Cyberpsychol. Behav. Soc. Netw.* **2015**, *18*, 618–624. [CrossRef] [PubMed]
27. Borzekowski, D.L.G. Considering children and health literacy: A theoretical approach. *Pediatrics* **2009**, *124* (Suppl. 3), S282–S288. [CrossRef] [PubMed]
28. Fox, S. *Online Health Search 2006*; PEW Internet & American Life Project: Washington, DC, USA, 2006.
29. European Commission. *European Citizens' Digital Health Literacy*; European Union: Brussels, Belgium, 2014.
30. Rennis, L.; McNamara, G.; Seidel, E.; Shneyderman, Y. Google it!: Urban community college students' use of the Internet to obtain self-care and personal health information. *Coll. Stud. J.* **2015**, *49*, 414–426.
31. Kontos, E.; Blake, K.D.; Chou, W.-Y.S.; Prestin, A. Predictors of eHealth usage: Insights on the digital divide from the Health Information National Trends Survey 2012. *J. Med. Internet Res.* **2014**, *16*, e172. [CrossRef] [PubMed]
32. Nölke, L.; Mensing, M.; Krämer, A.; Hornberg, C. Sociodemographic and health-(care-)related characteristics of online health information seekers: A cross-sectional German study. *BMC Public Health* **2015**, *15*, 31. [CrossRef] [PubMed]
33. Nguyen, A.; Mosadeghi, S.; Almario, C.V. Persistent digital divide in access to and use of the Internet as a resource for health information: Results from a California population-based study. *Int. J. Med. Inform.* **2017**, *103*, 49–54. [CrossRef] [PubMed]
34. Baumann, E.; Czerwinski, F.; Reifegerste, D. Gender-specific determinants and patterns of online health information seeking: Results from a representative German health survey. *J. Med. Internet Res.* **2017**, *19*, e92. [CrossRef] [PubMed]
35. Carroll, J.K.; Moorhead, A.; Bond, R.; LeBlanc, W.G.; Petrella, R.J.; Fiscella, K. Who uses mobile phone health apps and does use matter? A secondary data analytics approach. *J. Med. Internet Res.* **2017**, *19*, e125. [CrossRef] [PubMed]

36. Levin-Zamir, D.; Leung, A.Y.M.; Dodson, S.; Rowlands, G. Health literacy in selected populations: Individuals, families, and communities from the international and cultural perspective. *Inf. Serv. Use* **2017**, *37*, 131–151. [CrossRef]
37. Neter, E.; Brainin, E. eHealth literacy: Extending the digital divide to the realm of health information. *J. Med. Internet Res.* **2012**, *14*, e19. [CrossRef] [PubMed]
38. Knapp, C.; Madden, V.; Wang, H.; Sloyer, P.; Shenkman, E. Internet use and eHealth literacy of low-income parents whose children have special health care needs. *J. Med. Internet Res.* **2011**, *13*, e75. [CrossRef] [PubMed]
39. Zibrik, L.; Khan, S.; Bangar, N.; Stacy, E.; Novak Lauscher, H.; Ho, K. Patient and community centered eHealth: Exploring eHealth barriers and facilitators for chronic disease self-management within British Columbia's immigrant Chinese and Punjabi seniors. *Health Policy Technol.* **2015**, *4*, 348–356. [CrossRef]
40. Chung, S.; Park, B.K.; Nahm, E.-S. The Korean eHealth Literacy Scale (K-eHEALS): Reliability and validity testing in younger adults recruited online. *J. Med. Internet Res.* **2018**, *20*, e138. [CrossRef] [PubMed]
41. Diviani, N.; Dima, A.L.; Schulz, P.J. A psychometric analysis of the Italian version of the eHealth Literacy Scale using item response and classical test theory methods. *J. Med. Internet Res.* **2017**, *19*, e114. [CrossRef] [PubMed]
42. Lee, S.-Y.D.; Arozullah, A.M.; Cho, Y.I. Health literacy, social support, and health: A research agenda. *Soc. Sci. Med.* **2004**, *58*, 1309–1321. [CrossRef]
43. Hernán-García, M.; Botello-Díaz, B.; Marcos-Marcos, J.; Toro-Cárdenas, S.; Gil-García, E. Understanding children: A qualitative study on health assets of the Internet in Spain. *Int. J. Public Health* **2015**, *60*, 239–247. [CrossRef] [PubMed]
44. Aponte, J.; Nokes, K.M. Electronic health literacy of older Hispanics with diabetes. *Health Promot. Int.* **2017**, *32*, 482–489. [CrossRef] [PubMed]
45. Sorensen, L.; Gavier, M.; Helleso, R. Latina breast cancer survivors informational needs: Information partners. *Stud. Health Technol. Inform.* **2009**, *146*, 727. [PubMed]
46. Hayat, T.Z.; Brainin, E.; Neter, E. With some help from my network: Supplementing eHealth Literacy with social ties. *J. Med. Internet Res.* **2017**, *19*, e98. [CrossRef] [PubMed]
47. Wharf Higgins, J.; Begoray, D. Exploring the borderlands between media and health: Conceptualizing "Critical Media Health Literacy". *J. Media Lit. Educ.* **2012**, *4*, 136–148.
48. Gordon, C.S.; Jones, S.C.; Kervin, L.; Lee, J.K. Empowering students to respond to alcohol advertisements: Results from a pilot study of an Australian media literacy intervention. *Aust. N. Z. J. Public Health* **2016**, *40*, 231–232. [CrossRef] [PubMed]
49. Zoellner, J.M.; Hedrick, V.E.; You, W.; Chen, Y.; Davy, B.M.; Porter, K.J.; Bailey, A.; Lane, H.; Alexander, R.; Estabrooks, P.A. Effects of a behavioral and health literacy intervention to reduce sugar-sweetened beverages: A randomized-controlled trial. *Int. J. Behav. Nutr. Phys. Act.* **2016**, *13*, 38. [CrossRef] [PubMed]
50. Lopes, F.; Araújo, R. Power to health reporters: Health literacy as a tool to avoid pressures from news sources. *Port. J. Public Health* **2018**, *35*, 193–201. [CrossRef]
51. Stellefson, M.; Hanik, B.; Chaney, B.; Chaney, D.; Tennant, B.; Chavarria, E.A. eHealth literacy among college students: A systematic review with implications for eHealth education. *J. Med. Internet Res.* **2011**, *13*, e102. [CrossRef] [PubMed]
52. Paek, H.-J.; Hove, T. Social cognitive factors and perceived social influences that improve adolescent eHealth literacy. *Health Commun.* **2012**, *27*, 727–737. [CrossRef] [PubMed]
53. Xie, B. Effects of an eHealth literacy intervention for older adults. *J. Med. Internet Res.* **2011**, *13*, e90. [CrossRef] [PubMed]
54. Xie, B. Older adults, e-health literacy, and collaborative learning: An experimental study. *J. Am. Soc. Inf. Sci.* **2011**, *62*, 933–946. [CrossRef]
55. Xie, B. Experimenting on the impact of learning methods and information presentation channels on older adults' e-health literacy. *J. Am. Soc. Inf. Sci.* **2011**, *62*, 1797–1807. [CrossRef]
56. Watkins, I.; Xie, B. eHealth literacy interventions for older adults: A systematic review of the literature. *J. Med. Internet Res.* **2014**, *16*, e225. [CrossRef] [PubMed]
57. Vayena, E.; Dzenowagis, J.; Brownstein, J.S.; Sheikh, A. Policy implications of Big Data in the health sector. *Bull. World Health Organ.* **2018**, *96*, 66–68. [CrossRef] [PubMed]

58. Sørensen, K.; Pelikan, J.M.; Röthlin, F.; Ganahl, K.; Slonska, Z.; Doyle, G.; Fullam, J.; Kondilis, B.; Agrafiotis, D.; Uiters, E.; et al. Health literacy in Europe: Comparative results of the European health literacy survey (HLS-EU). *Eur. J. Public Health* **2015**, *25*, 1053–1058. [CrossRef] [PubMed]
59. Paasche-Orlow, M.K.; Parker, R.M.; Gazmararian, J.A.; Nielsen-Bohlman, L.T.; Rudd, R.E. The prevalence of limited health literacy. *J. Gen. Intern. Med.* **2005**, *20*, 175–184. [CrossRef] [PubMed]
60. Paakkari, L.; Paakkari, O. Health literacy as a learning outcome in schools. *Health Educ.* **2012**, *112*, 133–152. [CrossRef]
61. Bandura, A. *Social Learning Theory*; Prentice-Hall: Englewood Cliffs, NJ, USA, 1977; ISBN 978-0-138-16744-8.
62. De Wit, L.; Fenenga, C.; Giammarchi, C.; di Furia, L.; Hutter, I.; de Winter, A.; Meijering, L. Community-based initiatives improving critical health literacy: A systematic review and meta-synthesis of qualitative evidence. *BMC Public Health* **2017**, *18*, 40. [CrossRef] [PubMed]
63. Rudd, R.E.; Rosenfeld, L.; Simonds, V.W. Health literacy: A new area of research with links to communication. *Atl. J. Commun.* **2012**, *20*, 16–30. [CrossRef]

© 2018 by the authors. Licensee MDPI, Basel, Switzerland. This article is an open access article distributed under the terms and conditions of the Creative Commons Attribution (CC BY) license (http://creativecommons.org/licenses/by/4.0/).

Article

Progress in Implementing National Policies and Strategies for Health Literacy—What Have We Learned so Far?

Anita Trezona [1,*], Gill Rowlands [2] and Don Nutbeam [3]

1. School of Health and Social Development, Deakin University, Melbourne 3125, Australia
2. Institute of Health and Society, Newcastle University, Newcastle NE1 7RU, UK; Gill.Rowlands@newcastle.ac.uk
3. School of Public Health, University of Sydney, Sydney 2006, Australia; don.nutbeam@sydney.edu.au
* Correspondence: anita.trezona@gmail.com

Received: 16 May 2018; Accepted: 18 July 2018; Published: 23 July 2018

Abstract: Health literacy has been a prominent issue on the agenda of the World Health Organization (WHO) for almost two decades. WHO recently established a strong global mandate for public policy action on health literacy by positioning it as one of three key pillars for achieving sustainable development and health equity in the Shanghai Declaration on Health Promotion. Several countries have national health literacy policies, with many others expected to develop them in the immediate future. It is, therefore, timely to examine current policy approaches to health literacy. The purpose of this study was to analyze a selection of existing policy documents for their strengths, limitations and themes, and offer observations about their potential to improve health literacy and health outcomes. In doing so our intention is to offer lessons and advice from early adopters that will have usefulness for future policy development and implementation. We selected six policies for review; Australia, Austria, China, New Zealand, Scotland, and the United States. We used a set of criteria to guide a systematic analysis of policy documents for their context, intended target audiences, objectives, proposed actions and interventions, evidence of financial investment and intentions to monitor outcomes. We observed a number of common features that provide helpful signposting for future policy development in other countries. All represent a response to perceived deficiencies in the quality of patient communication and patient engagement. Most present health literacy as a universal challenge, with some also identifying groups who are of higher priority. They all recognize the importance of professional education in improving the quality of communication, and most recognize that the health literacy responsiveness of the health system needs to be improved. However, there was significant variability in linking resources to specific strategies and actions, as well as in the systems for monitoring progress and accountability for progress. This variability reflects important contextual differences between countries and health systems. However, this lack of specificity will likely have an impact on the priority given to improving health literacy and on the long-term sustainability of defined actions to improve health literacy in populations.

Keywords: health literacy; policy; policy analysis

1. Introduction

Health literacy has become a subject of wide interest in the past decade, and several countries have current national health literacy policies or have incorporated health literacy as a priority issue within broader health strategies. It is not difficult to understand why. For researchers interested in health and disease causality, "health literacy" has become a convenient way of describing a measurable variable that can be used to understand and explain variation in health and disease outcomes. For clinicians, work over many years, mainly in the US, has established health literacy as an identifiable and manageable risk in clinical care, of particular importance in the management of long-term and complex conditions that depend upon successful patient engagement and management. For public health practitioners, health literacy is conceptually attractive in its fit with contemporary health promotion, understood as a personal "asset" that can be developed through educational and other interventions to support greater personal and community control over a range of determinants of health.

There is no doubt that wide scientific interest in health literacy has underpinned the policy interest. Over the past 20 years there has been a proliferation of studies that have provided definitions [1,2], conceptual models [3–5], and measurement tools [6–8]. Others have described the relationship between health literacy and health outcomes [9] and population prevalence [10,11]. This research has produced consistent evidence that low health literacy is a public health challenge across all parts of the world, and that it is modifiable through effective educational intervention and health system improvement.

This scientific interest has been mirrored by the growing interest of national and international organizations including, specifically, the World Health Organization (WHO) throughout this period. This was first evident from background work in support of a global conference on health promotion in Jakarta, Indonesia in 1997 [12] becoming a "key action" identified in the WHO Bangkok Charter for Health Promotion in a Globalized World [13]; and most recently described as one of three central strategies in the 2016 WHO Shanghai Declaration on promoting health in the 2030 Agenda for Sustainable Development [14].

The Shanghai Declaration has established a clear global mandate for the prioritization of health literacy within public policy, promoting the role and responsibility of governments to act. Countries and regions are already responding to this call to action [15], and the recently commissioned WHO Health Evidence Network synthesis report on Health Literacy Policy in the WHO European region [16], as well as the discussion generated through the first WHO Community of Practice on Health Literacy, provides evidence of the demand for guidance on effective health literacy policy development [17,18].

The policies and strategies that have emerged vary according to the way in which different countries and localities conceptualize health literacy and respond to perceived needs.

Each of the existing national policies and strategies has different origins, influences and processes that have informed their development and implementation, and have invariably been influenced by the political and health system contexts in which they were developed.

Policies articulate the intentions of governments to address public issues, including the priorities to be addressed and the courses of action to be taken [19]. These may take the form of broad informal policy statements, or more formalized documents such as policy frameworks, strategic plans or action plans. While health policies vary significantly in design and scope, most will or should contain common, observable elements. For example, they should establish a clear purpose, measurable goals and objectives, and actionable strategies [19]. They should also establish targets and specify mechanisms for monitoring, evaluating and reporting on implementation progress and policy outcomes [20]. This may include guidance to stakeholders on their roles and responsibilities in implementing the policy [21]. These elements can be objectively observed and reviewed for strengths and weaknesses, and general and specific lessons.

Policy responses to health literacy are likely to proliferate in the coming years, and it is timely to examine the early lessons emerging from those countries that have moved first in their public policy responses. The purpose of this study is to analyze a selection of existing policy documents for their strengths, limitations and themes, and offer observations about their potential to improve health literacy and health outcomes. In doing so our intention is to offer lessons and advice from early adopters that will have usefulness for future policy development and implementation.

2. Methods

Policy analysis is a retrospective, descriptive process of explaining various aspects of a particular policy. This may include the context, processes, actors and stakeholders (including their values and power), or the policy content such as the stated goals, intentions, actions and strategies [19–21]. Documentary analysis, or policy document analysis is a common approach to analyzing the content of policies, which can be useful for assessing the extent to which they contain the elements necessary to support successful implementation and achievement of the intended outcomes. Quantitative and qualitative methods can be used in policy document analysis [21]. Quantitative methods seek to systematically quantify the policy information according to predetermined categories, for example how many policies contain a concept of interest. Qualitative policy analysis is also a systematic process that aims to identify key concepts and themes. For example, Fisher et al. [22] undertook a qualitative analysis of health policy documents to determine the extent to which they address the social determinants of health and health inequities.

We undertook a review and analysis of six policy documents between August and November 2017. We selected health literacy policies from Australia, Austria, China, New Zealand, Scotland, and the United States for both practical and methodological reasons. Firstly, they were publicly available at the time of review and published in either English or German. Secondly, they were developed and implemented in diverse contexts, reflecting varying political and economic systems and conditions, and different healthcare systems, structures and public health approaches. Thirdly, the countries are sited in three WHO Regional groupings (Western Pacific, Europe and the Americas).

We adapted the policy analysis framework developed by Trezona et al. [23] to guide a systematic qualitative analysis of the six policy documents in this study. The authors developed the framework specifically for the purpose of analyzing the way in which policy documents prioritize, operationalize and resource health literacy. They then tested the utility of the framework by applying it to a set of Australian health policies. The framework has been tested and shown to be useful for analyzing policy documents containing health literacy, thus we determined it to be suitable for this study. However, the framework was previously applied quantitatively to rate and rank policy documents. We considered a qualitative approach to be more appropriate for achieving the aim of this study, therefore we adopted a number of criteria from the framework to guide a qualitative analysis and data extraction process. These were the criteria relating to policy objectives or priorities, proposed actions and interventions, allocation of resources and intentions to monitor policy outcomes. We also added criteria relating to the policy context and target audiences. The full list of analysis criteria is shown in Table 1.

Table 1. Criteria for analyzing and extracting data from policy documents.

1	What is the name of the policy?
2	When was it published?
3	Who published the policy (i.e., government department)?
4	What was the policy context in which it was developed?
5	Who are the intended target audiences of the policy (i.e., consumers, health professionals, hospitals)?
6	What are the stated objectives or priority areas of the policy?
7	What are the stated actions/interventions/strategies for addressing health literacy?
8	Does the document explicitly state the allocation of funding to support policy implementation?
9	Does the policy explicitly state a commitment to monitoring/measuring the policy outcomes? If so, what monitoring/measurement mechanisms are proposed?

The authors undertook the first round of analysis by extracting data from the six policy documents and organizing it in data collection sheets according to the above criteria. In order to verify the accuracy of the data extraction and interpretation, we invited key informants from the six countries to comment on the data presented in the data collection sheets. Specifically, they were asked to comment on whether the findings had been misinterpreted or misrepresented, or if there was critical information missing from the results. We received feedback from five of the six countries (we were unable to get feedback from our key informant in New Zealand). This feedback was generally positive regarding the accuracy of the representation of the policy, and our interpretation of its key elements. It also enabled us to improve the accuracy of our analysis by reporting information that was not explicitly stated in the policy documents, such as governance and oversight responsibilities, sources and level of expenditure related to the policy, and monitoring and evaluation mechanisms that are in place. We have also made specific references to information provided by key informants where this was not verifiable through currently accessible documents.

We present case studies for each country to provide an overview of their policy approach and observations about their strengths and weaknesses. We then compare and contrast the policies to describe the similarities and differences between the objectives and actions described, and to reveal trends in approaches to health literacy policy development across countries.

3. Results

A descriptive summary of each country's policy is presented below. This includes the policy title, year of publication and publishing organization, a brief description of the context in which the policy was developed, and an overview of the high-level policy priorities, objectives, and/or action areas.

3.1. Australia

Federal, state and territory and local governments have a shared responsibility for health governance in Australia, including policy development and implementation, and the management of healthcare systems. Their respective roles are specified in the National Healthcare Agreement [24] The federal government has responsibility for the three core elements of Australia's universal public health system: (i) The national public health insurance scheme (Medicare), which provides free or subsidized benefits for most medical, diagnostic and allied health services; (ii) The Pharmaceutical Benefits Scheme (PBS) which provides subsidized prescription medications; and (iii) The private health insurance rebate, which covers private hospital services and many out-of-hospital services not covered by Medicare [25]. State and territory governments are primarily responsible for public hospitals, ambulance services, community health services and mental healthcare.

The federal government is responsible for developing policies that set a national public health agenda, whereas state and territory governments set the public health agenda for their jurisdictions, as well as develop the program and funding guidelines that mandate the way services are expected to operate, including specific targets for service delivery. National advisory and regulatory bodies also play a significant role in shaping the priorities and direction of healthcare in Australia, and in monitoring the performance of the healthcare system.

In 2014 the *National Statement on Health Literacy* was released in Australia [26]. The Australian Commission on Safety and Quality in Healthcare (ACSQHC) is a corporate Commonwealth entity, jointly funded by the federal and state and territory governments in Australia. Its role is to ensure safe and high-quality health systems, including through the establishment of the National Safety and Quality Health Service Standards [27] and the ongoing accreditation of healthcare services. The ACSQHC is not a governing body, therefore the National Statement does not constitute a formal government policy, however it was endorsed by all federal, state and territory health ministers, signaling their at least in-principle commitment to addressing health literacy in Australia.

The ACSQHC developed the National Statement in order to increase an understanding of health literacy across relevant sectors, and promote a coordinated and collaborative approach to systematically addressing it nationally [26]. The document describes three strategic areas: (i) Embedding health literacy into systems; (ii) Ensuring effective communication; and (iii) Integrating health literacy into education. It also lists a range of actions divided into the role of consumers, healthcare providers, healthcare organizations, government organizations and policymakers (including regulatory and advisory bodies). The National Statement is reinforced by the incorporation of health literacy into the National Safety and Quality Health Service Standards. These standards are reviewed and revised regularly in consultation with the Australian Government, state and territory partners, consumers, the private sector and other stakeholders, and endorsed by all health ministers in Australia [28].

3.2. Austria

Responsibility for healthcare governance in Austria is shared between a number of institutions at federal and provincial levels. The federal government plays a central role in the development of legislation, with many implementation responsibilities delegated to provincial governments and social security institutions. Public health services are jointly provided by federal, provincial and local authorities, and supported by a compulsory, universal health and social insurance system. Ten national health targets currently guide healthcare reform in Austria to ensure coordinated planning, implementation and cross-sectoral action [29].

Health literacy is one of ten health targets for Austria, which were drafted in 2012 at the direction of the Federal Health Commission of Austria and the Austrian Council of Ministers [30]. In 2014 the Ministry of Health released the policy *National Health Target No. 3: Improving Population Health Literacy*. The policy is now being implemented in a two-fold approach, in which the aspects relating to the healthcare field are being implemented through the ongoing healthcare reform process, for which the Austrian Ministry of Health, the Austrian 'Länder' (Federal subdivisions) and social insurance have shared responsibility. The aspects relating to the 'health in all policies' dimensions of health literacy are being implemented through the intersectoral Austrian Health Literacy Platform [30].

The policy aims to improve health literacy for all people living in Austria, with a specific focus on vulnerable populations and sub-policies targeted to specific groups. The document describes three priority areas (articulated as sub-policies): (i) improve the health literacy-friendliness of healthcare services; (ii) improve individual health literacy (especially vulnerable groups); and (iii) improve health literacy-friendliness of the production and service sector. Actions under priority one include the implementation of a national strategy on improving the quality of communication in healthcare, promotion of the application of standard criteria (15 indicators) for good quality health information, the development of Austrian web portal on trustworthy health information, and making low threshold health consultation available through a 24-h telephone-based consultation service. Actions under priority two include health literacy-coaching for clients of health insurance companies, strengthening the responsibility of the education sector to lay the foundations for health literacy in schools, and supporting healthcare interactions of people who speak German (mother tongue) as a second language through a video interpreting service. Actions have not been articulated for priority three. However, it will focus on making it easier for consumers to make healthy decisions by providing good quality consumer information on products [30].

3.3. China

The Chinese National Government has overall responsibility for health legislation, policy development and administration in China, with local governments (provinces, cities, counties and towns) responsible for providing healthcare services. The National People's Congress is responsible for health legislation, but policies may also be implemented by the State Council and Central Committee of the Communist Party. The National Health and Family Planning Commission (at the federal and local level) oversees healthcare delivery, including quality and safety, and administration of the Center for Disease Control and Prevention. In terms of health system financing, China has a publicly funded health insurance scheme, which is financed and provided by local governments and covers primary, specialist, emergency department, hospital care, mental healthcare, prescription and traditional medicine. The public health insurance scheme is complemented by a rapidly growing private health insurance scheme [31].

China released its *National Plan of Health Literacy Promotion Initiatives* for Chinese Citizens in 2008, which together with the 'Health Literacy for Chinese Citizens–Basic Knowledge and Skills Trial' (combining initiatives for health professionals and urban and rural residents) represents the Ministry of Health of the People's Republic of China's commitment to addressing health literacy, as well as the guiding document for the implementation of health literacy initiatives by all Provincial Departments of Health, autonomous regions, municipalities, Xinjiang Production and Construction Corps, the cities specifically designated in the State Plan, and the Chinese Center for Disease Control and Prevention [32].

The first part of the document outlines the objectives, targets and measures for the policy, and sets out the governance and accountability expectations for implementation of the policy by administrative departments at county, city and district levels. The second part of the document summarizes a range of content topics, divided into three sections: (i) basic knowledge and concepts; (ii) healthy lifestyles and behaviors; and (iii) basic skills, which presumably form the topics to be included in initiatives implemented at local levels.

The National Plan was developed for the purpose of promoting and popularizing the 'Health Literacy for Chinese Citizens-Basic knowledge and skills Trial', with four key objectives or targets:

1. To establish a health sector leading, multi-sector social participatory working-network of Health Literacy Promotion Initiatives with a coverage rate of 100 percent, 80 percent, and 60 percent in province, city/prefecture and county level respectively.
2. At least 80 percent of the professionals in the working-network to be trained.
3. To establish a Chinese citizens' health literacy surveillance and evaluation system.
4. At least 60 percent of counties all over the country will carry out communication activities of 'Health Literacy 66' (the basic health knowledge and skills that have been identified for all Chinese citizens) [32].

The document also describes five key action areas or 'tasks' to be implemented as part of the policy, which can be briefly summarized as establish and improve the working network (leadership and governance), strengthen capacity building activities (workforce development), conduct communication activities, carry out health literacy surveillance, and develop demonstrative models (demonstration sites).

3.4. New Zealand

In New Zealand, the health system is largely publicly funded with the federal government responsible for setting the health policy agenda, service requirements and public funding allocation, while geographically defined district health boards are responsible for planning and delivering services. The Ministry of Health has overall responsibility for the health and disability systems, with support from specific purpose agencies such as the Health Promotion Agency and The Health Quality and Safety Agency [33].

While New Zealand does not have a specific health literacy policy, health literacy is incorporated as a key priority in the *New Zealand Health Strategy 2016–2026* [29]. The Strategy is required by New Zealand legislation that governs publicly funded health and disability services, which together with the New Zealand Disability Strategy, provides a framework for the delivery of all health and disability services. The Health Strategy is comprised of two documents; the main document establishes the broad 'future directions' for the health system and the companion document details the 'roadmap of actions' [34].

Health literacy is incorporated into the 'people-powered theme', one of five strategic themes within the strategy. The theme promotes building health literacy and active two-way engagement, with a broad focus on ensuring people have access to and can understand the information they need to manage their care, enabling individuals to make choices about their care, partnering with people to design services based on their needs and preferences, and communicating effectively and providing navigation support. Two action areas specifically relating to health literacy are described, one that focuses on individuals by providing health information to support self-management (including the use of digital technologies), and one that focuses on making the health system more health literacy responsive [35].

3.5. Scotland

The Scottish Government is responsible for healthcare legislation and financing, as well as setting national objectives and priorities for the National Health Service (NHS). NHS Health Boards (there are 14 across Scotland) are responsible for delivering health services that achieve the national objectives and priorities, which includes planning and commissioning hospital and community health services. The NHS Health Boards establish community health partnerships at a local level to ensure local authorities and patients are involved in healthcare delivery [36].

The Scottish Government released its first health literacy policy in 2014 with *Making it Easy: A Health Literacy Action Plan for Scotland*, the aim of which was for health and social care services to systematically address health literacy as a priority to improve health and reduce health inequalities, and for all people in Scotland to have the confidence, knowledge, understanding and skills needed to live well [37]. The Action Plan formed part of a broader policy agenda, contributing to the goals of Scotland's 2020 Vision for Health and Social Care Policy, the NHS Scotland Healthcare Quality Strategy, and upholding the Patient Rights Act.

The first Action Plan was comprised of four key actions areas: (i) Increase workforce awareness and capabilities to address health literacy; (ii) Promote the development and spread of existing and new health literacy tools, innovations and technologies; (iii) Develop a National Health Literacy Resource including a 'clearinghouse' and community of practice; (iv) Establish a National Demonstrator Site.

Building on the progress made with the first action plan, the Scottish Government recently released its second action plan *Making it Easier: A Health Literacy Action Plan for Scotland 2017–2025* [38], which is a key element of its agenda to better support people through shared decision making. Its aim is to improve health literacy practice across the health and care system by removing barriers, making services easier to navigate, making information more responsive to need, and ensuring the design of services are informed by health literacy needs.

The second action plan describes three overarching action areas: (i) Share the learning from Making it Easy; (ii) Embed ways to improve health literacy in policy and practice; and (iii) Shift the culture by developing more health literacy responsive organizations and communities.

3.6. United States

In the United States, the health system is funded through a mix of public and private financing mechanisms, with the majority of the population relying on private insurance. The Affordable Care Act (2010) has been a key reform, and aims to achieve universal coverage, greater affordability and higher quality care, and establishes a shared responsibility for health insurance provision between the government, employers and individuals. In terms of health system governance, the United States (U.S.) Department of Health and Human Services is the principal federal government agency responsible for healthcare in the U.S. It is made up of a number of agencies and institutions, including the Centers for Medicare and Medicade Services (which play a central role in administering aspects of the public insurance schemes), the Centre for Disease Control and Prevention, and the Agency for Healthcare Research and Quality [39].

The U.S. Department of Health and Human Services (Office of Disease Prevention and Health Promotion) released the *U.S. National Action Plan to Improve Health Literacy* in 2010 [40], which aims to stimulate a society-wide movement to create a health literate America. The Action Plan is built on a vision of a society in which everyone has access to accurate health information, person-centred health information and services are delivered and lifelong learning to promote good health is supported. The document describes seven goals for achieving this vision:

1. Develop and disseminate health and safety information that is accurate, accessible, and actionable
2. Promote changes in the healthcare system that improve health information, communication, informed decision making, and access to health services
3. Incorporate accurate, standards-based, and developmentally appropriate health and science information and curricula in child care and education through the university level
4. Support and expand local efforts to provide adult education, English language instruction, and culturally and linguistically appropriate health information services in the community
5. Build partnerships, develop guidance, and change policies
6. Increase basic research and the development, implementation, and evaluation of practices and interventions to improve health literacy
7. Increase the dissemination and use of evidence-based health literacy practices and interventions.

These goals provide the frame for action, with a set of strategies outlined under each goal (154 in total), grouped according to the stakeholders with a potential role in implementing them [39].

3.7. Data Analysis

Results of the data analysis processes are presented in Table 2. The 'Priority Areas' column includes information that was expressed in the policy document as a priority, goal, objective or strategic area. The 'Actions/Strategies' have been summarized into key themes identified within the policy document, rather than the full list of actions. Data were only included in 'Funding Allocation' and 'Monitoring and Evaluation' columns if these were explicitly stated in the policy document. Our key informants were able to provide us with additional information, which is discussed later.

Table 2. Analysis of selected policy documents.

Country	Target Audiences	Priority Areas #	Actions/Strategies	Funding Allocation *	Monitoring & Evaluation (M&E) *
Australia	• Healthcare providers • Healthcare organizations • Organizations that support healthcare workers • Government organizations • Education providers • Social services	• Embedding health literacy into systems • Ensuring effective communication • Integrating health literacy into education	• Increase consumer knowledge and skills through education • Improve the skills and practices of the health workforce • Provide and support professional development • Develop and implement health literacy policies (organization level) • Improve healthcare design and delivery • Advocate for funding allocation for health literacy initiatives	Not explicitly stated in the policy	Not explicitly stated in the policy.
Austria	• People living in Austria • Vulnerable groups	• Improve the health literacy-friendliness of healthcare services • Improve individual health literacy (especially vulnerable groups) • Improve health literacy-friendliness of the production and service sector	• National strategy to improve quality of communication in healthcare • Apply standard criteria when developing health information • Develop web portal • Provide telephone-based consultation service • Health literacy coaching for clients of health insurance companies, strengthen role of education sector in health literacy • Provide video interpreting service • Provide good quality consumer information on products	Not explicitly stated in the policy	Yes, in line with monitoring of all ten Austrian Health Targets. Includes monitoring progress intervention implementation and regular analysis of defined indicators. Will include use of the health literacy survey scheduled for 2019.
China	• Health professionals • Health organizations and health education institutes • Autonomous regions and municipalities • Urban and rural residents • Chinese citizens across the whole country	• To establish a health sector leading, multi-sector social participatory working-network of Health Literacy Promotion Initiatives with a coverage rate of 100 percent, 80 percent, and 60 percent in province, city/prefecture and county level respectively • At least 80 percent of the professionals in the working-network to be trained • To establish a Chinese citizens' health literacy surveillance and evaluation system • At least 60 percent of counties all over the country will carry out communication activities of 'Health Literacy 66'	• Establish and improve the working network (leadership and governance) • Strengthen capacity building activities (workforce development) • Conduct communication activities • Carry out health literacy surveillance • Develop demonstration models (demonstration sites)	Yes. Centrally funded through government, including for related initiatives (Health Literacy 66 and the Basic knowledge and skills trial). Health administrative departments at all levels are also required to incorporate local Health Literacy Promotion Initiatives into the health sector's annual budget to ensure their implementation.	Yes. Ministry of Health conducts monitoring and evaluation of the "Health Literacy Promotion Initiatives" to assess policy implementation. Autonomous regions and municipalities health administrative departments are required to undertake M&E according to the local conditions. The policy includes actions to set up M&E capability, including systems, technical support and training for professionals. A health literacy 'surveillance' system has been implemented.

Table 2. Cont.

Country	Target Audiences	Priority Areas #	Actions/Strategies	Funding Allocation *	Monitoring & Evaluation (M&E) *
New Zealand	<ul><li>Government agencies</li><li>National bodies; i.e., Health Quality and Safety Commission New Zealand</li><li>Maori and Pacific health providers</li><li>District health boards</li><li>Primary healthcare services</li><li>Disability services</li><li>Social care services</li></ul>	<ul><li>People have access to and can understand the information they need to manage their care</li><li>Enable individuals to make choices about their care</li><li>Partner with people to design services based on their needs and preferences</li><li>Communicate effectively and providing navigation support</li></ul>	<ul><li>Support self-management of health through the use of digital technologies, such as social media, mobile applications and video games (7 sub-actions)</li><li>Make the health system more responsive, including through shared decision making, cultural competence and increased engagement (7 sub-actions)</li></ul>	Not explicitly stated in the policy	Yes, the policy states that the Ministry of Health will monitor work undertaken on the actions in the roadmap. It states that a set of measures on health outcomes and equity will be used to track progress, however these are not contained within the document.
Scotland	<ul><li>People working in health and social care</li></ul>	<ul><li>Remove barriers (to access)</li><li>Make services easier to navigate</li><li>Making information more responsive to needs</li><li>Ensure the design of services is informed by health literacy needs</li></ul>	<ul><li>Public awareness of health literacy</li><li>Use of health literacy tools and techniques by professionals providing care</li><li>Provide better information at point of entry and discharge from services</li><li>Shared care planning and support</li><li>Promote a culture of shared decision-making</li><li>Support way-finding and navigation</li><li>Build networks of health literacy champions</li><li>Build the skills of the workforce (health and social care)</li><li>Build organizational health literacy responsiveness (undertake organizational assessments)</li></ul>	Not explicitly stated in the policy	Not explicitly stated in the policy.

Table 2. *Cont.*

Country	Target Audiences	Priority Areas #	Actions/Strategies	Funding Allocation *	Monitoring & Evaluation (M&E) *
United States	• Professionals • Public and private sector organizations Communities • Policymakers • Educators • Librarians • Clinicians • Social services providers • Researchers	• Develop and disseminate health and safety information that is accurate, accessible, and actionable • Promote changes in the healthcare system that improve health information, communication, informed decision making, and access to health services • Incorporate accurate, standards-based, and developmentally appropriate health and science information and curricula in child care and education through the university level • Support and expand local efforts to provide adult education, English language instruction, and culturally and linguistically appropriate health information services in the community • Build partnerships, develop guidance, and change policies • Increase basic research and the development, implementation, and evaluation of practices and interventions to improve health literacy • Increase the dissemination and use of evidence-based health literacy practices and interventions	The action areas of the plan align with the goals, with 158 strategies listed across the 7 action areas, summarized as: • Develop and distribute high quality, accessible and culturally appropriate health information • Improve health information, communication, and decisions making in the healthcare environment and improve access to health services • Incorporate health information into child care and education curricula • Provide adult education, English language programs, and culturally appropriate services in the community • Build partnerships and develop guidelines and policies that support and promote health literacy • Increase research and evaluation on interventions to improve health literacy • Increase the uptake of evidence-based health literacy practices and interventions	Not explicitly stated in the policy	Not explicitly stated in the policy.

* Key informants provided useful additional information regarding funding and monitoring/evaluation, which is verifiable but not evident from the published document. We refer to this in the discussion. # 'Priority Areas' includes information that was expressed in the policy document as a priority, goal, objective or strategic area.

4. Discussion

The very existence of this first group of national health literacy policies and national strategies indicates that governments in significantly different parts of the world have recognized the need to respond to the personal and societal challenges represented by inadequate health literacy in populations. It is too early in the cycle of implementation to make definitive observations about the impact of these policies on health literacy in each of the countries. At this early stage, our goal was to consider the policies against established criteria for describing and assessing a health policy and to make some early observations that may be useful to countries considering the development of similar policies or national strategies.

From our analysis, we can observe that these policies all have some common features. All represent a response (at least in part) to perceived deficiencies in the quality of patient communication and patient engagement in the healthcare system. These responses range from structured guidelines and standards for healthcare organizations (such as in Australia), to the more instrumental (such as the "initiatives" and "demonstration sites" identified in the China strategy) [32] through to more aspirational statements (such as those reflected in the U.S. strategy) [39]. Most present health literacy as a universal challenge (applying to all patients and/or communities), with some also identifying groups who are higher priorities (for example children and young people in the U.S. Strategy) and/or at greater risk (for example Austria) [30]. All recognize the importance of professional education in improving the quality of communication, with Australia, China and Scotland having explicit commitments.

Most policies and strategies recognize that the responsiveness of the health system to variations in patient health literacy needs to be improved. These make clear that organizational change is required, with the necessary action expressed in different forms, such as "embedding health literacy into systems' (Australia), "making the health system more responsive" (New Zealand); "building organizational health literacy responsiveness" (Scotland), and "promoting changes in the healthcare system" (U.S.).

China, the United States and to some extent Austria also have policies that overtly seek to influence and improve health literacy in the wider community, and identify a range of actions to support this. These range across improvements to adult literacy and language programs (U.S.), strengthening the role of the education sector in health literacy and providing better quality consumer information on products (Austria), through to more generic calls to public awareness of health literacy (Scotland).

Thus far, only China has undertaken population health surveys on an annual basis and these show modest but continuing gains in health knowledge and skills that are consistent with "Health Literacy 66" [32]. Of the other countries, Austria has baseline information on a population level from the European Health Literacy Survey [11], and Australia is undertaking a population survey in 2018 that might be used to monitor future change. The US has some data on some issues for some populations, but not universal population data on health literacy that is related to its national strategy.

Relative to the examples from China and Australia, the strategies in the U.S., New Zealand and Scotland appear to be more "enabling", with less prescribed pathways for implementation, and variable mechanisms for monitoring and accountability. In Austria and New Zealand, the health literacy policy is embedded in a wider health and healthcare strategy, with some specific, funded activities, and a system for monitoring on a population level.

The other policies offer less obvious connections between objectives and practical actions. The U.S. has set clear targets for improving health literacy and has developed a comprehensive and integrated strategy to achieve those outcomes. But ownership and accountability are much less clear, and responsibility for action is diffuse. Some new resources are connected to the strategy, but not in an obvious and systematic form. The Scottish and New Zealand policies are clearly connected to the healthcare system with implied responsibility, but less well-defined ownership, accountability and resourcing.

Some strategies come with dedicated funding to support expected actions. China presents the clearest example of funding aligned to specific programs and activities, with Austria also identifying dedicated funding in support of the policy. The others are not systematically linked to new or dedicated funding, reflecting an underlying expectation that existing resources will be used differently or repurposed to support the ambitions of the policy. In the U.S. resources have been allocated to support some elements of the strategy, for example through enhanced funding for health literacy research.

As "first movers" in the development of national health literacy policies, the governments of these six countries are to be commended. These are all important public statements of priorities by government that have actual or implied commitment of resources and provide a mechanism for public accountability. When examined against established criteria for describing and assessing a policy some significant variations can be observed.

Based on publicly accessible information, the policy from China appears to be the most complete in having clearly defined goals, linked strategies and actions for different levels of government, some dedicated resources, and a system for monitoring and accountability. Australia has a highly structured approach to working with healthcare services based on an established system for monitoring health system standards and backed by an accreditation process, but this approach is inevitably limited in its reach and impact with the wider population. Austria has a more complete and detailed national strategy, some commitment of resources that are linked to identified priorities, but not such a clear system for monitoring progress and accountability against the stated priorities. The U.S. has an impressively comprehensive strategy but less obvious systems for linking resources and defined action to the achievement of the strategy. Scotland and New Zealand both have approaches that are embedded within the health system but recognize the need for action beyond healthcare. Both are commendably enabling and aspirational, but currently lack detail on resourcing, monitoring and accountability.

These differences undoubtedly reflect the significant differences in healthcare systems, and in political preferences. For example, the contrast in approach taken by China and the U.S. reflects the significant differences in political and social structures in those countries, and the healthcare systems that emerge from such diversity. Australia, Austria, Scotland, and New Zealand have different forms of universal healthcare delivered through devolved governance structures. These health systems require significant but variable direct government investment and tend to be responsive to policies that are more enabling than prescriptive, more devolved than centralized.

Limitations

In deciding on which policy statements to include in the review we were inevitably constrained by the availability of sufficient English and German language material to be able to review and make comparative observations. The structure that we used to examine the available information assisted us in making comparative observations but inevitably restricted our ability to reflect the fundamentally different social and political context in which policy is formed and acted upon. We were able to obtain some of this feedback by using "key informants" in each of the countries and have tried to add this to the discussion, but inevitably some of the subtle and nuanced differences between countries and their political systems are likely to have been lost in this process. This is most obvious when considering the tools and mechanisms for national policy implementation that vary so markedly between countries. Those countries with significantly devolved decision-making and relatively limited national policy implementation incentives (such as the U.S.), contrast markedly with countries having more centralized policy-making and well-defined structures for local implementation (such as China).

The increasing recognition of the potential for health literacy to promote health and improve health services/systems is driving the emergence of new policies all the time. We are aware that since completing this review, policies have been issued in Germany, and are under development in Belgium, the Czech Republic, the Russian Federation and Portugal, making this review both topical and timely [16].

5. Conclusions

This first group of policy statements on health literacy provide a rich resource for current analysis and future learning. Each can be assessed against objective criteria but must also be understood as highly context specific. There are many positives in all of the examples we have examined, particularly in respect of the public acknowledgement of the challenge to improve health literacy, the priority given to the responsiveness of the health system, and the stimulus to improve the education and training of front-line staff in the health system (and beyond).

Policies focused on improving the effectiveness of health services carry strong political weight, in promising improved clinical quality and safety, and better health outcomes for patients. A broader focus on developing health literacy through community health education was harder to find but has greater potential to develop health literacy skills with wider application across the life-course. The absence of a clear, substantial and practical commitment to building health literacy in community populations was a notable deficit in most of the policies. Both approaches are necessary to advance health literacy in populations.

There was significant variability in linking resources to specific strategies and actions, in the systems for monitoring progress, and in accountability for progress. This variability reflects some of the important contextual differences between countries and health systems. However, this lack of specificity will often have an impact on the priority given to improving health literacy relative to other, more "urgent" and politically higher-profile priorities that have more immediate and visible impact on healthcare delivery (for example reducing patient waiting times). This, in turn, can have an impact on the long-term sustainability of defined actions to improve health literacy in populations as its visibility slips.

Author Contributions: Conceptualization, D.N., A.T., G.R.; Methodology, A.T., D.N., G.R.; Formal Analysis, A.T., G.R.; Investigation, A.T., G.R., D.N.; Data Curation, A.T.; Writing–Original Draft Preparation, A.T., D.N., G.R.; Writing–Review & Editing, A.T., D.N., G.R.; Visualization, A.T.; Project Administration, G.R., A.T.

Funding: This research received no external funding.

Acknowledgments: We would like to acknowledge and thank Andrew Pleasant and Jany Rademakers for their advice on our approach to this study. We would also like to acknowledge and thank Christina Dietscher, Cindy Brach, Cynthia Baur, Naomi Poole and Tian Xiangyang for providing feedback and advice as key informants in this study.

Conflicts of Interest: The authors declare no conflict of interest.

References

1. Institute of Medicine. Health Literacy: A Prescription to End Confusion, Institute of Medicine. Retrieved 23 May 2004. Available online: http://www.nationalacademies.org/hmd/Reports/2004/Health-Literacy-A-Prescription-to-End-Confusion.aspx (accessed on 23 May 2013).
2. Peerson, A.; Saunders, M. Health literacy revisited: What do we mean and why does it matter? *Health Promot. Int.* **2009**, *24*, 285–296. [CrossRef] [PubMed]
3. Sorensen, K.; Van den Broucke, S.; Fullam, J.; Doyle, G.; Pelikan, J.; Slonska, Z.; Brand, H.; (HLS-EU) Consortium Health Literacy Project European. Health literacy in public health: A systematic review and integration of definitions and models. *BMC Public Health* **2012**, *12*, 80. Available online: http://www.biomedcentral.com/1471-2458/12/80 (accessed on 17 April 2013). [CrossRef] [PubMed]
4. Paasche-Orlow, M.; Wolf, M. The causal pathways linking health literacy to health outcomes. *Am. J. Health Behav.* **2007**, *31*, S19–S26. [CrossRef] [PubMed]
5. Nutbeam, D. Health literacy as a public health goal: A challenge for contemporary health education and communication strategies into the 21st century. *Health Promot. Int.* **2000**, *15*, 259–267. [CrossRef]
6. Osborne, R.H.; Batterham, R.W.; Elsworth, G.R.; Hawkins, M.; Buchbinder, R. The grounded psychometric development and initial validation of the Health Literacy Questionnaire (HLQ). *BMC Public Health* **2013**, *13*, 658. Available online: http://www.ncbi.nlm.nih.gov/pubmed/23855504 (accessed on 3 March 2014). [CrossRef] [PubMed]

7. Davis, T.C.; Crouch, M.A.; Long, S.W.; Jackson, R.H.; Bates, P.; George, R.B.; Bairnsfather, L.E. Rapid assessment of literacy levels of adult primary care patients. *J. Fam. Med.* **1991**, *23*, 433–435.
8. Parker, R.M.; Baker, D.W.; Williams, M.V.; Nurss, J.R. The test of functional health literacy in adults: A new instrument for measuring patients' literacy skills. *J. Gen. Intern. Med.* **1995**, *10*, 537–541. [CrossRef] [PubMed]
9. Berkman, N.D.; Sheridan, S.L.; Donahue, K.E.; Halpern, D.J.; Viera, A.; Crotty, K.; Holland, A.; Brasure, M.; Lohr, K.N.; Harden, E.; et al. Health Literacy Interventions and Outcomes: An Updated Systematic Review, Agency for Healthcare Research and Quality. 2011. Available online: http://effectivehealthcare.ahrq.gov/ehc/products/151/671/Health_Literacy_Update_FinalTechBrief_20110502.pdf (accessed on 20 May 2013).
10. Murray, S.; Rudd, R.; Kirsch, I.; Yamamoto, K.; Grenier, S. *Health Literacy in Canada: Initial Results from the International Adult Literacy and Skills Survey*; Canadian Council on Learning: Ottawa, ON, Canada, 2007; Available online: http://www.ccl-cca.ca/pdfs/HealthLiteracy/HealthLiteracyinCanada.pdf (accessed on 23 April 2013).
11. HLS-EU Consortium. *Comparative Report on Health Literacy in Eight EU Member States: The European Health Literacy Survey HLS-EU*; HLS-EU Consortium: Vienna, Austria, 2012; Available online: http://ec.europa.eu/chafea/documents/news/Comparative_report_on_health_literacy_in_eight_EU_member_states.pdf (accessed on 13 May 2013).
12. World Health Organization. The Jakarta Declaration on Leading Health Promotion into the 21st Century. In Proceedings of the Fourth International Conference on Health Promotion, Jakarta, Indonesia, 21–25 July 1997; World Health Organization: Geneva, Switzerland, 1997.
13. World Health Organization. The Bangkok Charter for Health Promotion in a Globalized World. In Proceedings of the Sixth Global Conference on Health Promotion, Bangkok, Thailand, 7–11 August 2005; World Health Organization: Geneva, Switzerland, 2005.
14. World Health Organization. Shanghai Declaration on Promoting Health in the 2030 Agenda for Sustainable Development. In Proceedings of the 9th Global Conference on Health Promotion, Shanghai, China, 21–24 November 2016; World Health Organization: Geneva, Switzerland, 2016.
15. Budhathoki, S.S.; Pokharel, P.K.; Good, S.; Limbu, S.; Bhattachan, M.; Osborne, R.H. The potential of health literacy to address the health related UN sustainable development goal 3 (SDG3) in Nepal: A rapid review. *BMC Health Serv. Res.* **2017**, *17*, 237. Available online: http://www.ncbi.nlm.nih.gov/pubmed/28347355 (accessed on 27 March 2017). [CrossRef] [PubMed]
16. Rowlands, G.; Russell, S.; O'Donnell, A.; Kaner, E.; Trezona, A.; Rademakers, J.; Nutbeam, D. *What is the Evidence on Existing Policies and Linked Activities and Their Effectiveness for Improving Health Literacy at National, Regional and Organizational Levels in the WHO European Region? WHO Regional Office for Europe Health Evidence Network (HEN) Synthesis Report (Report 57) (In Press)*; WHO Regional Office for Europe: Copenhagen, Denmark, 2018.
17. World Health Organization. *WHO Global Coordination Mechanism on the Prevention and Control of NCDs*; retrieved 28 July 2016; World Health Organization: Geneva, Switzerland, 2016; Available online: http://www.who.int/global-coordination-mechanism/working-groups/working-group-3-3/en/ (accessed on 28 July 2016).
18. World Health Organization. *NCDs and Health Literacy*; retrieved 1 April 2018; World Health Organization: Geneva, Switzerland, 2018; Available online: https://communities.gcmportal.org/ncd-health-literacy (accessed on 1 April 2018).
19. Keleher, H. Policy for Health. In *Understanding Health*, 4th ed.; Keleher, H., Ed.; Oxford University Press: Melbourne, Australia, 2016.
20. Cheung, K.K.; Mirzaei, M.; Leeder, S. Health policy analysis: A tool to evaluate in policy documents the alignment between policy statements and intended outcomes. *Aust. Health Rev. Publ. Aust. Hosp. Assoc.* **2010**, *34*, 405–413. [CrossRef] [PubMed]
21. Buse, K.; Mays, N.; Walt, G. Doing Policy Analysis. In *Making Health Policy*, 2nd ed.; Buse, K., Mays, N., Walt, G., Eds.; Open University Press: Maidenhead, UK, 2012.
22. Fisher, M.; Baum, F.; MacDougall, C.; Newman, L.; McDermott, D. A qualitative methodological framework to assess uptake of evidence on social determinants of health in social policy. *Evid. Policy* **2015**, *11*, 491–507. [CrossRef]
23. Trezona, A.; Dodson, S.; Mech, P.; Osborne, R.H. Development and testing of a framework for analysing health literacy in public policy documents. *Glob. Health Promot.* **2018**. [CrossRef] [PubMed]

24. Council of Australian Governments. *National Healthcare Agreement*; Council of Australian Governments: Canberra, Australia, 2012. Available online: http://www.federalfinancialrelations.gov.au/content/npa/health/_archive/healthcare_national-agreement.pdf (accessed on 6 October 2017).
25. Australian Institute of Health and Welfare. *Australia's Health 2016*; AIHW: Canberra, Australia, 2016. Available online: https://www.aihw.gov.au/reports/australias-health/australias-health-2016/contents/summary (accessed on 5 October 2017).
26. Australian Commission on Safety and Quality in Health Care. *National Statement on Health Literacy: Taking Action to Improve Safety and Quality*; retrieved 1 February 2015; Australian Commission on Safety and Quality in Health Care: Sydney, Australia, 2014. Available online: http://www.safetyandquality.gov.au/wp-content/uploads/2014/08/Health-Literacy-National-Statement.pdf (accessed on 1 February 2015).
27. Australian Commission on Safety and Quality in Health Care. *Governance*; retrieved 1 August 2015; Australian Commission on Safety and Quality in Health Care: Sydney, Australia, 2015. Available online: http://www.safetyandquality.gov.au/about-us/governance/ (accessed on 1 August 2015).
28. Australian Commission on Safety and Quality in Health Care. *NSQHS Standards*, 2nd ed.; retrieved 1 April 2018; Australian Commission on Safety and Quality in Health Care: Sydney, Australia, 2018. Available online: https://www.safetyandquality.gov.au/our-work/assessment-to-the-nsqhs-standards/nsqhs-standards-second-edition/ (accessed on 1 April 2018).
29. Austrian Federal Ministry of Health. *The Austrian Health Care Stystem: Key Facts*; Austrian Ministry of Health: Vienna, Austria, 2013. Available online: https://www.bmgf.gv.at/cms/home/attachments/3/4/4/CH1066/CMS1291414949078/austrian_health_care_key_facts_2013.pdf (accessed on 25 June 2018).
30. Federal Ministry of Health and Women's Affairs. *Österreichische Plattform Gesundheitskompetenz*; Federal Ministry of Health and Women's Affairs: Vienna, Austria, 2016. Available online: https://oepgk.at/ (accessed on 1 November 2017).
31. Fang, H. *International Health Care Stystem Profiles: The Chinese Health Care System*; The Commonwealth Fund: New York, NY, USA, 2018; Available online: https://international.commonwealthfund.org/countries/china/ (accessed on 25 June 2018).
32. Ministry of Health the People's Republic of China. *National Plan of Health Literacy Promotion Initiatives for Chinese Citizens 2008–2010*; Ministry of Health the People's Republic of China: Beijing, China, 2008.
33. Gauld, R. *International Health Care Stystem Profiles: The New Zealand Health Care System*; The Commonwealth Fund: New York, NY, USA, 2018; Available online: https://international.commonwealthfund.org/countries/new_zealand/ (accessed on 25 June 2018).
34. New Zealand Ministry of Health. *New Zealand Health Strategy: Future Direction*; retrieved 7 February 2017; New Zealand Ministry of Health: Wellington, New Zealand, 2016. Available online: http://www.health.govt.nz/publication/new-zealand-health-strategy-2016 (accessed on 7 February 2017).
35. New Zealand Ministry of Health. *New Zealand Health Strategy: Roadmap of Actions 2016*; retrieved 1 June 2017; New Zealand Ministry of Health: Wellington, New Zealand, 2016. Available online: https://www.health.govt.nz/new-zealand-health-system/new-zealand-health-strategy-roadmap-actions-2016 (accessed on 1 June 2017).
36. Scottish Government. *NHSScotland-How It Works*; Scottish Government: Edinburgh, Scotland, UK, 2018. Available online: http://www.ournhsscotland.com/our-nhs/nhsscotland-how-it-works (accessed on 25 June 2018).
37. Scottish Government. *Making It Easy: A Health Literacy Action Plan for Scotland*; retrieved 12 June 2015; Scottish Government: Edinburgh, Scotland, 2014. Available online: http://www.gov.scot/resource/0045/00451263.pdf (accessed on 12 June 2015).
38. Scottish Government. *Making it Easier: A Health Literacy Action Plan for Scotland*; retrieved 10 August 2017; Scottish Government: Edinburgh, Scotland, 2017. Available online: https://www.alliance-scotland.org.uk/wp-content/uploads/2017/11/Making-It-Easier-A-Health-Literacy-Plan-for-Scotland.pdf (accessed on 10 August 2017).

39. The Commonwealth Fund. *International Health Care Stystem Profiles: The United States Health Care System*; The Commonwealth Fund: New York, NY, USA, 2018; Available online: https://international.commonwealthfund.org/countries/united_states/ (accessed on 25 June 2018).
40. U.S. Department of Health and Human Services. *National Action Plan to Improve Health Literacy*; retrieved 20 May 2013; U.S. Department of Health and Human Services: Washington, DC, USA, 2010. Available online: http://www.health.gov/communication/hlactionplan/pdf/Health_Literacy_Action_Plan.pdf (accessed on 20 May 2013).

© 2018 by the authors. Licensee MDPI, Basel, Switzerland. This article is an open access article distributed under the terms and conditions of the Creative Commons Attribution (CC BY) license (http://creativecommons.org/licenses/by/4.0/).

Article

Developing and Applying Geographical Synthetic Estimates of Health Literacy in GP Clinical Systems

Gill Rowlands [1,*], David Whitney [2] and Graham Moon [3]

1. Institute of Health and Society, Newcastle University, Newcastle-upon-Tyne NE2 4BN, UK
2. Division of Health and Social Care Research, King's College London, London WC2R 2LS, UK; d.whitney@nhs.net
3. Department of Geography and Environment at the University of Southampton, Southampton SO17 1BJ, UK; g.moon@soton.ac.uk
* Correspondence: gill.rowlands@newcastle.ac.uk; Tel.: +44-191-208-1300

Received: 6 June 2018; Accepted: 1 August 2018; Published: 10 August 2018

Abstract: *Background*: Low health literacy is associated with poorer health. Research has shown that predictive models of health literacy can be developed; however, key variables may be missing from systems where predictive models might be applied, such as health service data. This paper describes an approach to developing predictive health literacy models using variables common to both "source" health literacy data and "target" systems such as health services. *Methods*: A multilevel synthetic estimation was undertaken on a national (England) dataset containing health literacy, socio-demographic data and geographical (Lower Super Output Area: LSOA) indicators. Predictive models, using variables commonly present in health service data, were produced. An algorithm was written to pilot the calculations in a Family Physician Clinical System in one inner-city area. The minimum data required were age, sex and ethnicity; other missing data were imputed using model values. *Results*: There are 32,845 LSOAs in England, with a population aged 16 to 65 years of 34,329,091. The mean proportion of the national population below the health literacy threshold in LSOAs was 61.87% (SD 12.26). The algorithm was run on the 275,706 adult working-age people in Lambeth, South London. The algorithm could be calculated for 228,610 people (82.92%). When compared with people for whom there were sufficient data to calculate the risk score, people with insufficient data were more likely to be older, male, and living in a deprived area, although the strength of these associations was weak. *Conclusions*: Logistic regression using key socio-demographic data and area of residence can produce predictive models to calculate individual- and area-level risk of low health literacy, but requires high levels of ethnicity recording. While the models produced will be specific to the settings in which they are developed, it is likely that the method can be applied wherever relevant health literacy data are available. Further work is required to assess the feasibility, accuracy and acceptability of the method. If feasible, accurate and acceptable, this method could identify people requiring additional resources and support in areas such as medical practice.

Keywords: health literacy; synthetic area estimates; general practice

1. Introduction

The WHO defines health literacy as "the cognitive and social skills which determine the motivation and ability of individuals to gain access to, understand and use information in ways which promote and maintain good health" [1]. Low health literacy affects a significant proportion of English adults; 6 in 10 (61%) adults aged between 16 and 65 years of age in England lack the literacy and numeracy skills to fully understand common health-related information [2].

Research has shown that, compared with people with adequate health literacy, people with low health literacy are more likely to die prematurely [3], have one or more long-term health conditions

(LTHCs) [4], find any LTHCs more limiting [4], and find compliance with prescribed medication more challenging [5]. Furthermore, health literacy is also associated with lifestyle, with people with lower health literacy being more likely to exhibit unhealthy behaviours such as low levels of physical activity, poor diet/obesity, and harmful alcohol consumption [4]. Lower health literacy is also associated with lower rates of participation in disease prevention programmes such as screening, immunisation, and public health information campaigns [5].

Bodies commissioning health care in England have a legal duty to reduce health inequalities [6]. As data suggest a strong link between socio-demographic deprivation and low levels of health literacy [2], interventions focused on health literacy may have the potential to contribute to a reduction in health inequalities.

In order to understand and address the challenges of low health literacy within the health system, identification of individuals at risk of low health literacy has the potential to be useful at both population and individual patient levels. Previous work has demonstrated that statistical techniques can be applied to health literacy datasets to identify socio-demographic characteristics predictive of low health literacy in the U.S., Europe and England [7–10]. The predictive models produced from such "source" datasets, which could be described as "stage 1 models", can only be applied in systems that contain key predictive variables, in particular education level. Education level is rarely collected in routine medical practice, precluding the use of these methods in this setting.

This project aimed to explore the accuracy and feasibility of an alternative approach, which could be described as a "stage 2" predictive model. This model used only data routinely collected in the "target" system (in this case medical care practice) and present in the "source" health literacy dataset, i.e., individual socio-demographic details and geographical area of residence. As the model included geographical area of residence, area levels of health literacy could also be estimated using this approach. We explored accuracy at both individual patient and local area level. The study was undertaken in Lambeth, an inner-city borough in London, England. Lambeth is the 22nd most deprived of the 326 boroughs in England [11], with 45% if the population identifying as being in the "non-White" ethnic group, compared to 13% in England and Wales as a whole [11,12].

2. Materials and Methods

Lambeth DataNet (LDN) [13] is a database of pseudonymised, patient-level, primary care data covering over 360,000 people extracted from 46 GP practices serving the inner London Borough of Lambeth. It aims to provide health care service commissioners, public health, and researchers with high quality contemporaneous primary care data to improve local services and reduce inequalities. LDN does not contain any Patient Identifiable Data (PID); post/ZIP code of residence is converted to Lower Super Output Area (LSOA) of residence and Index of Multiple Deprivation (IMD) [14]. Lower Super Output Areas are standard small-area UK census geography areas, each covering areas of residence for approximately 1600 people [15].

Previous work has identified the literacy and numeracy skill levels required by working-age adults in England to fully understand and use health information in common circulation [2]. Rowlands et al. describe a health literacy "competency threshold": the literacy and numeracy skills required to fully understand and use health information in common circulation [2]; i.e., functional health literacy [16].

National small area estimates of health literacy were developed for LSOAs. The estimates were developed using the 2011 Skills for Life Survey (SfL) [17] and 2011 English census data [18], with embedded participant health literacy levels developed and reported previously by Rowlands et al. [2], and a multilevel synthetic estimation method widely used in past work, inter alia, on the estimation of small-area smoking prevalence [19–21]. Variables used in the estimates were age, sex, ethnicity, whether or not English was the first language, and deprivation of the area of residence. The synthetic estimation produced LSOA-level estimates of the proportion of the adult working-age population below the health literacy competency threshold for each LSOA in England, and a predictive model enabling the risk of an individual below the health literacy competency threshold to be determined. As the SfL survey only included working-age adults (16 years to 65 years), estimates were only calculated for this age range. The coefficients in the resulting model were converted to risk percentages for each cell in the age by sex, by ethnicity, by language preference, and by deprivation table. The intercept was the category hypothesised to have the lowest risk of having a health literacy level below the competency threshold. The Deviance Information Criterion (DIC) was calculated to assess the effectiveness of the model [22].

The predictive model required, at a minimum, patient age, sex and ethnicity data; other variables in the model, i.e., LSOA of residence and language preference, were not essential, but, if present, increased the accuracy of the estimation.

The algorithm used to import the risk scores derived from the predictive model into the patient records was a script file written for the R software package. The R script took a single input table, i.e., the individual patient-level data with demographic characteristics, and, after processing, returned the table in the original format with an additional column showing the health literacy risk scores. The R script also included basic data validation to check that characteristics in the input (patient) table were all available and in the expected format to prevent incorrect or unexpected results. More details of the algorithm are given in the supplementary file and Table S1.

The proportion of people below the health literacy threshold in Lambeth was compared with the proportion in the rest of England.

The validity of the model was assessed at two levels: geographical (LSOA) and individual. At LSOA level, the mean percentage risk score of adults aged 16 years to 65 years in the LSOAs according to the risk calculation using the LDN database was calculated and subtracted from the small-area estimate of risk. To eliminate boundary effects of patients living in one borough and registering with a GP practice in another borough, LSOAs were excluded where the GP registered population in the Lambeth DataNet database was >+15%/−15% of the latest ONS population estimates. To check the reliability of the algorithm coding at the individual level, a sample of 0.37% of people (n = 1013) was identified for accuracy estimation. There were 600 possible permutations of the demographic characteristics; however, 87 of these permutations were "empty", i.e., with no matching patient records. One patient record was randomly selected from each of the remaining 513 permutations. A further 500 records were randomly selected from the remaining records. These 1013 records were then checked manually against lookup tables to establish the accuracy of the score.

The characteristics of individuals for whom the minimum data set for calculation of the health literacy risk score was available were compared with the characteristics of individuals for whom the risk score could not be calculated. Statistical significance was assessed using χ^2 tests, and the strength of the association was assessed using Cramers V.

Ethics

Lambeth DataNet is a patient-level database which does not contain personal identifiable data (PID) [13]. This study did not involve the removal of data from its agreed location (NHS Lambeth Clinical Commissioning Group (CCG)) [23], nor did it involve the access to the database by any individuals not already granted access to data for the purposes of supporting Lambeth CCG business intelligence. The project was approved by the Lambeth DataNet steering group (a body made up of local GPs, public health professionals, commissioning managers, and patient/public representation, responsible for overseeing the development and use of the database) on 22 September 2015 and the Lambeth CCG information governance steering group were informed [24].

As no PID were held, the project did not require NHS Ethics Approval [25].

3. Results

The 2011 census data for Lambeth showed 225,113 residents aged between 16 years and 65 years, of whom 156,626 (69.58%) were estimated to be below the health literacy threshold. Census data for the rest of England showed 34,329,091 residents aged between 16 years and 65 years, of whom 21,168,166 (62.07%) were estimated to be below the health literacy threshold.

On the data extraction date (31 March 2014), LDN contained the data of 364,009 people, of whom 275,706 were in the age range 16 years to 65 years. Of the 275,706 people aged 16 years to 65 years, a risk score could be calculated for 228,610 people (82.92%); in the remaining 47,096 people (17.08%), the risk score could not be calculated due to one or more missing variables essential for risk score calculation (i.e., age, sex or ethnicity). As per Lambeth CCG information Governance regulations, any patients for whom sex was not available were removed from further analyses.

3.1. Predictive Model

The coefficients and fit statistics for the model are shown in Table 1. The reference category was white males, aged 16 to 24 years, with English as a first language, living in a "least-deprived" area. The DIC statistic suggests that the model represents a significant improvement over a "null" model with no covariates.

Table 1. Coefficient and fit statistics of predictive model.

Variable	Coefficient (Logit)	Standard Error
Intercept (white males, aged 16 to 24 years, with English as a first language, living in a "least-deprived" area)	−1.010	0.108
Age		
25–34	−0.196	0.103
35–44	−0.262	0.101
45–54	0.213	0.100
55–65	0.383	0.099
Gender		
Female	−0.147	0.057
Ethnicity		
South Asian	0.366	0.152
Black	0.518	0.178
Other	0.220	0.180
First language		
Non-English Speaker	0.876	0.125
Deprivation of area of residence		
Deprivation IMD Quartile 2	0.456	0.085
Deprivation IMD Quartile 3	0.735	0.097
Deprivation IMD Quartile 4 (most deprived)	1.244	0.090
Area-level variance	0.146	0.044
Units: Areas	828	
Units: Individuals	5815	
Estimation	MCMC	
DIC Full Model (Null Model)	7484.964 (7800.871)	
Chain Length	500,000	

IMD: Index of Multiple Deprivation; DIC: Deviance Information Criterion.

3.2. Algorithm Accuracy

For the 109 LSOAs included in the analysis, the mean difference in the percentage health literacy risk score (i.e., the percentage of residents calculated to be below the health literacy competency threshold) arising from the application of the algorithm was subtracted from the national small area estimates. The mean difference was +1.8/−1.8 percentage points (SD 3.8). Individual-level validation using 1013 records confirmed the accuracy of the process.

The missing data preventing the calculation of a risk score for individuals is shown in Table 2. All but 1 person had sex recorded. For the remaining 47,096 individuals with missing data, all were missing ethnicity data, of whom 88 people were also missing an IMD score due to either an un-linkable postcode (i.e., the postcode had been entered incorrectly by the General Practices or the LSOA was not in England) or was missing entirely.

Comparison of the characteristics of individuals for whom a risk score could be calculated with individuals for whom the risk score could not be calculated are shown in Table 3. This shows that individuals for whom a risk score could not be calculated due to missing data were statistically significantly more likely to be older, male, and to live in more deprived areas; however, the Cramer's V scores were all very low, indicating that the strengths of the associations were low.

Table 2. Missing data preventing risk score calculation.

Missing Data Variable	n
missing ethnicity only	47,008
missing IMD only	0
missing ethnicity and IMD	88
missing sex	1
total missing	47,097

Table 3. Comparison of socio-demographic characteristics for individuals for whom a risk score could be calculated compared with individuals for whom a risk score could not be calculated.

Socio-Demographic Characteristic	People with Sufficient Data for Risk Score % (n)	People without Sufficient Data for Risk Score % (n)	χ^2, df	p	Cramers V
Total	82.92 (228,610)	17.08 (47,097)			
Age					
16 years to 44 years	83.23 (164,294)	16.77 (33,094)	48.91, 1	$p < 0.0001$	0.013
45 years to 65 years	82.12 (64,316)	17.88 (14,002)			
Gender					
Female	85.22 (117,198)	14.78 (20,328)	1025.19, 1	$p < 0.0001$	0.061
Male	80.63 (111,412)	19.37 (26,768)			
Index of Multiple Deprivation					
1 = most deprived	82.32 (99,138)	17.68 (21,291)	36.87, 1 *	$p < 0.0001$ *	0.015
2	83.48 (101,880)	16.52 (20,158)			
3	83.13 (25,780)	16.87 (5230)			
4 = least deprived	83.68 (1687)	16.32 (329)			

* χ^2 test for trend.

4. Discussion

4.1. Summary of Main Findings

This study shows that it is feasible to develop predictive models from "source" health literacy datasets, using variables in common with "target" systems such as health systems, and then to apply these to identify individual- and area-level risk of low health literacy. On the basis of a sample of 1013 records, a check confirmed that the algorithm was coded correctly. At LSOA area level, there was a mean difference between the register-based algorithm and a small population-based estimate of the percentage of residents below the health literacy threshold of 1.8 percentage points. This difference likely arises from three factors. Firstly, the Lambeth DataNet data were extracted in 2014, whereas the census data on which the multilevel synthetic estimates were based was collected in 2011; migration and other elements of urban change will result in differences in the population base that would be expected to increase as the temporal distance from the census date increases. Secondly, there will be differences between the resident (census) population and that registered with GPs; under-registration is a known theme in inner city areas and is likely to particularly involve groups with low health literacy. Thirdly, the multilevel synthetic estimates used data not included in the risk predictions arising from the Lambeth DataNet data, in particular language preference. Given these factors, there is a strong correspondence between the synthetic estimates and risk prediction model.

This project has shown that, in the setting used in this project, ethnicity recording is essential for the synthetic estimates to be applied. Collection and recording of patient ethnicity is now a requirement in General Practice in England, and has resulted in over 90% recording in newly registered patients [26]; however, it is not known what current levels of recording are in longer-established patients, and whether their socio-demographic characteristics differ significantly from newly registered patients. This study found that the 17.08% of the population for whom the health literacy risk score could not be calculated due to missing ethnicity data were older, male or living in more deprived areas than the rest of the population, although the strength of these associations was weak. Some members of this "missing data" population may be longer-established residents, likely to be older and living in more deprived areas, while others may be recent arrivals, more likely to be male and living in more deprived areas; all may be at significant risk of falling below threshold levels of health literacy. Consequently, it may be that people for whom the risk of poor health literacy cannot be computed should be considered at risk.

4.2. Strengths and Limitations of This Study

This study used high-quality robust data. The 2011 national census and national English literacy and numeracy survey data [17] were used for the synthetic estimates, and the Lambeth DataNet is a high-quality dataset extracted directly from Primary Care clinical systems [13]. The synthetic estimation techniques have been demonstrated as accurate and robust in previous studies [19–21].

Some limitations must, however, be acknowledged. Lambeth is an atypical borough with high levels of socio-economic deprivation, a high proportion of people from Black and Minority Ethnic groups, and lower health literacy levels when compared to the rest of England. This study requires replication in other localities to assess its wider usefulness. In addition, it must be recognised that the synthetic estimate model gives a risk score for health literacy, and not a definitive "diagnosis" for individuals. Any score applied to individuals should thus be treated as a guide only, and adjustment of communication should be made to ensure that health messages and other communications are received and understood.

4.3. Implications for Practice and Research

This study highlights the importance of accurate and full collection of socio-demographic data, including postcodes, in areas of practice, such as health care, where health literacy may be key to the provision of high-quality care. While not a diagnostic tool, at an individual level, the synthetic estimates and algorithm could be used to highlight, and thus provide additional resources for, patients and clients at risk of low health literacy. At an area level, the method described here could be used to allocate staff and budgetary resources to geographical areas (such as health trusts and authorities providing social care) providing services to populations with high health literacy needs.

The models developed in this project are dependent on the datasets that form the basis of the models, i.e., the health literacy dataset and census data, combined with a knowledge of socio-demographic and geographical data present in the target data (in the case, health service data). Specifically, the "health literacy" outcome will reflect the way in which health literacy has been measured in the source dataset; in this case functional health literacy. However, the methods described here could theoretically be applied in any setting where there are baseline health literacy and census datasets, and where sufficient data are collected routinely in (for example) health care settings to enable the models to be built. Further research would need to be undertaken to assess the robustness of the resultant models in these settings.

5. Conclusions

This study explored the development and application of synthetic estimates for health literacy to primary care data in an inner-city area with high socio-economic deprivation and a high proportion of people from people from minority ethnic groups. If the findings are replicated in areas with different socio-demographic profiles, the methods described here may aid the delivery of resources and care to populations with low health literacy, and facilitate more health literacy research.

Supplementary Materials: The following are available online at http://www.mdpi.com/1660-4601/15/8/1709/s1, Supplementary information and Table S1: Characteristics used to determine the health literacy score.

Author Contributions: G.R. developed the original idea, D.W. and G.M. developed and applied the methodology, G.R. and D.W. undertook the analysis, and all authors contributed to the interpretation of the results. G.R. led on writing the paper, with contributions from D.W. and G.M.

Funding: This research received no external funding.

Conflicts of Interest: The authors declare no conflict of interest.

References

1. Dodson, S.; Good, S.; Osborne, R.H. *Health Literacy Toolkit for Low and Middle-Income Countries: A Series of Information Sheets to Empower Communities and Strengthen Health Systems*; World Health Organization, Regional Office for South-East Asia: New Delhi, India, 2015.
2. Rowlands, G.; Protheroe, J.; Winkley, J.; Richardson, M.; Seed, P.T.; Rudd, R. A mismatch between population health literacy and the complexity of health information: An observational study. *Br. J. Gen. Pract.* **2015**, *65*, e379–e386. [CrossRef] [PubMed]
3. Bostock, S.; Steptoe, A. Association between low functional health literacy and mortality in older adults: Longitudinal cohort study. *BMJ* **2012**, *344*, e1602. [CrossRef] [PubMed]
4. Sorensen, K.; Pelikan, J.M.; Rothlin, F.; Ganahl, K.; Slonska, Z.; Doyle, G.; Fullam, J.; Kondilis, B.; Agrafiotis, D.; Uiters, E.; et al. Health literacy in Europe: Comparative results of the European health literacy survey (HLS-EU). *Eur. J. Public Health* **2015**, *25*, 1053–1058. [CrossRef] [PubMed]
5. Berkman, N.D.; Sheridan, S.L.; Donahue, K.E.; Halpern, D.J.; Viera, A.; Crotty, K.; Viswanathan, M. Health literacy interventions and outcomes: An updated systematic review. In *Evidence Report/Technology Assessment*; Agency for Healthcare Research and Quality: Rockville, MD, USA, 2011; Volume 199.
6. *Health and Social Care Act 2012*; Department of Health (England), UK Government, The Stationery Office: London, UK, 2012.
7. Hanchate, A.D.; Ash, A.S.; Gazmararian, J.A.; Wolf, M.S.; Paasche-Orlow, M.K. The Demographic Assessment for Health Literacy (DAHL): A new tool for estimating associations between health literacy and outcomes in national surveys. *J. Gen. Intern. Med.* **2008**, *23*, 1561–1566. [CrossRef] [PubMed]
8. Martin, L.T.; TRuder, T.; Escarce, B.; Ghosh-Dastidar DSherman, M.; Elliott, C.E.; Bird, A.; Fremont, C.; Gasper, C.; Culbert, A.; Lurie, N. Developing predictive models of health literacy. *J. Gen. Intern. Med.* **2009**, *24*, 1211–1216. [CrossRef] [PubMed]
9. Van der Heide, E.; Uiters, E.; Sorensen, K.; Rothlin, F.; Pelikan, J.; Rademakers, J.; Boshuizen, H. Health literacy in Europe: The development and validation of health literacy prediction models. *Eur. J. Public Health* **2016**, *26*, 906–911. [CrossRef] [PubMed]
10. Laursen, K.R.; Seed, P.T.; Protheroe, J.; Wolf, M.S.; Rowlands, G.P. Developing a method to derive indicative health literacy from routine socio-demographic data. *J. Healthc. Commun.* **2016**, *1*. [CrossRef]
11. Lambeth. *State of the Borough 2016*; Lambeth Council: London, UK, 2016.
12. Ethnicity and National Identity in England and Wales: 2011. Available online: https://www.ons.gov.uk/peoplepopulationandcommunity/culturalidentity/ethnicity/articles/ethnicityandnationalidentityinenglandandwales/2012-12-11 (accessed on 9 May 2018).
13. Lambeth Datanet. Available online: http://www.lambethccg.nhs.uk/your-health/Information-for-patients/Pages/DataNet.aspx (accessed on 21 June 2018).
14. McLennan, D.; Barnes, H.; Noble, M.; Davies, J.; Garratt, E.; Dibben, C. *The English Indices of Deprivation 2010*; Department for Communities and Local Government: London, UK, 2011.

15. Census Geography. An Overview of the Various Geographies Used in the Production of Statistics Collected via the UK Census. Available online: https://www.ons.gov.uk/methodology/geography/ukgeographies/censusgeography (accessed on 18 June 2018).
16. Nutbeam, D. Health literacy as a public health goal: A challenge for contemporary health education and communication strategies into the 21st century. *Health Promot. Int.* **2000**, *15*, 259–267. [CrossRef]
17. Harding, C.; Romanou, E.; Williams, J.; Peters, M.; Winkley, J.; Burke, P.; Hamer, J.; Jeram, K.; Nelson, N.; Rainbow, R.; Bond, B.; Shay, M. *The 2011 Skills for Life Survey: A Survey of Literacy, Numeracy and ICT Levels in England*; Department for Business Innovation and Skills: London, UK, 2012.
18. 2011 Census. Available online: https://www.ons.gov.uk/census/2011census (accessed on 9 May 2018).
19. Twigg, L.; Moon, G.; Jones, K. Predicting small-area health-related behaviour: A comparison of smoking and drinking indicators. *Soc. Sci. Med.* **2000**, *50*, 1109–1120. [CrossRef]
20. Twigg, L.; Moon, G. Predicting small area health-related behaviour: A comparison of multilevel synthetic estimation and local survey data. *Soc. Sci. Med.* **2002**, *54*, 931–937. [CrossRef]
21. Twigg, L.; Moon, G.; Walker, S. *The Smoking Epidemic in England*; Health Development Agency: London, UK, 2004.
22. Spiegelhalter, D.J.; Best, N.G.; Carlin, B.P.; Linde, A. The deviance information criterion: 12 years on. *J. R. Stat. Soc.* **2014**, *76*, 485–493. [CrossRef]
23. NHS Lambeth Clinical Commissioning Group. Available online: http://www.lambethccg.nhs.uk/Pages/Home.aspx (accessed on 16 July 2018).
24. *Information Governance Framework*; Lambeth Clinical Commissioning Group: London, UK, 2018. Available online: http://www.lambethccg.nhs.uk/news-and-publications/publications/Documents/Policies,%20procedures%20and%20frameworks/Information%20Governance%20Framework%20v1.2%20Dec%202017.pdf (accessed on 4 December 2017).
25. Health Research Authority Decision Tool. Available online: http://www.hra-decisiontools.org.uk/research/ (accessed on 4 December 2017).
26. Mathur, R.; Grundy, E.; Smeeth, L. *Availability and Use of UK Based Ethnicity Data for Health Research*; National Centre for Research Methods Working Paper; National Centre for Research Methods and the Economic and Social Research Council: Southampton, UK, 2013.

© 2018 by the authors. Licensee MDPI, Basel, Switzerland. This article is an open access article distributed under the terms and conditions of the Creative Commons Attribution (CC BY) license (http://creativecommons.org/licenses/by/4.0/).

Article

Barriers to Breast Cancer Screening among Diverse Cultural Groups in Melbourne, Australia

Jonathan O'Hara [1], Crystal McPhee [1], Sarity Dodson [1,2], Annie Cooper [3], Carol Wildey [1], Melanie Hawkins [1], Alexandra Fulton [1], Vicki Pridmore [3], Victoria Cuevas [3], Mathew Scanlon [3], Patricia M. Livingston [1], Richard H. Osborne [1] and Alison Beauchamp [4,5,6,*]

1. Health Systems Improvement Unit, Centre for Population Health Research, School of Health and Social Development, Deakin University, Geelong 3220, Australia; jonathan.ohara@deakin.edu.au (J.O.); crystal.mcphee@deakin.edu.au (C.M.); sdodson@hollows.org (S.D.); carol.wildey@semphn.org.au (C.W.); melanie.hawkins@deakin.edu.au (M.H.); alexandra.fulton@tgarage.com.au (A.F.); trish.livingston@deakin.edu.au (P.M.L.); richard.osborne@deakin.edu.au (R.H.O.)
2. The Fred Hollows Foundation, Melbourne 3053, Australia
3. BreastScreen Victoria, Melbourne 3053, Australia; acooper@breastscreen.org.au (A.C.); vickip@breastscreen.org.au (V.P.); vcuevas@breastscreen.org.au (V.C.); mscanlon@breastscreen.org.au (M.S.)
4. Department of Rural Health, Monash University, Moe 3825, Australia
5. Department of Medicine-Western Health, The University of Melbourne, St Albans 3021, Australia
6. Australian Institute for Musculoskeletal Science (AIMSS), The University of Melbourne and Western Health, St Albans 3021, Victoria, Australia
* Correspondence: alison.beauchamp@monash.edu

Received: 3 July 2018; Accepted: 5 August 2018; Published: 7 August 2018

Abstract: This study explored the association between health literacy, barriers to breast cancer screening, and breast screening participation for women from culturally and linguistically diverse (CALD) backgrounds. English-, Arabic- and Italian-speaking women ($n = 317$) between the ages of 50 to 74 in North West Melbourne, Australia were recruited to complete a survey exploring health literacy, barriers to breast cancer screening, and self-reported screening participation. A total of 219 women (69%) reported having a breast screen within the past two years. Results revealed that health literacy was not associated with screening participation. Instead, emotional barriers were a significant factor in the self-reported uptake of screening. Three health literacy domains were related to lower emotional breast screening barriers, feeling understood and supported by healthcare providers, social support for health and understanding health information well enough to know what to do. Compared with English- and Italian-speaking women, Arabic-speaking women reported more emotional barriers to screening and greater challenges in understanding health information well enough to know what to do. Interventions that can improve breast screening participation rates should aim to reduce emotional barriers to breast screening, particularly for Arabic-speaking women.

Keywords: health literacy; HLQ; breast cancer; breast cancer screening; mammography; Italian; Arabic; CALD

1. Introduction

Breast cancer is the most commonly diagnosed cancer for women globally and the second leading cause of cancer mortality for Australian women [1,2]. Breast screening programs provide an opportunity for early breast cancer detection and contribute to increased survivorship and reduced breast cancer mortality [3,4]. While controversy exists regarding the effectiveness of mammography [5,6], women need to be adequately informed about the benefits of screening alongside the potential harm of false positive results and unnecessary treatment when deciding to participate in breast screening [7,8].

The National BreastScreen Australia Program, a population-based breast cancer screening program, invites women aged 50 to 74 to have a free mammogram every two years [9]. The program is widely promoted by delegated state and territory breast cancer screen promotion organisations [10], and eligible women receive invitation and reminder letters at the address registered on the electoral roll. Letters have been found to be highly effective in engaging women in screening [11]. However, despite significant promotional efforts to increase screening participation, the Australian Institute of Health and Welfare reported in 2016 that Australia-wide breast screening participation rates had not increased from 54% since 2010 [12]. A significant proportion of eligible women remain under-screened and an exploration of potential determinants is warranted, including whether targeted approaches are required for specific cultural groups.

A variety of emotional, knowledge, and structural factors have been identified as barriers to women's participation in breast cancer screening [13,14]. These barriers may be exacerbated for women from culturally and linguistically diverse (CALD) backgrounds who may have English language limitations or cultural and family factors that could impact upon their decision to screen [15].

Emotional barriers include anxiety driven by personal beliefs [13,14] and negative expectations, such as concerns related to perceived disrespect from screening providers and feelings of embarrassment [16]. Physical discomfort during previous mammograms has also been associated with under-screening [17]. Knowledge barriers include a lack of breast cancer risk awareness, not understanding the importance of screening regardless of current symptoms, and believing misinformation, such as 'screening is harmful' or that 'there is no cure for breast cancer' [18,19]. Structural barriers refer to practical challenges associated with making appointments, accessing screening services, and managing priorities, such as family commitments [16]. Financial barriers include direct costs of screening, and non-medical out of pocket costs associated with screening participation. While cost is often significant barrier to participation in screening elsewhere [20–22], direct costs are not a barrier to screening for Australian women given that the Australian program is free of charge.

Health literacy may provide a framework to better understand a woman's vulnerability to breast screening barriers and under-screening. Health literacy is defined as the personal characteristics and social resources needed for individuals and communities to access, understand, and use information and services to make decisions about health [23,24]. Health literacy includes the capacity to communicate, assert, and enact these decisions. Previous breast screening research that explored health literacy focused on reading, writing, and numeracy skills related to comprehension of health information (known as functional health literacy) and identified associations with non-participation in breast screening [21,25,26]. Individuals with low functional health literacy were more likely to hold fatalistic cancer attitudes, less likely to identify the purpose of cancer screening procedures, and less inclined to engage with information about health conditions that they do not have [27].

In recent years, measurement of health literacy has advanced and it is now recognised as a multidimensional concept [28]. Health literacy includes a wide range of skills and resources that people use to engage with information, healthcare providers and services (see Table 1) [29–31]. These broader concepts may present further insights into the barriers to breast cancer screening. Women without reliable breast cancer screening information or adequate support from healthcare professionals may be more vulnerable to emotional barriers such as embarrassment, discomfort, and fear; women with less ability to find, understand, and appraise health information may be more susceptible to knowledge-related screening barriers; and women who lack social support or the skills needed to navigate healthcare services may be more likely to encounter structural barriers to screening. This framework for understanding risk factors related to under-screening for breast cancer may reveal new insights into women's health literacy challenges and offer opportunities to develop new interventions that better support their participation in breast screening.

The aim of this study was to explore if women from CALD backgrounds with lower health literacy reported greater emotional, knowledge, or structural barriers that may inhibit their participation in breast cancer screening. A further aim was to identify if women from CALD backgrounds with lower health literacy were more likely to report under-screening than women with higher health literacy.

2. Materials and Methods

2.1. Study Design

This study applied a cross-sectional survey design and targeted English-, Arabic-, and Italian-speaking women living or working in North West Melbourne, Australia. In this region of Melbourne, approximately 3.0% of the population speak Arabic and 3.3% speak Italian [32]. Surveys were administered in English, Arabic, and Italian with the assistance of bilingual Community Engagement Officers.

2.2. Study Setting

North West Melbourne has been identified by the Department of Health and Human Services (Victoria) Under-Screened Program as having lower than acceptable screening rates. This paper reports on a baseline survey results of the Ophelia (optimise health literacy and access) BreastScreen study: a collaborative project with the Department of Health and Human Services (Victoria), BreastScreen Victoria and Deakin University. BreastScreen Victoria is a public program that provides screening services (mammography) via many clinics (private and public providers) across the State. The Ophelia BreastScreen study aims to develop evidence-based, tailored interventions founded on consumer and provider health literacy strengths and limitations to improve breast screening uptake among women with CALD backgrounds. An additional cohort was included (Aboriginal and Torres Strait Islander women), and these findings will be reported separately.

2.3. Ethical Approval

Data were collected from March 2016 to September 2016. This study was approved by Deakin University (DUHREC project ID 2015-317) and Melbourne Health (HREC/16/MH/24. Project ID 2016.44). Informed written, implied, or verbal consent was obtained from all participants.

2.4. Participant Recruitment

Purposive sampling was used to recruit English-, Arabic-, and Italian-speaking women, eligible for breast screening between the ages of 50 to 74, living or working in North West Melbourne, Australia. Participant recruitment was guided by a multicultural Project Advisory Committee with representatives across community and service organisations. Invitations to participate were distributed through cultural social clubs and organisations, community centres, neighbourhood houses, community events, local radio, local newspapers, social media, and large employers of women in the target groups.

Paper-based surveys were delivered face-to-face in community settings (self-administered or with assistance from a Community Engagement Officer) and disseminated through community groups (a postage-paid envelope was provided for return of the survey). An online survey was promoted via project partners and community organisations. Computer assisted telephone interviews (CATI) were conducted by Italian-speaking data collectors to support the recruitment of Italian women. Surveys were provided to participants in English, Italian, and Arabic.

2.5. Measures

The Health Literacy Questionnaire (HLQ) is a widely-used multidimensional health literacy assessment tool for research and health service improvement [31]. The HLQ measures nine domains of health literacy, identifying strengths and challenges related to engagement with health information and services (see Table 1). The HLQ consists of 44 items across nine scales, with each scale containing four to six items. A four-point response scale is used to assess domains 1 to 5 (strongly disagree to strongly agree), and a five-point scale is used to assess domains 6 to 9 (cannot do or always difficult to always easy). The HLQ has a strong and reproducible theoretical structure that has been found to be robust in several studies [33–36]. The HLQ was translated using a formal forward and (blind) back translation procedure, with the forward translators guided by a detailed item intent document.

Table 1. Health Literacy Questionnaire (HLQ) domains with high and low descriptors.

No.	Low Level of the Construct	High Level of the Construct
1	*Feeling understood and supported by healthcare providers*	
	People who are low on this domain are unable to engage with doctors and other healthcare providers. They do not have a regular healthcare provider and/or have difficulty trusting healthcare providers as a source of information and/or advice.	Has an established relationship with at least one healthcare provider who knows them well and who they trust to provide useful advice and information and to assist them to understand information and make decisions about their health.
2	*Having sufficient information to manage my health*	
	Feels that there are many gaps in their knowledge and that they do not have the information they need to live with and manage their health concerns.	Feels confident that they have all the information that they need to live with and manage their condition and to make decisions.
3	*Actively managing my health*	
	People with low levels do not see their health as their responsibility, they are not engaged in their healthcare and regard healthcare as something that is done to them.	Recognise the importance and are able to take responsibility for their own health. They proactively engage in their own care and make their own decisions about their health. They make health a priority.
4	*Social support for health*	
	Completely alone and unsupported for health.	A person's social system provides them with all the support they want or need for health.
5	*Appraisal of health information*	
	No matter how hard they try, they cannot understand most health information and get confused when there is conflicting information.	Able to identify good information and reliable sources of information. They can resolve conflicting information by themselves or with help from others.
6	*Ability to actively engage with healthcare providers*	
	Are passive in their approach to healthcare, inactive i.e., they do not proactively seek or clarify information and advice and/or service options. They accept information without question. Unable to ask questions to get information or to clarify what they do not understand. They accept what is offered without seeking to ensure that it meets their needs. Feel unable to share concerns. The do not have a sense of agency in interactions with providers.	Is proactive about their health and feels in control in relationships with healthcare providers. Is able to seek advice from additional healthcare providers when necessary. They keep going until they get what they want. Empowered.
7	*Navigating the healthcare system*	
	Unable to advocate on their own behalf and unable to find someone who can help them use the healthcare system to address their health needs. Do not look beyond obvious resources and have a limited understanding of what is available and what they are entitled to.	Able to find out about services and supports so they get all their needs met. Able to advocate on their own behalf at the system and service level.
8	*Ability to find good health information*	
	Cannot access health information when required. Is dependent on others to offer information.	Is an 'information explorer'. Actively uses a diverse range of sources to find information and is up to date.
9	*Understanding health information well enough to know what to do*	
	Has problems understanding any written health information or instructions about treatments or medications. Unable to read or write well enough to complete medical forms.	Is able to understand all written information (including numerical information) in relation to their health and able to write appropriately on forms where required.

Source: Osborne et al. (2013) [31].

After defining the term 'mammogram', four survey items measured self-reported breast screening participation. These included "have you ever had a mammogram (or breast screen) to check for breast cancer?" and "if you have had a mammogram (or breast screen), when was your last one? (0–1 years, 2–3 years, 4–5 years, 6+ years, I have never had a mammogram)". Further items enquired if participants recalled receiving a screening invitation letter from BreastScreen Victoria, and if the location of their last mammogram was at a BreastScreen Victoria clinic or at another private health service.

Eleven breast screening survey statements were used to assess emotional, knowledge, and structural barriers to breast screening. A broad list of statements was assembled from a review of publications describing barriers to breast screening [16,37,38]. From these, a summary list of statements considered to reflect barriers for women from CALD backgrounds was selected (see Table 2). Agreement with each breast screening belief statement was assessed using a five-point Likert scale ranging from strongly agree to strongly disagree. For the analysis of all breast screening survey statements, strongly agree and agree responses were assigned a value of "1". Strongly disagree and disagree responses were assigned a value of "0". Recoded responses for each type of breast screening barrier were summed together to produce counts of the three types of breast screening barriers.

Table 2. Breast screening belief statements.

Emotional barriers to screening
1. I would not want to know if I have cancer
2. I put off having a breast screen because I have had a bad experience, or people I know have had a bad experience
3. I put off having a breast screen because I'm worried it will be very painful or uncomfortable
4. I put off having a breast screen because I'm worried they might find cancer
5. I put off having a breast screen because it is embarrassing
6. I have an objection to mammograms
Knowledge barriers to screening
7. Breast cancer screening could reduce my chance of dying from breast cancer
8. Breast cancer can often be cured
9. It is recommended that women my age have a breast screen
Structural barriers to screening
10. It is easy to arrange a breast screen
11. It is too difficult for me to get to a breast screen clinic

The survey included demographic questions covering date of birth, living circumstances, country of birth, home postcode, language spoken at home, self-assessed English proficiency, educational attainment, and current employment status. Health status questions included the presence of chronic health issues and self-rated overall health (from 1, poor, to 5, excellent).

2.6. Analysis

Univariate comparisons of continuous variables between groups were conducted using Welch's analysis of variance (ANOVA) and Games–Howell post-hoc tests to avoid the assumption of equal variances and sample size. Comparisons of categorical variables were conducted across the three language groups using cross-tabulations. Chi-square results were evaluated using p-values ($p < 0.05$) and adjusted standardised residuals (>1.96). For cross-tabulations with expected cell sizes of less than five, Fisher's exact test was used.

Multiple Poisson regression (with log link function) was used to assess associations with the three types of breast screening barriers. Multiple logistic regression was used to assess associations with participation in breast screening. Age, completion of secondary education, language group, English ability, number of comorbidities, and the nine domains of the HLQ were controlled for in all multiple regression analyses. The multiple logistic regression also included counts for the three types of breast screening barriers as covariates. Regression results are presented with 95% confidence intervals (CIs). All statistical procedures were conducted using the R language and environment for statistical computing [39].

3. Results

3.1. Participants

In total, 377 surveys were completed. Women who reported a previous breast cancer diagnosis ($n = 29$), were aged 75 or over ($n = 22$), or who did not report their breast screening attendance ($n = 9$)

were excluded from analyses. Data from 317 women were analysed. This total sample consisted of three cultural groups, defined by whether English ($n = 105$), Arabic ($n = 60$), or Italian ($n = 152$) was spoken at home.

Table 3 highlights demographic differences between the cultural groups. Compared to English- and Italian-speaking women, fewer Arabic-speaking women reported that they were currently employed or able to speak English very well. Arabic-speaking women also reported lower self-rated overall health and more chronic health conditions, including arthritis, diabetes, and cardiovascular problems. None of the Arabic-speaking women were born in Australia. Italian-speaking women reported a higher average age than the English-speaking women, and a lower proportion reported attaining a university-level education.

Table 3. Participant demographics.

Demographics	All Women		Cultural group						Cross-Tabulation and ANOVA
			English		Arabic		Italian		
	n	%	n	%	n	%	n	%	
Number of participants	317	100%	105	33%	60	19%	152	48%	
Age (Mean, SD)	61.07	6.89	60.78	6.31	59.28	7.04	61.98	7.1	$F(2154.8) = 3.27, p = 0.041$
Born in Australia	144	45%	81	77%	0	0%	63	41%	$x2(2) = 93.153, p < 0.001$
Lives alone	50	16%	19	18%	12	20%	19	12%	$x2(2) = 2.342, p = 0.31$
Not currently employed	207	65%	56	53%	47	78%	104	68%	$x2(2) = 13.712, p < 0.001$
Has a healthcare card	150	47%	36	34%	46	77%	68	45%	$x2(2) = 27.125, p < 0.001$
Education									
Did not finish primary school	19	6%	0	0%	12	20%	7	5%	$x2(12) = 61.874, p < 0.001$
Finished primary school	34	11%	0	0%	13	22%	21	14%	
Finished some of secondary school	64	20%	24	23%	9	15%	31	20%	
Finished secondary school	65	21%	21	20%	6	10%	38	25%	
Certificate, diploma, or apprenticeship	52	16%	23	22%	6	10%	23	15%	
Undergraduate university	43	14%	18	17%	6	10%	19	12%	
Postgraduate university	39	12%	19	18%	7	12%	13	9%	
Health									
Number of comorbidities (Mean, SD)	1.24	0.9	1.15	0.83	1.63	1.29	1.15	0.7	$F(2132.1) = 3.87, p = 0.023$
Fair or poor self-rated health	90	28%	14	13%	40	67%	36	24%	$x2(2) = 56.602, p < 0.001$
Cardiovascular problems	22	7%	5	5%	8	13%	9	6%	$x2(2) = 4.813, p = 0.090$
Arthritis	96	30%	21	20%	28	47%	47	31%	$x2(2) = 12.916, p = 0.002$
Diabetes	39	12%	8	8%	15	25%	16	11%	$x2(2) = 11.545, p = 0.003$
Depression	37	12%	9	9%	14	23%	14	9%	$x2(2) = 9.787, p = 0.007$
Anxiety	35	11%	10	10%	12	20%	13	9%	$x2(2) = 6.107, p = 0.047$
How well do you speak English?									
Very well	221	70%	98	93%	14	23%	109	72%	$x2(6) = 118.631, p < 0.001$
Well	59	19%	5	5%	20	33%	34	22%	
Not well	28	9%	0	0%	19	32%	9	6%	
Not at all	6	2%	0	0%	6	10%	0	0%	
Received a breast screening invitation	248	78%	88	84%	39	65%	121	80%	$x2(4) = 11.213, p = 0.024$
Breast screening participation									
Screened within the past 2 years	219	69%	74	70%	29	48%	116	76%	$x2(4) = 17.731, p < 0.001$
Under-screened	75	24%	26	25%	22	37%	27	18%	
Never screened	23	7%	5	5%	9	15%	9	6%	

Note: Results in bold are significant, $p < 0.05$.

3.2. Screening Participation

Just over two thirds of women in the sample reported participating in breast screening within the past two years (Table 3). A greater proportion of Arabic-speaking women reported either under-screening or never screening. No significant differences in screening participation were found between English- and Italian-speaking women. A greater proportion of women who had under-screened or never screened also reported not receiving a screening invitation.

3.3. HLQ Scales and Barriers to Breast Screening

Table 4 demonstrates that, on average, Arabic-speaking women reported significantly greater difficulty for HLQ scale 7, *navigating the healthcare system*, scale 8, *finding good health information*, and scale 9, *understanding health information well enough to know what to do*, compared to English- and Italian-speaking women. Arabic-speaking women also reported a significantly greater number of emotional and structural barriers to breast screening (Table 4).

Table 4. Descriptive statistics for the HLQ scales and barriers to breast screening.

Item	All Women	Cultural Group			ANOVA
		English	Arabic	Italian	
	n = 317 (100%)	n = 105 (33%)	n = 60 (19%)	n = 152 (48%)	
HLQ [scale range]					
1. Feeling understood and supported by healthcare providers [1–4]	3.20 (0.51)	3.25 (0.54)	3.23 (0.51)	3.15 (0.48)	$F(2150.8) = 1.15, p = 0.319$
2. Having sufficient information to manage my health [1–4]	3.08 (0.46)	3.09 (0.45)	3.08 (0.54)	3.06 (0.42)	$F(2143.5) = 0.12, p = 0.884$
3. Actively managing my health [1–4]	3.04 (0.52)	3.03 (0.56)	3.03 (0.62)	3.04 (0.44)	$F(2138.2) = 0.04, p = 0.958$
4. Social support for health [1–4]	3.07 (0.52)	3.05 (0.55)	3.14 (0.63)	3.07 (0.45)	$F(2136.1) = 0.45, p = 0.640$
5. Appraisal of health information [1–4]	3.00 (0.46)	2.98 (0.46)	3.08 (0.52)	2.97 (0.43)	$F(2144.5) = 0.98, p = 0.379$
6. Ability to actively engage with healthcare providers [1–5]	3.87 (0.71)	3.89 (0.72)	3.86 (0.67)	3.87 (0.71)	$F(2154.6) = 0.04, p = 0.964$
7. Navigating the healthcare system [1–5]	3.71 (0.65)	3.80 (0.61)	3.45 (0.64)	3.75 (0.65)	$F(2152.5) = 6.03, p = 0.003$
8. Ability to find good health information [1–5]	3.71 (0.70)	3.88 (0.59)	3.39 (0.77)	3.71 (0.71)	$F(2147.8) = 9.04, p < 0.001$
9. Understanding health information well enough to know what to do [1–5]	3.86 (0.69)	4.09 (0.59)	3.52 (0.72)	3.83 (0.69)	$F(2149.1) = 14.43, p < 0.001$
Barriers to breast screening [count range]					
Emotional [0–6]	0.51 (1.07)	0.46 (0.99)	1.25 (1.59)	0.25 (0.67)	$F(2124.1) = 11.83, p < 0.001$
Knowledge [0–3]	0.13 (0.41)	0.11 (0.42)	0.20 (0.55)	0.11 (0.34)	$F(2134.3) = 0.69, p = 0.502$
Structural [0–2]	0.19 (0.45)	0.10 (0.34)	0.50 (0.68)	0.12 (0.34)	$F(2133.5) = 9.28, p < 0.001$

Note: Results in bold are significant, $p < 0.05$; ANOVA = Analysis of Variance.

3.4. HLQ Scale Associations with Barriers to Breast Screening

Multiple Poisson regression results in Table 5 highlight significant associations between the HLQ scales and barriers to breast screening. A lower number of emotional breast screening barriers were reported by women who had higher scores for scale 1, *feeling understood and supported by healthcare providers*, 4, *social support for health*, and 9, *Understanding health information well enough to know what to do*. A lower number of knowledge barriers were reported by women who had higher scores for scale 1, *feeling understood and supported by healthcare providers*. A greater number of structural barriers were reported by women who had higher scores for scale 5, *appraisal of health information*.

Differences between cultural groups were also present. Compared with English and Italian-speaking women, Arabic-speaking women reported a 94% higher number of emotional barriers and an 85% higher number of structural barriers. Italian-speaking women reported a lower number of emotional barriers. Women who reported receiving a screening invitation letter had a lower number of emotional barriers. Additionally, women with greater comorbidities reported greater number of emotional barriers.

Table 5. Association between health literacy, barriers to breast screening and being up-to-date with breast screening participation.

	Barriers to Breast Screening			Up-To-Date Breast Screening Participation	
	Emotional	Knowledge	Structural		
	Poisson Regression			Logistic Regression	
	Score Ratio [95% CI]			Unadjusted OR [95% CI]	Adjusted OR [95% CI]
[Intercept]					0.15 [0.00–8.36]
Age	1.00 [0.97–1.02]	1.01 [0.97–1.06]	0.98 [0.95–1.02]	**1.07 [1.03–1.11]**	1.04 [0.99–1.10]
Completed secondary education	1.15 [0.78–1.72]	1.43 [0.76–2.75]	0.77 [0.47–1.27]	0.86 [0.52–1.42]	0.88 [0.42–1.85]
Arabic-speaking	**1.94 [1.24–3.04]**	1.21 [0.55–2.62]	**1.85 [1.06–3.27]**	**0.33 [0.18–0.59]**	0.60 [0.24–1.50]
Italian-speaking	**0.60 [0.39–0.91]**	0.71 [0.39–1.31]	0.65 [0.38–1.10]	**1.94 [1.19–3.18]**	1.10 [0.56–2.13]
Reported receiving a breast screening invitation	**0.55 [0.39–0.77]**	0.66 [0.38–1.17]	0.71 [0.47–1.09]	**3.84 [2.19–6.81]**	**3.46 [1.81–6.67]**
Number of comorbidities	**1.27 [1.12–1.43]**	0.97 [0.71–1.26]	1.11 [0.92–1.31]	**0.74 [0.57–0.96]**	0.80 [0.56–1.12]
HLQ					
1. Feeling understood and supported by healthcare providers	**0.50 [0.31–0.80]**	**0.43 [0.21–0.88]**	0.64 [0.36–1.15]	1.50 [0.93–2.43]	2.05 [0.90–4.79]
2. Having sufficient information to manage my health	1.15 [0.70–1.91]	1.74 [0.75–4.13]	1.61 [0.87–3.05]	1.28 [0.76–2.18]	1.04 [0.41–2.57]
3. Actively managing my health	0.92 [0.62–1.36]	1.12 [0.60–2.11]	0.74 [0.46–1.21]	1.43 [0.90–2.29]	1.19 [0.58–2.48]
4. Social support for health	**0.60 [0.40–0.92]**	1.16 [0.59–2.35]	1.04 [0.61–1.80]	1.31 [0.83–2.09]	1.18 [0.53–2.59]
5. Appraisal of health information	1.28 [0.77–2.13]	0.88 [0.39–1.98]	**2.44 [1.31–4.63]**	0.86 [0.51–1.46]	0.55 [0.21–1.35]
6. Ability to actively engage with healthcare providers	1.15 [0.78–1.72]	0.98 [0.53–1.84]	0.96 [0.59–1.56]	1.19 [0.84–1.66]	1.19 [0.55–2.63]
7. Navigating the healthcare system	1.35 [0.85–2.17]	0.90 [0.43–1.89]	1.25 [0.72–2.20]	1.10 [0.75–1.59]	0.78 [0.32–1.85]
8. Ability to find good health information	1.28 [0.81–2.07]	1.16 [0.58–2.40]	0.97 [0.57–1.64]	1.03 [0.73–1.45]	1.10 [0.47–2.60]
9. Understanding health information well enough to know what to do	**0.57 [0.38–0.86]**	0.75 [0.39–1.43]	0.64 [0.39–1.05]	1.03 [0.72–1.46]	0.63 [0.29–1.35]
Barriers to breast screening					
Emotional				**0.59 [0.46–0.74]**	**0.72 [0.54–0.94]**
Knowledge				0.82 [0.48–1.47]	1.14 [0.58–2.26]
Structural				**0.42 [0.25–0.70]**	0.57 [0.30–1.09]

Note: Results in bold are significant, $p < 0.05$; OR = Odds ratio.

3.5. HLQ Scale Associations with Up-To-Date Breast Screening Participation

Results from logistic regression analyses evaluating associations with up-to-date breast cancer screening participation are presented in Table 5. Overall, no significant associations between health literacy and up-to-date breast screening participation were identified across all unadjusted and multivariate results. Results revealed that up-to-date screening was positively associated with receiving a screening invitation and negatively associated with emotional screening barriers. Receiving a screening invitation increased the odds of up-to-date screening by 246% (OR = 3.46, 95% CI = 1.81, 6.67), when all other demographic variables, HLQ scales, and barriers to breast screening were held constant. Each additional reported emotional barrier decreased the odds of up-to-date screening by 28% (OR = 0.72, 95% CI = 0.54, 0.94), when other values were held constant.

4. Discussion

This study investigated potential barriers to breast screening in a multicultural Australian context. Overall, Arabic-speaking women reported greater health literacy challenges and lower up-to-date breast screening participation than both English- and Italian-speaking women. However, findings suggest no evidence of a direct association between the many dimensions of health literacy and screening participation. Previous research has identified negative relationships between functional health literacy and screening participation [21,25,26], but this is the first study to have examined associations between a wide range of robust measures of health literacy and participation in breast cancer screening. These findings may reflect differences in the research contexts because previous studies were conducted in the United States of America where there is no free, comprehensive national breast screening program [21,22].

Consistent with previous research, emotional barriers were the most important barriers for up-to-date breast screening participation [14,38,40]. As previously found in the context of Arabic-speaking women [41], knowledge barriers were not associated with screening participation for any cultural group. Compared with English- and Italian-speaking women, Arabic-speaking women reported more emotional and structural barriers to breast screening, even when considering whether or not they reported receiving a screening invitation. The lower screening participation reported by Arabic-speaking women is partially explained by reports of a higher number of emotional barriers and a lower proportion of screening invitations received. Furthermore, Arabic-speaking women reported a higher prevalence of arthritis, diabetes, depression, anxiety, and a greater number of comorbid conditions overall, which may have limited their mobility and access to breast screening facilities.

Four health literacy domains were significantly associated with the three types of breast screening barriers. Domain 1, *feeling understood and supported by healthcare providers*, was related to fewer emotional and knowledge barriers. Direct recommendations to attend breast screening by health care providers are effective in increasing breast screening attendance [42]; however, even just maintaining an ongoing relationship with one or more health care providers has been found to increase the likelihood of screening [43]. Domain 4, *social support for health*, was related to fewer emotional barriers. Previous research has identified social support as a contributor to breast screening participation [44].

Domain 5, *appraisal of health information*, was related to a greater number of structural barriers. This suggests that women who reported a greater tendency to think critically about the information they received and if it was right for them may also perceive greater obstacles to arranging and attending a breast screen appointment. Domain 9, *understanding health information well enough to know what to do*, was also related to lower emotional barriers. This ability enables women to interpret available information, potentially reducing their emotional concerns and overall anxiety about breast screening [13]. The availability of this information, in the form of a screening invitation letter, may also reduce emotional concerns.

Overall, findings from this study indicate that cultural groups were an important factor in predicting emotional screening barriers, structural screening barriers, and breast screening participation. The potential links between emotional, knowledge, and structural barriers with the health literacy abilities of using, understanding, and accessing health information and services were not supported in this sample and context. The structure of breast screening services and the minimal demands they place on women's ability to access, understand, and use health information and services may reduce the impact of health literacy challenges on ongoing breast screening participation.

Screening invitations had a greater positive association with up-to-date screening participation than all other investigated factors, which is consistent with the findings from a systematic review [11]. However, invitation letters written in English may have been a barrier to women from non-English speaking backgrounds. Women unable to read screening invitations provided in English are unlikely to report that they received these invitations, and this may explain why a smaller proportion of Arabic-speaking women reported receiving an invitation. Screening invitations written in multiple languages may help non-English speaking women to make their first contact with breast screening providers. Additionally, the use of the electoral roll as a register for screening invitation will only be relevant to those women who are enrolled to vote. Arabic-speakers have been found to be less likely to enroll due to language barriers [45]. Furthermore, recent migrants may be more likely to change address and their language difficulties may result in postal addresses being misreported.

A strength of this study was that the participant sample was based on targeted recruitment with extensive support from community organisations. Bilingual resources and staff supported broad participant recruitment within each cultural group. Among the women included in the study sample, self-reported rates of up-to-date breast screening participation for English- and Italian-speaking women (73% and 75%, respectively) were higher than rates Australia-wide (54%); however, previous research has found self-reported breast screening participation in minority groups to be accurate [46]. The sample may not be representative of women from their respective communities. Given the purposive sampling frame used in this study, caution should be taken with extrapolating the findings to other regions or other cultural groups. Population-based research may be warranted to confirm the current findings and to support the development of interventions that seek to increase breast cancer screening among disadvantaged and migrant groups. In addition, breast screening survey statements were not based on a previously validated measure and no validation of self-reported screening rates were undertaken.

5. Conclusions

Emotional screening barriers were negatively associated with up-to-date breast screening participation. Screening invitations were positively associated with up-to-date breast screening participation. These factors explained differences in screening participation across the three cultural groups. However, Arabic-speaking women reported the most difficulty with all three of these factors. Women with lower health literacy were not more likely to under-screen. However, they did report more breast screening barriers than women with higher health literacy. Future research should explore the nature of emotional barriers, particularly for Arabic-speaking women, and how these might be overcome. Emotional barriers to breast cancer screening appear to be an important target for interventions to increase participation rates, particularly for Arabic-speaking women. For these interventions to be most effective, it is important that they are culturally-sensitive and designed collaboratively with community members and other stakeholders [47].

Author Contributions: The overall study design was devised by A.B., R.H.O., S.D., A.C., C.W., V.P., V.C., M.S., P.M.L. and managed by A.B., C.W. managed data collection and community engagement. J.O. conducted data analyses and led the writing of drafts. M.H. and C.M. assisted in the development of the first draft. All authors contributed to the second and subsequent drafts including interpretation of the results. All authors approved the final manuscript.

Funding: This research received no external funding.

Acknowledgments: This study was commissioned by BreastScreen Victoria through the Department of Health and Human Services (Victoria). Richard Osborne was funded in part by a NHMRC Senior Research Fellowship #APP1059122. Alison Beauchamp is funded in part by a NHMRC MRFF TRIP fellowship #APP1150745. The authors would like to thank BreastScreen Victoria, the Department of Health and Human Services (Victoria), all members of the Consumer Advisory Group, all members of the Project Management Group, and all of the participants throughout North West Melbourne for their time and support.

Conflicts of Interest: The authors declare no conflict of interest.

References

1. Australian Institute of Health and Welfare. *Cancer in Australia 2017*; Australian Institute of Health and Welfare: Canberra, Australia, 2017.
2. World Health Organisation Breast Cancer: Prevention and Control. Available online: http://www.who.int/cancer/detection/breastcancer/en/index1.html (accessed on 1 December 2017).

3. Nelson, H.D.; Fu, R.; Cantor, A.; Pappas, M.; Daeges, M.; Humphrey, L. Effectiveness of breast cancer screening: Systematic review and meta-analysis to update the 2009 U.S. Preventive services task force recommendation. *Ann. Intern. Med.* **2016**, *164*, 244–255. [CrossRef] [PubMed]
4. Morrell, S.; Taylor, R.; Roder, D.; Dobson, A. Mammography screening and breast cancer mortality in Australia: An aggregate cohort study. *J. Med. Screen.* **2012**, *19*, 26–34. [CrossRef] [PubMed]
5. Nelson, H.D.; Pappas, M.; Cantor, A.; Griffin, J.; Daeges, M.; Humphrey, L. Harms of breast cancer screening: Systematic review to update the 2009 U.S. Preventive services task force recommendation. *Ann. Intern. Med.* **2016**, *164*, 256–267. [CrossRef] [PubMed]
6. Houssami, N. Overdiagnosis of breast cancer in population screening: Does it make breast screening worthless? *Cancer Biol. Med.* **2017**, *14*, 1–8. [CrossRef] [PubMed]
7. Myers, E.R.; Moorman, P.; Gierisch, J.M.; Havrilesky, L.J.; Grimm, L.J.; Ghate, S.; Davidson, B.; Montgomery, R.C.; Crowley, M.J.; McCrory, D.C.; et al. Benefits and Harms of Breast Cancer Screening. *JAMA* **2015**, *314*, 1615. [CrossRef] [PubMed]
8. Welch, H.G.; Passow, H.J. Quantifying the Benefits and Harms of Screening Mammography. *JAMA Intern. Med.* **2014**, *174*, 448. [CrossRef] [PubMed]
9. Shah, T.A.; Guraya, S.S. Breast cancer screening programs: Review of merits, demerits, and recent recommendations practiced across the world. *J. Microsc. Ultrastruct.* **2016**, *5*, 59–69. [CrossRef] [PubMed]
10. Brown, R.L.; Baumann, L.J.; Helberg, C.P.; Han, Y.; Fontana, S.A.; Love, R.R. The simultaneous analysis of patient, physician and group practice influences on annual mammography performance. *Soc. Sci. Med.* **1996**, *43*, 315–324. [CrossRef]
11. Baron, R.C.; Melillo, S.; Rimer, B.K.; Coates, R.J.; Kerner, J.; Habarta, N.; Chattopadhyay, S.; Sabatino, S.A.; Elder, R.; Leeks, K.J. Intervention to Increase Recommendation and Delivery of Screening for Breast, Cervical, and Colorectal Cancers by Healthcare Providers. A Systematic Review of Provider Reminders. *Am. J. Prev. Med.* **2010**, *38*, 110–117. [CrossRef] [PubMed]
12. Australian Institute of Health and Welfare. *BreastScreen Australia Monitoring Report 2013–2014*; Australian Institute of Health and Welfare: Canberra, Australia, 2016.
13. Consedine, N.S.; Magai, C.; Krivoshekova, Y.S.; Ryzewicz, L.; Neugut, A.I. Fear, anxiety, worry, and breast cancer screening behavior: A critical review. *Cancer Epidemiol. Prev. Biomark.* **2004**, *13*, 501–510.
14. Consedine, N.S.; Magai, C.; Neugut, A.I. The contribution of emotional characteristics to breast cancer screening among women from six ethnic groups. *Prev. Med.* **2004**, *38*, 64–77. [CrossRef] [PubMed]
15. Beauchamp, A.; Buchbinder, R.; Dodson, S.; Batterham, R.W.; Elsworth, G.R.; McPhee, C.; Sparkes, L.; Hawkins, M.; Osborne, R.H. Distribution of health literacy strengths and weaknesses across socio-demographic groups: A cross-sectional survey using the Health Literacy Questionnaire (HLQ). *BMC Public Health* **2015**, *15*, 678. [CrossRef] [PubMed]
16. Sarma, E.A. Barriers to screening mammography. *Health Psychol. Rev.* **2015**, *9*, 42–62. [CrossRef] [PubMed]
17. Whelehan, P.; Evans, A.; Wells, M.; MacGillivray, S. The effect of mammography pain on repeat participation in breast cancer screening: A systematic review. *Breast* **2013**, *22*, 389–394. [CrossRef] [PubMed]
18. Azaiza, F.; Cohen, M. Health Beliefs and Rates of Breast Cancer Screening among Arab Women. *J. Women's Health* **2006**, *15*, 520–530. [CrossRef] [PubMed]
19. Temple-Smith, M.J.; Banwell, C.L.; Gifford, S.M.; Presswell, N.T. Promoting health beyond recruitment: Beliefs and attitudes to breast and cervical cancer screening services among Italian-born women in Melbourne. *Health Promot. J. Aust.* **1995**, *5*, 31–36.
20. Gesink, D.; Mihic, A.; Antal, J.; Filsinger, B.; Racey, C.S.; Perez, D.F.; Norwood, T.; Ahmad, F.; Kreiger, N.; Ritvo, P. Who are the under- and never-screened for cancer in Ontario: A qualitative investigation. *BMC Public Health* **2014**, *14*, 495. [CrossRef] [PubMed]
21. Komenaka, I.K.; Nodora, J.N.; Hsu, C.H.; Martinez, M.E.; Gandhi, S.G.; Bouton, M.E.; Klemens, A.E.; Wikholm, L.I.; Weiss, B.D. Association of health literacy with adherence to screening mammography guidelines. *Obstet. Gynecol.* **2015**, *125*, 852–859. [CrossRef] [PubMed]
22. Lee, S.; Chen, L.; Jung, M.Y.; Baezconde-Garbanati, L.; Juon, H.-S. Acculturation and Cancer Screening Among Asian Americans: Role of Health Insurance and Having a Regular Physician. *J. Community Health* **2014**, *39*, 201–212. [CrossRef] [PubMed]
23. Nutbeam, D. Health literacy as a public health goal: A challenge for contemporary health education and communication strategies into the 21st century. *Health Promot. Int.* **2000**, *15*, 259–267. [CrossRef]

24. Dodson, S.; Good, S.; Osborne, R.H.; Batterham, R.; Beauchamp, A.; Belak, A.; Cheng, C.; Garad, R.; Hawkins, M.; Komarek, L.; et al. *Health Literacy Toolkit for Low- and Middle-Income Countries: A Series of Information Sheets to Empower Communities and Health Systems*; World Health Organization: Geneva, Switzerland, 2015; ISBN 9789290224754.
25. Fernandez, D.M.; Larson, J.L.; Zikmund-Fisher, B.J. Associations between health literacy and preventive health behaviors among older adults: Findings from the health and retirement study. *BMC Public Health* **2016**, *16*, 596. [CrossRef] [PubMed]
26. Sentell, T.; Braun, K.L.; Davis, J.; Davis, T. Health literacy and meeting breast and cervical cancer screening guidelines among Asians and whites in California. *Springerplus* **2015**, *4*, 432. [CrossRef] [PubMed]
27. Morris, N.S.; Field, T.S.; Wagner, J.L.; Cutrona, S.L.; Roblin, D.W.; Gaglio, B.; Williams, A.E.; Han, P.J.K.; Costanza, M.E.; Mazor, K.M. The Association Between Health Literacy and Cancer-Related Attitudes, Behaviors, and Knowledge. *J. Health Commun.* **2013**, *18*, 223–241. [CrossRef] [PubMed]
28. Jordan, J.E.; Buchbinder, R.; Osborne, R.H. Conceptualising health literacy from the patient perspective. *Patient Educ. Couns.* **2010**, *79*, 36–42. [CrossRef] [PubMed]
29. Altin, S.V.; Finke, I.; Kautz-Freimuth, S.; Stock, S. The evolution of health literacy assessment tools: A systematic review. *BMC Public Health* **2014**, *14*, 1207. [CrossRef] [PubMed]
30. Batterham, R.W.; Hawkins, M.; Collins, P.A.; Buchbinder, R.; Osborne, R.H. Health literacy: Applying current concepts to improve health services and reduce health inequalities. *Public Health* **2016**, *132*, 3–12. [CrossRef] [PubMed]
31. Osborne, R.H.; Batterham, R.W.; Elsworth, G.R.; Hawkins, M.; Buchbinder, R. The grounded psychometric development and initial validation of the Health Literacy Questionnaire (HLQ). *BMC Public Health* **2013**, *13*, 658. [CrossRef] [PubMed]
32. North Western Melbourne Primary Health Network Community profile—Language Spoken at Home. Available online: https://profile.id.com.au/nwmphn/language?WebID=10 (accessed on 6 August 2018).
33. Hawkins, M.; Gill, S.D.; Batterham, R.; Elsworth, G.R.; Osborne, R.H. The Health Literacy Questionnaire (HLQ) at the patient-clinician interface: A qualitative study of what patients and clinicians mean by their HLQ scores. *BMC Health Serv. Res.* **2017**, *17*, 309. [CrossRef] [PubMed]
34. Kolarcik, P.; Cepova, E.; Madarasova Geckova, A.; Elsworth, G.R.; Batterham, R.W.; Osborne, R.H. Structural properties and psychometric improvements of the Health Literacy Questionnaire in a Slovak population. *Int. J. Public Health* **2017**, 1–14. [CrossRef] [PubMed]
35. Maindal, H.T.; Kayser, L.; Norgaard, O.; Bo, A.; Elsworth, G.R.; Osborne, R.H. Cultural adaptation and validation of the Health Literacy Questionnaire (HLQ): Robust nine-dimension Danish language confirmatory factor model. *Springerplus* **2016**, *5*, 1232. [CrossRef] [PubMed]
36. Nolte, S.; Osborne, R.H.; Dwinger, S.; Elsworth, G.R.; Conrad, M.L.; Rose, M.; Härter, M.; Dirmaier, J.; Zill, J.M. German translation, cultural adaptation, and validation of the Health Literacy Questionnaire (HLQ). *PLoS ONE* **2017**, *12*, e0172340. [CrossRef] [PubMed]
37. Stoll, C.R.T.; Roberts, S.; Cheng, M.-R.; Crayton, E.V.; Jackson, S.; Politi, M.C. Barriers to Mammography Among Inadequately Screened Women. *Health Educ. Behav.* **2015**, *42*, 8–15. [CrossRef] [PubMed]
38. Magai, C.; Consedine, N.; Conway, F.; Neugut, A.; Culver, C. Diversity matters: Unique populations of women and breast cancer screening. *Cancer* **2004**, *100*, 2300–2307. [CrossRef] [PubMed]
39. Team, R.C. *R: A Language and Environment for Statistical Computing*; R Foundation for Statistical Computing: Vienna, Austria, 2018.
40. Nadalin, V.; Maher, J.; Lessels, C.; Chiarelli, A.; Kreiger, N. Breast screening knowledge and barriers among under/never screened women. *Public Health* **2016**, *133*, 63–66. [CrossRef] [PubMed]
41. Kwok, C.; Endrawes, G.; Lee, C.F. Cultural Beliefs and Attitudes About Breast Cancer and Screening Practices Among Arabic Women in Australia. *Cancer Nurs.* **2016**, *39*, 367–374. [CrossRef] [PubMed]
42. Peterson, E.B.; Ostroff, J.S.; DuHamel, K.N.; D'Agostino, T.A.; Hernandez, M.; Canzona, M.R.; Bylund, C.L. Impact of provider-patient communication on cancer screening adherence: A systematic review. *Prev. Med.* **2016**, *93*, 96–105. [CrossRef] [PubMed]
43. Cardarelli, R.; Kurian, A.K.; Pandya, V. Having a Personal Healthcare Provider and Receipt of Adequate Cervical and Breast Cancer Screening. *J. Am. Board Fam. Med.* **2010**, *23*, 75–81. [CrossRef] [PubMed]

44. Documet, P.; Bear, T.M.; Flatt, J.D.; Macia, L.; Trauth, J.; Ricci, E.M. The Association of Social Support and Education With Breast and Cervical Cancer Screening. *Health Educ. Behav.* **2015**, *42*, 55–64. [CrossRef] [PubMed]
45. Victorian Electoral Commission. *Barriers to Enrolment and Voting, and Electronic Voting among Arabic-Speaking and Turkish Communities*; Victorian Electoral Commission: Sydney, Australia, 2012.
46. Nandy, K.; Menon, U.; Szalacha, L.A.; Park, H.; Lee, J.; Lee, E.E. Self-Report Versus Medical Record for Mammography Screening Among Minority Women. *West. J. Nurs. Res.* **2016**, *38*, 1627–1638. [CrossRef] [PubMed]
47. Macnamara, J.; Camit, M. Effective CALD community health communication through research and collaboration: An exemplar case study. *Commun. Res. Pract.* **2017**, *3*, 92–112. [CrossRef]

© 2018 by the authors. Licensee MDPI, Basel, Switzerland. This article is an open access article distributed under the terms and conditions of the Creative Commons Attribution (CC BY) license (http://creativecommons.org/licenses/by/4.0/).

Article

A Qualitative Study of the Development of Health Literacy Capacities of Participants Attending a Community-Based Cardiovascular Health Programme

Verna B. McKenna *, Jane Sixsmith and Margaret M. Barry

Health Promotion Research Centre, Discipline of Health Promotion, National University of Ireland Galway, H91 CF50 Galway, Ireland; jane.sixsmith@nuigalway.ie (J.S.); margaret.barry@nuigalway.ie (M.M.B.)
* Correspondence: verna.mckenna@nuigalway.ie

Received: 20 April 2018; Accepted: 30 May 2018; Published: 2 June 2018

Abstract: Health literacy is a critical determinant of health, which can empower individuals and lead to engagement in collective health promotion action and is also a crucial component in the self-management of illness. The current study moves beyond a focus on functional health literacy and presents findings from a longitudinal qualitative (LQ) study consisting of three phases. This paper presents findings from the second phase of the study, which assessed the development of health literacy capacities of individuals attending a structured cardiovascular risk reduction programme in Ireland. The study objectives were to: explore perceptions of changes in interactions and information exchange within health consultations; identify the facilitators associated with changes in health literacy capacities; assess developments in engagement with broader contexts for health literacy capacities. A LQ study design was undertaken, which employed repeat interview methodology with 19 participants (aged 36–76 years) 12 weeks after beginning a structured cardiovascular risk reduction programme. Health literacy levels were assessed using the HLS-EU 47 item instrument in phase 1 (68% limited health literacy (HL), 32% adequate health literacy). A semi-structured interview guide, (informed by Sørensen's conceptual model of health literacy), was used to explore the development of health literacy and to identify changes in knowledge, attitudes and experiences over time. Thematic analysis was used, informed by aspects of Saldaña's framework for longitudinal qualitative data analysis. All participants reported having acquired increased understanding of issues relevant to their health and self-care. Participants described health literacy capacities that incorporate aspects of all levels of health literacy (functional, interactive and critical). Core themes were identified corresponding to changes in these levels: re-engagement with health information and increased understanding of risk and protective factors (changes in functional health literacy); changes in interactions with healthcare providers (HCP) (changes in interactive health literacy); enhanced psychological insights and understanding the broader determinants of health (changes in critical health literacy). Findings support the development of health literacy capacities across the functional, interactive and critical health literacy domains. Participants are capable of locating responsibility for health beyond the individual level and are making sense of knowledge within their own social contexts. Individuals, regardless of their initial health literacy levels, are capable of engaging with broader issues that can impact on their health and can be supported to develop these critical health literacy capacities.

Keywords: health literacy; critical health literacy longitudinal qualitative research; determinants of health

1. Introduction

Health literacy is a critical determinant of health that can empower individuals and lead to engagement in collective health promotion action [1]. It is also a crucial component in the self-management of illness [2]. Regarded as an asset, it is seen as central to lifelong engagement with health, building cognitive and social skills as well as the motivation necessary to navigate healthcare systems, disease prevention and health promotion throughout the life course [3–5]. While there is increasing recognition of the need to support the development of individuals' health literacy capacities and minimise environmental demands in both healthcare and broader societal contexts [6–12], there is still relatively little known about the barriers and facilitators in this process [13,14]. Research has highlighted the need to move beyond a focus on functional health literacy capacities in order to gain a greater insight into how the social and cultural context of individuals' lives can facilitate the development of health literacy capacities, [12,15,16]. Some recent studies have examined this in adult-based educational settings [17,18]. This paper draws on the health literacy model developed by Sørensen et al. [5] to explore the different dimensions of health literacy within healthcare, disease prevention and health promotion settings. In this study, health literacy is defined as being' linked to literacy and entails peoples' knowledge, motivation and competencies to access, understand, appraise, and apply health information in order to make judgements and take decisions in everyday life concerning healthcare, disease prevention and health promotion to maintain or improve quality of life during the life course' [5]. The current study addresses health literacy 'capacities', which refer specifically to the skills, abilities and potentialities of individuals to effectively access, understand, appraise and use information [6,19,20]. This definition aims to capture and embrace the depth of health literacy as an asset.

Increased insight is needed into how the development of health literacy capacity can be facilitated. The current study sets out to do this and presents findings from a longitudinal qualitative study, consisting of three phases (see Table 1 below), which examines developments in the health literacy of individuals over time. This study entails an in-depth qualitative exploration of the development of health literacy over time for a group of individuals managing their health and illness in the context of their everyday lives. There is a paucity of such longitudinal qualitative studies in the current health literacy literature.

Table 1. Overview of timeline, sample and methods for overall longitudinal qualitative study.

Time Points	Sample	Methods
Phase 1: (Baseline: Beginning of programme)	26 Participants	HLS-EU survey and interview completed [21]
Phase 2: (End of programme @12 weeks)	19 Participants	Interview completed
Phase 3: (One-year follow-up @12 months)	17 Participants	HLS-EU survey and interview completed [21]

This study makes an important contribution to the field of health literacy research as it is a qualitative in-depth and longitudinal study that follows individuals over time to examine developments in health literacy as they manage their health and illness in the context of their everyday lives. Findings from the first phase have been previously reported [22] and indicated a high level of limited health literacy for the population sample (65%). Both psychological factors, including perceptions of control and confidence in managing health, and structural factors such as access to health services and the impact of urban/rural environments, were found to impact on individuals' use of health literacy capacities. Relationships with healthcare providers, mainly the general practitioner (GP), and the quality of that relationship, were also identified as being crucial in using health literacy skills. This paper presents on the second phase of the study, which assesses the development and perceptions of changes in health literacy capacities of individuals attending a structured cardiovascular risk reduction programme. The study aim was not to evaluate the impact of the programme per se. Rather, the programme was used as a 'vehicle' to engage individuals as they managed their health and illness over a 12-month period. The study objectives were to:

explore perceptions of changes in interactions and information exchange within health consultations; identify the facilitators associated with changes in health literacy capacities; assess developments in engagement with broader contexts for health literacy capacities.

2. Methods

2.1. Study Design

This paper describes phase two of a longitudinal qualitative study design, which employed repeat interview methodology at three separate time points (see Table 1) to examine developments in the health literacy of individuals over time. Findings from time point 2 (T2) are outlined in this paper.

2.2. Participants

In this study, purposeful sampling was employed in order to select individuals attending a community-based structured cardiovascular risk reduction programme. Purposeful sampling is used in qualitative research to select individuals/sites for study that can purposefully inform an understanding of the research problem and central phenomenon in the study [23]. The sample in this study were selected in order to obtain the views and experiences of people with a range of risk factors for cardiovascular disease, as well as those with established disease (see Table 2). Twenty-six individuals were interviewed in phase one and nineteen of these were subsequently interviewed again at the 12-week point due to attrition of seven participants. The 12-week programme integrates the care of individuals with established heart disease and those at high multi-factorial risk of developing the disease, into a local community-based programme [24] that was originally developed at Imperial College London following the EUROACTION trial [25]. The programme is delivered by a multidisciplinary team comprising nurse specialists, dieticians and exercise specialists and incorporates weekly group exercise classes and educational workshops. The workshops address a range of topics including the risk factors for coronary heart disease and stroke, healthy eating, alcohol use, weight management, physical activity, stress management, food labels, maintaining change and cardiac medications. Participants also have weekly meetings with the multidisciplinary team [24]. Initial recruitment took place in conjunction with the programme nurse, who identified individuals who were cognitively able to participate and were able to communicate through the English language. A unique feature of the programme is that the partners of referred patients are also invited to complete the programme, and three partners were included in phase 2 of this study. Recruitment for this study took place between May 2014 and March 2015.

2.2.1. Profile of Study Participants

All of the participants ($n = 19$) had completed a 12-week cardiovascular disease (CVD) risk reduction programme and were referred through various pathways including general practice and hospital departments such as cardiology, stroke, and endocrinology. Participants had a variety of risk factors including hypertension and elevated cholesterol and many were also overweight or obese. In addition the majority of participants had experienced one or more of the following conditions: established heart disease (stents fitted), heart failure, type 2 diabetes, cardiac arrhythmia and stroke. Participant characteristics, including health literacy levels recorded at phase one, are summarised in Table 2. The raw scores of the general health literacy index are categorised to denote the following levels of health literacy: inadequate, problematic, sufficient and excellent health literacy. In this study these were further combined to yield scores for limited (inadequate and problematic) and adequate (sufficient and excellent) levels of health literacy. The limited level of health literacy reported here (68%) is significantly higher than levels reported in the overall European Health Literacy survey (47%) and in the Irish sample of the European survey (40%) [2,26]. These findings correspond with those for population subgroups with lower education and social class levels, and higher rates of disease and health service use, which is consistent with this participant profile.

Table 2. Profile of study participants.

Participants (n)	19
Gender	n, %
Male	8 (42%)
Female	11 (58%)
Age (mean, range)	61 (36–76)
Education: highest level attained to date	n, %
Primary School	4 (21%)
Secondary School	10 (53%)
Diploma/certificate/Primary degree/postgraduate	5 (26%)
Social class [1]	n, %
I–II (High)	6 (32%)
III–IV (Medium)	1 (5%)
V–VII (Low)	12 (63%)
General health literacy level from HLS-EU measure [2]	n, %
Limited	13 (68%)
Adequate	6 (32%)
Length of time with risk factors/illness	n, %
6–9 months	7 (37%)
More than 1 year	12 (63%)
Health service access	n, %
Private health insurance	10 (53%)
Medical card only [3]	7 (37%)
Private AND medical card	2 (10%)

[1] [27]; [2] [21] [3] A medical card allows access to GP services, community health services, dental services, prescription medicines and hospital care free of charge under the General Medical Services Scheme for sub-groups of the population based on income levels/specific medical conditions [28,29].

2.2.2. Data Collection Procedures

Interviews

Twenty-six individuals were interviewed in phase one and 19 of these were subsequently interviewed again at the 12-week point. Retention issues and attrition of participants is common in qualitative longitudinal studies [30–32]. In this study, attrition was attributed to a combination of issues including limited engagement with the risk-reduction programme on the part of some participants and illness factors that prevented programme completion.

Semi-structured interview guides were used to explore the development of health literacy and to identify changes in knowledge, attitudes and experiences over time (see Appendix A). The development of the interview guide was informed by Sørensen's conceptual model of health literacy [5], in order to explore all the capacities associated with health literacy. Interview questions for phase 2, similar to phase 1, focussed on the areas of accessing, understanding, appraising and applying health information, and transcript data were initially categorised within these areas. In addition, questions were also included, in the form of probes, to explore further issues that had been identified in phase 1 (for example, concerns about upcoming treatment decisions). Saldaña's framework [33] (as outlined in Table 3 below) was used to guide the analytic process and to structure the data analysis. The interview schedule was piloted prior to commencement of data collection with a small number of individuals attending the structured programme. Only minor changes were made to the sequencing of questions.

Table 3. Saldaña framework [33] (aspects used in this analysis are bolded).

Framing Questions (5)
What is different from one round of data to the next?
When do changes occur?
What contextual and intervening conditions appear to influence and affect participant changes over time?
What are the dynamics of participant changes over time?
What preliminary assertions about participant changes can be made as the data analysis progresses?
Descriptive Qs (7)
What increases/emerges over time?
What is cumulative?
What kinds of surges/epiphanies occur?
What decreases/ceases over time?
What remains constant or consistent?
What is idiosyncratic?
What is missing?
Analytic and interpretive questions (4)
What changes are interrelated?
What changes oppose or harmonise with natural human development or constructed social processes?
What are participant or conceptual rhythms, e.g., cycles through time?
What is the through-line of the study?

All interviews took place in a private room at the community-based programme building and were conducted by the first author (Verna B. McKenna).

2.3. Data Analysis

All interviews were audio recorded digitally, transcribed verbatim and analysed using thematic analysis, which was facilitated through the use of N-vivo version 10 qualitative software. Qualitative validation criteria were applied in this study in line with established guidelines [34–36]. These included:

Credibility: Participants' perspectives were reported as accurately as possible and the participants own voice used. Review and refinement of themes through a consensus among the three authors.

Triangulation: convergence sought among multiple sources of information (interview transcripts, memos, relevant theory and authors) to verify interview data and to develop themes. A level of member checking achieved where key issues and themes arising at time point 1 were reviewed with the participants at start of time point 2 interviews.

Transferability: Detailed accounts of the data and the context of data collection provided.

Descriptive validity: Multiple reading of the transcripts and listening to recordings in line with the methodology of thematic analysis.

Interpretive validity: Made clear through the use of the participants own voice alongside the meaning attributed by the researcher.

Theoretical validity: Findings clearly set out within relevant theory in the field of health literacy.

Researcher reflexivity: Preliminary analysis between time points allowed researcher to reflect on personal assumptions related to health literacy and social contexts.

The study used a hybrid approach of inductive and deductive coding and theme development, employing a thematic analysis methodology as advocated by Braun and Clarke [37] whereby core themes, subthemes and categories were identified. Aspects of Saldaña's framework [33] (bolded in Table 3 above) were used in order to ensure that analysis captured the process of development and changes rather than presenting cross-sectional findings only [32,33]. By linking back to the previous dataset it was also possible to determine what changes or developments had occurred in terms of health literacy capacities (accessing, understanding, appraising and applying health information). The Saldaña framework [33] will be used more extensively for the overall longitudinal analysis of the entire dataset (time points 1–3). Preliminary analysis took place between interviews at time points 1 and 2 to allow reflexivity on the part of the researcher [38] as well as to focus on process and changes rather than on snapshots [32]. This preliminary analysis allowed the researcher to identify key issues that could then be returned to for further exploration in the second interview. This process was facilitated through the use of memos and field notes.

The analysis occurred both within each case and as a comparison between cases across the two time points. As such, the focus is not on gaining snapshots across time but to "ground the interviews in an exploration of processes and changes which look both forwards and backwards in time" [39] (p. 194), [40].

Credibility of findings was enhanced by returning to the original transcripts and through discussion with the other authors (Margaret M. Barry and Jane Sixsmith). A sample of transcripts were also read by Margaret M. Barry and initial codes, emerging themes and final themes reviewed and refined with both Margaret M. Barry and Jane Sixsmith through a negotiated consensus process.

2.4. Ethical Considerations

The study was independently reviewed and approved by the Research Ethics Committee, National University of Ireland, Galway in May 2013. All participants were provided with written and oral details of study participation and provided with written informed consent to participate in the study. Emphasis was placed on the voluntary nature of study participation, with the removal of all identifiers and assurance that all information would be anonymised. Due to the nature of longitudinal research, consent should be viewed as a process rather than an initial act [41]. In this study consent was requested from each individual at each time point. The Participant Information Sheet specifically set out that all participation was voluntary and that s/he was free to opt out of the study at any point.

3. Results

The interviews yielded rich data relating to developments in participants' experiences of accessing, understanding, appraising and applying health information across various health contexts. Themes are set out in Table 4 and described in detail below. Themes are also linked to changes across the functional, interactive and critical domains of health literacy and highlighted below. Reference to the literature to support the changes across levels is also included where appropriate. Quotation labels are numbered by participant (P) and partner (PP) and also denote gender (M: Male; F: Female) and health literacy level (A: Adequate; L: Limited).

3.1. Re-Engagement with Health Information

Participants found it possible to re-engage with health information. This was attributed to *how* information was communicated, which was regarded as being central to facilitating developments across the health literacy capacities of accessing, understanding, appraising and applying health information. Involvement in the structured programme was perceived to be a positive experience overall for the participants. Despite the fact that the majority had been managing illness and/or risk factors for a number of years, individuals reported being able to find new ways of accessing, understanding, appraising and applying health information. This was particularly clear in relation to information pertaining to exercise, food and nutrition, and medication use. These findings are indicative of changes in functional health literacy whereby participants are increasing their ability to respond successfully to the communication of factual information on health risks [4,42].

Table 4. Overview of themes and corresponding changes in levels of health literacy.

Theme	Health Literacy (HL) Level	Subtheme	Categories
Re-engagement with health information	Changes in functional HL	Qualities of communicator Forum/methods	Engaging Supportive Multiple methods used
Increased understanding of risk and protective factors	Changes in functional HL		Food and nutrition Exercise Medication and treatments Side-effects of medication Cholesterol Blood Pressure
Changes in interactions with healthcare providers (HCP)	Changes in interactive HL	More at ease in communicating with the HCP Reinforcement/reassurances	Increased knowledge and therefore confidence
Enhanced psychological insights	Changes in critical HL	Increased insights of personal control limits and opportunities	Self-efficacy and confidence Dealing with stress
		Emotional issues Facilitators of motivation	Anxiety/fear Peer comparisons
Understanding the broader determinants of health changes in critical health literacy	Changes in critical HL	Sharing information Infrastructures to support health	Safe access—walkways, cycling Food manufacturing/culture Government lobbying

In terms of the health information provided, comparisons were made to the more traditional or 'boring sell' (PP4FA). Although the information itself was not necessarily new, participants felt that it was the way it was delivered (more personalised and tailored health communication) that impacted positively on their ability to take it on board:

> I would have read lots of stuff and you'd hear stuff on the radio about healthy eating and all the rest of it but by actually handing you the packet of cereal that you buy every week and saying if you really look at it; and so it was really, really pertinent to where we were at rather than saying you should eat more of this, eat more of that. (PP4FA)

Participants, who at phase one had a recent diagnosis or illness event, were able to reflect back on the experience during the phase 2 interview. One participant described how she was now able to access information and reassurance regarding her husband's stroke and recovery that had not been available to her in the hospital setting including the knowledge that it was safe to engage in exercise:

> So we got an awful lot of information the first day we came—where the stroke was—they said it was in the front part of his brain—we didn't know that from the hospital, you know. . . . they said it was alright for him to do it (exercise), which was more—do you know we never got that from the hospital really—they never told us like from once he came home. (PP23FL)

Participants found that being able to communicate with programme staff helped them to understand and appraise information compared to reading information by themselves:

> Because the books are great but then when you've somebody to talk you through it as well it's good. (P1FL)

Yes, I would, I'd find it easier alright now to kind of eliminate down and say well, yeah, now that is a thing that I really need to look into a bit more. (P5FL)

3.2. Increased Understanding of Risk and Protective Factors

There were reported changes and developments in terms of understanding and awareness, which also led to application, i.e., how information was used. This in turn was linked to developments in engagement with and management of illness and risk factors. This was particularly evident in relation to food and nutrition, managing blood pressure and cholesterol levels, exercise, medication and treatments plans. These findings are also linked to changes in functional health literacy whereby participants are increasing their ability to act on the communication of factual information on health risks [4,42].

3.2.1. Food and Nutrition

Although managing diet is a crucial component of treatment plans for cardiovascular disease, participants had limited previous knowledge of how to correctly read and understand food labels. This was a key aspect of new learning for participants that they were then able to apply to their everyday lives:

Like checking out labels and food products and what's in some of the regular everyday foods that we just take for granted and don't even give a second thought to. Maybe sweet foods or not foods that you'd imagine would have sugars and fats and stuff in them. (P5FL)

They have it down as sodium or they have it down as something else and you're like, these are all the hidden things like. Then like the sugar, the way they have it under syrup or corn syrup or under; it can be under different names, just little things. (P1FL)

3.2.2. Medication Use and Managing Side Effects

Although many participants were on long-term medication/treatment plans (such as medications for cholesterol and blood pressure), they were able to acquire new learning in relation to their use of medications as well as improved understanding regarding side effects:

Just that there are different medications for the blood pressure and you don't have to stop at one; sometimes they combine two different things that you need, like two different tablets. (P1FL)

This participant also reflected on how her childhood experiences had influenced her view on medication use, which, although entrenched, had now shifted towards a prevention first approach:

Like I think because my own mam and dad, they were on loads of medication so as kids it was like medication would fix you and I think since here it's like why not prevent it before you get to the stage of medication ... (P1FL)

Participants in phase 1 had spoken about concerns regarding possible side effects of certain medications or treatment plans. They were now able to reflect on new learning regarding the possible side effects of different medications and how these could be managed. For others, this reinforced their opposition to certain medications:

I opted not to take (a statin) because I had read things about it ... you know, I kind of feel I've gone from never taking anything to suddenly taking medication, you know ... Yeah, I am always aware that I have responsibility but I will listen to research but I will also ask the question because I do, you know. (P8FL)

Well I started off with having high cholesterol and it was 7 this time last year and we had that conversation about statins and I wouldn't go on them and I went on my broccoli and my kale and it's down now to, presently, to 5.5 so I'm happy the way it's going. If I can keep bringing it down now it'll be great. (P12FL)

Others had seen positive changes in their medication regimens:

I'm off a lot of tablets I used to be on—a lot of my diabetic tablets that I was on have been more than halved. (P13MA)

So it's great that way and that way you can pass it on hopefully because I don't have to take my blood pressure tablets any more. (P1FL)

3.3. Changes in Interactions with HCP

Participants reported perceived changes in how they interacted with their GP. Participants identified increased confidence due to improved understanding of their conditions and/or having the reassurance of programme feedback to support them in their interactions with their GP. These findings reflect changes in the interactive or communicative level of health literacy whereby participants' motivation and self-confidence to act on information was increased. One participant reported that she felt better able to communicate with her GP because she now has more knowledge about health issues such as blood pressure:

Just like when we were talking about blood pressure I was like, I know how it is. . . . Yeah, because I'd know more about it, I'd be able to say well this, that or the other. I'd be able to say no and isn't this that and he'd be like, yeah, I'd be more comfortable about it because then I'd know what I'm talking about. (P1FL)

Participants reported increased confidence in asking questions and felt that the credence of having attended a risk reduction programme supported their new found knowledge and helped in decision-making related to their treatment plans:

Probably because I'm not just dealing with my own GP, there are other influences and I can kind of, and other people that I've got contact with here and I suppose that can sort of say well this has been said and what do you think? That to me I think is important because you know sometimes you do feel you're at the mercy sometimes of, you know, if you're just dealing with one person. . . . . I mean, that was the good thing of this, I kind of feel now I've got more than one area to pull on. (P8FL)

I suppose the reinforcement by the people here from what my GP was saying, you know, when you're dealing with one person I was able to kind of say to him 'can you leave me another month?' But they were very definite here, 'oh you actually need your medications increased.' So it was reinforced in two places. It was very definite, and I kind of knew they were right, you know. (P21FL)

Participants also commented on the contrast between the busy GP practice and the access to staff on the programme particularly for emotional support:

GPs are very busy, you know, you have so many things when you go in I feel of the medical type . . . but really you are conscious that they are so busy and there is so many more waiting to come in, that, no, you know, I don't think it's a good place to sort out feelings. (P21FL)

Another participant acknowledged that her communication/interactions with GP were more relaxed as she was less anxious now regarding her health condition:

> I was probably more relaxed this time than I would have been normally and I probably wouldn't, I probably allowed my GP to just get on with the job herself as opposed to interrogating the poor woman ... and at the same time, for example, I suppose I would have been less anxious in many ways; that would be an indication of me being more willing to trust that things are probably alright but no harm to check things out. (P2FA)

3.4. Enhanced Psychological Insights

This theme refers to individuals' increased insight regarding personal control limits and opportunities and also encompassed the areas of self-efficacy, emotional issues and facilitators of motivation. Similar to the findings from interviews in phase one, this theme was important in terms of its impact on individuals' abilities to utilise their health literacy capacities to their fullest potential. Having the potential to fully engage with and use health information became more possible through gaining an increased understanding of their own situation. These findings also show that participants are becoming more empowered as they navigate illness and health management and are increasingly using of critical health literacy skills in attempting to control aspects of personal and social health determinants.

3.4.1. Perceptions of Control and Self-Efficacy

Participants were able to reflect on developments in terms of the control they felt over their situations. One participant reflected on earlier challenges:

> Everything was kind of against me. I remember at one of the meetings now alright and what they kind of said to me well at least like, you're not in a great place but at least if you're doing something about it, you know, you should feel that bit better in yourself. You're trying to improve some of the situation anyway. (P5FL)

This participant also made the comparison to what she was then able to achieve:

> Maybe with them telling you and explaining to you that I suppose every point you come down in something or every month you're doing something that it sort of helps you along the way. (P5FL)

Another participant reflected on the importance of developing a greater understanding of health issues and having the time or space to pay attention to them:

> You see, I suppose for myself, you know, when you're busy, you're working you don't, I just didn't think about my health, you know. I'm realising because I've had a lot go on in the last while, if I want to live healthily and I suppose now too when I'm retired; I think when you're working sometimes you don't have so much control but now that I've retired I think my attitude has changed. (P8FL)

Another participant reflected on the role of stress and learning how to deal with it to have more control over health issues:

> I let stress develop, it was like a cancer, it was eating away at me. So in the last few weeks I've started letting it go completely over my head, positive things have come out of it, you know. I'm totally relaxed, totally chilled out, which I wasn't, and maybe that's why my blood pressure was away, you know. (P13MA)

Some participants also demonstrated a more comprehensive understanding of their situations and the factors that determine their health:

I can control my amount of exercise and diet, certain things you can control, but there are certain things you can't in life. You know like your situation. Or if you wanted to go and live somewhere else, or live alone, or not having the stress of this that or the other, then there is some things you can't control, you know, financially and that kind of thing. (P21FL)

Developments in self-efficacy linked to exercise performance were also apparent. This was most evident for participants with mobility and illness concerns in phase 1. These participants felt reassured that exercise was both safe and possible:

I never was in a gym, I never used a gym before, or exercised with other people, or that kind of thing—I never realised how good you can feel after! I didn't know that! I feel a bit braver. It made me feel, you know, that I could do it, and it's nice to exercise. (P21FL)

I feel that I have enough information about my illness, my sickness, I wouldn't call it an illness either, but my health, that I feel I'm in safe hands. And if I reduced my chances of getting a stroke by 20 percent in 12 weeks, what can I do in another [12 weeks]? Like, they wanted to get my blood, my heartbeat up to a certain thing, and they've done that. (P20FA)

3.4.2. Anxiety and Fears

While participants had previously referred to the impact of anxiety on dealing with illness, they were now able to reflect on how these fears had been assuaged.

One participant spoke about her fears following her husband's stroke and how this impacted her sense of control:

How do I put it? Like when the stroke came I didn't know what I knew anymore, or what, because he was such an unlikely candidate of getting a stroke. (PP23FL)

Participants also reflected on overcoming fears about illness:

So I just, I think I have a kind of a, I feel more confident that I'm not as bad as I thought I was, and that I know like that I can live a good life. I can look forward, I look forward now like to a better kind of a life for myself. (P20FA)

The symptoms that I presented with, were sort of symptoms that would be relevant to a mini stroke. And that sort of made me afraid. That if I take a long journey in the car or should, should I do this, should I do that, will I get more symptoms, will I get a stroke? That, it knocked my confidence. (P15FA)

This participant was now able to reflect with a more positive outlook, which she attributed to staff reassurance:

And they were all (saying) you know that might never happen again and your blood pressure is being monitored and your heart checks and cholesterol and diet ... it takes a while to readjust ... I'm smiling now and all that, but it did throw me ... But I've come out the other end now and I'm ok. (P15FA)

One participant with heart failure reflected on the fact that she was less fearful about taking part in activities:

And doing a bit more. But I'm not as nervous now about, say, taking off and doing more things by myself. Just up to the gym and keep doing it, and I knew that I could then, you know. (P21FL)

3.5. Understanding of Broader Determinants of Health

Participants demonstrated an increased ability to reflect on external factors that can impact on health. These were related to physical contexts, such as walkability issues and access to cycle lanes; health and public policies, e.g., in relation to childhood obesity, affordability of medicines; and legislation in relation to food labelling standards. These findings can also be related to changes in critical health literacy, as participants are critically analysing health information and using this in an attempt to exert greater control over personal and social health determinants [4,42].

3.5.1. Physical Contexts

Walking—Access and Road Safety Issues

Similar to the phase one findings, rural-dwelling participants were most critical of the lack of safe places to walk:

> Just somewhere for people to be able to go out walking that's safe, just a little footpath just for maybe three miles say and then everybody can go, because like it's there, it's safe. Women can bring their buggies, kids can go on bikes. (P1FL)

This participant went on to make a comparison between two different areas and the impact of having safe walkways:

> So like there's loads of walkways and people are more motivated up there. You look out the window, every three seconds there's somebody walking by; always movement, people are running or cycling or something but back in our place all you see is cars. It's a different place ... It would be great for everywhere because I know, say cities have it all but out in the country there's really nothing. (P1FL)

Similarly, from another participant:

> Paths would make lives better for people, a lot easier. So if you were walking with a child in a pram you just couldn't do it you know. And I mean an elderly person, my mother has one of those wheelers, she can't walk. Those little things would make life a lot easier you know. (P8FL)

Others, living in more urban areas appreciated access to scenic walkways and green spaces and not having to rely on a car:

> But the effort of getting into a car and driving, you just won't do that, whereas where we are we don't have that excuse. We do not need to get into the car to go to somewhere specific to do exercise. (P4FA)

> I actually love where I live, in that I'm beside a big green, I'm beside a big park, so I can walk, in five minutes from my house I can walk in a big field, and it's half a mile we'll say one way and the other, I can have a half mile to a mile walk. And that really is important to me. Or I can go down to a beach. And that is really a lifeline for me, being able to live where I'm living. So I think that really has an impact on your health, if you have somewhere nice to walk, I think, it's really important. (P21FL)

Cycling

Participants who regularly cycled commented on the lack of a completed cycling infrastructure, which impacted on safety:

> Once you go outside the city area back on the country roads like I'd be nervous enough now cycling. It would make it safer. Because you are taking your life in your hands if you get up on a bike ... the traffic is too busy. So from that point of view I would like to see something being done. (P16ML)

Food Culture/Food Manufacturing

A key learning in relation to food and nutrition was reading and understanding food labels, which led to reflection on broader issues such as the regulation of food labelling:

> I think they'd want to get that system brought in for all food manufacturers. But there would be too much opposition from the ones who have the bad food. So there's a stalemate there. So it's up to the government to bring it in by law and that's the only way it can happen. If they bring it in by law then they're compelled to put that red label on and put their product, whether it's red, amber or green. (P3ML)

Another participant commented on the role of policy with regard to childhood obesity.

> I would be very bothered about this new idea in the schools that they've a 'no running' policy now in 1 in 20 schools in the country. I think that's where it needs to start with the health. Now I know they do some of these sports things and that, but there should be an awful lot more. They're talking about having a sugar tax but then on the soft drinks and that but I think there should be a tax like cigarettes, you know, because it's ridiculous. (PP4FA)

Role of Government

One participant had taken part in a lobbying exercise to get the government to consider the provision of a medical card (free primary care access) for people with certain chronic diseases:

> So I sent that in and wrote all my own views on it and the list of complaints that I have, all the heart problems I have, the liver and so on. And then the list of all the drugs I have. In other words I pay the maximum of, it's over 1700 a year even with the allowance the government make, that's what it works out at. And I'm retired so you know I'd appreciate it if the government were to do that; give me a medical card for the drugs. So that's the one way I can appeal to the government. (P3ML)

Another commented on a lack of long-term health promotion planning at government level.

> And the other thing is that they're putting in a whole load of wind farms, which is fine and I'm in favour of wind farms and alternative energy, but our carbon footprint would go way down if we actually cycled in the places that we can cycle. So I think there's very little joined-up thinking in terms of health promotion. (P2FA)

Sharing Information

Some participants were actively sharing health information with extended family/friends and some were actively trying to change the health practices of others:

> So there's little bits here and there, even just me in the class here; I'm passing it along because there's 13 of us so I'm passing it on to them and their wives and their kids. So there's a whole bundle of people out there that's getting the information as well. Even the booklets that I get here I pass them on there and they're all reading them. Some things they might change, some they mightn't. You know that they are trying themselves as well because like a few of us started doing a few changes and you see them doing it as well; even like there's a few of my brothers and they've given up salt altogether. (P1FL)

> I do especially say to immediate family. I did, I spoke to my niece about it, I spoke to my sister. I'm very much a kind of pass it on, I think that's important. The more people who know, you know ... Passing it on, kind of giving people, say my sister, both sisters actually and also my sister's partner because he had a stent put in; I suppose I rang him then just this week and said are you aware that you really should have a blood test on a regular basis; well he was but he hadn't, so that kind of thing. (P8FL)

Participants recognised that dietary changes would also have a positive impact on other family members such as children and grandchildren.

> I've a young lad there, he's seven, he comes in [saying,] 'Granddad, I'm starving.' I say, 'go to the fridge there and get something for yourself.' And he'll pick the fruit and he'll eat it, whereas if it wasn't there he'd be looking for Tayto (crisps) or something like that. (P16ML)

> But there isn't as much around for them [grandchildren], there's no biscuits around or anything like that. Yeah. And I thought first that we'd try it—I thought it wouldn't last—but now it's nearly normal, do you know, that we don't have it. (PP23FL)

4. Discussion

The overall aim of this study was to explore developments in the use of health literacy skills for individuals in the context of managing risk factors for CVD. The findings are consistent with an approach that goes beyond the functional aspects of health literacy to capture broader social contexts [43]. The findings have generated important insights into factors that support developments for health literacy capacities and indicate that individuals with varying levels of health literacy can engage with self-management. Findings support the development of health literacy capacities across the functional, interactive and critical health literacy domains and engagement with health knowledge that goes beyond personal health management to the social determinants of health [5,42].

Although many participants had been managing risk factors and/or conditions for some time, they found that it was possible to re-engage with information that was presented in a very practical and relevant format and tailored to them. In terms of managing lifestyle factors associated with illnesses such as diabetes, CVD and stroke, having an understanding of the importance of good nutrition and diet is crucial, as well as the ability to apply that information [44]. Participants learnt how to read and interpret food labels and were able to apply this information to their everyday lives. This allows for a greater sense of control over self-care behaviours and participants, therefore, experienced changes in how they perceived control and self-efficacy in relation to managing their risk factors. These findings indicate that participants are becoming more empowered and support the conceptualisation of health literacy as an instrument in the empowerment process [45]. Other studies [46] have examined specifically the role of self-efficacy and health literacy in improving health outcomes and also advocate the need for self-management programmes to promote the development of self-efficacy. Numerous studies have postulated the links between self-efficacy, health literacy and self-care behaviours [8,47,48]. Work by Lee et al. [48] suggests that studies focusing only on the functional aspects of health literacy may not reflect the relevance of self-efficacy. Therefore, interventions need to also focus on the communicative and critical aspects of health literacy [7,48,49]. A recently developed health literacy communication training for healthcare professionals has also emphasised the inclusion of skills to enhance both interactive (shared decision-making) and critical health (enabling self-management) skills of healthcare providers [50]. Participants in this study described health literacy experiences that incorporate aspects of both communicative/interactive health literacy (i.e., the ability to extract meaning from different sources of information and share the information) and critical health literacy experiences (i.e., the ability to critically analyse information and apply it to decision-making process). Findings in the current study indicate that participants also experienced enhanced self-efficacy in managing their health regardless of their level of health literacy at the start of programme (i.e., whether adequate or limited). This is an important finding as it may indicate that persons with limited health literacy can engage well on structured programmes and develop their health literacy at all levels as a result.

Similar to findings from the Skilled for Health study [51], there was evidence that participants where actively 'cascading' or sharing their newly acquired information with their family and wider community. Edwards, Wood, Davies and Edwards, [52] in their study used the term *health literacy mediators* to describe individuals who passed on their health literacy skills. This is linked to distributed health literacy though in this instance it is about supporting others to become more health literate (rather than being supported).

Findings in relation to anxiety provide further support of findings from time point 1 [22], which highlighted the impact of illness-related anxiety and fears on the ability to fully utilise health literacy capacities. In the current study, participants reported how their concerns had been alleviated and they were thus able to engage with and utilise health information more effectively. This concurs with work by Dunn, Margaritis and Anderson [13], which emphasised the role of the HCP in the provision of social support and reduction of anxiety for patients with CVD. Further, they also point out that patients are then in a better position to be able to take on board and have a better understanding of their condition. Morgan et al. [53] also stress the need for self-management support to include the broader contexts of an individual's life so that management is not constrained within a narrow disease control approach [53]. Findings in this study support a view of participants, not as a patients but as active participants in their own health management, and more akin to being 'citizens in relation to the health promotion efforts in the community, the work place, the educational system, the political arena and the market place' [5] (p. 13).

Participants in this study participated in a community-based risk reduction programme, which provided them with the opportunity to make comparisons between typical healthcare encounters and those at the programme. There were many positives associated with how information was imparted; the group effect ('collective efficacy' as described by Bandura [54]), the accessibility and approachability of the staff; the time of staff; emotional support; social support; motivation etc. All of these factors would seem to be conducive to promoting effective self-management [53]. The programme also offered the opportunity to become more familiar with medication regimens and treatment plans including being aware of when and why changes to these were made. Overall, participants noted positive developments in their interactions with HCPs. These were attributed to having increased knowledge and understanding of one's condition as well as a sense of increased confidence regarding communication with the HCP.

All participants reported having acquired increased understanding of issues relevant to their self-care. Findings indicated that participants had a new level of engagement with the issues as they often were exposed to a new perspective or information presented in a new way.

One of the most important findings was in relation to participants' understanding of medications and side effects. It was noteworthy that participants continued to question the use of statins and continued to favour lifestyle approaches (where benefits seen). This understanding can be attributed to a combination of knowledge acquired both through the programme and through their own information-seeking.

An important finding in the current study is the engagement of participants with broader issues that can impact on health and the contextualisation of health issues. In terms of health literacy this is a shift towards critical health literacy whereby individuals start to address the demands and complexities of their social contexts [12]. These findings compare favourably to those reported by Rowlands et al. [16] where social determinants, social activity and the local community were viewed to influence the translation of knowledge into health behaviours. Participants were able to reflect on how physical and structural factors can directly affect one's health and wellbeing. Participants' responses also indicated that they are capable of locating responsibility (for health) beyond the individual level [55] and are making sense of knowledge within their own 'social space' [43] within their own family and community environments. This indicates that developments in health literacy have moved beyond the acquisition of knowledge to also use health literacy capacities as a resource for engaging in health at the community level [43,55]. The community-based programme offers the potential to develop critical health literacy and lends support to community-based programmes for the management of chronic illness. The potential to develop critical health literacy capacities is important. Beginning with having an increased insight into the limits and opportunities of one's personal control, it is evident that there is potential to develop this further as an important element of self-management. Future research could build on the value of the qualitative longitudinal approach and incorporate more of a participative methodology whereby individuals could map and elucidate the facilitators and barriers in the empowerment process as health issues are managed. It would also be useful to examine this approach with individuals outside of access to a structured programme so that comparisons between organisation/system demands on health literacy could be made.

4.1. Strengths

A strength of the current study is the qualitative perspective, which allows for a more in-depth examination of the development of health literacy capacities from the perspective of individual study participants. The longitudinal aspect of this study also allows us to identify the types of factors that can contribute to the positive development of health literacy for individuals over time. It is also possible to see that developments occurred regardless of initial health literacy levels. It is important that these developments are explored outside of the clinical encounter so that aspects of social and community contexts, where health and illness management and health promotion activities frequently occur, are also addressed.

4.2. Limitations

The relatively small sample and the attrition of study participants from phase 1 to phase 2 is an important study limitation. Attrition is a frequently reported issue in longitudinal studies, which in the case of this study resulted mainly from the illness experiences of participants and limited programme engagement in a small number of cases.

Only preliminary analysis was possible between interviews at time one and the completion of time 2 interviews due to time constraints and resource limitations. However, the keeping of memos and field notes following all interviews assisted in the overall analysis process. This study is focussed on a specific population sample who attended a risk reduction programme. It is possible that some of the positive effects in relation to the development of health literacy capacities evident at the completion of phase 2 are due in part to the effects of programme participation. The fact that participants had just completed the 12-week programme is likely to have influenced their perceptions regarding positive outcomes.

5. Conclusions

Study findings demonstrate that, overall, participants have become more empowered in managing their health and self-care. Developments in terms of perceived confidence and self-efficacy were apparent, which in turn impacted on positive relations with HCPs. Crucially participants have also demonstrated an increased ability to critically reflect on social and environmental issues that can support or impede their health opportunities. These findings support the idea that health literacy should be regarded as context and content specific and that critical health literacy can be achieved in the absence of high functional health literacy skills [56,57]. Findings also demonstrated that individuals have the capacity to acquire new insights and perspectives in managing health issues, even where the illness is not new. This can mitigate against resignation regarding long-term treatment plans and the promotion of their own health in a more active manner.

Author Contributions: V.B.M. conceived the study design, collected and analysed the data, and wrote the paper. M.M.B. and J.S. also contributed to study design, data analysis, and review of the paper.

Acknowledgments: An NUI Galway grant was used to support the open access publishing costs. The authors wish to thank the study participants and the staff of the community based organisation for their support in making the study possible. All views expressed in this article are those of the authors only and do not necessarily represent the views of NUI Galway, Ireland or any other organisation.

Conflicts of Interest: The authors declare no conflict of interest

Appendix A Interview Guide

1. How would you describe your experience of taking part in the programme (a structured CVD risk reduction and health promotion course)?
2. Can you tell me about how you have been getting information about your health/health issues in general since we last met?
3. How has your understanding changed in relation to your own health situation/relation to health issues in general?
4. Have you learnt anything that makes it easier to make judgements on what information is useful and what is not? How have you done this?
5. Tell me about how you have used any information from the course? What has helped/hindered this process?
6. Can you tell me about your understanding of health and well-being issues in general?
7. If it were possible to make any changes in your own neighbourhood, what might you do to make it more health promoting for yourself/your community?
8. Can you tell me what changes you see or feel in yourself as a result of participating in the programme?

References

1. World Health Organisation. *The Shanghai Declaration on Promoting Health in the 2030 Agenda for Sustainable Development*; World Health Organisation: Geneva, Switzerland, 2016.
2. Sorensen, K.; Pelikan, J.M.; Rothlin, F.; Ganahl, K.; Slonska, Z.; Doyle, G.; Fullam, J.; Kondilis, B.; Agrafiotis, D.; Uiters, E.; et al. Health literacy in Europe: Comparative results of the European health literacy survey (HLS-EU). *Eur. J. Public Health* **2015**, *25*, 1053–1058. [CrossRef] [PubMed]
3. Nutbeam, D. Health promotion glossary. *Health Promot. Int.* **1998**, *13*, 349–364. [CrossRef]
4. Nutbeam, D. The evolving concept of health literacy. *Soc. Sci. Med.* **2008**, *67*, 2072–2078. [CrossRef] [PubMed]
5. Sørensen, K.; Van Den Broucke, S.; Fullam, J.; Doyle, G.; Pelikan, J.; Slonska, Z.; Brand, H. Health literacy and public health: A systematic review and integration of definitions and models. *BMC Public Health* **2012**, *12*, 80. [CrossRef] [PubMed]
6. Institute of Medicine. *Health Literacy: A Prescription to End Confusion*; National Academies Press: Washington, DC, USA, 2004.
7. Ishikawa, H.; Yano, E. Patient health literacy and participation in the health-care process. *Health Expect.* **2008**, *11*, 113–122. [CrossRef] [PubMed]
8. Paasche-Orlow, M.K.; Wolf, M.S. The causal pathways linking health literacy to health outcomes. *Am. J. Health Behav.* **2007**, *31*, 19–26. [CrossRef]
9. Baker, D. The meaning and the measure of health literacy. *J. Gen. Intern. Med.* **2006**, *21*, 878–883. [CrossRef] [PubMed]
10. Rudd, R.E. Needed action in health literacy. *J. Health Psychol.* **2013**, *18*, 1004–1010. [CrossRef] [PubMed]
11. Rudd, R.E. The evolving concept of health literacy: New directions for health literacy studies. *J. Commun. Healthc.* **2015**, *8*, 7–9. [CrossRef]
12. De Wit, L.; Fenenga, C.; Giammarchi, C.; di Furia, L.; Hutter, I.; de Winter, A.; Meijering, L. Community-based initiatives improving critical health literacy: A systematic review and meta-synthesis of qualitative evidence. *BMC Public Health* **2017**, *18*, 40. [CrossRef] [PubMed]
13. Dunn, P.; Margaritis, V.; Anderson, C.L. Understanding health literacy skills in patients with cardiovascular disease and diabetes. *Qual. Rep.* **2017**, *22*, 33–46.
14. Edwards, M.; Wood, F.; Davies, M.; Edwards, A. The development of health literacy in patients with a long-term health condition: The health literacy pathway model. *BMC Public Health* **2012**, *12*, 130. [CrossRef] [PubMed]
15. Freedman, D.; Bess, K.; Tucker, H.; Boyd, D.; Tuchman, A.; Wallston, K. Public health literacy defined. *Am. J. Prev. Med.* **2009**, *36*, 446–451. [CrossRef] [PubMed]

16. Rowlands, G.; Shaw, A.; Jaswal, S.; Smith, S.; Harpham, T. Health literacy and the social determinants of health: A qualitative model from adult learners. *Health Promot. Int.* **2017**, *32*, 130–138. [CrossRef] [PubMed]
17. Muscat, D.M.; Morony, S.; Smith, S.K.; Shepherd, H.L.; Dhillon, H.M.; Hayen, A.; Trevena, L.; Luxford, K.; Nutbeam, D.; McCaffery, K.J. Qualitative insights into the experience of teaching shared decision making within adult education health literacy programmes for lower-literacy learners. *Health Expect.* **2017**, *20*, 1393–1400. [CrossRef] [PubMed]
18. Muscat, D.M.; Smith, S.; Dhillon, H.M.; Morony, S.; Davis, E.L.; Luxford, K.; Shepherd, H.L.; Hayen, A.; Comings, J.; Nutbeam, D.; et al. Incorporating health literacy in education for socially disadvantaged adults: An Australian feasibility study. *Int. J. Equity Health* **2016**, *15*, 84. [CrossRef] [PubMed]
19. Mancuso, J.M. Impact of health literacy and patient trust on glycemic control in an urban USA population. *Nurs. Health Sci.* **2010**, *12*, 94–104. [CrossRef] [PubMed]
20. Centers for Disease Control and Prevention. What is Health Literacy? 2016. Available online: https://www.cdc.gov/healthliteracy/learn/index.html (accessed on 15 December 2017).
21. HLS-EU Consortium. *Comparative Report of Health Literacy in Eight EU Member States*; The European Health Literacy Survey; HLS-EU; HLS-EU Consortium: Maastricht, The Netherlands, 2012.
22. McKenna, V.B.; Sixsmith, J.; Barry, M.M. The relevance of context in understanding health literacy skills: Findings from a qualitative study. *Health Expect.* **2017**, *20*, 1049–1060. [CrossRef] [PubMed]
23. Creswell, J. *Qualitative Inquiry & Research Design: Choosing Among Five Approaches*; SAGE: Los Angeles, CA, USA, 2013.
24. Gibson, I.; Flaherty, G.; Cormican, S.; Jone, J.; Keirns, C.; Walsh, A.M.; Costelleo, C.; Windle, J.; Connolly, S.; Crowley, J. Translating guidelines to practice: Findings from a multidisciplinary preventive cardiology programme in the west of Ireland. *Eur. J. Prev. Cardiol.* **2014**, *21*, 366–376. [CrossRef] [PubMed]
25. Connolly, S.; Holden, A.; Turner, E.; Fiumicelli, G.; Stevenson, J.; Hunjan, M.; Mead, A.; Kotseva, K.; Jennings, C.S.; Jones, J.; et al. MyAction: An innovative approach to the prevention of cardiovascular disease in the community. *Br. J. Cardiol.* **2011**, *18*, 171–176.
26. Doyle, G.; Cafferkey, K.; Fullam, J. *The European Health Literacy Survey: Results from Ireland*; UCD: Dublin, Ireland, 2012.
27. Central Statistics Office. *This Is Ireland: Highlights from Census 2011, Part 2*; Stationary Office: Dublin, Ireland, 2012.
28. Health Service Executive. Medical Cards. Available online: https://www.hse.ie/eng/cards-schemes/medical-card/ (accessed on 16 January 2018).
29. Department of Public Expenditure and Reform. *General Medical Services Scheme*; Irish Government Economic and Evaluation Service: Dublin, Ireland, 2016.
30. Murray, S.A.; Kendall, M.; Carduff, E.; Worth, A.; Harris, F.M.; Lloyd, A.; Cavers, D.; Grant, L.; Sheikh, A. Use of serial qualitative interviews to understand patients' evolving experiences and needs. *BMJ* **2009**, *339*, b3702. [CrossRef] [PubMed]
31. Hermanowicz, J.C. The longitudinal qualitative interview. *Qual. Sociol.* **2013**, *36*, 189–208. [CrossRef]
32. Calman, L.; Brunton, L.; Molassiotis, A. Developing longitudinal qualitative designs: Lessons learned and recommendations for health services research. *BMC Med. Res. Methodol.* **2013**, *13*, 14. [CrossRef] [PubMed]
33. Saldana, J. *Longitudinal Qualitative Research: Analyzing Change through Time*; AltaMira Press: Walnut Creek, CA, USA, 2003.
34. Guba, E.G. Criteria for assessing trustworthiness of naturalistic inquiries. *Educ. Commun. Technol. A J. Theory Res. Dev.* **1981**, *29*, 75–91.
35. Maxwell, J.A. Understanding and validity in qualitative research. *Harvard Educ. Rev.* **1992**, *62*, 279–300. [CrossRef]
36. Creswell, J.W.; Miller, D.L. Determining validity in qualitative inquiry. *Theory Pract.* **2000**, *39*, 124–130. [CrossRef]
37. Braun, V.; Clarke, V. Using thematic analysis in psychology. *Qual. Res. Psychol.* **2006**, *3*, 77–101. [CrossRef]
38. Carduff, E.; Murray, S.A.; Kendall, M. Methodological developments in qualitative longitudinal research: The advantages and challenges of regular telephone contact with participants in a qualitative longitudinal interview study. *BMC Res. Notes* **2015**, *8*, 142. [CrossRef] [PubMed]
39. Neale, B.; Flowerdew, J. Time, texture and childhood: The contours of longitudinal qualitative research. *Int. J. Soc. Res. Methodol.* **2003**, *6*, 189–199. [CrossRef]

40. Bowman, M.A.; Neale, A.V. Exciting research studies on practical medical problems and health services delivery. *J. Am. Board Fam. Med.* **2011**, *24*, 221–223. [CrossRef] [PubMed]
41. France, A.; Bendelow, G.; Williams, S. A "risky" business: Researching the health beliefs of children and young people. In *Researching Children's Perspectives*; Lewis, A., Lindsay, G., Eds.; Open University Press: Buckingham, UK, 2000; pp. 151–162.
42. Nutbeam, D. Health literacy as a public health goal: A challenge for contemporary health education and communication strategies into the 21st century. *Health Promot. Int.* **2000**, *15*, 259–267. [CrossRef]
43. Renwick, K. Critical health literacy in 3D. *Front. Educ.* **2017**, *2*, 40. [CrossRef]
44. Meyer, S.B.; Coveney, J.; Ward, P.R. A qualitative study of CVD management and dietary changes: Problems of 'too much' and 'contradictory' information. *BMC Fam. Pract.* **2014**, *15*, 25. [CrossRef] [PubMed]
45. Crondahl, K.; Eklund Karlsson, L. The nexus between health literacy and empowerment: A scoping review. *SAGE Open* **2016**, *6*. [CrossRef]
46. Huynh-Hohnbaum, A.-L.T.; Marshall, L.; Villa, V.M.; Lee, G. Self-management of heart disease in older adults. *Home Health Care Serv. Q.* **2015**, *34*, 159–172. [CrossRef] [PubMed]
47. Osborn, C.Y.; Paasche-Orlow, M.K.; Bailey, S.C.; Wolf, M.S. The mechanisms linking health literacy to behavior and health status. *Am. J. Health Behav.* **2011**, *35*, 118–128. [CrossRef] [PubMed]
48. Lee, Y.-J.; Shin, S.-J.; Wang, R.-H.; Lin, K.-D.; Lee, Y.-L.; Wang, Y.-H. Pathways of empowerment perceptions, health literacy, self-efficacy, and self-care behaviors to glycemic control in patients with type 2 diabetes mellitus. *Patient Educ. Couns.* **2016**, *99*, 287–294. [CrossRef] [PubMed]
49. Inoue, M.; Takahashi, M.; Kai, I. Impact of communicative and critical health literacy on understanding of diabetes care and self-efficacy in diabetes management: A cross-sectional study of primary care in Japan. *BMC Fam. Pract.* **2013**, *14*, 40. [CrossRef] [PubMed]
50. Kaper, M.S.; Sixsmith, J.; Koot, J.A.R.; Meijering, L.B.; van Twillert, S.; Giammarchi, C.; Bevilacqua, R.; Barry, M.M.; Doyle, P.; Reijneveld, S.A.; et al. Developing and pilot testing a comprehensive health literacy communication training for health professionals in three European countries. *Patient Educ. Couns.* **2018**, *101*, 152–158. [CrossRef] [PubMed]
51. The Tavistock Institute. *Evaluation of the Second Phase of the Skilled for Health Programme*; The Tavistock Institute: London, UK, 2008; Available online: http://www.tavinstitute.org/projects/evaluation-of-phase-two-skilled-for-health/ (accessed on 1 August 2017).
52. Edwards, M.; Wood, F.; Davies, M.; Edwards, A. 'Distributed health literacy': Longitudinal qualitative analysis of the roles of health literacy mediators and social networks of people living with a long-term health condition. *Health Expect.* **2013**, *18*, 1180–1193. [CrossRef] [PubMed]
53. Morgan, H.M.; Entwistle, V.A.; Cribb, A.; Christmas, S.; Owens, J.; Skea, Z.C.; Watt, I.S. We need to talk about purpose: A critical interpretive synthesis of health and social care professionals' approaches to self-management support for people with long-term conditions. *Health Expect.* **2016**, *20*, 243–259. [CrossRef] [PubMed]
54. Bandura, A. Exercise of human agency through collective efficacy. *Curr. Dir. Psychol. Sci.* **2000**, *9*, 75–78. [CrossRef]
55. Sykes, S.; Wills, J.; Rowlands, G.; Popple, K. Understanding critical health literacy: A concept analysis. *BMC Public Health* **2013**, *13*, 150. [CrossRef] [PubMed]
56. Smith, S.K.; Nutbeam, D.; McCaffery, K.J. Insights into the concept and measurement of health literacy from a study of shared decision-making in a low literacy population. *J. Health Psychol.* **2013**, *18*, 1011–1022. [CrossRef] [PubMed]
57. Chinn, D. Critical health literacy: A review and critical analysis. *Soc. Sci. Med.* **2011**, *73*, 60–67. [CrossRef] [PubMed]

 © 2018 by the authors. Licensee MDPI, Basel, Switzerland. This article is an open access article distributed under the terms and conditions of the Creative Commons Attribution (CC BY) license (http://creativecommons.org/licenses/by/4.0/).

Article

Effects of the Conceptual Model of Health Literacy as a Risk: A Randomised Controlled Trial in a Clinical Dental Context

Linda Stein [1,*], Maud Bergdahl [1], Kjell Sverre Pettersen [2] and Jan Bergdahl [1,3]

[1] Department of Clinical Dentistry, Faculty of Health Sciences, UiT—The Arctic University of Norway, 9019 Tromsø, Norway; maud@jmbergdahl.se (M.B.); janl@jmbergdahl.se (J.B.)
[2] Department of Nursing and Health Promotion, Faculty of Health Sciences, OsloMet—Oslo Metropolitan University, 0130 Oslo, Norway; spetters@oslomet.no
[3] Department of Psychology, Umeå University, 901 87 Umeå, Sweden
* Correspondence: linda.stein@uit.no; Tel.: +47-776-49-142

Received: 2 July 2018; Accepted: 31 July 2018; Published: 1 August 2018

Abstract: Numerous conceptual models of health literacy have been proposed in the literature, but very few have been empirically validated in clinical contexts. The aim of this study was to test the effects of the conceptual model of health literacy as a risk in a clinical dental context. A convenience sample of 133 Norwegian-speaking adults was recruited. Participants were randomly allocated to an intervention group ($n = 64$, 54% women, mean age = 50 years) and a control group ($n = 69$, 49% women, mean age = 46 years). Clinical measurements were conducted pre-intervention and six months post-intervention. In the intervention group, communication regarding patients' oral health was tailored to their health literacy levels using recommended communication techniques, whereas the control group received brief information not tailored to health literacy levels. The ANCOVA showed significant between-group effects, finding reduced post-intervention mean gingival ($p < 0.000$) and mean plaque ($p < 0.000$) indices in the intervention group when controlling for baseline index scores. The adjusted Cohen's d indicated large effect sizes between the intervention group and the control group for both the mean gingival index (-0.98) and the mean plaque index (-1.33). In conclusion, the conceptual model of health literacy as a risk had a large effect on important clinical outcomes, such as gingival status and oral hygiene. The model may be regarded as a suitable supplement to patient education in populations.

Keywords: health literacy; patient education; dentistry; oral health; RCT

1. Introduction

Oral diseases remain a burden, despite great improvements in oral health in recent decades. Dental caries, or tooth decay due to acid-producing oral bacteria, is one of the most common preventable chronic diseases worldwide, and people are susceptible to it beginning in childhood and continuing throughout their lifetime [1]. Dental caries affects 60 to 90% of school-aged children and the vast majority of adults and accounts for oral pain, tooth loss and large expenses for both individuals and society [2]. Gingivitis, or inflammation of the gums, affects 50 to 90% of adults worldwide, depending on the precise definition considered [3]. Left untreated, gingivitis may progress to periodontitis, an inflammation below the gums and along the roots of the teeth, causing destruction of the teeth's supporting ligaments and bone [4]. This process ultimately leads to a loosening of the teeth and potential tooth loss. Both dental caries and gingivitis are initially preventable and reversible diseases and can be halted at any stage if the bacterial biofilm covering the tooth surface, the dental plaque, is removed [3,4]. Adequate daily oral hygiene routines are important to prevent these common diseases and improve clinical status. However, this requires rather specialised skills, as well as an understanding of oral health information. In short, it requires health literacy.

Literacy and its association with health have recently gained increased attention. The WHO considers literacy to be one of the strongest predictors of health, along with age, income, employment status, education level and race or ethnic group [5]. The prevalence of limited health literacy is high, even in economically developed countries. In Europe, the European Health Literacy Project (HLS-EU) recently reported limited health literacy among 47% of respondents in its international survey [6]. Systematic reviews found that limited health literacy is associated with poor health outcomes across different diseases, greater difficulty participating in shared decision-making, less understanding regarding the importance of preventive behaviour and poorer self-management of disease [7,8].

Oral health literacy is defined as the degree to which individuals have the capacity to obtain, process and understand basic oral health information and services needed to make appropriate health decisions [9]. Importantly, oral health literacy has been identified as a potential barrier to effective disease prevention, diagnosis and treatment [10]. The burden of limited health literacy in different health contexts is considered enormous, and the potential to reduce poor outcomes through intervention has been emphasised [11]. The literature has presented numerous conceptual models of health literacy, though very few have been empirically validated [12]. The central tenet is that identifying low levels of health literacy will foster the implementation of tailored interventions to improve health outcomes [7,13]. In a paper on the evolving concept of health literacy, Nutbeam presented two conceptual models inspired by several previously developed models [13]. One of the models positions health literacy as a risk factor that needs to be identified and appropriately managed in clinical care, while the other positions health literacy as an asset to be built and an outcome to health education. To the best of our knowledge, no clinical trial has yet been published assessing the effects of the risk model on clinical outcomes, such as gingival status or oral hygiene. Thus, the objective of this study was to test the effects of the conceptual model of health literacy as a risk in a clinical dental setting. Based on the model, we hypothesised that patients provided with communication sensitive to oral health literacy would improve their gingival status and oral hygiene.

2. Materials and Methods

2.1. Study Design

The study was designed as a randomised, examiner- and participant-blinded, controlled clinical trial. Clinical oral health measurements to assess oral hygiene and gingival health were conducted pre-intervention and six months post-intervention. To be eligible for inclusion, participants had to be older than 20 years, have no severe visual impairments, and have mastery of the Norwegian language. Participants were recruited from a list of adults who had volunteered to be enrolled as dental students' patients at the University Dental Clinic, but had not yet been diagnosed or started any form of dental treatment. Due to the large age differences among eligible individuals, a stratified randomisation was considered necessary to balance the control and intervention groups with respect to age. Pair matching across groups was performed using gender and an age range of five years. The allocation was concealed by having a person who had no information regarding the participants' oral health and was not a member of the research team perform the randomisation procedure. To detect medium-size effects (Cohen's d = 0.5) with a power of 0.80 (α = 0.05, two-tailed), an a priori sample size power calculation was conducted using the software G*Power 3 [14] (Institut für Experimentelle Psychologie, Dusseldorf, Germany). The calculation indicated that a sample size of 64 participants per group was required. We followed the CONSORT guidelines to properly design, conduct and report the clinical trial. The study was registered in the international online database clinicaltrials.gov (ID: NCT 01118143). Ethical approval was granted by the Regional Ethical Committee for Medical and Health Research, Tromsø, Norway (2010/31-11), and the study was conducted in accordance with the World Medical Association Declaration of Helsinki.

2.2. Trial Procedure

Individuals who returned signed consent forms by mail after receiving written information about and invitations to participate in the study were invited to the dental clinic at the Public Dental Service Competence Centre of Northern Norway, Tromsø, Norway, for study participation. As inadequate comprehension of informed consent is common among study participants [15], the study information was repeated orally, and efforts were made to make sure the participants understood both the advantages and disadvantages of the study, that participation was voluntary and that their decision would not affect their future care at the University Dental Clinic [16]. Participants were allocated to either the intervention or the control group prior to the pre-intervention appointment. All pre-intervention characteristics were collected during the same visit. First, oral health literacy was assessed. Second, clinical examinations were performed. Interventions took place immediately after the clinical measurements. Finally, participants filled out a self-administered questionnaire. Post-intervention measurements were scheduled six months after the pre-intervention measurements. The recruitment of participants started in May 2010 and ended in June 2011, when the number of participants reached that required by the power calculation. The data collection period lasted from June 2010, when the first baseline measurements were conducted, until the last follow-up measurements were completed in February 2012.

2.3. Measurements

Oral health literacy (range: 1 to 5) was assessed using the Adult Health Literacy Instrument for Dentistry (AHLID) [17]. The AHLID is a newly developed and validated Norwegian interview instrument. It consists of printed oral health information texts, medicine prescriptions, post-treatment information and brochures on dental diseases, all frequently used for the benefit of adult dental patients to complement communication with dental professionals. Participants were asked to read ten different health information texts and answer questions related to their content. The texts and accompanying questions corresponded to five different levels of oral health literacy ranging from 1 (lowest) to 5 (highest). The AHLID interview guide was used to score the participants according to these levels. The interviews took place in a suitable room free from disturbing noises and dental equipment. All AHLID interviews were conducted by the same dental researcher, who was also the principal investigator.

Clinical parameters included dentition status, gingival status and oral hygiene status. Dental status was examined using the WHO criteria to account for the numbers of decayed, missing and filled teeth (DMFT) [18]. The gingival index [19] was utilised to objectively measure gingival status, and the plaque index [20] was used to objectively measure oral hygiene status. These indices are well known and have been used worldwide since the 1960s. Mean gingival and mean plaque index scores for each participant were obtained by registering four tooth surfaces (distal, buccal, mesial and lingual/palatal) on all present teeth, except third molars. For oral hygiene, the amount of plaque was measured, and for gingival status, the amount of bleeding for these sites was measured. Importantly, for both indices, scores from the four sites of all teeth were added and then divided by the present number of teeth to create the mean variables for oral hygiene and gingival bleeding, according to the method described by Silness and Löe [19,20]. Background variables, such as gender, age, income, education level and smoking status, were collected using a self-administered questionnaire. The same trained dental hygienist performed all clinical examinations on all participants pre- and post-intervention. The dental hygienist was calibrated by a dentist and senior clinical researcher to minimise measurement errors. To examine reproducibility of the indices, plaque and gingival indices were calculated by registering scores obtained by the dental hygienist who performed all analyses and the dentist/senior researcher prior to the study. For this intra-examiner reliability measure, six index teeth in 10 volunteering individuals, not involved in the study, were assessed. The kappa coefficient scores were 0.70 for gingival index and 0.78 for plaque index, representing substantial agreement. The dental hygienist was blinded to group allocation and participants' oral health literacy levels.

The primary study outcome variable was the mean gingival index score, and its secondary outcome variable was the mean plaque index score.

2.4. Interventions

2.4.1. Communication According to the Model (Intervention Group)

For participants in the intervention group, communication regarding their gingival status and oral hygiene was carried out according to the conceptual model of health literacy as a risk [14] (Figure 1). Utilising this model, the first step was an assessment of health literacy. A clinical environment sensitive to health literacy was emphasised by considering the participants' health literacy level, as the clinician's sensitivity can improve patients' access to health care and enhance the quality of patient–clinician interactions. As a consequence, the clinician was more skilled to provide patient education that was tailored to individual needs and capacities. Tailored communication increases patients' capability for self-management, which in turn may lead to improved clinical outcomes. Health literacy tools are typically organised into four categories: Improving spoken communication, improving written communication, improving self-management and empowerment and improving supportive systems [21]. Communication techniques utilised in the intervention group included speaking in plain, non-medical language; confirming understanding using the "teach-back" approach by having patients repeat information back in their own words; and showing patients how to operate dental devices. Furthermore, open-ended questions were used to avoid yes/no answers [22,23]. Radiographs, pictures and models of teeth and jaws were used as visual supplements to the oral conversations when considered necessary for comprehension [24]. Because the effect of printed or written health information materials is considered greater when the information is personalised [25], all participants in the intervention group were provided with an individualised take-home message. Inspired by the "Ask me three" approach [26], the take-home message concentrated on three important questions: "What is my main problem?", "What do I need to do?" and "Why is it important for me to do this?" The written message was written in bullet points. The participants were provided with the recommended oral hygiene devises free of charge. The same person who conducted all AHLID interviews also performed the interventions, which lasted from 3 to 10 min each.

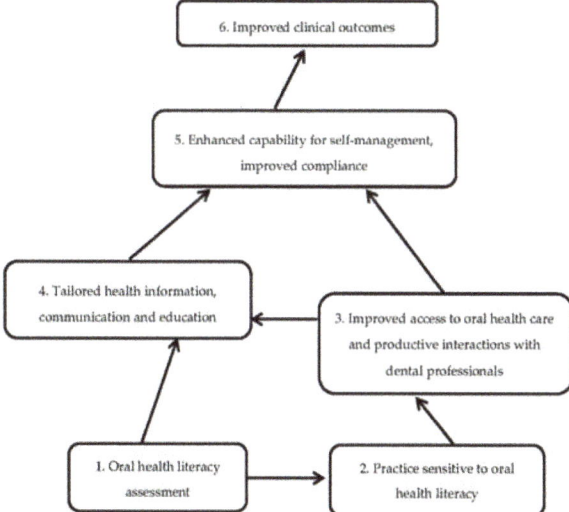

Figure 1. Model for the study adapted to oral health literacy from the Conceptual model of health literacy as a risk, proposed by Nutbeam [13].

2.4.2. General Communication (Control Group)

Participants in the control group received information regarding their gingival status and oral hygiene according to standard practice in general dentistry. Brief information was delivered orally, and no written information was provided. The communication was not sensitive to oral health literacy and did not follow the conceptual model of health literacy as a risk. The same person who conducted all AHLID interviews and performed the interventions for the intervention group also communicated with the control group. The oral communications lasted for about 3 to 4 min each.

2.5. Statistical Analyses

Descriptive statistics were performed on the pre-intervention characteristics of the study participants in both groups. Differences between the intervention and control groups were tested with an independent sample t-test for continuous variables and a chi-square test for categorical variables. Paired sample t-tests were performed on both groups separately to investigate within-group effects on the pre-intervention and post-intervention mean gingival index and mean plaque index. An analysis of covariance (ANCOVA) was used to evaluate between-group treatment effects on mean gingival and plaque index. Pre-intervention measures were entered as covariates to adjust for differences between groups in pre-intervention scores. Within- and between-group effect sizes were measured using Cohen's d. A Cohen's d of 0.2 was considered a small effect, 0.5 was considered a medium effect and 0.8 was considered a large effect [27]. p-Values lower than 0.05 were considered statistically significant. Statistical analyses were performed using IBM SPSS Statistics software for Windows (version 21.0, IBM SPSS Inc., Chicago, IL, USA). Within-group effect sizes were calculated using Becker's effect size calculator separately for the mean gingival index and the mean plaque index [28]. Between-group effect sizes were calculated separately for the mean gingival index and the mean plaque index using the adjusted mean difference between the intervention group and the control group divided by the estimated pooled standard deviation obtained from the square root of the MS error of the ANCOVA model.

3. Results

A total of 133 adults were randomly allocated for study participation: 64 in the intervention group and 69 in the control group. Two participants from each group were lost to follow-up due to drop-outs, and an additional three participants were lost in the control group due to other reasons (Figure 2). All participants were analysed in the group to which they were randomised. The participants' pre-intervention characteristics are presented by group allocation in Table 1. There were no significant baseline differences between the groups with respect to gender, age, level of education, oral health literacy level, smoking status, chronic disease, DMFT or plaque index. However, the intervention group had a significantly higher mean gingival index ($p < 0.001$). Paired-sample t-tests showed that the mean gingival index decreased significantly from the pre-intervention to the post-intervention measurement in the intervention group ($p < 0.000$), but not in the control group ($p = 0.480$). Regarding the mean plaque index, a significant decrease was seen in both the intervention group ($p < 0.000$) and the control group ($p < 0.000$) (Table 2). The within-group effect size for the gingival index was zero in the control group, but large in the intervention group. The plaque index effect size was large in the intervention group and small in the control group (Table 2). The ANCOVA showed a significant between-group effect, indicating that reduction in both the post-intervention mean gingival index and the mean plaque index was significantly greater for the intervention group than the control group when controlling for baseline index scores (Table 3). The adjusted Cohen's d indicated large between-group effect sizes for both the mean gingival index and the mean plaque index.

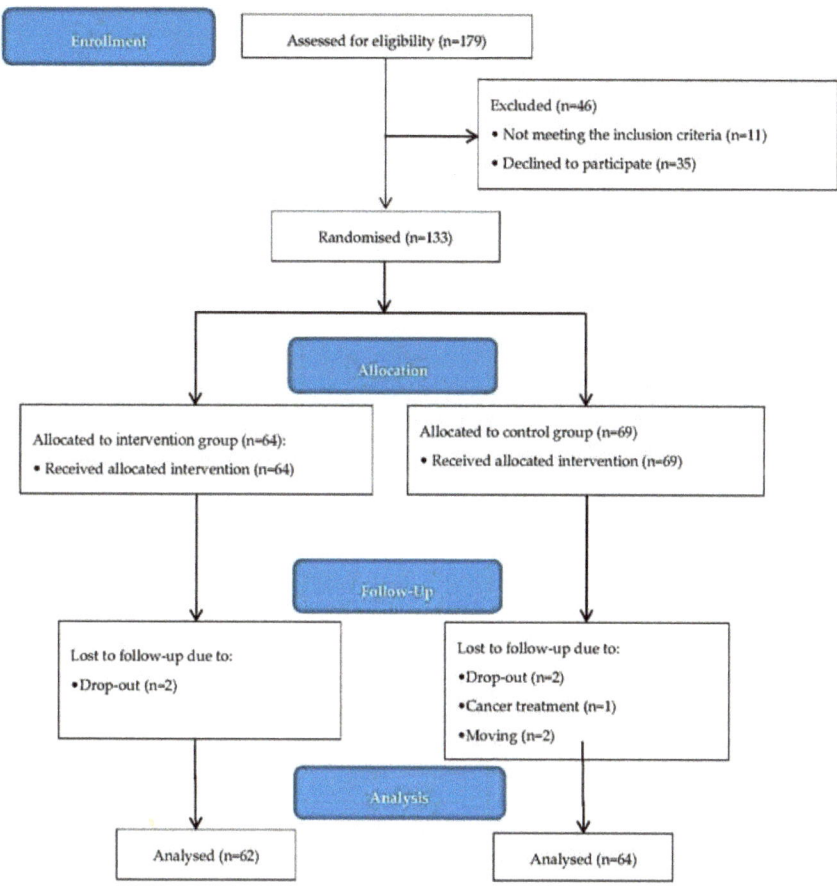

Figure 2. Flow chart of study participants.

Table 1. Pre-intervention characteristics of study participants.

Characteristics	Intervention Group ($n = 64$)	Control Group ($n = 69$)	p-Value [a]
Gender			0.394
Men	46%	51%	
Women	54%	49%	
Age (years) [b]	49.53 ± 14.97	46.35 ± 14.23	0.211
Education level			0.917
Elementary school	19%	16%	
High school	36%	38%	
University/University college	45%	46%	
Oral health literacy level [b]	3.02 ± 0.72	2.96 ± 0.88	0.675
Smoker	15%	27%	0.095
Chronic disease	45%	44%	0.832
DMFT [b]	18.19 ± 6.62	17.94 ± 6.36	0.828
Gingival index [b]	1.34 ± 0.29	1.16 ± 0.35	0.001
Plaque index [b]	0.53 ± 0.36	0.48 ± 0.36	0.420

[a] Independent sample t-test for continuous data. Chi-square test for categorical data; [b] Values are mean ± DS.

Table 2. Within-group measurements and effects of primary and secondary outcome variables.

Group	Pre-Intervention Gingival Index [a]	Post-Intervention Gingival Index [a]	p-Value [b]	Cohen's d	Pre-Intervention Plaque Index [a]	Post-Intervention Plaque Index [a]	p-Value [b]	Cohen's d
Intervention (n = 62)	1.34 ± 0.29	0.72 ± 0.42	0.000	−1.775	0.53 ± 0.36	0.08 ± 0.13	0.000	−1.663
Control (n = 64)	1.16 ± 0.35	1.12 ± 0.46	0.480	−0.098	0.48 ± 0.36	0.34 ± 0.35	0.000	−0.394

[a] Values are mean ± SD. [b] p-values obtained from paired-sample t-tests performed for separate groups.

Table 3. Between-group effects of interventions on primary and secondary outcome variables.

Outcome Variable	Group	ANCOVA-Adjusted Mean (95% CI)	MS Error	p-Value	Adjusted Cohen's d
Gingival index	Intervention (n = 62)	0.70 (0.591–0.815)	0.190	0.000	−0.98
	Control (n = 64)	1.13 (1.020–1.242)			
Plaque index	Intervention (n = 62)	0.07 (0.019–0.125)	0.045	0.000	−1.33
	Control (n = 64)	0.35 (0.294–0.399)			

4. Discussion

The hypothesis of this study was that patients provided with communication sensitive to oral health literacy according to the conceptual model of health literacy as a risk would improve their gingival status and oral hygiene compared to the control group. Our findings support the hypothesis. The participants' pre-intervention characteristics (Table 1) reveal that the intervention group had a higher mean gingival index score. This can be seen as a weakness of the study; however, an ANCOVA analysis was used to adjust these baseline differences. A significant post-intervention reduction in the gingival index score was observed in the intervention group, but not in the control group. Both groups exhibited a significant decrease in the mean plaque index, although the decrease was more pronounced in the intervention group. We interpret the decrease in the plaque index for the control group as a non-specific effect of trial participation due to the consequence of being observed (i.e., the Hawthorne effect). Although the Hawthorne effect should not affect the assessment of the difference between intervention and control, it may result in an inflated estimate of effect size in routine clinical settings due to an over-estimation of the responses from both groups [29]. All participants were aware that participation involved a repeated measurement of oral health variables. It might be reasonable to assume that some participants payed extra attention to and spent more time on their oral hygiene on the day of measurement, resulting in less plaque. Gingival status is a more reliable measure of sustained behaviour over time, since the presence of bacterial plaque in contact with the gingiva will cause gingivitis if not removed on a regular basis. The post-intervention measure showed a significant reduction in the gingival index score in the intervention group, but not the control group. This result indicates that communication sensitive to oral health literacy can effectively improve oral health outcomes, as hypothesised. The improved oral health was likely due to enhanced capability for self-management and motivation, leading to improved compliance [13].

A recent review of oral health promotion trials in relation to oral hygiene and gingival health found no clear indication that any particular type or style of educational approach was more effective than others [30]. However, no oral health literacy interventions had been published at the time of this study; therefore, they are not included in the review. Since the study, a handful of oral health literacy intervention studies have been published. Ju et al. [31] tested the efficacy of an oral health literacy intervention based on Bandura's Social Cognitive Theory to enhance oral health literacy among indigenous Australian adults and concluded that the intervention was partially successful in improving oral health literacy and oral health-literacy related outcomes after multiple imputations. Vilella et al. [32] evaluated the effect of oral health literacy on the retention of health information in pregnant women. The results suggested that low oral health literacy has a negative effect on information retention, but that only spoken oral health interventions can address differences in literacy levels. These studies provide new knowledge of vulnerable populations, but neither includes clinical outcomes. In the broader health context, a systematic review of interventions designed to mitigate the effect of low health literacy found that common features of interventions that changed distal outcome (i.e., biomarkers of disease) had a solid theoretical basis, emphasised skill-building and were delivered by a health professional [33]. Our study included these features, and the results regarding distal outcomes (i.e., the gingival index and the plaque index) support the design of health literacy studies. Furthermore, most of the interventions included in the systematic review occurred in a single session focused on making health information more understandable to patients with low health literacy, which used visual aids and/or handouts with materials written in simpler language to complement conversations between health professionals and their patients [30]. Participants in the intervention group were provided with these communication techniques during the dental encounter. All techniques were well known and should be easy to conduct in a clinical dental setting. However, a recent national survey from the U.S. concluded that the routine use of communication techniques, including some techniques thought to be most effective for patients with limited literacy skills, is low among dentists [34]. Another study assessing dental hygienists' communication techniques found routine use of only one-third of the recommended communication techniques for patients with low health literacy [35]. These studies support the need to train health professionals in communicating with patients with low health literacy. Furthermore, it has been argued that the barriers caused by limited health literacy in a clinical context may be as much a problem of insufficient clinician competence to reduce unnecessary complexity and improve communication skills as they are a problem of limited health literacy skills in patients [36]. Implementing clinical practice sensitive to patients' health literacy, as proposed in the conceptual model of health literacy as a risk, might be an important step to reduce these barriers in clinical encounters.

The strengths of this study include its Randomised controlled trial (RCT) design and good follow-up rates. Limitations include its convenience sample of persons seeking care at a university dental clinic. Compared to the general population, these individuals may be more interested in oral health and more motivated to participate in a study, which may influence the results. At baseline, the intervention group had a higher mean gingival index than the control group, which may be seen as a weakness in the randomisation process. The groups were randomised using age and gender stratifications. Since periodontal problems typically increase with age, the age stratification was used, but there were still differences in the gingival index. In future studies, periodontal status might be considered in the stratification. Longer follow-up times and additional repeated measurements would also have been beneficial; however, such measures were limited due to a lack of resources. The drop-out rate was similar and low for both groups, which can be interpreted as indicating that the study instructions were followed and that both groups received the same care. The participants were blinded to group allocation, but the researcher who performed the interventions was not. This fact could have influenced the results in favour of the intervention group. Most importantly, however, the clinical examiner was blinded to group allocation, which is a strength of the study. Another strength is that both groups received the intervention from the same researcher, resulting in more consistent interpersonal interactions. This may have reduced the unwanted effects of the intervention. On the other hand, one cannot be sure of whether the positive effects achieved in this study on gingival status and oral hygiene in the intervention group are due exclusively to the approaches made. For instance, a study from the dental context [37] demonstrated associations among patients' degree of self-efficacy, their oral health literacy and their dental neglect (negative correlation). Nutbeam [13], thus, commented in his conceptual model that actions to improve health literacy should be focused on developing age- and context-specific health knowledge and that strong self-efficacy is necessary to implement increased health knowledge in ways that enable people to exert greater control over their health and health-related decisions. Therefore, the patients' degree of self-efficacy should have favourably been assessed in this study. On the other hand, it would be reasonable to include health literacy in intervention studies testing other models. One editorial emphasised that oral health researchers must develop and test new theories and models instead of conducting interventions based on the same well-established theories [38]. Furthermore, a recent systematic review of psychological approaches to behaviour change for improved oral hygiene concluded that understanding the benefits of behaviour change and the seriousness of the disease are important predictors for the likelihood of behaviour change [39].

The model on which we based this intervention focuses on the direct pathways between health literacy and health outcomes. We do recognise that other circumstances may mediate the effects of the intervention. Conceptualising health literacy as an individual risk does have limitations and improving health literacy in a population involves more than the transmission of health information, although this certainly remains a fundamental task [13]. Focusing on individual behavioural change and managing barriers to health literacy in a clinical context are important; however, clinical approaches alone can never be sufficient to enhance oral health in populations. Upstream public health actions are also required.

5. Conclusions

To the best of our knowledge, this is the first randomised control trial to test the effects of the conceptual model of health literacy as a risk in a clinical dental context. Our findings should, therefore, be seen a first step to provide evidence, and we hope that they will encourage other researchers to perform similar studies. In conclusion, the conceptual model of health literacy as a risk demonstrates a significant improvement in important clinical outcomes, such as gingival status and oral hygiene, in adult patients. The hypothesis that patients provided with communication sensitive to oral health literacy will improve their gingival status and oral hygiene was supported. The model may be considered a suitable clinical supplement to health literacy-based patient education in populations.

Author Contributions: L.S., M.B. and J.B. designed the RCT study. L.S. performed the interventions and wrote the main parts of the manuscript. J.B. and L.S. performed the statistical analyses. M.B. and K.S.P. commented on the manuscript draft and implemented aspects of clinical dentistry and health literacy theory, respectively.

Funding: The trial was funded by the Department of Clinical Dentistry, UiT—The Arctic University of Norway. The publication charges for this article were funded by a grant from UiT's publication fund.

Acknowledgments: The authors are grateful to the staff at the Public Dental Service Competence Centre of Northern Norway, Tromsø, Norway, as well as to the staff at the University Dental Clinic, Tromsø, Norway. We sincerely thank dental hygienist Hilde Nyborg for her participation in the clinical examinations.

Conflicts of Interest: The authors declare no conflict of interest.

References

1. Kidd, E.; Fejerskov, O. *Essentials of Dental Caries*; Oxford University Press: Oxford, UK, 2016.
2. Petersen, P.E.; Bourgeois, D.; Ogawa, H.; Estupinan-Day, S.; Ndiaye, C. The global burden of oral diseases and risks to oral health. *Bull. World Health Organ.* **2005**, *83*, 661–669. [PubMed]
3. Pihlstrom, B.L.; Michalowicz, B.S.; Johnson, N.W. Periodontal diseases. *Lancet* **2005**, *366*, 1809–1820. [CrossRef]
4. Selwitz, R.H.; Ismail, A.I.; Pitts, N.B. Dental caries. *Lancet* **2007**, *369*, 51–59. [CrossRef]
5. World Health Organization. Health Literacy. The Solid Facts. Available online: http://www.thehealthwell.info/node/534072 (accessed on 3 April 2018).
6. HLS-EU Consortium. Comparative Report of Health Literacy in Eight EU Member States. The European Health Literacy Project. Available online: http://www.healthliteracy.ie/wp-content/uploads/2012/09/HLS-EU_report_Final_April_2012.pdf (accessed on 14 April 2018).
7. Berkman, N.D.; Sheridan, M.D.; Donahue, M.D.; Halpern, D.J.; Crotty, K. Low health literacy and health outcomes: An updated systematic review. *Ann. Int. Med.* **2011**, *155*, 97–107. [CrossRef] [PubMed]
8. Easton, P.; Entwistle, V.A.; Williams, B. Health in the hidden population of people with low literacy. A systematic review of the literature. *BMC Public Health* **2010**, *10*, 459. [CrossRef]
9. U.S. Department of Health and Human Services. *A National Call to Action to Promote Oral Health*; U.S. Department of Health and Human Services, Public Health Service, Centre for Disease Control and Prevention, National Institutes of Health, National Institutes of Dental and Craniofacial Research: Rockville, MD, USA, 2003.
10. Podschun, G. National plan to improve health literacy in dentistry. *J. Calif. Dent. Assoc.* **2012**, *40*, 317–320. [PubMed]
11. U.S. Department of Health and Human Services. National Action Plan to Improve Health Literacy. Available online: http://www.health.gov/communication/hlactionplan/ (accessed on 29 October 2017).
12. Sørensen, K.; Van den Broucke, S.; Fullam, J.; Doyle, G.; Pelikan, J.; Slonska, Z.; Brand, H. Health literacy and public health: A systematic review and integration of definitions and models. *BMC Public Health* **2012**, *12*. [CrossRef] [PubMed]
13. Nutbeam, D. The evolving concept of health literacy. *Soc. Sci. Med.* **2008**, *67*, 2072–2078. [CrossRef] [PubMed]
14. Faul, F.; Erdfelder, E.; Lang, A.-G.; Buchner, A. G*Power 3: A flexible statistical power analysis program for the social, behavioral, and biomedical sciences. *Behav. Res. Methods* **2007**, *39*, 75–191. [CrossRef]
15. Jackson, R.D.; Echert, G.J. Health literacy in an adult dental research population: A pilot study. *J. Public Health Dent.* **2008**, *68*, 196–200. [CrossRef] [PubMed]
16. Sugarman, J.; Paasche-Orlow, M. Confirming comprehension of informed consent as a protection of human subjects. *J. Gen. Intern. Med.* **2006**, *21*, 898–899. [CrossRef] [PubMed]
17. Stein, L.; Pettersen, K.S.; Bergdahl, M.; Bergdahl, J. Development and validation of an instrument to assess health literacy in Norwegian adult dental patients. *Acta Odontol. Scand.* **2015**, *73*, 530–538. [CrossRef] [PubMed]

18. World Health Organization. *WHO Oral Health Country/Area Profile Programme (CAPP)*; WHO: Geneva, Switzerland, 2000. Available online: http://www.who.int/oral_health/databases/malmo/en/ (accessed on 20 March 2017).
19. Silness, J.; Löe, H. Periodontal disease in pregnancy II. Correlation between oral hygiene and periodontal condition. *Acta Odontol. Scand.* **1964**, *22*, 121–135. [CrossRef] [PubMed]
20. Löe, H.; Silness, J. Periodontal disease in pregnancy I. Prevalence and severity. *Acta Odontol. Scand.* **1963**, *21*, 533–551. [CrossRef] [PubMed]
21. Tapp, H.; Dunlin, M.; Plescia, M. Chronic disease self-management. In *Chronic Illness Care*; Daaleman, T., Herlton, M., Eds.; Springer: Cham, Switzerland, 2018.
22. Tamura-Lis, W. Teach-back for quality education and patient safety. *Urol. Nurs.* **2013**, *33*, 267–271. [PubMed]
23. Schillinger, D.; Piette, J.; Grumbach, K.; Wang, F.; Wilson, C.; Daher, C.; Leong-Grotz, K.; Castro, C.; Bindman, A.B. Closing the loop. Physician communication with diabetic patients who have low health literacy. *Arch. Intern. Med.* **2003**, *163*, 83–90. [CrossRef] [PubMed]
24. Houts, P.S.; Doak, C.C.; Doak, L.G.; Loscalzo, M.J. The role of pictures in improving health communication: A review of research on attention, comprehension, recall and adherence. *Patient Educ. Couns.* **2006**, *61*, 173–190. [CrossRef] [PubMed]
25. Haynes, R.B.; Ackloo, E.; Sahota, N.; McDonald, H.P.; Yao, X. Interventions for enhancing medication adherence. *Cochrane Database Syst. Rev.* **2008**, *2*. [CrossRef]
26. DeWalt, D.A.; Brouckou, K.A.; Hawk, V.; Brach, C.; Hink, A.; Rudd, R.; Callahan, L. Developing and testing the health literacy universal precautions toolkit. *Nurs. Outlook* **2011**, *59*, 85–94. [CrossRef] [PubMed]
27. Cohen, J. *Statistical Power Analysis for the Behavioral Sciences*; Academic Press: New York, NY, USA, 1988.
28. Becker, L.A. Becker's Effect Size Calculator. Available online: http://www.uccs.edu/~lbecker/ (accessed on 14 October 2017).
29. McCarney, R.; Warner, J.; Iliffe, S.; van Haselen, R.; Griffin, M.; Fisher, P. The Hawthorne effect: A randomized, controlled trial. *BMC Med. Res. Methodol.* **2007**, *7*. [CrossRef] [PubMed]
30. Watt, R.G.; Marinho, V.C. Does oral health promotion improve oral hygiene and gingival health? *Periodontol 2005*, *37*, 34–47. [CrossRef] [PubMed]
31. Ju, X.; Brennan, D.; Parker, E.; Mills, H.; Kapellas, K.; Jamieson, L. Efficacy of an oral health literacy intervention among indigenous australian adults. *Commun. Dent. Oral Epidemiol.* **2017**, *45*, 413–426. [CrossRef] [PubMed]
32. Vilella, K.D.; Fraiz, F.C.; Benelli, E.M.; Assunção, L.R. Oral health literacy and retention of health information among pregnant women: A randomised controlled trial. *Oral Health Prev. Dent.* **2017**, *15*, 41–48. [PubMed]
33. Sheridan, S.L.; Halpern, D.J.; Viera, A.J.; Berkman, N.D.; Donahue, K.E.; Crotty, K. Interventions for individuals with low health literacy: A systematic review. *J. Health Commun.* **2011**, *16* (Suppl. 3), 30–54. [CrossRef] [PubMed]
34. Rozier, R.G.; Horowitz, A.M.; Podschun, G. Dentist-patient communication techniques used in the United States: The results of a national survey. *J. Am. Dent. Assoc.* **2001**, *142*, 518–530. [CrossRef]
35. Flynn, P.; Schwei, K.; VanWormer, J.; Skryzpcak, K.; Acharya, A. Assessing dental hygienists' communication techniques for use with low oral health literacy patients. *J. Dent. Hyg.* **2016**, *90*, 162–169. [PubMed]
36. Paasche-Orlow, M.K.; Wolf, M. Promoting health literacy research to reduce health disparities. *J. Health Commun.* **2010**, *15* (Suppl. 2), 34–41. [CrossRef] [PubMed]
37. Lee, J.Y.; Divaris, K.; Baker, A.D.; Rozier, R.G.; Vann, W.F., Jr. The relationship of oral health literacy and self-efficacy with oral health status and dental neglect. *Am. J. Public Health* **2012**, *102*, 923–929. [CrossRef] [PubMed]
38. Noar, S.M. Letter to the editor: Charting the course forward: Promising trends in health behavior theory application. *J. Public Health Dent.* **2011**, *73*, 83–85. [CrossRef] [PubMed]
39. Newton, T.J.; Asimakopoulou, K. Managing oral hygiene as a risk factor for periodontal disease: A systematic review of psychological approaches to behaviour change for improved plaque control in periodontal management. *J. Clin. Periodontol.* **2015**, *42*. [CrossRef] [PubMed]

© 2018 by the authors. Licensee MDPI, Basel, Switzerland. This article is an open access article distributed under the terms and conditions of the Creative Commons Attribution (CC BY) license (http://creativecommons.org/licenses/by/4.0/).

Article

Is It Possible to "Find Space for Mental Health" in Young People? Effectiveness of a School-Based Mental Health Literacy Promotion Program

Luísa Campos [1,2,*], Pedro Dias [1,2], Ana Duarte [1], Elisa Veiga [1,2], Cláudia Camila Dias [3,4] and Filipa Palha [1,2,5]

1. Faculty of Education and Psychology, Universidade Católica Portuguesa, Rua Diogo Botelho, 1327, 4169-005 Porto, Portugal; pdias@porto.ucp.pt (P.D.); aiduarte@porto.ucp.pt (A.D.); eveiga@porto.ucp.pt (E.V.); fpalha@porto.ucp.pt (F.P.)
2. Research Centre for Human Development, Rua Diogo Botelho, 1327, 4169-005 Porto, Portugal
3. Department of Community Medicine, Information and Health Decision Sciences, Faculty of Medicine of the University of Porto, 4200-319 Porto, Portugal; camila@med.up.pt
4. CINTESIS—Center for Health Technology and Services Research, Alameda Prof. Hernâni Monteiro, 4200-319 Porto, Portugal
5. ENCONTRAR+SE—Association for the Promotion of Mental Health, Rua Professor Melo Adrião 106, 4100-340 Porto, Portugal
* Correspondence: mcampos@porto.ucp.pt

Received: 27 March 2018; Accepted: 5 July 2018; Published: 6 July 2018

Abstract: Lack of knowledge regarding, and the stigma associated with, mental disorders have been identified as major obstacles for the promotion of mental health and early intervention. The present study aimed to evaluate the effectiveness of a school-based intervention program focused on the promotion of mental health literacy (MHL) in young people ("Finding Space for Mental Health"). A sample of 543 students (22 classes), aged between 12 and 14 years old, participated in the study. Each class of students was randomly assigned to the control group (CG; $n = 284$; 11 classes) or the experimental group (EG; $n = 259$; 11 classes). MHL was assessed using the Mental Health Literacy questionnaire (MHLq), which is comprised of three dimensions—Knowledge/Stereotypes, First Aid Skills and Help Seeking, and Self-Help Strategies. The scores on these dimensions can also be combined to give an overall or total score. Participants from the EG attended the MHL promotion program (two sessions, 90 min each) delivered at one-week intervals. Sessions followed an interactive methodology, using group dynamics, music, and videos adapted to the target group. All participants responded to the MHLq at three points in time: pre-intervention assessment (one week prior to the intervention), post-intervention assessment (one week after the intervention) and follow-up assessment (six months after the intervention). The intervention effectiveness and the differential impact of sociodemographic variables on the effectiveness of the program were studied using a Generalized Estimation Equation (GEE). Results revealed that participants from the EG demonstrated, on average, significantly higher improvement in MHL from pre-intervention to follow-up when compared to participants from the CG. Different sociodemographic variables affected the effectiveness of the program on distinct dimensions of the MHLq. Overall, "Finding Space for Mental Health" showed efficacy as a short-term promotion program for improving MHL in schools.

Keywords: mental health literacy; effectiveness; young people; promotion

1. Introduction

In recent years, the literature has highlighted a growing concern about the number of children and youth who are experiencing mental health problems [1,2]. From a preventative perspective, it has become evident that there is an urgent need to intervene as early as possible in order to promote positive mental health and well-being [3,4]. This evidence is reinforced, in particular, by the fact that most mental disorders develop during youth, and it is estimated that about half of all cases of diagnosed mental disorders in adulthood started by the age of 14 [5–8].

With these factors in mind, several countries are currently investing not only in structures for the treatment of mental disorders, but also in the promotion of mental health and prevention of mental health problems both in at-risk groups and in the general population [9]. One of the five priority areas addressed by the EU's Joint Action for Mental Health and Well-Being [10], launched in 2013, was the promotion of mental health in schools. This effort in treatment, prevention and promotion faces important challenges which are well reported in the literature—including the lack of adequate knowledge of mental health issues (mental health literacy) and the stigma associated with mental health problems [4,11].

The term mental health literacy was first introduced in 1997 by Jorm and colleagues and defined as "knowledge and beliefs about mental disorders which aid their recognition, management and prevention" [12]. It is known that the general population, and in particular young people, have low levels of mental health literacy (MHL) (e.g., [13]): they have difficulties in identifying mental disorders and their underlying causes, risk factors, and associated protective factors, and can develop incorrect beliefs about the effectiveness of therapeutic interventions, often resulting in a decrease in the likelihood of seeking help [14,15]. Additionally, the stigma associated with mental health problems becomes apparent to people at an early age [16]. However, the attitudes of young people are malleable and can be changed more easily than those of adults [17], and this therefore represents an important opportunity to invest in the promotion of mental health literacy at this age.

According to Wright, Jorm, Harris and McGorry [18], the recognition of mental health problems and associated psychological disorders is the most predictive factor for whether a young person seeks help. This predictor is of particular relevance because of the need to address the serious consequences to mental health that the delay in seeking help may entail [15,19,20].

Researchers from several countries have created programs for the promotion of mental health for young people, most of which were developed in a school context, whose main objective is to promote improved mental health by increasing MHL and reducing the stigma associated with mental health problems [21]. Overall, evaluation studies of these programs have demonstrated their effectiveness in improving MHL levels, although limitations have been identified in most studies—absence of focus groups and pilot studies with the target group; weak internal validity, causal assessment, and quality of evidence; and lack of long term follow-up, thus highlighting the need to develop new work that meets more stringent design criteria (e.g., [22–24]).

Evidence also suggests that some specific variables may influence the development of MHL, such as gender and prior contact with people who have mental health problems. With regards to gender, results from different studies suggest that young women have higher levels of MHL (e.g., [25–28]), presenting with more positive attitudes and less stereotypes in relation to people with mental disorders, when compared with young men [26,28,29]. In a study developed by Pinfold et al. [11] it was pointed out that, after an intervention to promote MHL, female participants obtained higher gains in MHL when compared to male participants.

Additionally, higher levels of MHL are consistently reported in people who refer knowing someone with a mental health problem (e.g., [30–32]). This prior contact seems to increase the impact of MHL promotion interventions with young people [11].

This article presents results regarding the effectiveness of a school-based intervention program focused on the promotion of mental health literacy in a group of young people, developed in the project "Finding Space for Mental Health" [21,33]. The specific objectives of this research were: (1) to evaluate the effectiveness of the intervention in the promotion of MHL; and (2) to analyze the impact of the variables of gender and previous contact with people with mental health problems, as well as to explore the potential impact of other sociodemographic variables of the participants, including year of schooling and type of school in the intervention results. We hypothesized that: (1) students who participate in the mental health literacy promotion program would display significant increases in MHL after the intervention, maintaining them at follow-up, compared to students who did not participate; (2) girls and students who have had previous contact with someone with a mental health problem would show higher increase in MHL after the program, compared to boys and to students who didn't have previous contact with mental health problems.

2. Materials and Methods

2.1. Participants

Five-hundred and forty-three youngsters from 22 school classes were randomly divided into two groups—11 classes in the experimental group (EG: n = 259, 48%) and 11 classes in the control group (CG: n = 284, 52%), before pre-intervention assessment. The participants were aged between 12–14 years (mean age = 13.04, SD = 0.79), and were attending the third cycle of their basic education (26% in the seventh year, 37% in the eighth year, 37% in the ninth year) at one of eight schools in northern Portugal. The majority of the participants were male (52%) and attended state-funded schools (74%) (The English definition of public vs state-funded schools was used in this work—a public school is a school in which students have to pay to study and a state-funded school is a school that is free for students as the government pays for their study).

Concerning the professional situation of the parents, 86% were employed.

With regards to contact with mental health problems, 236 (44%) said they knew someone with a mental health problem, 161 (30%) reported not knowing anyone, and 139 (26%) did not know. As to the degree of proximity to a person with a mental health problem, 103 (42%) of the young people reported knowing a relative, 98 (39%) pointed out a friend, 8 (3%) said it was themselves, 37 (15%) pointed out another person, and 2 (1%) identified that several people with a mental health problem were known to them.

When questioned about the mental health problems experienced by the people they identified, 14% said they did not know. From the answers given by those who did know, 29 distinct problems were reported, some of them corresponding to mental disorders (e.g., "Depression", n = 41), neurological problems (e.g., "Stroke", n = 3) or other physical health problems (e.g., "Heart Problem", n = 1).

Finally, there were no significant associations between the variables of the groups (experimental vs. control) and the sociodemographic variables, except for the type of school (public school vs. state-funded school) (Table 1).

The number of participants after the intervention decreased to 239 (EG) and 263 (CG), and during the follow-up assessment further decreased to 211 (EG) and 176 (CG), respectively. This was due to the school absence of some students in post-intervention assessment and to school year transition by students between post-intervention and follow-up (some students were transferred to a new school). No students who stayed in the same class/school refused to participate in the follow-up assessment.

2.2. Intervention

The intervention program, named "Finding Space" was composed of two sessions, lasting 90 min each and delivered at one-week intervals in the students' classrooms (each class had between 20 to 25 students), conducted by a trained psychologist in collaboration with one masters-level psychology student. The sessions followed an interactive methodology using group dynamics, music, and videos which were adapted to the target group. Each session had specific goals. The first session included: (1) presentation of the project; (2) establishment of group rules; (3) exploration of students' knowledge and beliefs about physical and mental health and illness; (4) exploration of the signs of mental health problems and their impact; (5) identification of risk factors for mental health; (6) identification of symptoms and signs of five mental disorders (depressive disorder, generalized anxiety disorder, anorexia, schizophrenia, and substance-related disorder); and (7) promotion of nonstigmatized behaviors towards mental disorders, addressing the social inclusion of people with mental health disorders. The second session aimed to: (1) explore inadequate beliefs related to mental disorders; (2) raise students' awareness of mental health problems and their impact; (3) identify formal and informal help-seeking options; (4) promote first aid skills towards people with mental health problems; and (5) address self-help strategies and explore mental health promoting behaviors. The program was previously designed and tested with the target group, through the development of a pilot study, in order to identify participants' needs, and to guarantee message (e.g., "wording") and methodology accuracy. This pilot study, developed with students aged 12–14 years old, included two stages: (1) focus groups; (2) pilot-intervention with impact evaluation (pre-post intervention assessment) [33]. Information about the program and its manual can be found at http://www.fep.porto.ucp.pt/pt/AbrirEspacoSaudeMental?msite=12.

Table 1. Differences between the experimental group and control group regarding sociodemographic variables (pre-test).

	Control Group		Experimental Group		p-Value [1]
	n	(%)	n	(%)	
Gender					0.731
Male	148	(53%)	130	(51%)	
Female	133	(47%)	124	(49%)	
School Year					0.936
7th year	74	(26%)	64	(25%)	
8th year	105	(37%)	98	(38%)	
9th year	105	(37%)	97	(37%)	
Type of Education					<0.001
State-Funded School	245	(86%)	154	(59%)	
Public School	39	(14%)	105	(41%)	
Parents' professional situation					0.770
Employed	221	(86%)	240	(85%)	
Unemployed	36	(14%)	42	(15%)	
Knowledge of anyone with a mental health problem					0.317
Yes	114	(57%)	122	(62%)	
No	86	(43%)	75	(38%)	
Degree of Proximity					0.617
Relative	49	(40%)	54	(43%)	
Friend	45	(37%)	53	(42%)	
Him/herself	5	(4%)	3	(2%)	
Other	23	(19%)	16	(13%)	

[1] Chi-square test.

2.3. Measures

The MHLq—Mental Health Literacy questionnaire—was used to evaluate the effectiveness of the mental health promotion program [32].

The MHLq consists of two sections; in the first section sociodemographic data are collected, namely the date of birth, gender, year of schooling, and area of residence of the young person, and the professions and professional status of the parents. In this section, three questions are also given concerning knowledge of someone with a mental disorder, identification of the mental health disorder/problem, and relationship with the identified person.

The second section evaluates mental health literacy and consists of 33 multiple-choice items on a five-point Likert scale (from 1 = strongly disagree to 5 = strongly agree), organised in three dimensions: (1) Knowledge/Stereotypes (18 items); (2) First Aid Skills and Help Seeking (10 items); and (3) Self-Help Strategies (5 items).

The questionnaire assesses: (1) knowledge about mental health issues, including general characteristics of mental health problems, prevalence, signs and symptoms, and risk factors for mental disorders, as well as protective factors/mental health promoters; (2) knowledge of three specific mental disorders—depression, anxiety, and schizophrenia; (3) stereotypes associated with mental disorders; and (4) behavioral intentions (predisposition to help, behavioral promoters of mental health/self-help strategies, behaviors promoting the seeking of formal and/or informal help). At the follow-up stage three questions were added to the questionnaire in order to confirm participation in the intervention sessions and to measure satisfaction with the intervention, as well as request suggestions for improvement.

Higher values in all dimensions and for the total MHLq score correspond to higher levels of mental health literacy.

3. Procedures

3.1. Data Collection

The MHLq was applied one week before (pre-test), one week after (post-test) and six months after (follow-up) the intervention. It was carried out in a classroom setting by one of the researchers from the project team for "Finding Space for Mental Health".

This study was approved by the Portuguese Data Protection Authority (ID 11098/2011) and by the Portuguese Ministry of Education (ID 0128800003).

Informed consent was given by participants and by the students' caregivers, prior to their inclusion in the project. In order to pair participants in the three assessment moments, students were asked to provide five digits from their cell phone number (4th, 5th, 7th, 8th, and 9th digits).

After the follow-up assessment, students from the control group had the opportunity to attend the intervention program.

3.2. Analytic Plan

Continuous variables are described by the mean and standard deviation.

To evaluate the effectiveness of the intervention over the three moments in time (pre, post, follow-up), multivariate models (GEE, or generalized estimating equations) were applied, with the identity as a function of connection, i.e., a linear evolution was assumed. GEE is a method that allows the analysis of repeated or longitudinal measurements, taking into account that the measurements in the same individual over time are correlated. GEE provides many benefits, namely (1) accounts for within-subject/within-cluster correlations; (2) allows for time-varying covariate; (3) allows for irregularly timed or mistimed measurements; (4) provides consistent (i.e., asymptotically unbiased) parameter and standard error associated with the covariates of the model even when the correct correlation structure was not pick; (5) fits marginal models; (6) normality assumptions are not required; and (7) allows missing data [34,35]. As covariables (variables for adjustment), the pre-test scores and the variables defined in the study were used as possible confounding factors (pre-test score, gender, school year, type of school and knowledge of anyone with a mental health problem).

In this study, sum scores for the MHLq dimensions and global score were calculated. In all hypothesis tests, a level of significance of $\alpha = 5\%$ was used. The analysis was performed using the statistical analysis program SPSS® v.20.0 (Statistical Package for the Social Sciences, Armonk, NY, USA).

4. Results

The presentation of the results is divided in two sections: (1) presentation of the descriptive statistics of the MHLq for the experimental and control group, at the three times of evaluation; and (2) presentation of the results regarding the effectiveness of the intervention and the impact of the sociodemographic variables on the results of the intervention.

4.1. Descriptive Statistics on the Overall Score and Scores on the Dimensions of Mental Health Literacy

Table 2 shows the means and standard deviations of the experimental and control groups, at the three evaluation times—pre, post and follow-up—in relation to the global score and the dimensions of mental health literacy evaluated by the MHLq.

Table 2. Descriptive statistics concerning the global score and dimensions of mental health literacy at the three evaluation times—pre, post and follow-up.

	Global Score		Knowledge/Stereotypes		First Aid Skills and Help Seeking		Self-Help Strategies	
	Control	Experimental	Control	Experimental	Control	Experimental	Control	Experimental
Pre								
Mean (sd)	130.86 (13.23)	129.75 (11.15)	69.39 (8.22)	69.00 (7.17)	41.60 (5.41)	41.58 (4.71)	19.94 (3.14)	19.17 (3.11)
n	284	259	284	259	284	259	283	259
Post								
Mean (sd)	130.58 (13.08)	140.10 (12.58)	69.02 (8.23)	75.91 (8.13)	41.64 (5.34)	42.74 (4.68)	19.91 (3.16)	21.44 (2.70)
n	263	239	263	239	263	239	263	239
Follow up								
Mean (sd)	134.77 (11.02)	137.76 (11.88)	72.19 (6.82)	75.36 (7.25)	41.81 (5.01)	41.52 (4.96)	20.77 (2.70)	20.89 (2.86)
n	176	211	176	211	176	211	176	211

Differences between groups in the pre-test were studied in relation to the global score and MHLq dimensions. The only significant differences were found in the dimension "Self-Help Strategies", in which the control group had higher initial values than the experimental group ($p < 0.001$).

4.2. Effectiveness of the Intervention and Impact of Sociodemographic Variables

Table 3 shows the results of the GEE models used to evaluate the effectiveness of the intervention, based on the data collected at the three evaluation times (pre, post and follow-up), for each of the dimensions and the global score of the MHLq. The results concerning the differential impact of sociodemographic variables on the outcome of the intervention are also presented, using multivariate models in which the coefficients presented are adjusted to all variables.

Participants in the experimental group had, on average, significantly higher gains compared to the control group, both in the global score ($\beta = 7.707$; 95% CI = 6.069; 9.345) and in all MHLq dimensions (Knowledge/Stereotypes $\beta = 5.693$; 95% CI = 4.682; 6.704; First Aid Skills and Help Seeking $\beta = 0.744$; 95% CI = 0.133; 1.356; Self-Help Strategies $\beta = 1.236$; 95% CI = 0.848; 1.624), demonstrating the effectiveness of the program through to follow-up.

In terms of the differential impact of the sociodemographic variables on the global score, it was observed that the participants who did not know someone with a mental health problem obtained lower gains than those who reported knowing someone with a mental health problem ($\beta = -1.992$; 95% CI = -3.949; -0.035).

Regarding the dimension of Knowledge/Stereotypes, it was observed that the students attending the ninth year had, on average, higher gains than students attending the seventh year ($\beta = 1.719$; 95% CI = 0.404; 3.034) and the participants who reported not knowing people with mental health problems showed, on average, gains that were significantly lower than those of the participants who reported knowing someone with these types of problems ($\beta = -1.699$; 95% CI = -2.935; -0.463).

With regards to the First Aid Skills and Help Seeking dimension, the results indicated that female participants showed, on average, gains that were significantly higher than the male participants ($\beta = 0.777$; 95% CI = 0.146; 1.407), and those enrolled in public schools showed, on average, gains that were significantly lower than the students from state-funded schools ($\beta = -0.769$; 95% CI = -1.462; -0.076).

Table 3. Study of intervention effectiveness and the differential impact of sociodemographic variables based on Generalized Estimating Equations using repeated measurements (pre, post and follow-up) adjusted for some variables (Pre-test scores, Gender, School Year, Type of School and knowledge of anyone with a mental health problem) for global score and dimensions of mental health literacy.

		Global Score (n = 508)			Knowledge/Stereotypes (n = 508)			First Aid Skills and Help Seeking (n = 508)			Self-Help Strategies (n = 507)		
		β	95% CI	p	β	95% CI	p	β	95% CI	p	β	95% CI	p
Group	Control	Ref	-		Ref	-		Ref	-		Ref	-	
	Experimental	7.707	6.069; 9.345	<0.001	5.693	4.682; 6.704	<0.001	0.744	0.133; 1.356	0.017	1.236	0.848; 1.624	<0.001
Pre-Test score		0.523	0.442; 0.604	<0.001	0.505	0.420; 0.590	<0.001	0.589	0.523; 0.654	<0.001	0.420	0.347; 0.492	<0.001
Gender	Male	Ref			Ref			Ref			Ref		
	Female	1.429	−0.199; 3.057	0.085	0.750	−0.267; 1.767	0.149	0.777	0.146; 1.407	0.016	−0.168	−0.543; 0.208	0.382
School Year	7th year	Ref			Ref			Ref			Ref		
	8th year	0.778	−1.344; 2.900	0.472	1.086	−0.251; 2.423	0.110	0.086	−0.722; 0.894	0.835	−0.313	−0.821; 0.195	0.227
	9th year	1.500	−0.504; 3.505	0.142	1.719	0.404; 3.034	0.010	−0.499	−1.296; 0.297	0.219	0.610	0.115; 1.104	0.016
Type of School	State-Funded School	Ref			Ref			Ref			Ref		
	Public School	−1.612	−3.487; 0.263	0.092	−0.724	−1.928; 0.480	0.239	−0.769	−1.462; −0.076	0.030	−0.124	−0.583; 0.335	0.595
Knowledge of anyone with mental health problem	Yes	Ref			Ref			Ref			Ref		
	No	−1.992	−3.949; −0.035	0.046	−1.699	−2.935; −0.463	0.007	−0.214	−0.943; 0.514	0.564	−0.108	−0.538; 0.321	0.621
	Don't Know	−1.467	−3.444; 0.510	0.146	−1.129	−2.384; 0.126	0.078	−0.228	−0.970; 0.515	0.548	−0.114	−0.582; 0.354	0.633

Type of Model: scale response: linear; Ref—Category of reference; 95% CI—95% confidence interval; Reading example: β = 7.707—an expected difference in global score comparing experimental to control group of the same gender, school year, type pf school and knowledge of anyone with mental health problem.

Finally, on the Self-Help Strategies dimension, it was verified that the participants attending the ninth year obtained, on average, significantly higher gains than the participants of the seventh year group ($\beta = 0.610$; 95% CI = 0.115; 1.104).

5. Discussion

5.1. Effectiveness of Intervention

The present study involved 543 participants and aimed to evaluate the effectiveness of an intervention program to promote mental health literacy with youngsters from 12–14 years of age in a school context, as well as to explore the impact of sociodemographic variables on the intervention results.

GEE analysis informed us about the effectiveness of the intervention. As hypothesized, the participants of the EG had, on average, significantly higher values in the global score and in all dimensions of the MHLq compared to the CG, considering the evolution throughout the three evaluation times (pre, post, and follow-up). These results suggest that the intervention was effective, similar to the results found from other programs focused on promoting mental health literacy (e.g., [29,36]).

More specifically, there was a significant increase in Knowledge/Decrease of Stereotypes (Dimension 1). The literature has previously revealed the usefulness of short interventions to increase knowledge about mental health problems in young people (e.g., [11,29]).

As for the results obtained in Dimension 2—First Aid Skills and Help Seeking—the young people who benefited from the intervention were more likely to seek appropriate help for mental health problems, as well as to help others who present with them, and these results are also in line with the literature (e.g., [13]).

For Dimension 3—Self-Help Strategies—there was a statistically significant increase in the knowledge of self-help strategies in the EG, as reported in similar studies (e.g., [29]). These results can be explained by a positive view of the use of self-help strategies in young people and the general population, increasing the chance that people will show an interest in learning new forms of self-help as a way of coping with adversity arising from mental health problems like anxiety [4].

5.2. Exploration of the Impact of Sociodemographic Variables on Intervention Effectiveness

With regards to the hypothesized differences in gender, they were only statistically significant in the demand for First Aid Skills and Help Seeking. These results are in line with what is suggested in the literature, which indicates that in comparison to girls, boys show less intention to seek help and are less likely to help someone in need [25,26].

However, although the literature indicates that the intervention tends to have a greater impact for girls (e.g., [27,29]), in the present study there was a positive impact for both genders, in the global score and in the dimensions of Knowledge/Stereotypes and Self-Help Strategies.

On the variable of type of school, young people who attended public schools had, on average, significantly lower gains in the First Aid Skills and Help Seeking dimensions than those attending state-funded schools.

State-funded and public schools seem to be associated with lower and higher socioeconomic status (SES) [37], respectively. Previous research showed an influence of SES on MHL, with people with low SES tending to know less about the symptoms and prevalence of different mental health problems [38,39]. Preliminary results from the "Finding Space for Mental Health" project indicated that students from state-funded schools presented initially with lower levels of knowledge related to mental health problems, when compared to students from public schools [40]. As far as we know, no studies have focused on the influence of this variable on the impact of MHL promotion interventions. Future mental health promotion interventions and research on their effectiveness should consider school context specificities.

Regarding the variable of year of schooling, the oldest year group (ninth year) presented gains, on average, that were significantly higher in the dimension of Knowledge/Stereotypes and in the Self-Help Strategies dimension when compared to the younger youths (seventh grade). This result is in line with our previous research [32], where differences in MHL between 14–17 year old and 11–13 year old participants were found, with older students demonstrating higher scores in the Knowledge/Stereotypes and Self-Help Strategies dimensions, and the MHLq global score. Although this project is focused on a narrow age-span (12–14 year-old), it is interesting to notice age differences in the impact of the intervention concerning specific dimensions of MHL, which might be attributable to the rapid cognitive and socioemotional developmental changes in adolescence. This points to the importance of adjusting intervention strategies focused on the different dimensions of MHL according to the age and developmental stage of participants.

Finally, concerning the hypothesis regarding the impact of previous knowledge of someone with a mental health problem on the effectiveness of the intervention, young people who reported knowing people with a mental health problem had, on average, significantly higher gains than those who did not know someone with a mental health problem, on the Global Score and on the Knowledge/Stereotypes dimension. Previous research (e.g., [30–32]) showed higher levels of MHL in people who indicated knowing someone with a mental health problem. It is possible that young people who have already had contact with people with mental health problems are more willing to understand and discuss informative content on this subject and, consequently, benefit more from interventions of this type. The design of future interventions should take into account previous level of contact with mental health problems amongst those for whom the intervention is designed.

In future studies, some of the limitations of the present study may be addressed, namely those related to the lack of information concerning some variables that could also impact the effectiveness of the intervention, such as students' socioemotional developmental characteristics, family SES and other parental variables, as well as identification of possible health-related programs developed in schools they attend. Furthermore, new research should explore the impact of the intervention program in specific groups of students, such as adolescents at risk of developing mental health problems, assessing their help-seeking behavior as a potential outcome. A larger dissemination of this program through the integration of its content into school curricula would also be an interesting research subject, already been studied by some authors [41]. Finally, considering the ubiquity of technology in young peoples' lives, it is relevant to test the differential effectiveness of this intervention program, comparing its current delivery model to an updated model that includes technologically-mediated communication with the participants between sessions.

6. Conclusions

This study evaluated a school-based intervention program at three moments in time—pre-intervention, post-intervention and follow-up (six months after the intervention), using an experimental design that utilized assessment instruments adapted to the population, as recommended in the literature [22,42].

The results presented in this study should contribute to the broader discussion of how the promotion of mental health literacy in young people needs to be addressed. There is an urgent need to implement interventions that demonstrate positive impacts in the promotion of mental health literacy with young people—specifically in the increase of knowledge and reduction of stereotypes related to mental health problems, promotion of positive attitudes towards first aid skills and help-seeking behaviors, and development of self-help strategies.

Differences were observed in the gains from the intervention due to sociodemographic variables—gender, schooling year, previous contact with mental health problems, and school type (public vs. state funded).

The results of the study reinforce the usefulness of the most current and comprehensive version of the MHL concept, (e.g., not focusing exclusively on increasing knowledge about a particular disorder), as well as the need to take into account developmental and contextual variables in MHL promotion programs.

Author Contributions: L.C. contributed to the conception and design of the research, to the design of the experiments, supervised the data collection and interpretation of the data, reviewed the literature and wrote the manuscript. P.D. contributed to the design of the experiments, analysis and interpretation of the data, reviewed the literature and wrote the manuscript. F.P. contributed to the conception and design of the research, to the design of the experiments, reviewed the literature, and revised the manuscript. A.D. contributed to data collection and analysis, reviewed the literature, and revised the manuscript. E.V. contributed to the design of the research and revised the manuscript. C.C.D. carried out the data analyses and produced the tables and revised the manuscript. All authors approved the final version of the document.

Funding: This study was funded by the Portuguese Foundation for Science and Technology (PTDC/PSI-PCL/112526/2009) and developed by the Faculty of Education and Psychology of the Universidade Católica Portuguesa, in partnership with ENCONTRAR+SE—Association for the promotion of mental health. The publication of this manuscript was supported by the Portuguese Foundation for Science and Technology (UID/CED/4872/2016).

Acknowledgments: The authors would like to thank the support from: Anthony Jorm (consultant of the research project), António Fonseca, Raquel Matos, Maria Xavier, Vânia Sousa Lima, Bárbara César Machado (experts in psychology), schools where data collection occurred, as well as their boards, teachers and students; and master students—Inês Silva, Ana Catarina Ferreira, Miriam Medina, Sara Pinho, Júlio Roma Torres, Ana Filipa Assunção, and Marta Luís.

Conflicts of Interest: The authors declare no conflicts of interest.

References

1. Kieling, C.; Baker-Henningham, H.; Belfer, M.; Conti, G.; Ertem, I.; Omigbodun, O.; Rohde, L.A.; Srinath, S.; Ulkuer, N.; Rahman, A. Child and adolescent mental health worldwide: Evidence for action. *Lancet* **2011**, *378*, 1515–1525. [CrossRef]
2. World Health Organization. Mental Health Promotion in Young People—An Investment for the Future. 2010. Available online: http://www.euro.who.int/__data/assets/pdf_file/0013/121135/E94270.pdf (accessed on 23 May 2018).
3. Brauner, C.; Stephens, C. Estimating the prevalence of early childhood serious emotional/behavioral disorders: Challenges and recommendations. *Public Health Rep.* **2006**, *121*, 303–310. [CrossRef] [PubMed]
4. Jorm, A. Mental Health Literacy: Empowering the community to take action for action for better mental health. *Am. Psychol.* **2012**, *67*, 231–243. [CrossRef] [PubMed]
5. World Health Organization. Mental Health Action Plan 2013–2020. 2013. Available online: http://www.who.int/mental_health/publications/action_plan/en/ (accessed on 23 May 2018).
6. Kessler, R.C.; Berglund, P.; Demler, O.; Jin, R.; Merikangas, K.R.; Walters, E.E. Lifetime prevalence and age-of-onset distributions of DSM-IV disorders in the National Comorbidity Survey Replication. *Arch. Gen. Psychiatry* **2005**, *62*, 593–602. [CrossRef] [PubMed]
7. Belfer, M.L. Child and adolescent mental disorders: The magnitude of the problem across the globe. *J. Child Psychol. Psychol.* **2008**, *49*, 226–236. [CrossRef] [PubMed]
8. World Health Organization. Social Cohesion for Mental Well-Being among Adolescents. 2008. Available online: http://www.euro.who.int/__data/assets/pdf_file/0005/84623/E91921.pdf (accessed on 1 March 2018).
9. Boyle, F.M.; Donald, M.; Dean, J.H.; Conrad, S.; Mutch, A.J. Mental health promotion and non-profit health organisations. *Health Soc. Care Community* **2007**, *15*, 553–560. [CrossRef] [PubMed]
10. Joint Action—Mental Health and Wellbeing. 2013. Available online: https://www.mentalhealthandwellbeing.eu/ (accessed on 28 February 2018).
11. Pinfold, V.; Toulmin, H.; Thornicroft, G.; Huxley, P.; Farmer, P.; Graham, T. Reducing psychiatric stigma and discrimination: Evaluation of educational interventions in UK secondary schools. *Br. J. Psychiatry* **2003**, *182*, 342–346. [CrossRef] [PubMed]
12. Jorm, A.; Korten, A.; Jacomb, P.; Christensen, H.; Rodgers, B.; Pollitt, P. "Mental health literacy": A survey of the public's ability to recognise mental disorders and their beliefs about the effectiveness of treatment. *Med. J. Aust.* **1997**, *166*, 182–186. [PubMed]
13. Hart, L.M.; Mason, R.J.; Kelly, C.M.; Cvetkovski, S.; Jorm, A.F. 'Teen Mental Health First Aid': A description of the program and an initial evaluation. *Int. J. Ment. Health Syst.* **2016**, *10*. [CrossRef] [PubMed]

14. Jorm, A.F.; Barney, L.J.; Christensen, H.; Highet, N.J.; Kelly, C.M.; Kitchener, B.A. Research on mental health literacy: What we know and what we still need to know. *Aust. N. Z. J. Psychiatry* **2006**, *40*, 3–5. [CrossRef] [PubMed]
15. Kelly, C.M.; Jorm, A.F.; Wright, A. Improving mental health literacy as a strategy to facilitate early intervention for mental disorders. *Med. J. Aust.* **2007**, *187*, 26–30.
16. European Commission & Portuguese Ministry of Health—Background Document for the Thematic Conference—Promoting Social Inclusion and Combating Stigma for Better Mental Health and Well-Being. 2010. Available online: http://ec.europa.eu/health/mental_health/docs/ev_20101108_bgdocs_en.pdf (accessed on 27 February 2018).
17. Corrigan, P.; Watson, A. How children stigmatize people with mental illness. *Int. J. Soc. Psychiatry* **2007**, *53*, 526–546. [CrossRef] [PubMed]
18. Wright, A.; Jorm, A.; Harris, M.G.; McGorry, P.D. What's in a name? Is accurate recognition and labelling of mental disorders by young people associated with better help-seeking and treatment preferences? *Soc. Psychiatry Psychiatr. Epidemiol.* **2007**, *42*, 244–250. [CrossRef] [PubMed]
19. Cheng, H.; Wang, C.; McDermott, R.; Kridel, M.; Rislin, J. Self-Stigma, Mental Health Literacy, and Attitudes toward Seeking Psychological Help. *J. Couns. Dev.* **2018**, *96*, 66–71. [CrossRef]
20. Kutcher, S. Child and Youth Mental Health: Investing in the Front End. *Can. J. Psychiatry* **2017**, *62*, 232–234. [CrossRef] [PubMed]
21. Campos, L.; Palha, F.; Lima, V.S.; Dias, P.; Duarte, A.; Veiga, E. School-based Innovative Practices for the Promotion of Social, Emotional and Learning Skills in Portugal. In *Innovative Practices and Interventions for Children and Adolescents with Psychosocial*, 1st ed.; Kourkoutas, E., Hart, A., Eds.; Cambridge Scholars Publishing: Newcastle Upon Tyne, UK, 2015; pp. 152–183, ISBN 1-4438-7250-4.
22. Campos, L. Commentary on the paper, 'Evaluation of a campaign to improve awareness and attitudes of young people towards mental health issues' (Livingston et al., 2012). *Educ. Health* **2013**, *31*, 45–50.
23. Salerno, J. Effectiveness of universal school-based mental awareness programs among youth in the United States: A systematic review. *J. School Health* **2016**, *86*, 922–931. [CrossRef] [PubMed]
24. Wei, Y.; Hayden, J.A.; Kutcher, S.; Zygmunt, A.; McGrath, P. The effectiveness of school mental health literacy programs to address knowledge, attitudes and help seeking among youth. *Early Interv. Psychiatry* **2013**, *7*, 109–121. [CrossRef] [PubMed]
25. Chandra, A.; Minkovitz, C.S. Stigma starts early: Gender differences in teen willingness to use mental health services. *J. Adolesc. Health* **2006**, *38*, 754. [CrossRef] [PubMed]
26. Cotton, S.M.; Wright, A.; Harris, M.G.; Jorm, A.F.; McGorry, P.D. Influence of gender on mental health literacy in young Australians. *Aust. N. Z. J. Psychiatry* **2006**, *40*, 790–796. [CrossRef] [PubMed]
27. Martínez-Zambrano, F.; García-Morales, E.; García-Franco, M.; Miguel, J.; Villellas, R.; Pascual, G.; Arenas, O.; Ochoa, S. Intervention for reducing stigma: Assessing the influence of gender and knowledge. *World J. Psychiatry* **2013**, *3*, 18–24. [CrossRef] [PubMed]
28. Williams, B.; Pow, J. Gender differences and mental health: An exploratory study of knowledge and attitudes to mental health among Scottish teenagers. *Child Adol. Ment. H-UK* **2007**, *12*, 8–12. [CrossRef]
29. Skre, I.; Friborg, O.; Breivik, C.; Johnsen, L.; Arnesen, Y.; Wang, C. A school intervention for mental health literacy in adolescents: Effects of a non-randomized cluster controlled trial. *BMC Public Health* **2013**, *13*, 873. [CrossRef] [PubMed]
30. Lauber, C.; Nordt, C.; Falcato, L.; Rössler, W. Do people recognise mental illness? *Eur. Arch. Psychiatry Clin. Neurosci.* **2003**, *253*, 248–251. [CrossRef] [PubMed]
31. Angermeyer, M.; Matschinger, H.; Corrigan, P. Familiarity with mental illness and social distance from people with schizophrenia and major depression: Testing a model using data from a representative population survey. *Schizophr. Res.* **2004**, *69*, 175–182. [CrossRef]
32. Campos, L.; Dias, P.; Palha, F.; Duarte, A.; Veiga, E. Development and psychometric properties of a new questionnaire for assessing Mental Health Literacy in young people. *Univ. Psychol.* **2016**, *15*, 61–72. [CrossRef]
33. Campos, L.; Dias, P.; Palha, F. Finding Space to Mental Health—Promoting mental health in adolescents: Pilot study. *Educ. Health* **2014**, *32*, 23–29.
34. Fitzmaurice, G.M.; Laird, N.M.; Ware, J.H. *Applied Longitudinal Analysis*, 2nd ed.; Wiley-Interscience: Hoboken, NJ, USA, 2011; ISBN 0470380276.

35. Pepe, M.S.; Anderson, G.L. A cautionary note on inference for marginal regression models with longitudinal data and general correlated response data. *Commun. Stat.-Simul. C* **1994**, *23*, 939–951. [CrossRef]
36. Pinto-Foltz, M.D.; Logsdon, M.C.; Myers, J.A. Feasibility, acceptability, and initial efficacy of a knowledge-contact program to reduce mental illness stigma and improve mental health literacy in adolescents. *Soc. Sci. Med.* **2011**, *72*, 2011–2019. [CrossRef] [PubMed]
37. Organisation for Economic Co-operation and Development. Private Schools: Who Benefits? 2011. Available online: https://www.oecd.org/pisa/pisaproducts/pisainfocus/48482894.pdf (accessed on 15 February 2018).
38. Holman, D. Exploring the relationship between social class, mental illness stigma and mental health literacy using British national survey data. *Health* **2015**, *19*, 413–429. [CrossRef] [PubMed]
39. von dem Knesebeck, O.; Mnich, E.; Daubmann, A.; Wegscheider, K.; Angermeyer, M.; Lambert, M.; Karow, A.; Härter, M.; Kofahl, C. Socioeconomic status and beliefs about depression, schizophrenia and eating disorders. *Soc. Psychiatry Psychiatr. Epidemiol.* **2012**, *48*, 775–782. [CrossRef] [PubMed]
40. Campos, L.; Losada, A.; Pinho, S.; Duarte, A.; Palha, F.; Dias, P.; Veiga, E. Mental Health Literacy in students from public & private schools: Preliminary results from Finding Space to Mental Health. In Proceedings of the 1st World Congress on Children and Youth Health Behaviors, Viseu, Portugal, 23–25 May 2013.
41. Mcluckie, A.; Kutcher, S.; Wie, Y.; Weaver, C. Sustained improvements in students' mental health literacy with use of a mental health curriculum in Canadian schools. *BMC Psychiatry* **2014**, *14*, 379. [CrossRef] [PubMed]
42. Kutcher, S.; Wei, Y.; Coniglio, C. Mental Health Literacy: Past, Present, and Future. *Can. J. Psychiatry* **2016**, *61*, 154–158. [CrossRef] [PubMed]

© 2018 by the authors. Licensee MDPI, Basel, Switzerland. This article is an open access article distributed under the terms and conditions of the Creative Commons Attribution (CC BY) license (http://creativecommons.org/licenses/by/4.0/).

Article

Understanding Educational and Psychosocial Factors Associated with Alcohol Use among Adolescents in Denmark; Implications for Health Literacy Interventions

Claudia König [1], Mette V. Skriver [1], Kim M. Iburg [1] and Gillian Rowlands [2,*]

1. Department of Public Health, Aarhus University, Bartholins Allé 2, Bygning 1260, 8000 Aarhus C, Denmark; claudiakoe7@gmail.com (C.K.); mette.skriver@ph.au.dk (M.V.S.); kmi@ph.au.dk (K.M.I.)
2. Institute of Health and Society, Newcastle University, NE1 7RU Newcastle upon Tyne, UK
* Correspondence: gill.rowlands@newcastle.ac.uk; Tel.: +44-191-208-1300

Received: 25 June 2018; Accepted: 30 July 2018; Published: 6 August 2018

Abstract: *Background.* Alcohol misuse is a global public health priority, with a variation in prevalence and impact between countries. Alcohol misuse in adolescence is associated with adverse psychological, social and physical health. Adolescents in Denmark have higher alcohol consumption and problematic alcohol use than adolescents in other European countries. Associations between social determinants of health (SDH), psycho-social factors and alcohol consumption are complex and influenced by national context and cultures. This study explored these associations in Danish adolescents. *Method.* The European School Survey Project on Alcohol and Other Drugs (ESPAD) survey collects data on alcohol and substance use among 15–16-year-old European students. Data contributed by Danish students to the 2011 survey were analyzed. The outcomes of interest were alcohol consumption (any, intoxication and problematic). Health literacy was not directly measured, so self-described educational performance and knowledge about alcohol were used as proxies for health literacy. Exploratory factors thus included socio-demographic, health literacy-related (knowledge about alcohol, educational performance) and psycho-social factors, as well as expectancies of the effect of alcohol (both positive and negative) and self-reported health. Univariate and multivariate logistic regression analyses were undertaken. *Results.* Of the 2768 adolescents who participated in the survey, 2026 (80%) consumed alcohol during the last 30 days, 978 (38%) were intoxicated at least once during the last 30 days, and 1050 (41%) experienced at least one problem because of alcohol use during the last 12 months. Multivariable analysis showed that the factors associated with higher alcohol intake were gender, poor relationships with parents, expectancies of the impact of alcohol (both positive and negative), and the influence of peers and their alcohol use. Higher school performance was related to lower alcohol consumption. Low socio-demographic status was not associated with higher alcohol consumption. *Conclusions.* This study confirmed the high levels of alcohol intake, intoxication, and problem drinking amongst the Danish students in the survey and the complexity of the socio-demographic, psychosocial, health literacy-related, and environmental factors associated with alcohol behaviours. Approaches to addressing the issue of alcohol use in Danish adolescents will need to be multi-factorial, including supporting students to develop alcohol-related health literacy skills to enable them to make informed choices.

Keywords: health literacy; alcohol; adolescent; local context

1. Introduction

Alcohol is one of the world's top three priority areas in public health and is the third largest risk factor for disease and early death in Europe [1–3]. In childhood and adolescence, alcohol use is associated with adverse psychological, social and physical health consequences, including violence, accidents, injury, risky sexual behaviour, academic failure and increased risk of the use of other substances [4,5]. Alcohol may interfere with adolescent brain development and functioning [6]. Those who are early initiators, excessive drinkers and who have multiple risk behaviours are especially likely to experience adverse health outcomes [7]. Alcohol use in adolescence has been associated with alcohol consumption and health issues in later life [4,8,9].

Alcohol use in adolescence is common in many European countries [8,10–12], particularly so in Denmark with high levels of lifetime alcohol consumption (92%), alcohol consumption during the last 30 days (73%), 'heavy episodic drinking' (drinking more than five drinks on the same occasion) during the last 30 days (56%), and 'intoxication' during the last 30 days (32%) [12]. The minimum legal age of alcohol consumption in Denmark is 16 years.

The HBSC study on adolescents' health showed social inequalities for a number of health outcomes, with higher socioeconomic resources in general being associated with better health outcomes and positive social contexts with respect to family, peers and school [8,10]. However, associations between social determinants of health (SDH: the conditions in which people are born, grow, live, work and age [13]) and risk behaviors such as alcohol consumption are often more complex, and show contradictory results [8,10,14–21]. Additional factors increasing the complexity of understanding the reasons underlying alcohol consumption in adolescence are the associations with psycho-social factors such as social relationships to parents and friends [14,17,22,23]. The variation in alcohol consumption in adolescents between countries [12] is likely to reflect differences in environmental (i.e., national, cultural and legal) contexts.

Health literacy, 'the motivation, knowledge and competencies to access, understand, appraise and apply health information in order to make judgments and take decisions in everyday life concerning healthcare, disease prevention and health promotion to maintain or improve quality of life throughout the course of life' [24], may be another factor of importance in enabling informed alcohol consumption. Health literacy is gaining increasing focus internationally, as it empowers individuals and communities through enhancing capacities for promoting health and preventing and managing disease. It is seen as key to the delivery of health promotion strategies [25]. Health literacy can be viewed at several levels of cognitive capacities. Functional skills are the reading and writing skills needed to be able to function effectively in everyday situations; communicative/interactive skills are more advanced cognitive and literacy skills which, together with social skills, can be used to actively participate in everyday activities, to extract information and derive meaning from different forms of communication, and to apply new information to changing circumstances; and critical skills are more advanced cognitive skills which, together with social skills, can be applied to critically analyze information and to use this information to exert greater control over life events and situations [26]. It is being increasingly recognized that health literacy may be important in understanding—and developing interventions to address—risky alcohol consumption. 'Alcohol health literacy' has been defined as is 'the degree to which individuals have the capacity to obtain, process and understand knowledge about alcohol content, units, strengths and harms' [27]. This definition thus fits within 'functional health literacy' as described by Nutbeam [26]. At present, no wider definitions of alcohol health literacy (i.e., incorporation of the concept of interactive and critical alcohol health literacy) exist.

In summary, alcohol behavior in adolescents is an important cause of health, educational, legal and social problems. The reasons underlying alcohol consumption are complex and in addition are likely to be influenced by national and local alcohol-related contexts and cultures and health literacy. This study was an in-depth exploration of these associations in Denmark, a country with high levels of alcohol use in adolescents.

2. Materials and Methods

2.1. Design, Data Collection and Participants

Data were collected in 2011 by the European School Survey Project on Alcohol and Other Drugs (ESPAD), a project aiming to collect comparable data on substance use among 15–16-year-old European students [11]. Analyses were performed on Danish data. The study population were students in 9th grade public and private schools in Denmark, primarily aged 15–16 years, who participated in the 2011 ESPAD survey. Ninety-seven schools with a total of 2768 Danish students participated. The ESPAD report provides details on survey methodology and data quality [11].

2.2. Aim

The study aimed to explore associations between social determinants of health including health literacy as indicated by educational performance and knowledge about the risks of high levels of alcohol intake, psycho-social factors and alcohol consumption in Danish adolescents, in order to give recommendations for action to support safer alcohol consumption in this age-group.

2.3. Measures

For the analyses, the research team selected variables likely to be relevant, given published research in the area. Measures used in the analyses are described below. The test-retest reliability of the measurements used in ESPAD have been described [28]. Reliability has been described both within and between countries. Validity (in this case, the degree to which the survey measures what it is intended to measure, namely substance use in students) is high; whilst direct measures of alcohol and drug consumption (e.g., through saliva or urine sampling) are not taken, in post-survey interviewing and questionnaires, students have consistently reported truthful responses in earlier survey completions.

Health literacy was not directly measured in the survey. We thus identified those variables that mapped most closely onto the definition of health literacy; i.e., cognitive skills and alcohol knowledge [26,27]. Cognitive skills were captured through student educational performance, whilst alcohol knowledge was evaluated through student knowledge that consuming 4–5 alcoholic drinks a day is risky behavior. Students' educational performance was measured through self-report using the Danish education system grading system, categorized into 'below average' (grade less than 6), 'average' (grade 6–8,), and 'above average' (grade 9 or higher).

2.4. Socio-Demographic Factors

These included gender, age, educational attainment of the parent(s), and socio-economic status (SES). Parental educational attainment was grouped into low (lower secondary education), medium (upper secondary education), and high (medium long or higher education). SES was assessed by the perceived financial situation of the adolescents' family compared to other families in Denmark and grouped into three categories: 'better off', 'about the same', and 'less well off'.

2.5. Psycho-Social Factors

Respondents were asked how satisfied they usually were with their relationship with their mother, father and friends. Response categories ranged from 'very satisfied' to 'not at all satisfied' and answers were grouped into two categories: 'satisfied' and 'neither nor/not satisfied'. Respondents also reported how often during the last 12 months they had experienced serious problems with their parents and friends, categorized into never (0) and '1 or more occasions'.

Parental monitoring was measured by students' assessment of parents' knowledge of their whereabouts at weekends, grouped into two categories: 'know always/know quite often' and 'know sometimes/usually don't know'.

Peer alcohol consumption was measured through variables including both the alcohol consumption of friends and siblings. Respondents estimated how many of their friends drink alcoholic beverages or get drunk. The answers were categorized into 'none/a few/some' and 'most/all'). In addition, the students reported whether any of their older siblings drink alcoholic beverages or get drunk ('yes' or 'no').

2.6. Other Factors

Students' well-being and their knowledge related to alcohol consumption were included. Respondents rated their satisfaction with their own health and separately with themselves and their lives. Answers were categorized into 'satisfied' and 'neither nor/not satisfied'. Respondents also appraised the extent to which people risk harming themselves (physically or in other ways) if they have four or five drinks nearly every day (categorized: 'don't know/no risk' and 'risk'). Alcohol expectancies were measured by asking the students how likely it was that each of the following things would happen to them personally if they drank alcohol. Their answers were grouped into positive and negative alcohol expectancies as follows and categorized into 'likely' and 'unsure/unlikely'. Positive alcohol expectancies included feeling relaxed, feeling happy, feeling more friendly and out-going, having a lot of fun, and forgetting their problems. Negative alcohol expectancies included getting into trouble with police, harming their health, not being able to stop drinking, getting a hangover, doing something they would regret, feeling sick.

2.7. Alcohol Consumption

Outcome variables were chosen to reflect a gradient in severity of alcohol consumption i.e., (1) alcohol consumption during the last 30 days; (2) intoxication during the last 30 days; and (3) problems because of own alcohol use during the last 12 months. Alcohol consumption was measured through the number of occasions (if any) in which respondents had any alcoholic beverage to drink during the last 30 days; intoxication was measured through the number of occasions (if any) respondents had been intoxicated during the last 30 days; and 'problems from drinking' was measured through the number of occasions respondents had experienced one the following during the last 12 months because of their alcohol use: physical fights, accident or injury, serious problems with parents, serious problems with friends, performing poorly at school or work, being victimized by robbery or theft, trouble with police, being hospitalized or admitted to an emergency room, engaging in sexual intercourse without a condom, or engaging in sexual intercourse that was regretted the next day. The answers of all three outcome variables were categorized into never (0) and '1 or more occasions'.

2.8. Statistical Analysis

Initially, descriptive analyses of relevant variables were conducted. Following this, the relations between alcohol consumption and SDH, HL and psycho-social factors were studied using logistic regression analyses, both univariable and multivariable.

Univariable analyses explored the associations of explanatory variables (SDH, HL, psycho-social factors) and (1) alcohol consumption; (2) intoxication; and (3) problem drinking.

Multivariable analyses were then undertaken including all explanatory variables. To simplify the analysis, only one variable representing the students' school performance, i.e., average grade, was included.

Three sets of analyses were carried out, i.e., associations between SDH, HL, psycho-social factors and (1) alcohol consumption; (2) intoxication; and (3) problem drinking.

As a Supplementary Materials analysis, the dataset was divided by gender and all above described analyses were conducted to determine if results differed by gender.

All statistical analyses were performed using STATA (14.1). The level of significance was set at $p < 0.05$.

3. Results

3.1. General Characteristics

The sample contained responses from 2768 students, with approximately equal numbers of male and female students. Data on key variables are shown in Table 1. It should be noted that not all students answered every question.

Table 1. Description of sample and variables of interest.

Total	2768
Male Gender	1319 of 2750 (48.0%)
Alcohol intake	
Alcohol taken on ≥ 1 occasion in last 30 days	2026 of 2544 (79.64%)
Alcohol intoxication on ≥ 1 occasion in last 30 days	978 of 2548 (38.38%)
Have experienced problems from alcohol use during the last 12 months	1050 of 2550 (41.18%)
Alcohol environment	
Most or all friends drink alcohol	2410 of 2745 (87.80%)
Most or all friends get intoxicated	1927 of 2746 (70.17%)
Older siblings drink alcohol	1632 of 1867 (87.41%)
Older siblings get intoxicated	1436 of 1808 (79.42%)
Alcohol expectancies and beliefs	
Reporting that they are likely to experience positive outcomes from alcohol	2341 of 2523 (92.79%)
Reporting that they are unlikely to experience negative outcomes from alcohol	686 of 2511 (27.32%)
Socio-economic status	
Highest level of schooling father: Lower secondary education or less	606 of 1901 (31.88%)
Highest level of schooling mother: Lower secondary education or less	360 of 2082 (17.29%)
Families' wealth: Less well off than average	283 of 2697 (10.49%)
Health	
'Not satisfied' or 'neither satisfied nor dissatisfied' with own health	392 of 2739 (14.31%)
'Not satisfied' or 'neither satisfied nor dissatisfied' with themselves	654 of 2735 (23.91%)
Family and peer relationships	
'Not satisfied' or 'neither satisfied nor dissatisfied' with maternal relationship	303 of 2712 (11.17%)
'Not satisfied' or 'neither satisfied nor dissatisfied' with paternal relationship	450 of 2635 (17.08%)
Parents know sometimes or usually do not know where respondent is on Saturday nights	148 of 2746 (5.39%)
Have experienced 'serious problems' with parents on ≥ 1 occasion	752 of 2744 (27.41%)
'Not satisfied' or 'neither satisfied nor dissatisfied' with relationships with friends	205 of 2740 (7.48%)
Have experienced 'serious problems' with friends on ≥ 1 occasion	896 of 2742 (32.68%)
Health literacy proxies	
School performance† below average	436 of 2664 (16.37%)
Knowledge that 4–5 drinks a day brings health risks: answered 'no' or 'don't know'	115 of 2740 (4.20%)

Of note is the high levels of alcohol intake in the last 30 days ($n = 2026$, 79.64%), intoxication ($n = 978$, 38.38%), and experience of problems as a result of drinking alcohol ($n = 1050$, 41.18%), and high levels of alcohol exposure from peers ($n = 2410$, 87.8%) and siblings ($n = 1632$, 87.41%). A very high proportion of the students expected positive outcomes to arise from drinking alcohol ($n = 2341$, 92.79%), with 686 of students (27.32%) reporting that they expected not to experience negative consequences from drinking alcohol. When socio-economic factors are considered, whilst nearly one third ($n = 606$, 31.88%) came from families with low paternal education, only 283 (10.49%) felt that their family was 'less well off than average'. Many students reported negative family and peer relationships, including serious problems with either parent ($n = 752$, 27.41%) and/or friends ($n = 896$, 32.68%).

Only a very small number (115 students, 4.2%) did not recognize the fact that drinking 4–5 alcoholic drinks a day brought risks.

3.2. Univariable Analysis

Associations between explanatory variables (SDH, HL, psycho-social factors) and all three outcome variables (alcohol consumption, intoxication, problem drinking) from univariable logistic regression analyses can be accessed in Table S1 in the Supplementary Materials.

3.3. Multivariate Analyses

Table 2 provides an overview of the results of the multivariable analyses.

Table 2. Multivariable analyses.

Explanatory Variable	Drinking any Alcohol during the Last 30 Days OR (95% CI)	Been Intoxicated during the Last 30 Days OR (95% CI)	Problems Because of Own Alcohol Use during the Last 12 Months OR (95% CI)
Gender			
Male	Reference	Reference	Reference
Female	0.56 (0.37 to 0.84) *	0.79 (0.58 to 1.08)	0.64 (0.46 to 0.88) **
School performance †			
6–8.9 (average)	Reference	Reference	Reference
>9 (above average)	0.60 (0.39 to 0.93) *	0.88 (0.60 to 1.29)	0.58 (0.39 to 0.86) **
<6 (below average)	1.34 (0.67 to 2.69)	1.42 (0.89 to 2.26)	1.22 (0.75 to 1.98)
Father's education			
Medium long or higher education	Reference	Reference	Reference
Upper secondary education	0.66 (0.40 to 1.09)	1.10 (0.74 to 1.64)	1.19 (0.79 to 1.78)
Lower secondary education or less	0.84 (0.49 to 1.42)	0.96 (0.63 to 1.45)	1.40 (0.92 to 2.13)
Mother's education			
Medium long or higher education	Reference	Reference	Reference
Upper secondary education	1.39 (.88 to 2.21)	0.90 (0.63 to 1.29)	1.27 (0.88 to 1.84)
Lower secondary education or less	0.97 (0.53 to 1.79)	0.76 (0.48 to 1.22)	1.35 (0.83 to 2.18)
Wealth			
About the same	Reference	Reference	Reference
Better off	1.15 (0.76 to 1.74)	1.33 (0.97 to 1.83)	1.22 (0.88 to 1.70)
Less well off	0.74 (0.35 to 1.58)	0.96 (0.51 to 1.81)	1.10 (0.58 to 2.07)
Pos. alcohol expectancies (things happen to participants personally)			
Likely	Reference	Reference	Reference
Unsure/Unlikely	0.28 (0.14 to 0.56) **	0.25 (0.07 to 0.87) *	0.17 (0.05 to 0.60) **
Neg. alcohol expectancies (things happen to participants personally)			
Unsure/Unlikely	Reference	Reference	Reference
Likely	1.18 (0.77 to 1.81)	2.20 (1.50 to 3.21) **	2.80 (1.90 to 4.12) **
Belief risk			
Risk	Reference	Reference	Reference
No risk or do not know	0.22 (0.08 to 0.55) **	0.57 (0.22 to 1.52)	0.43 (0.16 to 1.18)
Satisfied health			
Satisfied	Reference	Reference	Reference
Not satisfied or neither nor	0.70 (0.40 to 1.23)	0.88 (0.56 to 1.37)	0.94 (0.59 to 1.51)
Satisfied themselves			
Satisfied	Reference	Reference	Reference
Not satisfied or neither nor	1.20 (0.73 to 1.97)	1.36 (0.93 to 1.99)	1.05 (0.71 to 1.57)
Parents know where their children are on Saturday			
Know always/quiet often	Reference	Reference	Reference
Know sometimes/Usually do not know	0.86 (0.27 to 2.74)	0.84 (0.39 to 1.81)	1.03 (0.41 to 2.56)
Satisfied relationship with mother			
Satisfied	Reference	Reference	Reference
Not satisfied or Neither nor	1.38 (0.61 to 3.11)	1.18 (0.69 to 2.04)	1.96 (1.08 to 3.56) *

Table 2. Cont.

Explanatory Variable	Drinking any Alcohol during the Last 30 Days	Been Intoxicated during the Last 30 Days	Problems Because of Own Alcohol Use during the Last 12 Months
	OR (95% CI)	OR (95% CI)	OR (95% CI)
Satisfied relationship with father			
Satisfied	Reference	Reference	Reference
Not satisfied or Neither nor	0.80 (0.44 to 1.45)	1.17 (0.74 to 1.86)	1.01 (0.62 to 1.63)
Satisfied relationship with friends			
Satisfied	Reference	Reference	Reference
Not satisfied or Neither nor	0.33 (0.17 to 0.65) **	0.43 (0.22 to 0.84) *	0.72 (0.37 to 1.39)
Serious problems with parents			
Zero occasions	Reference	Reference	Reference
1 or more occasion	1.60 (0.94 to 2.72)	1.28 (0.89 to 1.85)	1.62 (1.11 to 2.36) *
Serious problems with friends			
Zero occasions	Reference	Reference	Reference
1 or more occasion	1.62 (1.01 to 2.61) *	1.56 (1.11 to 2.19) *	2.65 (1.86 to 3.76) **
Friends drink			
Most/all	Reference	Reference	Reference
None/a few/some	0.40 (0.20 to 0.77) **	0.53 (0.21 to 1.35)	0.49 (0.22 to 1.10)
Friends get drunk			
Most/all	Reference	Reference	Reference
None/a few/some	0.92 (0.57 to 1.50)	0.27 (0.18 to 0.43) **	0.50 (0.33 to 0.75) **
Older siblings drink			
Yes	Reference	Reference	Reference
No	0.54 (0.24 to 1.22)	0.66 (0.28 to 1.55)	0.83 (0.36 to 1.93)
Older siblings get drunk			
Yes	Reference	Reference	Reference
No	0.71 (0.37 to 1.39)	0.61 (0.33 to 1.13)	0.56 (0.31 to 1.03)

[1] significant results * for $p < 0.05$ & ** for $p < 0.01$; † related to the Danish grading system.

The variables indicating an increased risk of any alcohol consumption and more risky alcohol consumption (recent intoxication or having ever experienced problems due to drinking) were male gender, consumption of alcohol by friends and experiencing problems with friends. Those whose friends drink any alcohol were more likely to drink alcohol themselves, but not to engage in more risky drinking, whilst those whose friends become intoxicated were more likely to engage in risky drinking themselves. In addition, those students who reported having experienced problems with peers were more likely to report any alcohol consumption and more risky drinking. Students who reported not being satisfied with the relationship with their mother and having experienced serious problems with parents were more likely to report risky drinking.

Students with poor school performance had higher levels of alcohol consumption and risky drinking, but this did not reach statistical significance. Students who reported their school performance as above average were less likely to have consumed alcohol in the last 30 days and to report problems arising from alcohol consumption. The same result was seen concerning intoxication, although the finding was not statistically significant; overall, a non-significant trend was seen whereby those with above-average self-reported school performance had a lower likelihood of drinking, intoxication and problems arising from alcohol use.

As might be expected, students who expected positive outcomes from alcohol drinking were more likely to drink at all and to exhibit risky drinking. In contrast, understanding the risk of high alcohol intake and having expectancies of negative outcomes of drinking alcohol showed the opposite effects to those expected. Almost all the students (95.8%) knew that consuming 4–5 drinks a day has health risks; knowledge of these risks was associated with an increased likelihood of having drunk any alcohol in the last 30 days, although not with reporting more risky drinking. Students with expectations of negative outcomes were more likely to have undertaken more risky drinking, but not more likely to have drunk at all in the last 30 days.

Parents' socioeconomic status (education and wealth) was not associated with either any alcohol consumption in the last 30 days or more risky drinking behavior.

3.4. Gender-Separated Analysis

Supplementary Materials analyses by gender were conducted. Results were similar and are therefore not described in detail here. Results are accessible in Table S2 in the Supplementary Materials.

4. Discussion

4.1. Key Results

Alcohol drinking in 15–16-year-olds in Denmark is very high, with nearly 80% of students having drunk alcohol in the last 30 days, and approximately 40% describing risky drinking i.e., intoxication in the last 30 days or ever having experienced problems due to drinking. Danish adolescents are living in a high-alcohol environment, with over 80% of students reporting that their peers drink and, for those reporting drinking in siblings, over 80% reporting that their siblings drink.

Drinking alcohol is more likely in those students who are male, who are in a peer group that drinks alcohol, and for those experiencing problems with friends and at home. Expecting positive outcomes from drinking alcohol is associated with more drinking, but, surprisingly, expecting negative outcomes from alcohol and being aware that high alcohol consumption is risky were also associated with more drinking. Knowledge of the risks of high alcohol consumption, which was almost universal, was associated with higher likelihood of drinking any alcohol but not of undertaking riskier drinking.

Whilst poor school performance was not statistically significantly associated with alcohol consumption and risky drinking, students reporting above average school performance were less likely to drink at all and to experience problems as a result of drinking.

Family socio-economic status was not associated with alcohol intake.

4.2. Strength and Limitations

The data for the statistical quantitative analysis were gathered in 2011 by the European study 'European School Survey Project on Alcohol and Other Drugs' (ESPAD), a project that collected extensive data on substance use among adolescents aged 15–16 years. This comprehensive dataset, from a large, well established study with reliable, well validated questions and high-quality data, provides an excellent opportunity to study hazardous alcohol consumption in the Danish setting.

However, a number of limitations need to be recognized when interpreting our results.

Firstly, when examining the associations between social determinants of health, variables used as proxy measures for health literacy, psychosocial factors and alcohol consumption, we considered only variables that were available from the ESPAD survey. Although we included a variety of socioeconomic and psychosocial variables, several other factors may affect alcohol use in adolescents and the influence of the social background may be wider. There may be other important factors that were not included in the study. Secondly, data was entirely self-reported by adolescents and may be subject to various types of biases. Thirdly, health literacy was not directly measured. The variables we used as proxies for health literacy, whilst closely associated with the current definition of alcohol health literacy (knowledge about the risks of alcohol) and interactive and critical skills (educational competence), are not direct measures and thus should be interpreted with caution. Finally, the cross-sectional nature of the data prevents any conclusions of causal relationships between social determinants of health, psychosocial factors and alcohol consumption.

4.3. How this Research Links to Current Knowledge

This study supported many of the findings in previous research, in particular the influence of peers on alcohol consumption [14,23], the protective effect of parental emotional support/parenting factors [14,17,22,29], the associations between positive alcohol expectancies and alcohol intake [30], and the weak association between alcohol consumption and socio-economic factors [14,23].

There were some important differences, however, between the findings in this study and previous research. Specifically, previous research from the U.S. has shown that the gender differences in alcohol consumption seen in adults (i.e., men consuming more alcohol and experiencing more alcohol-related problems than females [31]) are not seen in U.S. adolescents [32]. The study described here shows that, in Denmark, the gender pattern of alcohol drinking in adolescents mirrors that seen in adults, with male students drinking more than female students.

Another difference between the results of this Danish study and previous research is in the associations between negative alcohol expectancies and alcohol drinking. Whereas previous studies have shown that negative alcohol expectancies tend to have the expected associations with alcohol drinking (i.e., more negative alcohol expectancies are associated with lower drinking) [30], the findings from the present study showed the opposite association; expecting negative effects of drinking were associated with more alcohol drinking.

4.4. Interpretation

Our study shows that, in Denmark, an environment with high levels of alcohol availability and alcohol consumption, students aged 15 to 16 years who are at risk of high alcohol consumption and risky drinking are more likely to be in a peer group that drinks alcohol and to be experiencing problems with friends and at home. They are not likely to be performing poorly at school, or to come from socio-economically deprived backgrounds.

The results indicate the likely importance of legal and cultural contexts; whilst alcohol consumption at the age of 15 years is not legal in Denmark, it is extremely common, and students have very high exposure to alcohol. This may explain the contrast to, for example, findings for U.S. adolescents, where the legal age of drinking alcohol is much higher (21 years in many U.S. states compared to 16 years in Denmark), and students may have a lower exposure to alcohol from family and friends.

The results relating to health literacy may also reflect the 'alcohol environment' in which the students are living. Almost all (95.8%) of Danish students knew that taking 4–5 alcohol drinks a day is a risk to health; given the ubiquity of alcohol consumption amongst students, it is perhaps not surprising that this knowledge was not associated with less alcohol consumption in general, and it did not appear have any protective effect against riskier drinking. Educational competency, however, which may correspond to Nutbeam's 'interactive' and 'critical' health literacy, did appear to be associated with less overall drinking, and also with less risky drinking.

Our findings indicate that interventions to support 15 to 16-year-olds in Denmark to develop skills to make informed choices about alcohol consumption will need to be multifaceted. Any interventions need to consist of more than simply giving information about alcohol and its effects and developing skills to find and understand information about alcohol (functional health literacy). The finding that expecting negative outcomes from drinking and being aware of risks from high alcohol intake are both associated with a higher risk of drinking indicate that more complex issues are at play. The finding that students in alcohol-drinking peer groups are more likely to drink alcohol, as are students experiencing problems with friends and at home, together with the apparent protective effects of high education competence, indicate that approaches that develop wider cognitive competencies together with self-confidence in resisting peer pressure and ways to manage stressful situations within and outside the home, (i.e., critical alcohol health literacy—skills to critically analyze information and to use this information to exert greater control over alcohol drinking) should be the focus of interventions in this age group. Before such interventions can be developed, qualitative studies need to be undertaken with students themselves to better understand students' experiences, and to gather their insights on what approaches might help.

Finally, it is likely that the availability of alcohol, cultural issues, and legal frameworks in relation to alcohol will also play a part. It may be that the risk factors and socio-demographic associations will differ in different national settings and amongst different cultural groups.

5. Conclusions

In Danish society, adolescents have a high exposure to and cultural acceptance of alcohol drinking. In 15 to 16-year-olds, alcohol consumption, including riskier drinking patterns, is associated with peer-group exposure to alcohol and experiencing problems with friends and at home, and not with alcohol knowledge and socio-economic deprivation. Higher school performance is associated with lower alcohol drinking, including risky alcohol behaviors. In Danish settings, interventions to give adolescents the capacities to make and enact informed decisions about alcohol should focus on building critical alcohol health literacy—skills to critically analyze information about alcohol drinking and its risks and to use this information to exert greater control over alcohol consumption to reduce the risks of current and future harm—rather than simply focusing on increasing knowledge. In other countries, with different levels of alcohol exposure and availability and different alcohol cultures, the socio-demographic and psycho-social factors, and the impact of knowledge about and expectations of alcohol drinking may be different; analysis of local associations is required to develop interventions that are locally specific and culturally relevant.

Supplementary Materials: The following are available online at http://www.mdpi.com/1660-4601/15/8/1671/s1, Table S1: Univariable analysis. Factors associated with alcohol consumption, odds ratios and 95% confidence intervals, Table S2: Multivariable gender-separated analysis. Factors associated with alcohol consumption, odds ratios and 95% confidence intervals.

Author Contributions: Conceptualization, C.K., M.V.S., K.M.I. and G.R.; Methodology, C.K., M.V.S., K.M.I. and G.R.; Formal Analysis, C.K.; Writing-Original Draft Preparation, C.K.; Writing-Review & Editing, C.K., M.V.S., K.M.I. and G.R.; Supervision, G.R.

Conflicts of Interest: The authors declare no conflict of interest.

References

1. WHO. Global health risks. In *Mortality and Burden of Disease Attributable to Selected Major Risks*; World Health Organization: Geneva, Switzerland, 2009.
2. Anderson, P.; Baumberg, B. Alcohol in Europe. In *A Public Health Perspective*; Institute of Alcohol Studies: London, UK, 2006.
3. Anderson, P.; Møller, L.; Galea, G. Alcohol in the European Union. In *Consumption, Harm and Policy Approaches*; WHO Regional Office for Europe: Copenhagen, Denmark, 2012.
4. Boden, J.M.; Fergusson, D.M. The short and long-term consequences of adolescent alcohol use. In *Young People and Alcohol: IMPACT, Policy, Prevention and Treatment*; Saunders, J., Rey, J., Eds.; Wiley-Blackwell: Chichester, UK, 2011; pp. 32–46.
5. Jackson, C.; Geddes, R.; Haw, S.; Frank, J. Interventions to prevent substance use and risky sexual behaviour in young people: A systematic review. *Addiction* **2012**, *107*, 733–747. [CrossRef] [PubMed]
6. Ewing, S.W.; Sakhardande, A.; Blakemore, S.J. The effect of alcohol consumption on the adolescent brain: A systematic review of mri and fmri studies of alcohol-using youth. *Neuroimage Clin.* **2014**, *5*, 420–437. [CrossRef] [PubMed]
7. Janssen, I.; Dostaler, S.; Boyce, W.F.; Pickett, W. Influence of multiple risk behaviors on physical activity–related injuries in adolescents. *Pediatrics* **2007**, *119*, e672–e680. [CrossRef] [PubMed]
8. Inchley, J.; Currie, D.; Young, T.; Samdal, O.; Torsheim, T.; Augustson, L.; Mathison, F.; Aleman-Diaz, A.; Molcho, M.; Weber, M.; et al. Growing up unequal: Gender and socioeconomic differences in young people's health and well-being. In *Health Behaviour in School-Aged Children (HBSC) Study: Innternational Report from the 2013/2014 Survey*; WHO Regional Office for Europe: Copenhagen, Denmark, 2016.
9. Andersen, A.; Due, P.; Holstein, B.E.; Iversen, L. Tracking drinking behaviour from age 15–19 years. *Addiction* **2003**, *98*, 1505–1511. [CrossRef] [PubMed]

10. Currie, C.; Zanotti, C.; Morgan, A.; Currie, D.; Looze, M.D.; Roberts, C.; Samdal, O.; Smith, O.R.F.; Barnekow, V. Social determinants of health and well-being among young people. In *Health Behaviour in School-Aged Children (HBSC) Study: International Report from the 2009/2010 Survey*; WHO Regional Office for Europe: Copenhagen, Denmark, 2012.
11. Hibell, B.; Guttormsson, U.; Ahlström, S.; Balakireva, O.; Bjarnason, T.; Kokkevi, A.; Kraus, L. The 2011 ESPAD report. In *Substance Use Among Students in 36 European Countries*; The Swedish Council for Information on Alcohol and Other Drugs (CAN); The European Monitoring Centre for Drugs and Drug Addiction (EMCDDA), Council of Europe, Co-operation Group to Combat Drug Abuse and Illicit Trafficking in Drugs (Pompidou Group): Stockholm, Sweden, 2011.
12. Kraus, L.; Guttormsson, U.; Leifman, H.; Arpa, S.; Molinaro, S.; Monshouwer, K.; Trapencieris, M.; Vicente, J.; Arnarsson, Á.M.; Balakireva, O.; et al. ESPAD report 2015. In *Results from the European School Survey Project on Alcohol and Other Drugs*; European Monitoring Centre for Drugs and Drug Addiction (EMCDDA): Lisbon, Portugal, 2016.
13. CSDH. *Closing the Gap in a Generation: Health Equity Through Action on the Social Determinants of Health*; World Health Organization: Geneva, Switzerland, 2008.
14. Olumide, A.O.; Robinson, A.C.; Levy, P.A.; Mashimbye, L.; Brahmbhatt, H.; Lian, Q.; Ojengbede, O.; Sonenstein, F.L.; Blum, R.W. Predictors of substance use among vulnerable adolescents in five cities: Findings from the well-being of adolescents in vulnerable environments study. *J. Adolesc. Health Off. Publ. Soc. Adolesc. Med.* **2014**, *55*, S39–S47. [CrossRef] [PubMed]
15. Respress, B.N. Social Determinants of Adolescent Risk Behaviors: An Examination of Depressive Symptoms and Sexual Risk, Substance Use, and Suicide Risk Behaviors. 2011. Available online: https://etd.ohiolink.edu/pg_10?0::NO:10:P10_ACCESSION_NUM:case1270238396 (accessed on 27 July 2018).
16. Abel, T.; Hofmann, K.; Schori, D. Social and regional variations in health status and health behaviours among Swiss young adults. *Swiss Med. Wkly.* **2013**, *143*, w13901. [CrossRef] [PubMed]
17. Stafström, M. Influence of parental alcohol-related attitudes, behavior and parenting styles on alcohol use in late and very late adolescence. *Eur. Addict. Res.* **2014**, *20*, 233–240. [CrossRef] [PubMed]
18. Kolip, P.; Bucksch, J.; Deutsch, H.-T. Health risk behaviour in adolescence. *Monatsschr. Kinderheilkund.* **2012**, *160*, 657–661. [CrossRef]
19. Johansson, K.; San Sebastian, M.; Hammarström, A.; Gustafsson, P.E. Neighbourhood disadvantage and individual adversities in adolescence and total alcohol consumption up to mid-life-results from the northern Swedish cohort. *Health Place* **2015**, *33*, 187–194. [CrossRef] [PubMed]
20. Lakshman, R.; McConville, A.; How, S.; Flowers, J.; Wareham, N.; Cosford, P. Association between area-level socioeconomic deprivation and a cluster of behavioural risk factors: Cross-sectional, population-based study. *J. Public Health* **2011**, *33*, 234–245. [CrossRef] [PubMed]
21. Quon, E.C.; McGrath, J.J. Community, family, and subjective socioeconomic status: Relative status and adolescent health. *Health Psychol.* **2015**, *34*, 591–601. [CrossRef] [PubMed]
22. Roustit, C.; Chaix, B.; Chauvin, P. Family breakup and adolescents' psychosocial maladjustment: Public health implications of family disruptions. *Pediatrics* **2007**, *120*, e984–e991. [CrossRef] [PubMed]
23. Salvy, S.J.; Pedersen, E.R.; Miles, J.N.V.; Tucker, J.S.; D'Amico, E.J. Proximal and distal social influence on alcohol consumption and marijuana use among middle school adolescents. *Drug Alcohol Depend.* **2014**, *144*, 93–101. [CrossRef] [PubMed]
24. Sørensen, K.; Van den Broucke, S.; Fullam, J.; Doyle, G.; Pelikan, J.; Slonska, Z.; Brand, H. Health literacy and public health: A systematic review and integration of definitions and models. *BMC Public Health* **2012**, *12*, 80. [CrossRef] [PubMed]
25. World Health Organization. Shanghai declaration on promoting health in the 2030 agenda for sustainable development. In Proceedings of the 9th Global Conference on Health Promotion, Shanghai, China, 21–24 November 2016.
26. Nutbeam, D. Health literacy as a public health goal: A challenge for contemporary health education and communication strategies into the 21st century. *Health Promot. Int.* **2000**, *15*, 259–267. [CrossRef]
27. Rundle-Thiele, S.; Siemieniako, D.; Kubacki, K.; Deshapnde, S. Benchmarking alcohol literacy: A multi-country study. *Mod. Manag. Rev.* **2013**, *18*, 99–111. [CrossRef]

28. Hibell, B.; Andersson, B.; Bjarnson, T.; Balikireva, O.; Davidaviciene, A.; Muscat, R.; Nociar, A.; Sabroe, S.; Veresies, K. *Do They Tell the Truth? A Methodological Study in Seven Countries about the Validity in School Surveys*; The Swedish council for Information on Alcohol and Other Drugs: Stockholm, Sweden, 2000.
29. Viner, R.M.; Ozer, E.M.; Denny, S.; Marmot, M.; Resnick, M.; Fatusi, A. Adolescence and the social determinants of health. *Lancet* **2012**, *379*, 1641–1652. [CrossRef]
30. Chisolm, D.J.; Manganello, J.A.; Kelleher, K.J.; Marshal, M.P. Health literacy, alcohol expectancies, and alcohol use behaviors in teens. *Patient Educ. Couns.* **2014**, *97*, 291–296. [CrossRef] [PubMed]
31. Substance Abuse and Mental Health Services Administration, Office of Applied Studies. *Results from the 2007 National Survey on Drug Use and Health: National Findings*; Substance Abuse and Mental Health Services Administration, Office of Applied Studies: Rockville, MD, USA, 2008.
32. Johnston, L.D.; O'Malley, P.M.; Bachman, J.G.; Schulenberg, J.E. *Monitoring the Future National Results on Adolescent Drug Use: Overview of Key Findings*; National Institute on Drug Abuse: Bethesda, MD, USA, 2002.

© 2018 by the authors. Licensee MDPI, Basel, Switzerland. This article is an open access article distributed under the terms and conditions of the Creative Commons Attribution (CC BY) license (http://creativecommons.org/licenses/by/4.0/).

Article

Conditions and Dynamics That Impact Maternal Health Literacy among High Risk Prenatal-Interconceptional Women

Suzanne D. Thomas [1,*], Sandra C. Mobley [2], Jodi L. Hudgins [3], Donald E. Sutherland [4], Sandra B. Inglett [5] and Brittany L. Ange [6]

1. CSRA Nursing Associates, PC, 300 Gardners Mill Court, Augusta, GA 30907, USA
2. Department of Obstetrics & Gynecology, Medical College of Georgia, Augusta University, Augusta, GA 30912, USA; samobley@augusta.edu
3. Education and Networking, Enterprise Community Healthy Start, Augusta University, Augusta, GA 30912, USA; jhudgins@augusta.edu
4. Enterprise Community Healthy Start, The Perinatal Center, Augusta University, Augusta, GA 30912, USA; dsutherl@augusta.edu
5. Enterprise Community Healthy Start, College of Nursing, Augusta University, EC-5338, 987 St. Sebastian Way, Augusta, GA 30912, USA; singlett@augusta.edu
6. Department of Population Health, Division of Biostatistics and Data Science, Augusta University, Augusta, GA 30912, USA; bange@augusta.edu
* Correspondence: suzannedt1984@gmail.com

Received: 28 April 2018; Accepted: 25 June 2018; Published: 2 July 2018

Abstract: The purpose of the study was to describe conditions and dynamics in the lives of high-risk, low-income, Southern United States prenatal-interconceptional women (n = 37) in a home visiting program that promoted maternal health literacy progression. In the Life Course Health Development (LCHD) Model, conditions were risk and protective factors that impacted health. Dynamics drove the complex, epigenetic relationships between risk and protective factors. Maternal health literacy promotion helped participants address conditions and dynamics to create positive life changes. This research was a retrospective, mixed methods study of women's service records documenting care from prenatal admission to 24 months post-delivery. The Life Skills Progression Instrument (LSP) was scored to measure maternal health literacy progression. Ethnographic content analysis of visit notes triangulated with quantitative data enabled specificity of critical data elements. Subsequently, a complementary focus group was conducted with the Registered Nurse Case Managers (RNCM). Severe social conditions included devastating poverty, low educational achievement, transient housing, unstable relationships, incarceration, lack of continuous health insurance, and shortage of health care providers. Dynamics included severe psycho-social stressors, domestic violence, lack of employment, low income, low self-esteem and self-expectations, and social/family restraints upon women's intended positive changes. An important protective factor was the consistent, stable, evidence-informed relationship with the RNCM. Findings from the focus group discussion supported content analysis results.

Keywords: determinants of health; health disparities; health education; health literacy; health interventions; health promotion; social disadvantage

1. Introduction—Purpose and Theoretical Framework

The purpose of this study was to describe conditions and dynamics in the lives of high-risk, low-income, Southern United States prenatal-interconceptional women, who were enrolled in a U.S. government-funded home visiting program called Healthy Start. Healthy Start was originally charged with reducing infant mortality. In time, it became clear that medical care alone was not able to accomplish that goal, and that women and their infants needed a much broader approach to care. The Enterprise Community Healthy Start (ECHS) program chose to promote functional health literacy among the prenatal-interconceptional women who participated in the ECHS program. Prenatal meant from pregnancy conception to delivery. Interconceptional meant after delivery through 24 months of the infant's life. Increased functional health literacy among prenatal-interconceptional women was termed maternal health literacy progression.

Women or participants were considered to have high-risk conditions if their medical, social, environmental, physical, interpersonal, financial, educational, or any other socio-economic factors were judged as hazardous to the well-being of the woman or her fetus or infant. Thus, conditions were risk factors. Conditions also included factors that were protective or helpful in reducing risks to the woman and her fetus or infant. Dynamics described how risk and protective factors interacted. In theory, dynamics among risk and protective factors were powerful enough to limit or increase gene expression. Examples of dynamics included social or peer pressure, financial incentives or costs, physical or physiologic changes associated with pregnancy, and the search for safe housing, for love and belonging, and for reproduction. The Life Course Health Development Model (LCHD) described epigenetic interaction, which meant the ways that conditions and dynamics worked together to bring about changes in health development over the course of a person's life [1–3]. The programmatic goal of ECHS was to intervene in participants' lives to reduce their risks and bring about positive health developmental potentials for participants and their infants.

1.1. Maternal Health Literacy Progression

Functional health literacy was defined as a person's knowledge, skill, and ability to understand and apply health related information and to access health care services [4]. The recent return to home visitation as a model of service delivery showed promise to examine the unique setting where health related decisions and activities took place, to understand women's conditions and dynamics, and to strategize actions that promoted health [5,6]. Investigators conceptualized these health promotion strategies as two theoretical constructs in maternal health literacy [4,7–9]. First, Maternal Health Care Literacy was conceptualized as a participant's knowledge, skill, and access to health care, and her ability to manage her own and her infant's care; and second, Maternal Self Care Literacy was conceptualized as her self-health practices, self-esteem, use of resources, and knowledge of infant development. The home environment's uniqueness made it difficult to measure the impact of nursing services upon maternal health literacy. Thus, in 2005, ECHS adopted the Life Skills Progression Instrument (LSP) as a structure for care and as a means of recording observed changes in maternal health literacy among women who were participants in ECHS services [10]. Progression in maternal health literacy was understood to indicate participants' increasing health equity, so that participants' health outcomes were closer to those of higher income, better educated, low-risk women's health outcomes [1,11]. ECHS promoted maternal health literacy progression through health education and health counseling, referrals to community and medical resources, and support through a consistent long-term relationship between a participant and a Registered Nurse Case Manager (RNCM).

An initial study documented that greater than ninety percent of participants in the ECHS Program made positive maternal health literacy progression from their prenatal to their postpartum assessments. Following delivery through 24 months of the infant's life, participants faced new challenges, and approximately 35% ($n = 37$) did not meet the measured criterion for adequacy in maternal health literacy progression at their final assessment. However, these participants did meet the most critical measure of all: they and their infants survived pregnancy, birth, and the first two years of their infants' lives [4]. In this report investigators examined the conditions and dynamics in the lives of participants who did not reach adequacy in maternal health literacy progression, and how their Registered Nurses who served as case managers intervened to improve their long-term health development potentials.

1.2. Setting and Background

The ECHS service area consisted of two non-contiguous rural counties in east central Georgia, U.S. These two counties ranked among the poorest in health status and health outcomes in the state (156th and 144th of 157 counties ranked), and in the nation (37th of 50 states) [12]. One service county had a community hospital that provided delivery services, and there was a board-certified obstetrics physician who practiced in that county. All other deliveries were made in the regional medical center that was an average of 25 miles away for ECHS participants. There was no public transportation in the two counties. Little or no primary medical care for the underinsured and uninsured was available in the two service counties. There were health professional shortages in primary medical, dental, and mental health services [13].

Rates of U.S. teen pregnancy, abortion, and infant mortality fell during the data collection period of the study, 2005–2012. When infants were born preterm, at less than 37 weeks of gestation, they were much more likely to die before their first year of life. Preterm birth was the risk most closely associated with infant mortality and had its highest rates among non-Hispanic black NHB infants. Compared to the 2014 national rate of 9.57% [14,15], the preterm birth rate in the Southern state of Georgia was 10.8%, and, in the Augusta, GA Perinatal Region that encompassed the study population, the rate was 12.6%.

Interpregnancy interval was the time from delivery to the next pregnancy conception. Short interpregnancy intervals of less than nine months, and very short interpregnancy intervals of less than three months, were associated with both preterm birth and morbidity for women and infants. Teen pregnancy was an important risk factor for women and infants because most teens were not married, they had not completed their education, and they were not mature physically or emotionally. Although it was a goal of the U.S. Department of Health and Human Services (USDHHS) to reduce the rates of teen pregnancy, teen pregnancy rates were still very high in the U.S. and Georgia during the study period. Teens were the most likely age group to have short interpregnancy intervals [16,17].

Even though teen pregnancy, abortion, and infant mortality rates declined for all three ethnic and racial groups, those for NHB women and infants did not decline as rapidly. Thus, disparities widened among NHB women and infants and other ethnic and racial groups [18]. NHB women in Georgia suffered a preterm birth rate three times greater than that of non-Hispanic white (NHW) women. Over the years, the difference in the rate of premature births widened as the NHW prematurity rate declined faster than the NHB rate [15,19]. Thus, racial disparities grew in the U.S. and in Georgia among women and infants of color (NHB) compared to NHW women and to women of all other races or ethnic groups.

Another important goal of the U.S. DHHS was to prevent pregnancy-related death (MMR), which was the number of maternal deaths within one year of pregnancy per 100,000 live births. It was recorded as the maternal mortality ratio (MMR). In 2013, Georgia's MMR was 24.9 compared to the U.S.'s ratio of 17.3 [19,20]. The U.S. Centers for Disease Control and Prevention (CDC) reported wide racial disparities in MMR in the years 2011–2013. NHB women died at the rate of 43.5, while NHW women died at the rate of 12.7, and women of all other races and ethnic groups combined died at the rate of 14.4 [21]. These data demonstrated the great differences in MMR that occurred when NHB women were compared to women of other ethnic and racial groups.

The U.S. CDC routinely conducted surveys of women who delivered a live infant. The survey was called PRAMS or Pregnancy Risk Assessment and Monitoring System. Based on earlier studies from the PRAMS data, investigators knew that social and demographic risk factors for maternal or infant mortality rates included the following: low income, NHB race, poor mental health, interpersonal violence, and substance abuse [21].

Stress was a high risk factor associated with depression, hypertension, and alcohol, tobacco, and drug use. Severe stress during or after pregnancy occurred if a parent—mother or father of the baby—was incarcerated [22]. Among very poor people with little education, and few chances for employment, there were very few marriages. Without marriage, family relationships were uncertain and unstable. When a pregnant woman was not married, the absence of the baby's father contributed to the risks of maternal and infant morbidity [23,24].

Healthy Start programs, including the ECHS program, were charged with discovering what the problems were that led to so many women and infants dying and intervening to prevent their deaths. NHB women and their infants were a special focus since their rates were so much higher than others' rates. Investigators chose to examine this group of ECHS participants because they were at greatest risk of adverse outcomes.

2. Materials and Methods

2.1. Ethics

This research was conducted in accord with prevailing ethical principles and was approved by the Georgia Regents University (now Augusta University) Institutional Review Board. Original empirical research was conducted under Research Protocol #1010080 for evaluation of participant service and under Research Protocol #716980 for the RNCMs to participate as subjects in a focus group. These protocols were approved by the Institutional Review Board. Throughout the study, investigators protected participants' personal health information. Each investigator was required to demonstrate knowledge of and practice in the highest standards of ethical behavior in research prior to their participation in the study.

2.2. Design

The study was a mixed methods design with ethnographic retrospective content analysis of prenatal-interconceptional service records for 37 ECHS participants [25]. Using techniques appropriate for mixed methods design specified by Sandelowski [26], investigators: (1) triangulated content analysis data with multiple sources of quantitative data to specify critical data elements, (2) complemented content analysis with a focus group comprised of the RNCMs to further explicate findings from content analysis, and (3) upon the recommendation of the RNCMs, planned additional studies to follow up 23 of the 37 study group participants who returned to ECHS to have nursing services for their next pregnancy.

2.3. Study Participant Recruitment and Description

Participants were referred to ECHS by local and regional providers because of their high-risk prenatal status. Participants lived in two rural southeastern Georgia counties with limited community resources, and health professional shortages in primary medical, dental, and mental health services [27]. Services were provided during 2005–2012 from prenatal entry into case management and up to 24 months post-delivery. Study participants were twenty-eight (78.8%) NHB and nine (24.3%) NHWs. Entry into the study was determined by their inability to achieve the criterion for adequacy in maternal health literacy progression as evidenced by their final comprehensive postpartum numeric scores on the LSP instrument [10]. Education was an important indicator of a woman's readiness to learn parenting and self-care skills. Most ($n = 21$, 57%) participants had less than a twelfth-grade education; their ages ranged from 14 to 36 years (median = 18.5, mode = 19). Eleven of the 37 (29.7%) were less than 19 years of age when admitted to prenatal care. One teen was gravida 2; 10 teens, gravida 1. Mean gravidity was 1.8 pregnancies (s d ± 1.4). Mean gestational age at delivery was 38.6 weeks (s d ± 2.2); two (5.4%) delivered at <37 weeks gestation. Mean birthweight was 3095.6 g (s d ± 551.7), and four (10.8%) infants had <2500 g low or very low birthweights (range: 1360–2381 g).

Risk factors from initial prenatal screening included: severe social conditions (12), late or no prenatal care (8), standard body weight >20% (8), obesity (3), positive depression screen (6), depression (4), severe mental disorder (2), hypertension (4), tobacco dependence (3), gestational diabetes (3), last delivery <1 year ago (4), history of preterm labor (3), parent of a NICU (neonatal intensive care unit) graduate (2), previous preterm birth (2), previous cesarean birth (2), under age 15 at conception (2), and family history of breast cancer (2). Thirty-four women had 2 or more risks (median = 4, range = 1–8 risks).

2.4. Intervention

The ECHS intervention program promoted maternal health literacy by teaching participants to manage their own and their infant's health care, including self-care practices, use of resources, and promotion of infant development. RNCMs used and taught participants a think-link-respond approach to problem solving, thus teaching them to consider consequences and make deliberate choices instead of reacting to circumstances. This critical thinking skill gave participants the opportunity to make life changes.

The four RNCMs were culturally and linguistically similar to participants. They provided nursing services to consistently assigned participants, using collaborative, interactive one-on-one visits with participants in their homes, schools, community settings, and in RNCMs' private offices. RNCMs facilitated access to the health care system, served as advocates, made referrals, and tracked follow-through of referrals. RNCMs maintained communication with participants using cell phones to text and talk as needed.

RNCMs conducted ongoing health counseling and education. Content was structured around client-identified needs using the Beginnings Guides for Pregnancy and Parenting [28]. RNCMs stimulated problem solving skills using reflective function [29]. They monitored physical, psycho-social, and environmental status. Participants had home visitation nursing services for a range of 10.2–29.7 months (median = 20.7 months). RNCMs increased frequency and intensity of visits as indicated.

Based on Kotelchuck's Adequacy of Prenatal Care Utilization Index, thirty-one participants had adequate to adequate-plus medical prenatal care as indicated for very high-risk pregnancies; eight had late entry into prenatal care [30]. Referrals for maternal-fetal medical care or other specialized health care involved arranging private or Medicaid transportation to the regional perinatal center. Children were not allowed to ride on the Medicaid bus unless it was for their pediatric appointment. Participants had limited access to child care and were reluctant to be away from home when older children came home from school.

Insurance was critical for access to medical care in the United States. During the preconceptional period twenty participants had no health insurance and no access to medical care even though they had very high medical risks. The lack of health insurance before and after pregnancy accentuated their health risks. The untreated high risk medical problems observed in this young study group of women was reflective of the lack of health insurance and health services available in their communities. RNCMs assisted all participants to access health insurance and health care during and after pregnancy through advocacy, guidance, and persistent support.

2.5. Instrumentation

The LSP was a validated set of items that measured factors important for home visitation with mothers, infants, and families of young children (alpha range 0.64–0.96) [10]. Groups of items were not considered scales. Items were scored with a rubric on a relational, numeric scale (0–5). Individual items as well as the groups of items representing the constructs Maternal Health Care Literacy and Maternal Self Care Literacy were scored as "adequate" if scores were equal to or greater than four (≥ 4). Items that were used to represent Maternal Health Care Literacy and Maternal Self Care Literacy demonstrated a consistent meaning that represented the constructs accurately, as evidenced in practice outcomes [4,8]. RNCMs used the LSP to identify women with adequate versus inadequate maternal health literacy progression. LSP items, scoring frequencies, item descriptions and the sample selection process were presented in earlier reports [4,27].

2.6. Data Collection

ECHS adopted the LSP on 1 July 2005. Staff had initial and continuous training with the LSP throughout the study period in formal and informal sessions in monthly case conferences. Through the training process RNCMs developed a clinical subculture of shared meanings, procedures, scoring, and likely interventions based upon nursing process that demonstrated internal consistency among RNCMs' scores for like phenomena.

During the prenatal period, RNCMs observed and interacted with participants over a period of at least two months prior to scoring the prenatal LSP. Within the first two to four weeks after the infant was in the home, an initial postpartum LSP assessment was conducted. Subsequent LSP assessments were conducted every six months, although participants had multiple contacts between LSP assessments. RNCMs recorded all data within 24 h of the dates of contact in the perinatal database, an electronic health record created by and for the ECHS program. Access was password protected and limited to employees and nursing faculty. Provisions were in place for a participant to have a copy of her own data upon request.

RNCMs screened participants with the Beck Depression Inventory [31] and Edinburgh Postpartum Depression Survey [32] upon entry into prenatal care, during the third trimester, and soon after delivery. Both instruments demonstrated validity and reliability with multi-racial, multi-cultural perinatal populations. ECHS collected demographic and identifying data, as well as periodic risk assessments and items about social and financial support. ECHS also obtained information from outpatient medical care, public health visits, schools and social services, and hospital discharge summaries on prenatal, delivery, and interconceptional admissions for the participant and her newborn infant. All data were recorded in the perinatal data base.

2.7. Investigators' Reflexivity

The four Registered Nurse investigators shared personal orientations and motivations before they conducted the research. Rules for group process and privacy were established and consistently followed. Investigators had advanced preparation at the master's and doctoral level in nursing with research, teaching, clinical, and administrative nursing experience. The database manager was doctorally-level prepared in a health-related field. The statistician had a master's degree and was enrolled in doctoral studies. Each investigator had a unique contribution that was incorporated in the research process.

Investigators were females, white, middle-later age, middle income and either currently or previously married. RNCMs were females, black, young adult to middle age, middle income. Three were currently or formerly married, and one had never married. Participants were low-income, black (28), white (9), not married (35), married (2), teens (15), and adults (22), and had low educational achievement. RNCMs provided a bridge across the cultural, educational, social, and linguistic differences noted between investigators and participants.

2.8. Data Analysis

Content analysis was guided by Berg's ethnographic method [25]. Investigators worked from a COREQ outline to structure the process of the study [33]. The unit of analysis was the individual participant. Visit notes consisted of the written record of the RNCMs' activities and observations about participants' conditions, dynamics, and responses to care. Triangulation incorporated each participant's data from all sources that were collected and recorded in the perinatal data base prior to the date of each LSP score. Investigators did not critique RNCMs' work. The database manager transferred quantitative data to an Excel spreadsheet for analysis and printed qualitative data from individual records. Data were checked for accuracy. To maintain confidentiality, files were encrypted and shared among the research team on the university's secure server. Investigators met in a private conference room or joined meetings on a secure conference line [34].

One investigator analyzed LSP data using Microsoft EXCEL© (Microsoft Corporation, Redmond, WA, USA) to examine the 20 LSP items scored for each assessment for each woman on the two constructs, Maternal Health Care Literacy and Maternal Self Care Literacy. Participants were those who had a final postpartum score less than four (<4) that indicated inadequate progression in Maternal Health Care Literacy and/or Maternal Self Care Literacy. During content analysis sessions, investigators triangulated the scored LSP items at each assessment with the dates of changes in LSP item scores, and the date-related visit notes and other available data for the period preceding the LSP assessment.

Investigators created a form that was used for each participant's case review. In the first column categories were problems, responses to care, resources, possible intervention to strengthen resources, barriers, possible intervention to remove barriers, interventions attempted and outcomes, and investigator's professional opinion. In the second column, each section of notes identified RNCM's factual statements, RNCM's interpretation of facts, and investigators' statement of problems. A third column was used to record supporting data and literature references. Investigators reviewed each participant's data as a group.

During content analysis sessions, one investigator served as recorder using Microsoft Word© (Microsoft Corporation, Redmond, WA, USA), on a Toshiba laptop computer (Toshiba USA Corporate Office Headquarters, Toshiba America, Inc., 1251 Avenue of the Americas, Ste. 4110, New York, NY 10020, USA—manufactured in China 6060B1023401 CM-2). The recorder projected onto a blank wall investigators' observations, interpretations, and commentary in real time. Following each session, the recording investigator sent encrypted case review forms and notes to each investigator on the university's secure email server.

2.9. Design Complementarity

Following content analysis, investigators invited the RNCMs to participate in a focus group discussion at the end of the study that would serve as an external validity check for data interpretation [26]. Investigators did not contribute to the discussion. RNCMs had study questions in advance. (See Figure 1). Each RNCM had a list of the 37 participants whom they served. Their comments were recorded in their presence as they occurred, projected onto a blank wall, and clarified with their feedback. Responses were not subjected to further analysis. Minimal editing was done to preserve their meaning.

---

(1) Based on your years of clinical experience, please list 7 to 10 reasons you think that some Healthy Start clients did not achieve an adequate maternal health literacy score using the Life Skills Progression instrument.

(2) At the end of the discussion, please rank your responses.

Figure 1. Focus Group Questions. The recorder grouped and recorded RNCMs' ranked responses with their input.

2.10. Design Development

Design development is the third stage of the technical levels in mixed methods studies according to Sandelowski [26]. Investigators planned additional studies from existing data for 23 of the 37 study group participants who returned to ECHS for their next pregnancy.

3. Results

3.1. Content Analysis

3.1.1. Risks

Content analysis revealed multiple risks. Of the 37 participants in the study 35 (95%) had unstable family relationships that were characterized by severe social conditions. Common themes of severe social conditions included: extreme poverty, incarceration of seven fathers of babies (FOBs) and one participant; transient, inadequate housing, and/or crowding; domestic violence; lack of safety; lack of privacy; and no protection from others in the household. Not one of these participants was in charge of the place she stayed. Participants were functionally homeless, staying short periods with their relatives or the FOB's family, with no permanent home. Patterns of toxic stress were evidenced by anger, grief, depression, fighting, and drug use. Additional stressors were from family members' criminal activities and extreme multi-generational poverty. Participants and FOBs lacked skills for employment and/or had unstable employment in low-income jobs.

3.1.2. Protective Factors

The most important protective factor was the consistent, long-term relationship with the RNCM that was focused upon maternal health literacy progression. While pregnant, participants were enrolled in Medicaid and had access to medical care. The RNCMs worked closely with medical providers to monitor medical conditions and teach participants to implement medical recommendations. The RNCMs also worked closely with DFCS social workers, local law enforcement personnel, and other community resource persons to ensure the safety and security of participants and their infants. The RNCMs provided continuous support and guidance through cell phone communications. The RNCMs provided a semi-structured program of maternal health education, infant care, developmental monitoring, and referrals to needed resources as appropriate, by teaching, questioning, showing examples, and by health counseling. As persons with cultural and linguistic similarity who were successful role models, their guidance held the respect of participants and their families. Even so, the RNCMs had limited ability to intervene in participants' severe social conditions and dynamics.

3.1.3. Dynamics

The competition for owning the infant's right to an income tax credit was a driving force in the participants' finances. There was no or limited evidence of any FOBs' financial support. If the participant added the FOB's name to the infant's birth certificate, the FOB became legally liable for financial support, and others in the participant's household could not receive tax credit for supporting the infant.

Social pressure between participants and their babies' fathers created unstable, highly stressful family relationships with personal, social, financial, and legal implications. Participants reported that the FOB was "controlling", "FOB was upset with her", because she applied for child support, and "off and on relationship with FOB to get his support for their baby". Therefore, participants did not usually include the FOB's name on the infant's birth certificate.

Existing social structures within families limited participants' abilities to change. Typically, participants had poor responses to referrals for life improvements. Overwhelming barriers and stressors, including family members' resistance, defeated most efforts to change.

The demands of single parenting focused participants' resources upon their infants. Infant wellness and sick care, rather than postpartum and interconceptional maternal self-care, were high priority as evidenced by multiple health care contacts per child.

3.1.4. Patterns

Patterns were regularly occurring sets of conditions and dynamics by which families or household groups conducted their activities of daily living. When one or more family or group member benefitted at the expense of others, the pattern was dysfunctional. When family or group members were committed to the well-being of one another, the pattern was functional. Participants' development of skills for maternal health literacy was affected by family patterns. Two examples (exemplars) that illustrate how participants' conditions and dynamics affected their maternal health literacy are shown in Figures 2 and 3.

> Participant had multiple partners and a history of multiple sexually transmitted infections. Paternity was uncertain so she expected no support from FOB. Her two older teenaged sisters were currently pregnant. Participant's mother claimed financial support for all infants.
>
> Poor mental health: Father told her to "die." Participant reported self-mutilation by cutting, sadness, misery, anxiety, worry, and poor sleep patterns, but denied suicidal ideation.
>
> Low educational level: Participant was two grades behind in school and currently in alternative school for fighting.
>
> Response to RNCM interventions: The family had normalized this pattern and was resistant to change. Participant's mother refused to let her have counseling until RNCM intervened. At the end of nursing services, participant was in counseling, had one boyfriend, did not have a repeat pregnancy, and had help in school to bring her up to grade level.
>
> Investigators' Reflexivity: Investigators were disturbed by the details of participant's life, but her mother seemed to accept it as normal. Participant had 56 face-to-face contacts with health care workers in 23 months of nursing services. Risks were poverty, family pattern, multiple sexual partners, youth, low educational attainment, and very poor mental health. The RNCM was a strong protective factor.
>
> Dynamics: Participant's mother's resistance to change was overcome by RNCM's interventions and participant's resilience.

Figure 2. Exemplar: Health Consequences of Teen Pregnancy—A Dysfunctional Family Pattern. Intensive nursing care enabled this family to change to a more health-promoting family pattern.

> Risks and protective factors: Risks were crowding, multi-generational poverty, crime, abuse, poor mental health, smoking, and uncontrolled medical conditions. Protective factors were the resourcefulness of the participant and her father despite extreme deprivation, the stable, consistent relationship with the RNCM, specialized medical intervention, and coordinated care with multiple community agencies' involvement.
>
> Dynamics: The chaotic family pattern was characterized by crises that were stabilized with the help of intensive medical and community interventions.
>
> Crowding and family relationships: Four generations of nine people lived in a one-room house with only the participant's father's disability income. During the study period, the participant's father built two additional rooms onto the house, in order for the Department of Family and Children's Services (DFCS) caseworker to approve the infant's return to the home after surgery.
>
> Depression: Participant's depression scores (Beck 38 and Edinburgh 23) remained elevated from entry into care throughout the 24 month interconceptional period, despite treatment. History of family violence: Her adult daughter accused participant's father of sexual molestation and he attempted suicide. The daughter's boyfriend abused drugs and threatened to kill all of them if he was made to move out. The participant had a history of battering. There were frequent police calls and DFCS visits.

Figure 3. *Cont.*

> Multiple medical problems: Participant had uncontrolled diabetes that was worse in pregnancy. She smoked 10 cigarettes per day. In addition, the participant's father had multiple medical problems. Her infant was delivered at the rural county hospital with a known heart defect that required surgery, and then transferred to NICU at the regional medical center 25 miles away.
>
> Interventions and responses: The RNCM coordinated referral and travel for infant to have cardiac surgery in Atlanta, then planned for discharge and follow-up care with the cardiologist. Lack of infant safety: Despite repeated emphasis on infant safety measures, the baby fell off the bed four times.
>
> Investigators' reflexivity: Visit notes were disturbing on many levels.

Figure 3. Exemplar: Health Consequences of a Chaotic, Dysfunctional Family Pattern with Multi-Generational Poverty and Family Violence. Intensive nursing care enabled this family to change to a more health-promoting family pattern.

Figure 2 contains an example of a family pattern in which the matriarch of the household encouraged her teenage daughters to have multiple pregnancies with multiple FOBs. The matriarch then claimed the infants' tax credits to control the family finances. The teenaged daughters were unable to complete high school. They were exposed to multiple risks of sexually transmitted infection. And they and their infants were on a pathway to living the rest of their lives in severe poverty as was the participant's mother. (See Figure 2.)

Figure 3 shows the results of a disorganized family pattern in which individuals strived to meet their own needs at the expense of others, resulting in chaos and poor health. The jeopardy for the newborn infant was illustrated by the participant's delivery in a local community hospital with no advanced level of treatment when she knew that her infant had been diagnosed in utero (while she was pregnant) with a heart defect. Further jeopardy was seen in the infant's four times falling off the bed. The RNCM's timely intervention saved this infant's life more than once. (See Figure 3.)

3.2. Focus Group Results

RNCM's Focus Group Responses

Focus Group Results are shown in Figure 4. They were recorded in the RNCMs' own words as presented here. RNCMs' recommendations are presented in the final recommendations section of this report. (See Figure 4.)

The language in Figure 4 was a real-time recording of RNCMs' comments in their own words; some were colloquial statements. " ... wanted to do more ... " meant that some participants wanted to change their circumstances. " ... afraid to step out ... " meant that participants feared the consequences if they took recommended actions to change their circumstances. RNCMs' recommendations have been placed at the end of this report to emphasize their importance.

3.3. Additional Planned Studies and Interventions

Investigators planned to calculate interpregnancy intervals and note the impact of a second session of ECHS intensive home nursing services upon maternal health literacy progression scores. Additional interventions were developed and implemented, including a module on Reproductive Life Planning.

> a. Low education: They (participants) did not finish high school--they quit school early. A few had learning disabilities and still did not follow the RNCM's advice even though they explained things at their level.
>
> b. Lack of transportation related to unemployment: Unemployment or low-paying jobs meant that they had to depend on someone else for transportation. They refused Medicaid transportation because they would have to stay all day and their older children would get off the school bus before the participant got home. Children were not allowed on the Medicaid transit unless they had an appointment.
>
> c. Depression: Participants were depressed but they knew how to answer those screens. They said, "I am not crazy." Participants preferred mental health counselors who made home visits because they could talk with them privately.
>
> d. Family and Social Restraints: Some wanted to do more but their families would not let them. One participant was the primary care taker for her whole family. RNCM had to convince everyone in the household that RNCM could help, and if anyone objected, it was very difficult. If they accepted the RNCM, the whole family wanted care. Participants were depending upon another person—"some man"—to take care of them and when RNCM would make some suggestion about how to change things they were afraid to step out. Participants did not want to put their baby's daddy on the birth certificate. They said FOB was providing diapers. One RNCM asked, "Is that all you want?" Participants lived in someone else's house and were influenced by whoever ruled the household. Trying to find them after delivery was hard because they were transient and after delivery they would move.
>
> e. Short interpregnancy interval: Participants repeated pregnancy quickly. They did not keep appointments for postpartum or for family planning even though they could have had free care at Public Health. Some had multiple pregnancies following this one.

Figure 4. Results of Focus Group with RNCMs. The focus group with the RNCM providers was a complementary research strategy that clarified and extended the content analysis.

4. Discussion

Data illustrated the critical influence of sociodemographic factors upon the health of participants and infants and their inadequate maternal health literacy progression [35]. Severe social conditions affected 35 of 37 participants. Participants lived with devastating poverty. They had little control over the conditions and dynamics of their lives and had continuous struggles to survive, that reflected the high maternal and infant mortality rates in Georgia. Severe social conditions contributed to: chronic depression and intimate partner violence; early sexual activity with sexually transmitted infections and unplanned and/or unwanted pregnancies often with short interpregnancy intervals; poor educational achievement; and unstable housing with crowding and substandard living conditions. The potential impact on infants and children from these factors was well documented in the Adverse Childhood Experiences (ACE) study [36]. Profound negative impacts upon health, social, and economic wellbeing were known to result from childhood trauma [37]. These maternal participants experienced ACE and cascading generational risks that, without further intervention, forecast the lives of themselves and their children.

The dynamics of participants' decisions were seen in the power struggles to overcome their families' multi-generational patterns, the struggle for the tax and welfare benefits for the infant's support, uncontrolled sexual advances against participants, peer pressure, transient housing, the new boyfriend wanting the participant to have his child, and the search for love and belonging by both participants and FOBs [38]. Participants had little power to overcome others' resistance to their needs to change.

Participants had perpetual toxic lifestyles that families viewed as "normal" [39]. RNCMs' focus group comments confirmed that families resisted participants' efforts to change [40]. RNCMs provided a protective relationship by teaching participants to change their responses [41]. RNCMs modeled reflective functioning techniques to encourage participants to think critically and make decisions in terms of potential consequences [28]. Often absent, unemployed, or incarcerated, FOBs had little economic, social, or parental input into the participant's pregnancy or infant care [23]. The RNCM who asked, "Is that all you want?" cast a vision of higher expectations [42]. Participants looked to the RNCMs for answers and support [43]. RNCMs' discussion of participants' conditions and dynamics aligned with investigators' interpretations.

ECHS staff facilitated participants' obtaining health insurance during pregnancy and the postpartum period to enable access to medical care. Without continuous health insurance, participants began pregnancy and ended postpartum care with uncontrolled medical risks that were magnified by childbearing [2,44,45]. RNCMs' focus on facilitating insurance coverage, prenatal care, and transportation to appointments explains the adequate to adequate plus level of care received in spite of the challenges in this rural area.

4.1. Strengths of the Study

Critically important information was revealed through in-depth examination of the conditions and dynamics in the lives of participants who did not achieve adequate (≥ 4) maternal health literacy progression by the end of their initial case management period of service. The study revealed the value of intensive nursing care in the home that contributed to the safe maternal and infant outcomes that occurred.

An important strength of the study was found in the research group process that investigators employed. Investigators stated their reflexivity positions early in the research process. Reflexivity meant a statement of their values, their motivations for participating in the research, and their past personal and professional experiences that would influence how they would interpret data [46]. Team meetings were characterized by synergy in focused discussions. Investigators contributed to the intense review, discussion, and evaluation of the complex set of data available for each participant. From the investigators' interactions there emerged a worksheet for each participant. Notes and decisions were recorded in real time when the team of investigators reached a conclusion. Every voice was heard. Every voice held equal weight in the production of the worksheets.

Investigators adhered to data and not speculation or interpretation. If the RNCM who had recorded the data included an interpretation, it was regarded as a factual component of the data. Investigators shared their multiple perspectives from personal knowledge based on professional experience in evidence-based nursing practice.

Current technology was one key to the success of the ECHS program. Each RNCM and each participant had a cell phone that enabled them to have unlimited communications. The ECHS program leadership had developed and implemented an electronic health record that permitted recording and retrieving data from each contact. The development and publication of the LSP made possible the structure and measurement of maternal health literacy progression. Combined, these technological advances supported nursing care and enabled investigators to measure the impact of care.

Participants in this study were at very high risk of pregnancy related morbidity or mortality, which was of great concern in public health in the U.S. Close examination using mixed methods research revealed the underlying sociodeterminants of risks, protective factors, and dynamics that impacted maternal health literacy progression of participants and their infants. The work of the RNCMs demonstrated the intensive nursing care necessary to help participants overcome their circumstances.

4.2. Limitations of the Study

A small study group with a non-randomized study design cannot yield prescriptive information that can be generalized to a broader population. It can provide insights that others may use to inform future research, services, and program evaluation.

5. Conclusions

5.1. Summary

In summary, the study described conditions and dynamics that impacted a group of high-risk, low income, Southern U.S. Healthy Start participants who had not been able to achieve criterion—referenced adequacy in maternal health literacy progression. The ECHS program's RNCMs provided instruction for mothers and babies, encouraged rational decision-making, supported access to health care with insurance coverage, arranged transportation, and encouraged participants to make needed changes. RNCMs succeeded in helping women and infants survive and improve their life circumstances by reducing risks and addressing medical and social needs even though participants did not achieve the criterion-referenced standard for maternal health literacy.

5.2. Investigators' Recommendations

In order to build health equity among rural, Southern, NHB and NHW families, study results indicated the need to:

(a) Increase support for educational programs that enable participants and FOBs to have greater employment opportunities and greater control over the conditions and dynamics of their lives.
(b) Continue home visitation family care with long-term relationships using evidence-informed, intensive nursing, mental health, and other resources that make care accessible, available, and acceptable.
(c) Advocate for sustainable multi-generational policy and legislative changes that enable access to health care for all with individual accountability.

5.3. RNCMs' Recommendations in Their Own Words

In order to prevent maternal and infant deaths, we need to have:

(a) Mental health counselors who go to the home.
(b) Safe places to house teenage girls who are homeless.
(c) Intensive nursing services for the extremely high-risk women who need a lot more attention, need very high-frequency contact, and just need to talk. Long term contact relationships are important to help them stabilize and sustain positive changes.
(d) Wrap-around services for perinatal/postpartum women—counseling, job training, family planning, check-ups, and baby care—all in one place all in one day.

Author Contributions: Conceptualization, S.D.T. and S.C.M.; Data curation, D.E.S.; Formal analysis, S.D.T., S.C.M., J.L.H., S.B.I. and B.L.A.; Funding acquisition, S.D.T., S.C.M., J.L.H., D.E.S. and S.B.I.; Investigation, S.D.T., S.C.M., J.L.H., D.E.S. and S.B.I.; Methodology, S.D.T., S.C.M., S.B.I. and B.L.A.; Project administration, S.D.T., S.C.M., J.L.H. and S.B.I.; Resources, S.D.T., S.C.M. and S.B.I.; Software, S.C.M. and J.L.H.; Supervision, S.D.T., S.C.M. and J.L.H.; Validation, S.D.T., S.C.M., J.L.H., D.E.S. and S.B.I.; Visualization, S.D.T. and S.C.M.; Writing—original draft, S.D.T., S.C.M., J.L.H., D.E.S. and S.B.I.; Writing—review & editing, S.D.T., S.C.M., J.L.H., D.E.S., S.B.I. and B.L.A.

Funding: This research was supported in part by the Health Resources and Services Administration (HRSA) of the U.S. Department of Health and Human Services (HHS) under Grant number H40MC00129 from the Healthy Start Initiative, Maternal Child Health Bureau, Health Resources and Services Administration.

Acknowledgments: This information or content and conclusions are those of the authors and should not be construed as the official position or policy of, nor should any endorsements be inferred by HRSA, HHS or the U.S.

Government. We wish to acknowledge the contributions of the Registered Nurse Case Managers (RNCMs) who provided service to the participants in this study and who themselves served as subjects of a focus group for the study. We also wish to acknowledge Peter Shipman MLIS, for his assistance with referencing and style matters. We wish to acknowledge Barbara Dixson, Ph.D., English Department, University of Wisconsin, Stevens Point, who edited the manuscript for language and readability.

Conflicts of Interest: The authors declare no conflict of interest.

References

1. Braveman, P. What is health equity and how does a life-course approach take us further toward it? *Matern. Child Health J.* **2014**, *18*, 366–372. [CrossRef] [PubMed]
2. Posner, S.F.; Johnson, K.; Parker, C.; Atrash, H.; Biermann, J. The national summit on preconception care: A summary of concepts and recommendations. *Matern. Child Health J.* **2006**, *10*, 199–207. [CrossRef] [PubMed]
3. Halfon, N.; Larson, K.; Lu, M.; Tullis, E.; Russ, S. Lifecourse health development: Past, present, and future. *Matern. Child Health J.* **2014**, *18*, 344–365. [CrossRef] [PubMed]
4. Mobley, S.C.; Thomas, S.D.; Sutherland, D.E.; Hudgins, J.; Ange, B.L.; Johnson, M.H. Maternal health literacy progression among rural perinatal women. *Matern. Child Health J.* **2014**, *18*, 1881–1892. [CrossRef] [PubMed]
5. Byrd, M.E. Long-term maternal-child home visiting. *Public Health Nurs.* **1998**, *15*, 235–242. [CrossRef] [PubMed]
6. Olds, D.; Henderson, C.; Tatelbaum, R.; Chamberlin, R. Improving the life course development of socially disadvantaged mothers: A randomized trial of nurse home visitation. *Am. J. Public Health* **1988**, *78*, 1436–1445. [CrossRef] [PubMed]
7. Renkert, K.; Nutbeam, D. Opportunities to improve maternal health literacy through antenatal education: An exploratory study. *Health Promot. Int.* **2001**, *16*, 381–388. [CrossRef] [PubMed]
8. Smith, S.; Moore, E.J. Health literacy and depression in the context of home visitation. *Matern. Child Health J.* **2011**, *16*, 1500–1508. [CrossRef] [PubMed]
9. Smith, S.K.; Nutbeam, D.; McCaffery, K. Insights into the concept and measurement of health literacy from a study of shared decision-making in a low literacy population. *J. Health Psychol.* **2013**, *18*, 1011–1022. [CrossRef] [PubMed]
10. Wollesen, L.; Peifer, K. *Life Skills Progression LSP: An Outcome and Intervention Planning Instrument for Use with Families at Risk*; Paul, H., Ed.; Brookes Publishing Co.: Baltimore, MD, USA, 2006; p. 224.
11. Braveman, P.; Marchi, K.; Egerter, S.; Kim, S.; Metzle, M.; Stancil, T.; Libet, M. Poverty, near-poverty, and hardship around the time of pregnancy. *Matern. Child Health J.* **2010**, *14*, 20–35. [CrossRef] [PubMed]
12. Robert Wood Johnson Foundation; University of Wisconsin Population Health Institute. County Health Rankings and Roadmaps. University of Wisconsin Population Health Institute: Madison, WI, USA. Available online: http://www.countyhealthrankings.org (accessed on 25 March 2012).
13. Health Resources and Services Administration HPSA Find. Available online: https://datawarehouse.hrsa.gov/tools/analyzers/hpsafind.aspx (accessed on 02/26/2012).
14. Martin, J.A.; Hamilton, B.E.; Osterman, M.J.K. *Births in the United States, 2014*; National Center for Health Statistics: Hyattsville, MD, USA, 2015; pp. 1–8.
15. Online Analytical Statistical Information System (OASIS). Births. In Georgia Department of Public Health. Office of Health Indicators for Planning (OHIP): Atlanta, GA, USA. Available online: https://oasis.state.ga.us/ (accessed 22 March 2017).
16. Rawlings, J.S.; Rawlings, V.B.; Read, J.A. Prevalence of low birth weight and preterm delivery in relation to the interval between pregnancies among white and black women. *N. Engl. J. Med.* **1995**, *332*, 69–74. [CrossRef] [PubMed]
17. Copen, C.E.; Thoma, M.E.; Kirmeyer, S. Interpregnancy intervals in the United States: Data from the birth certificate and the national survey of family growth. *Natl. Vital Stat. Rep.* **2015**, *64*, 1–11. [PubMed]
18. March of Dimes Prematurity Awareness Summit. *How Can We Innovate Against the Odds?* March of Dimes: Atlanta, GA, USA, 2015.
19. Matthews, T.J.; MacDorman, M.F. Infant mortality statistics from the 2010 period linked birth/infant death data set. *Natl. Vital Stat. Rep.* **2013**, *62*, 1–26. [PubMed]
20. Gober, M. *Maternal Mortality in Georgia, 2012–2013*; Mercer University: Macon, GA, USA, 2018.

21. Centers for Disease Control and Prevention. Pregnancy Mortality Surveillance System. Available online: https://www.cdc.gov/reproductivehealth/maternalinfanthealth/pmss.html (accessed on 15 April 2018).
22. Dumont, D.M.; Wildeman, C.; Hedwig, L.; Gjelsvik, A.; Valera, P.A.; Clarke, J.G. Incarceration, maternal hardship, and perinatal health behaviors. *Matern. Child Health J.* **2014**, *18*, 2179–2187. [CrossRef] [PubMed]
23. Salihu, H.M.; August, E.M.; Mbah, A.K.; Alio, A.P.; Berry, E.L.; Aliyu, M.H. Impact of a Federal Healthy Start program on feto-infant morbidity associated with absent fathers: A quasi-experimental study. *Matern. Child Health J.* **2014**, *18*, 2054–2060. [CrossRef] [PubMed]
24. Salihu, H.M.; August, E.M.; Jeffers, D.F.; Mbah, A.K.; Alio, A.P.; Berry, E. Effectiveness of a Federal Healthy Start program in reducing primary and repeat teen pregnancies. *J. Pediatr. Adolesc. Gynecol.* **2011**, *24*, 153–160. [CrossRef] [PubMed]
25. Berg, B.L. *Qualitative Research Methods for the Social Sciences*, 4th ed.; Allyn and Bacon: Boston, MA, USA, 2001.
26. Sandelowski, M. Combining qualitative and quantitative sampling, data collection, and analysis techniques in mixed-methods studies. *Res. Nurs. Health* **2000**, *23*, 246–255. [CrossRef]
27. Thomas, S.D.; Hudgins, J.L.; Sutherland, D.E.; Ange, B.L.; Mobley, S.C. Perinatal program evaluations: Methods, impacts, and future goals. *Matern. Child Health J.* **2015**, *19*, 1440–1446. [CrossRef] [PubMed]
28. Smith, S.; Wollesen, L. *Beginnings Life Skills Development Curriculum: Home Visitor's Handbook*; Practice Development Inc.: Seattle, WA, USA, 2004.
29. Slade, A.; Sadler, L.S.; Mayes, L.C. Minding the baby: Enhancing parental reflective functioning in a nursing/mental health home visiting program. In *Enhancing Early Attachments: Theory, Research, Intervention, and Policy*; Guildford Press: New York, NY, USA, 2005; pp. 152–177.
30. Kotelchuck, M. An evaluation of the Kessner Adequacy of Prenatal Care Index and a proposed Adequacy of Prenatal Care Utilization Index. *Am. J. Public Health* **1994**, *84*, 1414–1422. [CrossRef] [PubMed]
31. Beck, A.T.; Mendelson, M.; Mock, J.E. An inventory for measuring depression. *Arch. Gen. Psychiatry* **1961**, *4*, 561–571. [CrossRef] [PubMed]
32. Cox, J.L.; Holden, J.M.; Sagovsky, R. Detection of postnatal depression. Development of the Edinburgh Postnatal Depression Scale (EPDS). *Br. J. Psychiatry* **1987**, *150*, 782–786. [CrossRef] [PubMed]
33. Tong, A.; Sainsbury, P.; Craig, J. Consolidated criteria for reporting qualitative research (COREQ): A 32-item checklist for interviews and focus groups. *Int. J. Qual. Health Care* **2007**, *19*, 349–357. [CrossRef] [PubMed]
34. National Academy of Sciences; National Academy of Engineering; Institute of Medicine. *Ensuring the Integrity, Accessibility, and Stewardship of Research Data in the Digital Age*; The National Academies Press: Washington, DC, USA, 2009; p. 162.
35. Lu, M.C.; Halfon, N. Racial and ethnic disparities in birth outcomes: A life-course perspective. *Matern Child Health J.* **2003**, *7*, 13–30. [CrossRef] [PubMed]
36. Felitti, V.J.; Anda, R.F.; Nordenberg, D.; Williamson, D.F.; Spitz, A.M.; Edwards, V.; Koss, M.P.; Marks, J.S. Relationship of childhood abuse and household dysfunction to many of the leading causes of death in adults: The Adverse Childhood Experiences (ACE) Study. *Am. J. Prev. Med.* **1998**, *14*, 245–258. [CrossRef]
37. Dietz, P.M.; Spitz, A.M.; Anda, R.F.; Williamson, D.F.; McMahon, P.M.; Santelli, J.S.; Nordenberg, D.F.; Felitti, V.J.; Kendrick, J.S. Unintended pregnancy among adult women exposed to abuse or household dysfunction during their childhood. *JAMA* **1999**, *282*, 1359–1364. [CrossRef] [PubMed]
38. Maslow, A. A theory of human motivation. *Psychol. Rev.* **1943**, *50*, 370–398. [CrossRef]
39. Center on the Developing Child. Toxic Stress—Key Concepts. Available online: https://developingchild.harvard.edu/science/key-concepts/toxic-stress/ (accessed on 15 April 2018).
40. Kershaw, T.; Murphy, A.; Lewis, J.; Diveny, A.; Albritton, T.; Magriples, U.; Gordon, D. Family and relationship influences on parenting behaviors of young parents. *J. Adolesc. Health* **2014**, *54*, 197–203. [CrossRef] [PubMed]
41. Barak, A.; Spielberger, J.; Gitlow, E. The challenge of relationships and fidelity: Home visitors' perspectives. *Child. Youth Serv. Rev.* **2014**, *42*, 50–58. [CrossRef]
42. Lewis, C.; Lamb, M.E. Fathers' influences on children's development: The evidence from two-parent families. *Eur. J. Psychol. Educ.* **2003**, *18*, 211–228. [CrossRef]
43. Jack, S.M.; DiCenso, A.; Lohfeld, L. A theory of maternal engagement with public health nurses and family visitors. *J. Adv. Nurs.* **2005**, *49*, 182–190. [CrossRef] [PubMed]
44. Atrash, H.; Johnson, K.; Adams, M.; Cordero, J.; Howse, J. Preconception care for improving perinatal outcomes: The time to act. *Matern. Child Health J.* **2006**, *10*, S3–S11. [CrossRef] [PubMed]

45. Lu, M.C.; Highsmith, K.; de la Cruz, D.; Atrash, H. Putting the "M" back in the Maternal and Child Health Bureau: Reducing maternal mortality and morbidity. *Matern. Child Health J.* **2014**, *19*, 1435–1439. [CrossRef] [PubMed]
46. Barry, C.A.; Britten, N.; Bradley, C.; Stevenson, F. Using reflexivity to optimize teamwork in qualitative research. *Qual. Health Res.* **1999**, *9*, 26–44. [CrossRef] [PubMed]

© 2018 by the authors. Licensee MDPI, Basel, Switzerland. This article is an open access article distributed under the terms and conditions of the Creative Commons Attribution (CC BY) license (http://creativecommons.org/licenses/by/4.0/).

Article

Understanding of Information about Medicines Use among Parents of Pre-School Children in Serbia: Parental Pharmacotherapy Literacy Questionnaire (PTHL-SR)

Stana Ubavić [1], Nataša Bogavac-Stanojević [2], Aleksandra Jović-Vraneš [3] and Dušanka Krajnović [4,*]

[1] Medicines and Medical Devices Agency of Serbia (ALIMS), 11221 Belgrade, Serbia; stana.ubavic@alims.gov.rs
[2] Department of Medical Biochemistry, Faculty of Pharmacy, University of Belgrade, 11221 Belgrade, Serbia; naca@pharmacy.bg.ac.rs
[3] Institute of Social Medicine, Faculty of Medicine, University of Belgrade, 11000 Belgrade, Serbia; aljvranes@yahoo.co.uk
[4] Department of Social Pharmacy and Pharmaceutical Legislation, Faculty of Pharmacy, University of Belgrade, 11221 Belgrade, Serbia
* Correspondence: dusica.krajnovic@pharmacy.bg.ac.rs; Tel.: +381-631150629

Received: 9 March 2018; Accepted: 16 April 2018; Published: 3 May 2018

Abstract: Parental health literacy plays an important role in children's health. Experiences from pharmacy practice show that is necessary to check if parents understand instructions about use of medicines for children. This study aimed to assess pharmacotherapy literacy of parents of pre-school children and to examine association of parental pharmacotherapy literacy level with parent's socio-demographic characteristics. The study was cross-sectional, conducted among parents of pre-school children (1–7 years of age), in kindergartens in several municipalities of Belgrade, Serbia, during regular parents meetings, from May to October 2016. Functional health literacy was measured by the Serbian version of the Short Test of Functional Health Literacy in Adults (S-TOFHLA). Parental pharmacotherapy literacy was assessed with newly constructed PTHL-SR questionnaire with good psychometric characteristics (Parental pharmacotherapy literacy questionnaire—Serbian). Overall, 813 parents participated in the study, mostly females (81.30%), between 30 to 40 years of age (70.85%) with two children (56.70%). Almost all of our study participants (99%) had adequate health literacy as assessed by S-TOFHLA. Mean score on PTHL-SR was 72.83% (standard deviation was 13.37), with better results among females than males (72% of women were in the group of highest PTHL-SR results). Our study showed that many parents (76.5%) knew the appropriate usage of non-prescription medicine for children, 57.2% parents were able to correctly calculate the dose of oral syrup for a child, and only 43.3% were able to interpret non-prescription dosage information written on the package. The majority of parents (61.3%) would make a dosage to child based on age and not on their weight. Every fifth parent with adequate functional health literacy measured by S-TOFHLA test, achieved the lowest results measured by PTHL-SR. Higher performance of the PTHL-SR was significantly correlated with education ($p < 0.001$), female sex ($p < 0.001$), married parents and those living in common-law ($p < 0.001$), older parents ($p < 0.05$) and parents who have more children ($p < 0.05$), and are non-smokers ($p < 0.05$). These results provide evidence that limitations in understanding common information about use of medicines are widespread among parents of pre-school children and encourage efforts for further investigation. PTHL-SR questionnaire may be a useful tool for identification of parents who need more instructions and assistance from healthcare providers, above all in providing better communication, written or spoken at community pharmacy settings.

Keywords: parents; pharmacotherapy; health literacy; health education; pre-school children

1. Introduction

Health literacy is the term which has been used for more than 40 years in the scientific literature to describe the relationship between patient literacy levels and their ability to comply with prescribed therapeutic regimens [1]. It means applying literacy and numerical skills to health related materials such as prescriptions, appointment cards, medicine labels, and directions for home health care [2]. Health literacy is related to context [3,4], and in the pharmacy setting, can greatly impact the safe and effective use of medicines [5]. Poor health literacy may include misunderstanding of written medicine instructions, inadequate adherence to prescribed regimens, and inability to follow advice from health professionals regarding side effects and possible contraindications [5,6]. Individuals with limited health literacy experience difficulties in understanding drug labels [6]. Even educated patients face problems interpreting labels and patient information leaflets, as these tasks require understanding and application of information [5], thus emphasizing that higher education is not a requisite for understanding medical information [7]. These facts highlight the need for defining a pharmacotherapy literacy as "an individual's capacity to obtain, evaluate, calculate, and comprehend basic information about pharmacotherapy and pharmacy related services necessary to make appropriate medication-related decisions, regardless of the mode of content delivery (e.g., written, oral, visual images and symbols)" [8].

In the pediatric population, poor pharmacotherapy literacy of parents can cause serious problems in treatment. A study conducted in France [9] showed that parent's knowledge and practices about use of medicines for treatment of fever differ from recommendations in patient leaflets and without consulting a pediatric or pharmacist. This emphasizes the fact that parents are frequently the ones deciding on the type of medicine administered to a child, especially in emergency situations [9].

Moreover, oral antibiotic medicines were incorrectly prepared and reconstituted by parents in about 50% of cases, resulting in a risk of overdose or underdose [10]. According to a recent study in Australia [11], almost half of parents could not accurately determine weight-based doses. Errors in medicine dose or frequency of dose to children occur very often in cases where adults are preparing the medicines [12].

It was found that the format and content of labels could be improved in order to help parents understand the information about medicines [13]. These studies implicate parental pharmacotherapy literacy as one of the key factors influencing incorrect medicine administration, wrong dosage delivery, and miss-timed medicine delivery [14].

Researchers in parental and caregiver health literacy have mostly focused on asthma, nutrition, diabetes, and children with special care needs [14–17].

In the study of Kumar et al. [18], parental health literacy and numeracy skills needed for understanding instructions related to nutrition, injury and preventive care of young children were assessed using the Parental Health Literacy Activities Test (PHLAT).

Studies that assessed health literacy among parents and caregivers of children were not specific for assessing their pharmacotherapy literacy related to use of medicines for pediatric population [19].

Stilley et al. developed and examined psychometric properties of a Medication Health literacy measure tool, similar to Newest Vital Sign, in order to assess health literacy related to understanding and using information on prescription medication labels [20].

Furthermore, there were no studies that examined pharmacotherapy literacy of parents of pre-school children in Serbia, or understanding of information about use of medicines in the pediatric population. The previous study in Serbia by Jovic-Vranes and Bjegovic-Mikanovic evaluated health literacy among primary care patients using S-TOFHLA and TOFHLA as instruments for assessment of health literacy [21,22]. S-TOFHLA showed a "ceiling effect" [23] however was not sufficient to characterize pharmacotherapy literacy.

Our aim was to investigate knowledge and understanding of information together with numerical skills about medicines among parents of pre-school children with a newly constructed and validated Parental pharmacotherapy literacy questionnaire written in the Serbian language (PTHL-SR) [24].

2. Materials and Methods

2.1. Study Population

This cross-sectional study was conducted among parents and caregivers of pre-school children (from 1 to 7 years old) in a few municipalities of the city of Belgrade, Serbia. The study populations were both male and female, at least 18 years old, living as a parent, caregiver or a legal representative, or in a close relation to a child, and speaking the Serbian language. Selection of kindergartens was done on a random basis, taking into account kindergartens from municipalities with highest and lowest average monthly salaries. The number of respondents for the sample was calculated based on number of children enrolled in kindergartens in the city of Belgrade. We calculated sample size for a simple random sampling plan without replacement [25]. To determine the sample size we used a 3% margin of error and a 95% confidence level. The proportion of a sample that will choose a given answer to a question was estimated at 72.5% according to the results from Jovic-Vranes and Bjegovic-Mikanovic study which examined health literacy in the Serbian adult populations [21,22]. The Finite Population Correction factor was used for the final sample size calculation. The population size of pre-school children in year 2013 in Belgrade was 98,207 [26]. Calculated sample size in this study was 844 but after inclusion of response rate of 70% the total final number of examined parents were 1205 with the expectation of receiving 844 surveys back from this sample.

We decided to survey in a kindergarten setting as it is the easiest way to access parents, and to administer the context specific questionnaire. In addition, kindergartens were chosen as a setting, keeping in mind that in the context of a hospital and pharmacy, parents are often under pressure due to medical problems of the child, and do not have enough time to fill-in the questionnaire.

2.2. Data Collection

From March 2016 to October 2016 in Belgrade, Serbia, the survey was conducted in 10 kindergartens in a few municipalities of the city of Belgrade, Serbia. Respondents gave informed consent to participate in the study. All data were collected and analyzed anonymously, in order to keep the privacy of the respondents, as stated in the procedure approved by the Committee for Biomedical Research Faculty of Pharmacy, Belgrade (321/2, 15 March 2016).

Parents had to complete: (a) the previously validated instrument for health literacy (Short Test of Functional Health literacy in adults, S-TOFHLA [21,22,27] (Serbian version), (b) the Pharmacotherapy literacy questionnaire in Serbian (PTHL-SR questionnaire) [24], and (c) a socio-demographic questionnaire which included questions about age, sex, education, employment status, self-estimation of health condition, the number of annual visits to pediatrician, presence of chronic diseases of child, breast feeding information and whether parents were smokers or not. Participants in the survey did not receive any monetary compensation.

The questionnaire was distributed by an interviewer (SU) who was trained to describe necessary information about the survey and research. A printed survey was offered and administered to parents at the scheduled regular parent-teacher meetings in the kindergarten. Parents were allowed unlimited time to complete the PTHL-SR and socio-demographic questionnaire, and 7 min for completion of S-TOFHLA (Serbian version).

2.3. Study Instrument

Health literacy was examined by S-TOFHLA as a continuous variable. It calculated the number of correct answers for each of 36 items in S-TOFHLA, for every participant in survey, in order to understand whether they have inadequate (≤ 16 correctly answered questions), marginal (17–22) or adequate (≥ 23) health literacy.

The PTHL-SR questionnaire included 14 questions and was developed and validated in our previous study [24]. Some of the questions included graphic presentations of a measuring device for dosage of liquid pediatric medicines and graphical presentation of packaging for medicines.

The graphic images were used as the aim of the study was it be carried out without the active participation of interviewers. Parents were excluded if they had vision problems or reported that they felt sick. Questions in PTHL-SR questionnaire encompassed four domains of pharmacotherapy literacy: knowledge, understanding, numeracy and access to medicine related information.

An overall score in PTHL-SR for each participant was calculated as the percentage of correct answers. In order to examine the influence of socio-demographic characteristics of parents on different levels of pharmacotherapy literacy we divided total scores in the PTHL-SR into three clusters according to terciles. The first cluster were scores with up to 8 (64%) correct answers (low total score in PTHL-SR), the second were scores between 9 and 10 (65–85%) of correct answers (medium score), and the third cluster were score results between 11 and 14 (86–100%) of correct answers (high score).

The percentage of correct answers for each question was calculated, and the percentage of correct answers within domains of pharmacotherapy literacy.

2.4. Statistical Analysis

Statistical testing of group differences for categorical variables was examined by the chi-squared test of independence. Calculated scores for knowledge, understanding of information, numeracy skills and total PTHL-SR were compared between the groups by Student's *t*-test for two samples and one way analysis of variance (ANOVA) with post hoc Tuckey-Kremer test. Using binary univariate and multivariate logistic regression analysis we determined the probability of socio-demographic characteristics to predict low PTHL-SR score. All calculations were performed using SPSS, version 22.0 (IBM Corp., Armonk, NY, USA).

3. Results

In total 1200 questionnaires were given to parents in kindergartens, and 856 were collected (71.33% response rate). Most of parents said that their reason for non-response was a lack of time. After excluding questionnaires with no or double answers, 813 questionnaires were analyzed.

The present study was context specific, performed outside of medical settings, (i.e., in kindergartens) to minimize pressure related to children's health conditions. In addition, we have used the S-TOFHLA test, designed to provide quick estimation of health literacy in medical or educational setting (kindergarten).

We found that 99% of parents had adequate functional health literacy assessed by S-TOFHLA (mean score was 33). Mean score of PTHL-SR was 72.83% (standard deviation was 13.37%). Mean PTHL-SR score is the percent of questions answered correctly. Only 25% of parents had less than 90% correct answers in S-TOFHLA, while 75% of parents had less than 85% correct answers in PTHL-SR questionnaire. Our survey showed that 21.5% of parents with adequate health literacy achieved by S-TOFHLA, had the lowest level of pharmacotherapy literacy achieved in PTHL-SR questionnaire.

All examined parents characteristics are summarized in Table 1. Most of the participants were women (81.30%), who were married (90.2%), between 31 and 40 years old (70.85%), with two children (56.70%). Only 9.8% were single parents (widows, divorced, parents without partners). Every fifth participant estimated their health condition as excellent. Most of respondents (56.6%) had a university degree (at least 16 years of education), 88.1% were employed and were non-smokers (70.2%). In addition to this, our results showed that 80% of parents are reading Patients leaflet instructions before use of medicines. Those who read are mostly non-smokers (71.9%) and parents with two and more children (57%).

Table 1. Socio-demographic characteristics of the parents in the survey.

Socio-Demographic Characteristics		No.	%
Sex	Male	152	18.7
	Female	661	81.3
Age (years)	18–29	59	7.26
	30–40	576	70.8
	41–50	161	19.8
	51–60	17	2.09
Number of children	One child	245	30.1
	Two children	461	56.7
	Three and more children	107	13.1
Marital state	Single parent [a]	80	9.8
	Married/Common-law	733	90.2
Education	University degree and higher [b]	460	56.6
	Middle school or less [c]	353	43.3
Employment	Employed	716	88.1
	Unemployed	97	11.9
Self-estimation of health status	Average and Bad	144	17.7
	Good	502	61.7
	Excellent	167	20.5
Chronic diseases	No	710	87.3
	Yes	103	12.7
Smoker	No	570	70.2
	Yes	243	29.8
Breast feeding of a first child	No	85	10.5
	Yes	728	89.5
Annual visits to pediatrician	1–2 times a year	270	33.2
	3–4 times	263	32.3
	5–6 times a year and more	280	34.5

In Table 1 are presented absolute and relative frequences. [a] Single parents (widows, divorced, living with a child alone). [b] University degee and higher (at least 16 years of education). [c] Middle school or less (8–12 years of education).

More than 90% of parents recognized the medicine shown in the picture, answered correctly the numerical skills questions and knew to mark an exact dose with a measuring device (97.7%, 94.8%, 96.3%, respectively). In addition, 94.7% of parents would seek information about medicines from a doctor or pharmacist and 94.8% of parents could correctly dose a liquid pediatric medicine using an oral syringe. Conversely, only 38.7% of parents would make a dosage to the child based on their weight and not on their age and only 43.3% were able to interpret the paracetamol dosage chart written on package. On other questions most of the parents answered correctly. Most of responders were able to correctly calculate the dose of oral syrup for a child based on a dosage regimen per kg, knew to correctly interpret the warning statement "Avoid sun while taking this medicine" and knew the appropriate usage of OTC medicine for the children (57.2%, 64% and 76.5%, respectively). 79.3% of parents correctly understood the warning statement about avoiding milk while taking medicine and 84.4% of parents would not give an aspirin to the pre-school children (neither to children up to 16 years). The list of questions and correct answers in PTHL-SR were shown in Table 2.

Parent's pharmacotherapy literacy expressed as a score per each domain (knowledge, understanding information, numeracy) and total PTHL-SR score was compared according to socio-demographic characteristics. A higher knowledge score was seen in females, married parents, in parents with university degrees and higher education and in non-smokers.

Table 2. List of questions and percent of correct answers in PTHL-SR questionnaire.

No	Question	Domain	% Correct
1	What is this medicine (ibuprofen) used for?	Knowledge	76.5
2	What does this medicine contain? (picture of paracetamol syrup)	Knowledge	97.7
3	Would you give an aspirin to a child of 6 years if it has a fever?	Knowledge	84.4
4	Your child has otitis and pain. How do you calculate the dose for a child/Where do you find information how much medicine for pain relief to give (per kg or per age)?	Knowledge	38.7
5	What is the highest temperature limit after you give antipyretic to a child?	Knowledge	89.3
6	Pharmacist told you to avoid milk and milk products while taking medicine. What does it mean to you?	Understanding	79.3
7	Avoid sun while taking medicine. What does it mean to you?	Understanding	64.0
8	Keep under 25 °C. After reconstitution, keep refrigerated up to 14 days. How will you store this medicine after reconstitution?	Understanding	83.4
9	You have to give medicine to a child 2 times a day. If your package has 10 items, how many medicines you will have after 3 days?	Numeracy	94.8
10	To mark the dosage for a child of 13 kg on measuring spoon.	Numeracy	96.3
11	To answer how much medicine is inside the oral syringe.	Numeracy	92.6
12	To calculate a dose of oral syrup for child based on dosage regimen per kg.	Numeracy	57.2
13	To interpret paracetamol dosage chart written on package, per weight.	Numeracy	43.3
14	Where did you get an information how much antipyretic to give to your child?	Access	94.7

In addition, knowledge scores were different between age groups. The youngest parents had significantly lower knowledge compared to parents in the group of 31–40 years old ($p = 0.007$) and parents aged 41–50 ($p < 0.001$). Married and higher educated responders showed higher scores for understanding of information compared to single responders and responders with middle school degrees. Scores for numeracy skills were higher in responders with University degree, in employed and non-smoking responders. Moreover, ages influenced numeracy skills score. The youngest parents had significantly lower numeracy skills compared to parents in the group of 31–40 years old ($p = 0.002$) and among parents aged 41–50 ($p = 0.027$). Higher performance of the total PTHL-SR score was shown in females, married parents, in parents with University degrees and higher education and in non-smokers. Parents with more than two children had higher total PTHL-SR scores than parents with one child ($p = 0.016$). Youngest responders had lower total PTHL-SR score than responders in the second and third groups ($p < 0.001$ for the both comparisons). Results of parent's pharmacotherapy literacy according to socio-demographic characteristics are presented in Table 3.

We divided total PTHL-SR score into three clusters (low, medium and high) and examined dependence of different levels of pharmacotherapy literacy on the socio-demographic characteristics of parents (Table 4). The large number of male responders (42.1%) was in the group with low pharmacotherapy level while only 28% females were in the same group ($p < 0.003$). One third of parents (33%) with highest educational grade (faculty and PhD studies) had the highest scores in PTHL-SR, but at the same time only 16% of parents with a lower level of education had the highest scores ($p < 0.001$). Furthermore, 42.5% of single parents (divorced, widows, parents without partners) were in the group with the lowest PTHL-SR scores, while only 29.3% of parents who are married or living in common-law were in the same group ($p = 0.044$). Responders who had excellent self-estimation of health status and non-smokers were in the majority in the high total score group, and in the minority in low total score group ($p = 0.048$ and $p = 0.001$, respectively). Dependance of total PTHL-SR score on socio-demographic characteristics is shown in Table 4.

Table 3. Parent's pharmacotherapy literacy according to socio-demographic characteristics.

Parents Characteristics	Knowledge X ± SD (Max Score: 5)	p Value	Understanding X ± SD (Max Score: 3)	p Value	Numeracy X ± SD (Max Score: 5)	p Value	Total Score X ± SD (Max Score: 14)	p Value
Sex								
Male	3.64 ± 1.02	<0.001	2.41 ± 0.89	0.243	3.81 ± 0.98	0.693	9.88 ± 2.06	0.019
Female	3.91 ± 0.88		2.50 ± 0.85		3.85 ± 0.91		10.27 ± 1.82	
Age (years)								
18–29	3.46 ± 1.21	<0.001	2.25 ± 0.97	0.105	3.44 ± 1.04	0.004	9.15 ± 2.43	<0.001
30–40	3.86 ± 0.87 *		2.53 ± 0.85		3.89 ± 0.89 *		10.28 ± 1.78 *	
41–50	4.04 ± 0.92 *		2.44 ± 0.86		3.83 ± 0.98 *		10.32 ± 1.86 *	
51–60	3.76 ± 0.83		2.41 ± 0.79		3.71 ± 0.98		9.88 ± 1.87	
Number of children								
One child	3.75 ± 0.98	0.050	2.41 ± 0.93	0.118	3.78 ± 0.94	0.057	9.94 ± 2.01	0.014
Two children	3.92 ± 0.89		2.50 ± 0.84		3.83 ± 0.92		10.25 ± 1.79	
Three children and more	3.89 ± 0.88		2.61 ± 0.81		4.04 ± 0.90		10.54 ± 1.83 *	
Marital status								
Single parent	3.61 ± 1.23	0.009	2.23 ± 0.99	0.006	3.86 ± 0.91	0.067	9.51 ± 2.50	<0.001
Married	3.89 ± 0.87		2.51 ± 0.85		3.66 ± 1.04		10.27 ± 1.78	
Education								
University degree and higher [a]	3.98 ± 0.82	<0.001	2.60 ± 0.83	<0.001	3.99 ± 0.86	<0.001	10.58 ± 1.67	<0.001
Middle school and less education [b]	3.71 ± 1.00		2.34 ± 0.89		3.64 ± 0.97		9.69 ± 1.99	
Employment								
Employed	4.01 ± 0.94	0.098	2.50 ± 0.85	0.122	3.87 ± 0.89	0.021 *	10.22 ± 1.79	0.296
Unemployed	3.84 ± 0.91		2.36 ± 0.96		3.64 ± 1.14		10.01 ± 2.37	
Self-estimation of health status								
Average and bad	3.85 ± 1.00	0.557	2.43 ± 0.88	0.299	3.71 ± 1.06	0.080	10.00 ± 2.26	0.079
Good	3.85 ± 0.91		2.47 ± 0.89		3.84 ± 0.91		10.17 ± 1.84	
Excellent	3.93 ± 0.84		2.57 ± 0.76		3.95 ± 0.85		10.46 ± 1.60	
Chronic diseases								
No	3.84 ± 0.92	0.089	2.48 ± 0.88	0.652	3.84 ± 0.94	0.553	11.94 ± 1.97	0.101
Yes	4.01 ± 0.91		2.52 ± 0.77		3.89 ± 0.84		12.27 ± 1.71	
Smoking								
No	3.91 ± 0.89	0.023	2.50 ± 0.85	0.573	3.91 ± 0.88	<0.001	10.33 ± 1.75	0.002 *
Yes	3.75 ± 0.96		2.46 ± 0.91		3.66 ± 1.01		9.88 ± 2.10	
Breast feeding of a first child								
Yes	3.88 ± 0.90	0.845	2.49 ± 0.84	0.945	3.90 ± 0.94	0.129	10.27 ± 1.88	0.520
No	3.82 ± 0.93		2.46 ± 0.96		3.88 ± 0.84		10.16 ± 1.98	
Annual visits to pediatrician								
1–2 times	3.90 ± 0.88	0.447	2.53 ± 0.90	0.770	3.88 ± 0.92	0.579	10.31 ± 1.83	0.352
3–4 times	3.89 ± 0.92		2.48 ± 0.87		3.86 ± 0.93		10.23 ± 1.92	
5–6 times and more	3.83 ± 0.94		2.45 ± 0.83		3.79 ± 0.93		10.07 ± 1.86	

Groups were compared by Student t test for two samples or one-way ANOVA test. * Significant difference between groups ($p \leq 0.05$), determined by Post Hoc Tukey-Kramer test. [a] University degree and higher (at least 16 years of education). [b] Middle school or less (8–12 years of education).

Table 4. Dependance of total PTHL-SR score from socio-demographic characteristics.

Parents Characteristics	Total Score			p Value
	Low	Medium	High	
Sex				
Male	42.1%	36.2%	21.7%	0.003
Female	28.0%	45.5%	26.5%	
Age (years)				
18–29	45.8%	42.4%	11.9%	
30–40	29.7%	43.4%	26.9%	0.07
41–50	28.0%	44.7%	27.3%	
51–60	35.3%	52.9%	11.8%	
Number of children				
One child	37.1%	40.0%	22.9%	
Two children	28.9%	44.7%	26.5%	0.082
Three children and more	23.4%	48.6%	28.0%	
Marital status				
Single parent	42.5%	33.8%	23.8%	0.044
Married	29.3%	44.9%	25.8%	
Education				
University degree and higher [a]	23.3%	43.7%	33.0%	<0.001
Middle school and less (8–12 years of education) [b]	40.2%	43.9%	15.9%	
Employment				
Employed	30.9%	43.6%	25.6%	0.916
Unemployed	28.9%	45.4%	25.8%	
Self-estimation of health status				
Average and bad	34.0%	43.1%	22.9%	
Good	32.7%	41.2%	26.1%	0.048
Excellent	21.6%	52.1%	26.3%	
Chronic diseases				
No	31.3%	43.2%	25.5%	0.562
Yes	26.2%	47.6%	26.2%	
Smoker				
No	30.9%	43.5%	25.6%	0.001
Yes	35.5%	42.1%	22.3%	
Breast feeding of a first child				
Yes	30.8%	42.6%	26.8%	0.912
No	28.2%	45.9%	25.9%	
Annual visits to pediatrician				
1–2 times	32.2%	38.5%	29.3%	
3–4 times	27.4%	47.1%	25.5%	0.266
5–6 times and more	32.1%	45.7%	22.2%	

[a] University degree and higher (at least 16 years of education). [b] Middle school or less (8–12 years of education).

Only 17.8% of males compared to 82.2% of females would ask a doctor or pharmacist for information about which medicines to give to a child for pain relief and fever. Other parents would search for information from different sources (e.g., neighbors, internet, newspapers). This finding suggests that broad access to information via INTERNET or newspapers are common among parents with lower health literacy, especially males.

Parents characteristics associated with lower PTHL-SR results are presented in Table 5. Men had almost 2 times higher probability for low PTHL-SR scores then women (OR 1.871; $p < 0.001$). Older parents had lower probability for low scores—parents older than 30 years had less than half probability for low scores (OR 0.500 for parents from 30 to 40 years and OR 0.460 for parents from 41 to 50 years) compared to parents younger than 30 years. Furthermore, the number of children in a family was associated with low PTHL-SR score; if number of children was higher probability for low total PTHL score was lower. Single parents had almost two times higher probability of low scores than married ones (OR 1.781, $p < 0.016$). Higher education and excellent self-estimation of health are less likely to achieve low total scores in PTHL-SR (OR 0.450 and OR 0.533, respectively).

Table 5. Parent's characteristics associated with lower PTHL-SR results.

Characteristic	OR	95% CI	p Value
Sex			
Male sex	1.871	1.300–2.693	<0.001
Age (years)			
30–40	0.500	0.291–0.861	0.012
41–50	0.460	0.248–0.852	0.014
Number of children			
2 children	0.686	0.494–0.953	0.025
3 children	0.516	0.308–0.866	0.012
Marital status			
Single	1.781	1.112–2.852	0.016
Married (Common-law)			
Education			
Higher education	0.450	0.333–0.610	<0.001
Self-estimation of health status			
Excellent	0.533	0.322–0.883	0.015

Furthermore, we determined independent predictors of low PTHL-SR scores after inclusion of significant socio-demographic characteristics in the logistic model. Significant independent predictors of the low PTHL-SR score were male gender, high education and number of children. Male gender was associated with higher probability [OR—1.79, 95% CI (1.239–2.588), $p = 0.002$] for low total score. High education [OR—0.471, 95% CI (0.349–0.636), $p < 0.001$] and higher number of children were associated with lower probability for low total score [OR for parents with two children —0.701, 95% CI (0.504–0.975), $p = 0.035$ and OR for parents with more than two children was 0.591 95% CI (0.356–0.981), $p = 0.042$].

4. Discussion

This is the first specific study that examines pharmacotherapy literacy of parents related to use of medicines for pre-school children in Serbia. We found that many parents of pre-school children in Serbia do not accurately understand basic information about medicines for their children, regardless whether the information is written or spoken.

Our results show that more than half of parents (56.7%) could not properly understand dosage regimen of OTC medicines written on the package and in Patient Information leaflets, especially warning statements (for example, about avoiding sun and milk during medical therapy). Previous study among pharmacy visitors in Australia [5], found that auxiliary label statements were misinterpreted among a majority of responders. Findings from the study by Emmerton et al. [11] suggested that half of parents could not accurately determine weight-based doses. In our study, almost two/third of parents would make dosage based on the age and not on the weight of the child, and every 4th parent did not know appropriate use of OTC medicine for children.

This indicates that information about medicines should be written in a simpler way [28] or that the majority of parents need more clarification from a pharmacist or pediatrician. Writing of information about medicines use in a simpler way and ease of communication between parents and healthcare professionals are the key measures that should be done in order to facilitate the use of medicines by parents in cases of acute illness or preventive care. These measures could also include visual aids for those with communication barriers [29], and the necessity to check if parents understood information of medicines [19], by determining if parents can explain information with their own words.

In our study, higher scores of PTHL-SR closely correlated with higher educational level, female sex, married parents, parents with more children, parents who estimated their health condition as excellent, non-smokers and those who visit pediatricians less times per year.

This study showed that parents with higher education level (university degree or higher with more than 16 years of education) had significantly better overall score in PTHL-SR as well as in knowledge, understanding and numeracy. The results are in line with previous studies on health literacy [13,15–18,20].

A previous study on health literacy in Serbia [22] highlighted that there is no significant difference in functional health literacy level between males and females. Our results highlight gender differences in pharmacotherapy literacy in the tested population. While 42% of men had the lowest PTHL-SR score, this was true for only 28% of women. Moreover, women had better scores in all defined domains: knowledge, understanding and numeracy in comparison to men ($p < 0.001$). This might be because women as mothers are predominantly taking care of ill children and because our survey responders were mostly women.

In general, older parents (41–50 years old) had the highest mean score in knowledge about pediatric medicines (4.04 ± 0.92, $p < 0.001$). This can be explained by the empirical knowledge about medicines use by older parents.

Our findings on parents with more than two children having better scores for knowledge and total PTHL-SR score, may also be related to previous experience and empirical knowledge gained during care and medication of children. This finding implies that healthcare professionals, especially pharmacists, could actively assist in helping younger parents who have one child, firstly in clarifying given information by repeating instructions. Parents have to be encouraged to become more educated, either by self-education through reliable sources of information or through educational campaigns organized by healthcare professionals. Interestingly, our study also showed that single parents are more likely to have lower pharmacotherapy literacy, especially in knowledge and understanding of medicines related information. This could be explained by the lack of mutual interaction when people can influence each other's behavior and could learn from each other.

Our study results confirmed findings from previous studies of health literacy [22] that people who estimated their health condition as excellent had an adequate functional health literacy, as well as the highest (26.3% of parents) overall scores measured by PTHL-SR questionnaire.

Furthermore, parents who smoke showed decreases overall scores in PTHL-SR together with limited knowledge and numerical skills. This correlates with a previous study conducted by Radic et al. in Serbia [30], where smoking was significantly frequent among less educated parents, both mothers and fathers.

Results of the PTHL-SR illustrated some more important facts. Every fourth parent in Serbia has difficulty in understanding common information written on the package or in Patient Information leaflets, especially warning statements (for example, about avoiding sun and milk during medical therapy). About 20% of parents do not read patient leaflet instructions, but rather rely on advice from a pharmacist or pediatrician.

Data presented showed that adequate health literacy results, as assessed by S-TOFHLA, are not an accurate indicator of parental pharmacotherapy literacy, especially in parents with a higher level of education.

This is primarily because the PTHL-SR tests understanding, knowledge, access to medicines related information and numeracy, while the S-TOFHLA test examine only reading comprehension and understanding of medical terms. PTHL-SR seems to be a more accurate measure of pharmacotherapy literacy among parents of pre-school children.

The results from our study emphasize the need for evaluation of medication labelling in order of improving instructions about pediatric medicines use, especially for parents with limited health and pharmacotherapy literacy. It is also a trigger to improve communication of health care professionals, particularly pharmacists, with aim to reduce errors in medication of pediatric patients made by parents.

Limitations

Certain limitations of the present study should be taken into consideration when interpreting results. As this is a cross-sectional study, we didn't correlate the PTHL-SR with clinical outcomes. However, the study shows that parents of pre-school children in Serbia have problems in appropriate dosing and understanding information about use of pediatric medicines.

The study does not investigate causes of low parental pharmacotherapy literacy, just correlation of low PTHL-SR results with socio-demographic characteristics of parents. Moreover, the study is done in an urban area, among parents with higher education degree. Future studies should consider parents outside urban area and further improvement of the PTHL-SR reliability and feasibility.

5. Conclusions

These results provide evidence that limitations in understanding common information about use of medicines are widespread among parents of pre-school children and encourage efforts for further investigation. The PTHL-SR questionnaire may be a useful tool for identification of parents who need more instructions and assistance from healthcare providers, above all in providing better written or spoken information at community pharmacy settings.

Author Contributions: D.K. conceived the study. D.K. and S.U. contributed to the design of the study and the acquisition of data. All authors contributed to the analysis and interpretation of data. S.U. wrote an initial draft of the manuscript. All authors contributed to the drafting of the manuscript or revised it critically, and have given final approval of the version published.

Acknowledgments: We thank pre-school institutions from the city of Belgrade and their staff who allowed survey in their settings. We also thank all parents who respond to questionnaire. The work of D.K. is partially supported by the grant of Ministry of Science and Education in Serbia, Grant Number 41004. We would also like to thank GSK International, Representative office, Belgrade, for financial support for obtaining license for using of S-TOFHLA instrument. We would also like to thank to the company Pharmanova Ltd, Obrenovac, Serbia and Hemofarm Vršac, a member of Stada group for part of financial support for Article Processing Charge for publication of this manuscript. This grant didn't produce any influence on method and results of our work during research.

Conflicts of Interest: The authors declare no conflict of interest. The founding sponsors had no role in the design of the study; in the collection, analyses, or interpretation of data; in the writing of the manuscript, and in the decision to publish the results.

References

1. Ad Hoc Committee on Health Literacy for the American Council on Scientific Affairs, American Medical Association. Health Literacy: Report of the Council on Scientific Affairs. *J. Am. Med. Assoc.* **1999**, *281*, 552–557.
2. Parker, R.M.; Baker, D.W.; Williams, M.V.; Nurss, J.R. The test of functional health literacy in adults: A new instrument for measuring patient's literacy skills. *J. Gen. Intern. Med.* **1995**, *10*, 537–541. [CrossRef] [PubMed]
3. Nutbeam, D. Health literacy as a public health goal: A challenge for contemporary health education and communication strategies into the 21st century. *Health Promot. Int.* **2000**, *15*, 259–267. [CrossRef]
4. Ghanbari, S.; Rameyankhani, A.; Montazeri, A.; Mehrabi, Z. Health Literacy Measure for Adolescents (HELMA): Development and Psychometric properties. *PLoS ONE* **2016**, *11*, e0149202. [CrossRef] [PubMed]
5. Emmerton, L.M.; Mampallil, L.; Kairuz, T.; McKauge, L.M.; Bush, R.A. Exploring health literacy competences in community pharmacy. *Health Expect.* **2012**, *15*, 12–22. [CrossRef] [PubMed]
6. Koster, E.S.; Philbert, D.; Bouvy, M.L. Health literacy among pharmacy visitors in The Netherlands. *Pharmacoepidemiol. Drug Saf.* **2015**, *24*, 716–721. [CrossRef] [PubMed]
7. Kindig, D. *Health Literacy: A Prescription to End Confusion*; National Academias Press: Washington, DC, USA, 2004.
8. King, S.R.; McCaffrey, D.J., III; Bouldin, A.S. Health literacy in the pharmacy setting: Defining pharmacotherapy literacy. *Pharm. Pract.* **2011**, *9*, 213–220.

9. Bertille, N.; Fournier-Charriere, E.; Pons, G.; Chalumeau, M. Managing fever in children: A national survey of parent's knowledge and practices in France. *PLoS ONE* **2013**, *8*, e83469. [CrossRef] [PubMed]
10. Berthe-Aucejo, A.; Girard, D.; Lorrot, M.; Bellettre, X.; Faye, A.; Mercier, J.C.; Brion, F.; Bourdon, O.; Prot-Labarthe, S. Evaluation of frequency of paediatric oral liquid medication dosing errors by caregivers: Amoxicillin and josamycin. *Arch. Dis. Child.* **2016**, *101*, 359–364. [CrossRef] [PubMed]
11. Emmerton, L.M.; Chaw, X.Y.; Kelly, F.; Kairuz, T.; Marriott, J.; Wheeler, A.; Moles, R. Management of children's fever by parents and caregivers: Practical measurements of functional health literacy. *J. Child Healthc.* **2014**, *18*, 302–313. [CrossRef] [PubMed]
12. Heubi, J.E.; Barbacci, M.B.; Zimmerman, H.J. Therapeutic misadventures with acetaminophen: Hepatoxicity after multiple doses in children. *J. Pediatr.* **1998**, *132*, 22–27. [CrossRef]
13. Yin, H.S.; Parker, R.M.; Wolf, M.; Mendelsohn, A.L.; Sanders, L.M.; Vivar, K.L.; Carney, K.; Cerra, M.E.; Dreyer, B.P. Health Literacy Assessment of Labeling of Pediatric Nonprescription Medications: Examination of Characteristics that May Impair Parent Understanding. *Acad. Pediatr.* **2012**, *12*, 288–296. [CrossRef] [PubMed]
14. Keim-Malpass, J.; Letzkus, J.C.; Kennedy, C. Parent/caregiver health literacy among children with special health care needs: A systematic review of the literature. *BMC Pediatr.* **2015**, *15*, 92. [CrossRef] [PubMed]
15. Pulgarón, E.R.; Sanders, L.M.; Patiño-Fernandez, A.M.; Wile, D.; Sanchez, J.; Rothman, R.L.; Delamater, A.M. Glycemic control in young children with diabetes: The role of parental health literacy. *Patient Educ. Couns.* **2014**, *94*, 67–70. [CrossRef] [PubMed]
16. Harrington, K.F.; Zhang, B.; Magruder, T.; Bailey, W.C.; Gerald, L.B. The Impact of Parent's Health Literacy on Pediatric Asthma Outcomes. *Pediatr. Allergy Immunol. Pulmonol.* **2015**, *28*, 20–26. [CrossRef] [PubMed]
17. Gibbs, H.D.; Kennett, A.R.; Kerling, E.H.; Qing, Y.; Gajewski, B.; Ptomey, L.T.; Sullivan, D.K. Assessing the Nutrition Literacy of Parents and its Relationship with Child Diet Quality. *J. Nutr. Educ. Behav.* **2016**, *48*, 505–509. [CrossRef] [PubMed]
18. Kumar, D.; Sanders, L.; Perrin, E.M.; Lokker, N.; Patterson, B.; Gunn, V.; Finkle, J.; Franco, V.; Choi, L.; Rothman, R.L. Parental Understanding of Infant Health Information: Health Literacy, Numeracy and the Parental Health Literacy Activities Test (PHLAT). *Acad. Pediatr.* **2010**, *10*, 309–316. [CrossRef] [PubMed]
19. Tran, T.P.; Robinson, L.M.; Keebler, J.R.; Walker, R.A.; Wadman, M.C. Health Literacy among Parents of Pediatric Patients. *West. J. Emerg. Med.* **2008**, *9*, 130–134. [PubMed]
20. Stilley, C.S.; Terhorst, L.; Flynn, W.B.; Fiore, R.M.; Stimer, E.D. Medication health literacy measure: Development and psychometric properties. *J. Nurs. Meas.* **2014**, *22*, 213–222. [CrossRef] [PubMed]
21. Jovic-Vranes, A.; Bjegović-Mikanović, V.; Marinkovic, J.; Vukovic, D. Evaluation of a health literacy screening tool in primary care patients: Evidence from Serbia. *Health Promot. Int.* **2014**, *29*, 601–607. [PubMed]
22. Jovic-Vranes, A.; Bjegović-Mikanović, V.; Marinkovic, J.; Kocev, N. Health literacy in a population of primary health-care patients in Belgrade, Serbia. *Int. J. Public Health* **2011**, *56*, 201–207. [CrossRef] [PubMed]
23. Morrison, A.K.; Schapira, M.M.; Hoffmann, R.G.; Brousseau, C. Measuring Health Literacy in Caregivers of Children: A Comparison of the Newest Vital Sign and S-TOFHLA. *Clin. Pediatr.* **2014**, *53*, 1264–1270. [CrossRef] [PubMed]
24. Ubavic, S.; Krajnovic, D.; Bogavac-Stanojevic, N. Pharmacotherapy literacy (PTHL-SR) questionnaire for parents of pre-school children in Serbia: Construction and psychometric characteristics. *Vojnosanit. Pregl.* **2018**. [CrossRef]
25. Moore, D.; McCabe, G. *Introduction to the Practice of Statistics*, 3rd ed.; W.H. Freeman and Company: New York, NY, USA, 1999.
26. Republic of Serbia—Institute for Statistics. Available online: http://www.stat.gov.rs/WebSite/public/ReportView.aspx (accessed on 29 January 2018).
27. Baker, D.W.; Williams, M.V.; Parker, R.M.; Gazmararian, J. Development of a brief test to measure functional health literacy. *Patient Educ. Couns.* **1999**, *38*, 33–42. [CrossRef]
28. Yin, H.S.; Johnson, M.; Mendelsohn, A.L.; Abrams, M.A.; Sanders, L.M.; Dreyer, B.P. The health literacy of parents in the United States: A nationally representative study. *Pediatrics* **2009**, *124*, 289–298. [CrossRef] [PubMed]

29. Schillinger, D.; Machtinger, E.; Wang, F.; Chen, L.; Win, K.; Palacios, J.; Rodriguez, M.; Bindman, A. Language, literacy and communication regarding medication in an anticoagulation clinic: Are pictures better than words? *J. Health Commun.* **2006**, *11*, 651–666. [CrossRef] [PubMed]
30. Radic, S.D.; Gvozdenovic, B.S.; Pesic, I.M.; Zivkovic, Z.M.; Skodric-Trifunovic, V. Exposure to tobacco smoke among asthmatic children: Parents' smoking habits and level of education. *Int. J. Tuberc. Lung Dis.* **2011**, *15*, 276–280. [PubMed]

© 2018 by the authors. Licensee MDPI, Basel, Switzerland. This article is an open access article distributed under the terms and conditions of the Creative Commons Attribution (CC BY) license (http://creativecommons.org/licenses/by/4.0/).

Article

Do Low Income Youth of Color See "The Bigger Picture" When Discussing Type 2 Diabetes: A Qualitative Evaluation of a Public Health Literacy Campaign

Dean Schillinger *, Jessica Tran and Sarah Fine

Department of Medicine and Center for Vulnerable, Populations University of California San Francisco, Zuckerberg San Francisco Hospital, 1001 Potrero Avenue San Francisco, CA 94118, USA; jessdqtran@gmail.com (J.T.); sarah.fine@ucsf.edu (S.F.)
* Correspondence: dean.schillinger@ucsf.edu; Tel.: +415-206-8940; Fax: +415-206-5586

Received: 3 February 2018; Accepted: 20 April 2018; Published: 24 April 2018

Abstract: As Type 2 diabetes spikes among minority and low-income youth, there is an urgent need to tackle the drivers of this preventable disease. *The Bigger Picture* (TBP) is a counter-marketing campaign using youth-created, spoken-word public service announcements (PSAs) to reframe the epidemic as a socio-environmental phenomenon requiring communal action, civic engagement and norm change. Methods: We examined whether and how TBP PSAs advance health literacy among low-income, minority youth. We showed nine PSAs, asking individuals open-ended questions via questionnaire, then facilitating a focus group to reflect upon the PSAs. Results: Questionnaire responses revealed a balance between individual vs. public health literacy. Some focused on individual responsibility and behaviors, while others described socio-environmental forces underlying risk. The focus group generated a preponderance of public health literacy responses, emphasizing future action. Striking sociopolitical themes emerged, reflecting tensions minority and low-income youth experience, such as entrapment vs. liberation. Conclusion: Our findings speak to the structural barriers and complexities underlying diabetes risk, and the ability of spoken word medium to make these challenges visible and motivate action. Practice Implications: Delivering TBP content to promote interactive reflection has potential to change behavioral norms and build capacity to confront the social, economic and structural factors that influence behaviors.

Keywords: health literacy; social marketing; type 2 diabetes; diabetes prevention; qualitative research

---

1. Introduction

Type 2 diabetes has drastically risen in the U.S. over the last decade, disproportionately affecting ethnic minority populations. The mean prevalence among adult minority populations with diabetes is 21.7%, in comparison to 11.3% among non-Hispanic whites [1]. Although Type 2 diabetes has historically been coined as "adult-onset" diabetes, it has increased by 30.5% in youth aged 10–19 years between 2001 and 2009 [2]. Among new cases of diabetes among youth, the vast majority of sub-types in white youth represent Type 1 (an autoimmune disease). In contrast, among minority youth, one–half to three-quarters of new cases represent Type 2 (a largely environmental disease) [3]. There is an urgent need to engage at-risk youth in preventing an illness that poses substantial risks for disabling complications.

Prevention efforts have primarily focused on individual behaviors and personal responsibility. However, encouraging youth to engage in healthy eating and physical activity is challenging. A limitation of previous approaches is an overemphasis on long-term health outcomes as the primary source of motivation. This focus on individual behavior change, despite the importance of the social, economic and environmental context in determining behaviors, reinforces the notion of "individual shame and blame" and contributes to a lack of effectiveness in engaging youth. Creating messages that align with values held closely by adolescents are much more likely to resonate with them and effect change [4]. Although adolescents might not be motivated by their health in the distant future, they are certainly not apathetic. While they are often regarded as being vulnerable to *hedonism* (focusing on pleasure and instant gratification), they do have strong drives towards *eudaimonism* (focusing on meaning and self-realization). Adolescents aspire to feel like socially conscious, autonomous people worthy of approval by their peers and others whose opinions they respect [4]. Such values include social justice, autonomy and defiance against authority. For example, the kinds of messages previously developed for the anti-tobacco Truth campaign—those that vilify the tobacco industry and its corporate henchmen and call out the targeting of minority consumers—represent attempts to tap into adolescent values of defiance against authority, the expression of autonomy, and social (in)justice. Moving adolescents towards healthier behaviors, such as not consuming soda or junk food, can become a way to "stick it to the man" and rebel against industry executives' authority. In The Bigger Picture campaign (see below), minority youth poets have created content that enables youth to see the "the bigger picture", e.g., the social and environmental forces that create and perpetuate diabetes, and motivates their peers to "take a stand against injustice", eliciting "righteous anger and action" for social change [5,6].

A recent study of U.S. media coverage related to Type 2 diabetes revealed that only 12% mentioned social or environmental contributors; the vast majority focus on individual choices, unhealthy behaviors, or genetics [7]. *The Bigger Picture* (TBP, www.thebiggerpictureproject.org) differs from traditional diabetes prevention campaigns in that it is a counter-marketing, public health literacy campaign that harnesses minority youth-created spoken-word performance pieces produced as short films (public service announcements, PSAs). Counter-marketing campaigns use health communications strategies to reduce the demand for unhealthy products by exposing the motives of their producers and portraying their marketing activities as outside the boundaries of civilized corporate behavior.

TBP brings together the Arts with Public Health to create authentic and compelling content that speaks to and resonates with youth values of defiance against authority and the struggle for social justice. We have previously described the development and implementation of TBP [8]. While TBP process is curated by spoken word poet mentors and health communication experts, the creative work itself is generated by minority youth poets. TBP encourages young viewers to "take a step back" and observe and reflect on the larger social, structural and environmental forces that shape behavior and determine disease risk (Table 1). PSAs get disseminated via live high school assemblies and workshops, and social media, with the goal of increasing public health literacy and positively influencing behavioral norms [4,9].

Individual health literacy focuses solely on improving knowledge and capacity so the individual makes better health decisions [10], and consists of three dimensions: functional, interactive and critical. *Public health literacy* is "the degree to which individuals and groups can obtain, process, understand, evaluate, and act upon information needed to make public health decisions that benefit the community" [11]. This construct consists of three dimensions—conceptual foundations, critical skills and civic orientation—and differs from the construct of individual health literacy. Public health literacy contextualizes individuals as parts of a whole in the social ecology, engaging more stakeholders in advocating for community-level changes to address population health concerns. In combination, both individual and public health literacy provide a broader framework to promote health and reduce health disparities. Understanding the degree to which low-income youth integrate TBP as conveying individual vs. public health literacy messages will likely determine the effectiveness of the campaign. In addition, examining whether the context in which youth are exposed and respond to TBP messages (individual reflection vs. group-based reflection) has important implications as to how to best deliver, refine and amplify TBP messages to achieve the campaign's goals.

2. Materials and Methods

2.1. Research Design

Since the focus of TBP is to shift discourse around Type 2 diabetes in youth away from individual "fault" or deficits, toward a more systemic, socio-ecological framework, we performed a non-experimental, qualitative study to examine whether and how TBP campaign PSAs advances health literacy among a sample of low-income, minority youth.

2.2. Sample

We recruited a convenience sample from *Youth Radio* (youthradio.org), identifying youth at the beginning of their Health Internship Program. *Youth Radio* is a non-profit media production organization in Oakland, CA that engages and trains low-income and minority youth in media literacy. In late 2014, the Program Coordinator asked her 13 health interns to participate in an interactive project on type 2 diabetes. The UCSF (University of California, San Francisco) study team offered these youth a $10 gift certificate to partake in a 1-h viewing of TBP PSAs, followed by a post-viewing questionnaire and a focus group discussion. The study was approved by the UCSF Institutional Review Board. We enrolled 10 of 13 potentially eligible youth, aged 15–20. They included 6 females and 4 males who were currently in high school or had completed high school education within the last 2 years. Six participants self-identified as African American, 2 as White, 1 as Mixed Race (Hispanic/Latino and African American), and 1 as Middle Eastern.

2.3. Intervention

We first delivered a 30-min non-facilitated presentation that included 9 representative TBP PSAs (average length 2:54 min, range 1:12–4:37). Genres of PSAs ranged from comedic parody to suspense; each PSA conveyed a central public health literacy message related to Type 2 diabetes. Table 1 lists the PSAs, including titles, genres, and intended public health messages. Table 1. Representative Bigger Picture Campaign Messages, Associated Adolescent Values, and Extent of PSAs' Success in Conveying Messages.

Table 1. Representative Bigger Picture Campaign Messages [a], Associated Adolescent Values, and Extent of PSAs' Success in Conveying Messages.

The Bigger Picture Campaign Spoken Word Piece and Film	Public Health Literacy Intended Public Health Message	Film Genre (and Accompanying Youth Value)	Participants Fully Understood the Film's Public Health Message	Participants Discussed a Theme Related, But Not Central, to the Film's Public Health Message	Participants Expressed an Unrelated Public Health Message	The Film Did Not Convey its Public Health Message
1. Pushin' Weight	Profit-hungry food industries target youth with addictive sugary foods.	Dark Parody (Defiance)	3/10 Key Quote: "how from a young age sugar is shown as good and how fast it gets addictive but how bad it is for you"	4/10 Key Quote: "Sugar consumption"	2/10 Key Quote: "controlling your weight by watching what you eat"	1/10 Key Quote: "A drug dealer showing everyone how to sell drugs"
2. Product of His Environment	Institutionally reinforced social conditions, such as poverty, food insecurity, and violence, increase diabetes risk.	Drama (Social Justice)	6/10 Key Quote: "a young boy, how he doesn't have access to food let alone healthy food so he starves and then only rarely can go to McDonalds so he is very unhealthy—and how messed up this cycle is"	2/10 Key Quote: "Not having enough money to provide healthy food"	1/10 Key Quote: "The biggest lesson is to eat right"	1/10 Key Quote: "About a black boy eating McDonalds and his father gets shot and he starts crying cause he broke and live in the hood"
3. Health Justice Manifesto	Policy call to action to address the Type 2 diabetes epidemic by challenging the government and corporations and advocating for the public's health rights	Documentary/Anthem (Social Justice, Autonomy and Empowerment)	6/9 Key Quote: "About young people encouraging others to eat healthy and fight for health rights" One participant did not respond to questions pertaining to this video	1/9 Key Quote: "This video was about how liquor stores are in neighborhoods and grocery stores isn't which makes people buy unhealthy food from liquor stores."	1/9 Key Quote: "It's much more likely for young people to get diabetes these days"	1/9 Key Quote: "A knock off of a commercial I saw about not drinking at a party"
4. Block O' Breakfast	Food and beverage industries utilize deceptive marketing and false advertisements to sell unhealthy, sugary and processed foods to young people.	Comedic Parody (Defiance)	3/10 Key Quote: "This videos was about how they advertise unhealthy food and that everything is not what it seems"	5/10 Key Quote(s): "How corporations pay the fee to be able to put all that junk in our neighborhood"	2/10 Key Quote: "bad breakfast that kids eat and what the effects can lead to"	0/10 N/A
5. Sole Mate	Prolonged, unmanaged Type 2 diabetes can lead to severe consequences, such as amputation of limbs. Increasing awareness can help prevent diabetes-related complications.	Horror (Social Justice)	7/10 Key Quote(s): "About diabetes causing amputation of body parts"	0/10 N/A	1/10 Key Quote(s): "stay healthy"	2/10 Key Quote: "How grateful we should be to be able to walk, but also to stop wars. There was too many messages"
6. Farm Livin'	We, as consumers, are clueless to what is happening behind the scenes of industrialized foods; we are being "fed" by profit-hungry corporations—like farm animals.	Documentary (Defiance)	3/9 Key Quote: "What people are eating, and what they do to the farm food for the consumers" One participant did not respond	3/9 Key Quote: "We don't know what we eat or what we are putting in our body"	2/9 Key Quote: "We as consumers are just as bad as what we consume"	1/9 Key Quote: "About a rapper that's chunky"

Table 1. Cont.

The Bigger Picture Campaign Spoken Word Piece and Film	Public Health Literacy Intended Public Health Message	Film Genre (and Accompanying Youth Value)	Participants Fully Understood the Film's Public Health Message	Participants Discussed a Theme Related, But Not Central, to the Film's Public Health Message	Participants Expressed an Unrelated Public Health Message	The Film Did Not Convey its Public Health Message
7. Death Recipe	Slavery and other forms of historical or contemporary forms of oppression shape dietary norms. Food addiction is a response to the stress and mental health problems that accompany oppression. Obesity and body image disorders are a result.	Autobiography/Testimonial (Social Justice and Defiance)	4/10 Key Quote: "How diabetes can be a part of culture or a family"	3/10 Key Quote: "a young lady who's fed up about the way food is"	1/10 Key Quote: "how young people dying at a younger age from diabetes"	2/10 Key Quote: "not so clear"
8. Quantum Field	Trying to be healthy in an environment not conducive to healthy living feels like living in a nightmare.	Suspense (Defiance)	2/9 Key Quote: "our addiction to fast food is real. So much so, it's odd when we wanna be healthy" One participant did not respond	1/9 Key Quote: "How it's hard to escape diabetes ... but possible"	1/9 Key Quote: "About unhealthy eating habits"	5/9 Key Quote: "that there's good and bad people"
9. The Corner	Inaccessibility of healthy food options in low-income neighborhoods makes "choice" an illusion.	Testimonial (Social Justice and Autonomy)	3/8 Key Quote(s): "corner store convenience boost risks of diabetes" Two participants did not respond to questions pertaining to this video	1/8 Key Quote: "The dilemma between junk food and healthy food"	2/8 Key Quote: "all that unhealthy food is leading to diabetes"	2/8 Key Quote: "It was about a dude at a grocery store"

[a] All films can be found at www.thebiggerpictureproject.org.

2.4. Participant Responses to TBP Messages

Immediately after watching each PSA, participants completed a questionnaire with open-ended questions that asked participants, for each PSA, to reflect on: (a) what they felt the PSA was about; (b) what the biggest lesson of the PSA was; (c) what they liked or did not like about the PSA; (d) whether the PSA changed how they felt about Type 2 diabetes; and (e) what changes they would make to the PSA, if any. Because these questions were posed after each of the 9 videos, respondents were provided with up to 30 min of non-viewing time to complete the questionnaire.

The *Youth Radio* Coordinator, a Masters-level experience facilitator, then conducted a 1-h focus group that largely mirrored the survey questions, eliciting participant reflections with respect to specific and general opinions of the PSAs, understandings about Type 2 diabetes, and intentions to change behavior, including barriers to and facilitators of change. Moderator-guided facilitation provided a safe and confidential forum for participants to openly discuss their personal experiences and perspectives, maximizing opportunities to share a wide range of positive and negative opinions. During the focus group, brief video clips of all 9 PSAs were shown to participants as reminders to trigger conversation. The focus group was audio-recorded and transcribed.

2.5. Analysis

With respect to individual responses to each TBP PSA, we evaluated the degree to which participants integrated public health messages based on their responses to the questions: "What was the video about?" and "What was the biggest lesson?" Responses were grouped into one of four categories: participants fully integrated the PSA's intended message; discussed a theme related, but not central, to the PSA's intended message; expressed an unrelated message; or did not perceive a message. We also mapped responses into the broader constructs of *individual health literacy* and *public health literacy*, identifying salient themes within the relevant dimensions of each form of health literacy.

Because we were interested in gaining insights into minority youth responses to the content of the PSAs from this public health communication campaign, the qualitative approach that we applied to the questionnaire and focus group data was exploratory and formative. Insofar as we did not have a specific hypothesis, we employed content analysis to identify emergent themes [12,13]. In a subsequent analytic phase, based on the overarching objective of the communication campaign and the patterns of youth responses that emerged, we mapped these themes onto distinct domains derived from the health literacy construct (see below).

Members of the research team (JT and SF)—one a pre-doctoral student in Medicine and the other a Masters-level communication expert—independently coded the open-ended questionnaire responses and the transcripts to identify recurring themes. Iterative discussions amongst the study investigators, including the Principal Investigator (DS), a health communication scientist and public health physician, then led to a final set of overarching, predominant public health and sociological themes. Finally, based on the conceptual frameworks of Nutbeam [10] and Freedman [11], relevant coded statements were independently assigned by JT and SF into one of: (a) three dimensions of individual health literacy; or (b) three dimensions of public health literacy, respectively. Any disagreements as to the assignment of these statements were adjudicated by DS, who was blinded as to the source of the statements (e.g., individual response vs. focus group setting).

We first coded the questionnaires and the focus group transcript line-by-line, categorizing responses by themes of the lowest complexity. We then organized the preliminary set of themes under overarching themes; to be considered an overarching theme, it needed to have at least 3 associated responses. Since the focus group discussion was often characterized by dualistic and competing perspectives on lived experiences as they relate to Type 2 diabetes, we also coded responses that reflected these tensions. Again, we mapped responses into the broader constructs of individual and public health literacy, identifying salient themes within health literacy dimensions.

Finally, as PSAs can be viewed in vivo by individuals alone or in a facilitated group setting, we assessed differences in patterns of response across settings. To compare the individual vs. group setting responses, we organized coded statements pertaining to particular constructs and dimensions of health literacy in order of frequency, determined by counts of coded statements and calculated as a percentage of total coded statements.

3. Results

3.1. Participants' Integration of Central Messages of PSAs from Post-Viewing Questionnaires

The percentage of participants who fully recognized a PSA's intended public health message ranged from 22.2% to 70%, with the PSA entitled *Quantum Field* being the least and the PSA entitled *Sole Mate* being the most understood (Table 1). On average, more participants' post-PSA questionnaire responses exhibited a complete understanding of the public health message (43%); a minority of participants expressed a theme related, but not central, to the public health message (15%) or described an unrelated public health message or no message (18%).

3.2. Prominent Public Health Themes

Four prominent themes related to factors associated with diabetes risk emerged from the initial coding framework of both individual and focus group responses: individual behaviors, built environment, financial barriers, and institutional factors. Below, we describe these themes; illustrative participant quotes can be found in Table 2.

Individual Behaviors. Proponents of this notion described how individuals have the choice to be healthy—to eat healthy and exercise—often assuming that they are in full control of their own health and well-being.

Built Environment. Some participants expressed understanding that Type 2 diabetes is not simply a result of individual behaviors and choices, but can also result from structural forces in the built environment [14]. Structural determinants included poor access to healthy food and drink options, e.g., the dearth of grocery stores and farmers' markets vs. excess of corner stores and fast food establishments; unsafe neighborhoods; and insufficient recreational space for physical activity.

Financial Barriers and Competing Demands. In the context of poverty and food insecurity, individuals' eating habits and choices are limited. Adults in low-income families are also often pressed for time, making cooking challenging. Therefore, some participants reported how youth often resort to high-caloric, nutrient-deficient food and beverages from the corner store for a fast "hunger fix" at a fraction of the price of healthier options.

Institutional Factors: Deceptive Marketing. Barriers at the institutional level involve deceptive marketing by profit-hungry food and beverage industries and lack of government regulation. Participants reported an understanding of how the food and beverage industry employs false advertising to sell unhealthy products to youth.

Table 2. Prominent Themes Emerging from Responses to Individual Questionnaires and Group Discussion and Illustrative Participant Quotes.

Primary Public Health Themes	Representative Quotes
Individual Behaviors	"I can blame you for having diabetes, but you can win because it's your way of living. That's how you want to live because if you want to live like a hoarder, go ahead. If you want to live this way, it's your choice to live. That's why I say it's within the individual"
Built Environment	"We know it's the individual's responsibility, but where restaurants are compared to where grocery stores is like strategically placed"
	"This video was about how liquor stores are in neighborhoods and grocery stores isn't, which makes (our) people buy unhealthy food from liquor stores."
Financial Barriers and Competing Demands	"These kids are hungry and they only go to certain places for food 'cause that's where they go. So if a kid only goes to the corner store because their parents don't cook and there's no grocery store close by, what are they supposed to do? They can go to a corner store for a $0.99 cent bag of chips ... it's convenient but it's not good."

Table 2. Cont.

Primary Public Health Themes	Representative Quotes
Institutional Factors: Deceptive Marketing	"I mean it shows how I look at it ... behind the scenes of the commercials of the food or ... the advertisement of the food."
Underlying Sociopolitical Themes	**Representative Quotes**
Entrapment vs. Liberation	"Even if people wanted to be healthy they don't have the opportunity to go about it like financially or physically because they have nowhere to go."
	"I want us to leave out of here with help and whatever we can."
Powerlessness vs. Empowerment	"It's ... much bigger than our own so we can't and—I hate to say it—that we can't really do anything. We write as many letters to the government as we want, but they're not going to take these liquor stores that have been here since I was a child. I'm sure somebody complained about them, they're still here."
	"I'm going to go tell somebody because it seems like—I didn't used to know why the life expectancy of African American people was shorter that white people, but now that look at all the factors, it starting to make sense to me. So if you tell somebody else, maybe they want to eat healthier or something like that or maybe they have a better idea than me."
	"(Let's) start a garden in your community ... (so) we have fresh produce in our garden. I mean we have in our garden, fresh produce I'd say that's what I can think of like community-wise"
Cultural Determinism vs. Cultural Relativism	"There's a lot of cultures that have things that Americans will look at and be like "Ugh! Why would you eat that?" but that's their culture regardless if it's healthy or not so it's kind of for Black People, that's our culture so, for you to say it's unhealthy ... It's so offensive."
	"I don't like that ... For the same reason, it was kind of tedious too and it's like, "Okay, we know, Black people know." That it's not usually the healthiest thing to eat, but that's culture."

3.3. Underlying Sociological Themes

In addition to these "surface-level" themes, we identified three additional themes that reflected the underlying sociopolitical tensions faced by these youth when responding to the PSAs; these were more complex themes that likely reflected their lived experience. Below, we describe these themes; illustrative participant quotes can be found in Table 2.

Entrapment vs. Liberation. Some participants reported they felt confined by the structural barriers in their surroundings, conditioning them to lead unhealthy lives. In contrast, other participants aspired toward liberation from these entrapments through increased health literacy and social activation.

Powerlessness vs. Empowerment. While there was an appreciation for the need to address diabetes as a social justice issue, some participants reported a sense of futility and frustration. They believed that social action instigates change, but not always generates positive outcomes. These individuals felt that the epidemic has no fixable solution: the same corner stores will still be there and healthy food will not get cheaper anytime soon. On the other hand, other participants wanted to channel knowledge into action, either through intended personal or community-level change.

Cultural Determinism vs. Cultural Relativism. Some responses demonstrated a conflict between cultural determinism (wherein a dominant culture decides what is "right" or "wrong" in terms of health or nutritional value) and cultural relativism (wherein beliefs and customs have relative values within that individual's social and cultural context). As such, some rejected PSA messages, articulating a rebellion against the dominant culture.

3.4. Differential Impact of Setting on Participant Responses

Figure 1 demonstrates the relative frequency of individual and public health literacy constructs emerging from questionnaire and group discussions. While there were more responses elicited in the individual setting than in the focus group setting, we observed a dramatic shift in content focus and emphasis between the two settings: from an individual health literacy construct (among individual responses) towards a public health literacy construct (among reflective group responses).

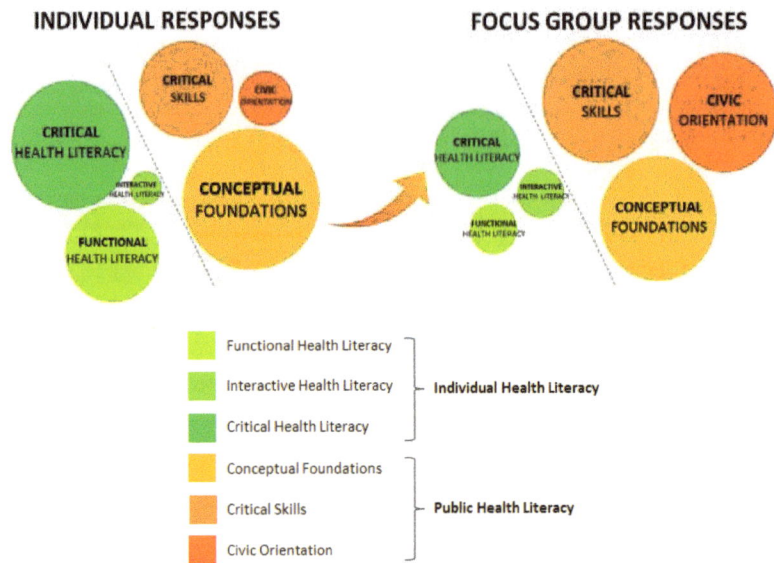

Figure 1. Distribution of Participant Responses in Individual vs. Focus Group Settings.

A total of 175 statements were coded from participants' individual questionnaire responses. Seventy-nine of those statements (45.1%) were classified under *individual health literacy*: 29 out of 79 (16.6%) pertained to functional, 3 (1.7%) interactive, and 47 (26.9%) critical health literacy. The remaining 96 statements (54.9%) were classified under *public health literacy*: 56 (32.0%) conceptual foundations, 30 (17.1%) critical skills, and 10 (5.7%) civic orientation.

A total of 56 statements were coded from the focus group responses: 14 statements (25%) related to *individual health literacy*, with 3 statements (5.4%) related to functional, 3 (5.4%) interactive, and 8 (14.3%) critical health literacy. Forty-two (75%) responses were categorized under *public health literacy*, with 15 statements (26.8%) related to conceptual foundations, 15 (26.8%) critical skills, and 12 (21.4%) civic orientation.

Table 3 demonstrates the dimensions of health literacy within the two constructs of heath literacy (individual and public), as articulated by respondents in the individual and focus group settings.

Table 3. Representative coded rubric of responses related to dimensions of health literacy obtained in the post-film survey and focus group responses.

Dimensions of Health Literacy	Individual Health Literacy Dimensions of Individual Health Literacy (Nutbeam, 2006): Functional, Interactive, and Critical Health Literacy	Public Health Literacy Dimensions of Public Health Literacy (Freedman, 2009): Conceptual Foundations, Critical Skills, and Civic Orientation
Conceptual Foundations		Theme: **Built Environment** (Please confirm whether the bold is necessary.) • "This video was about a boy that lives in a low income housing and had a unhealthy diet because there wasn't grocery stores around" (2) Theme: **Institutional Factors: Deceptive Marketing** • "How they [corporations] advertise the food, behind the scenes of the product" (4)

Table 3. *Cont.*

Dimensions of Health Literacy	Individual Health Literacy Dimensions of Individual Health Literacy (Nutbeam, 2006): Functional, Interactive, and Critical Health Literacy	Public Health Literacy Dimensions of Public Health Literacy (Freedman, 2009): Conceptual Foundations, Critical Skills, and Civic Orientation
Functional Health Literacy	Theme: **Individual Behaviors** • "The biggest lesson of this video was to show us how much sugar I eat" (1)	
Interactive Health Literacy	Theme: **Empowerment** • "Should come together to change the way we eat" (3) Theme: **Liberation** • "How it's hard to escape diabetes ... but possible" (8)	
Critical Skills	Theme: **Institutional Factors: Deceptive Marketing** • "Be careful on what you buy because the things they say is in there is really not" (4)	Theme: **Liberation** • "Do more research on the government and nutritions" (3) Theme: **Institutional Factors: Deceptive Marketing** • "from a young age sugar is shown as good and how fast it gets addictive" (1)
Civic Orientation		Theme: **Empowerment** • "we need to remove junk food places and put in more markets that sell cheaper healthier food" (2) Theme: **Financial Barriers and Competing Demands** • "low income neighborhoods are at higher risk for diabetes due to the lack of resources" (2)
Conceptual Foundations		Theme: **Built Environment** • "they can go to a corner store for a $0.99 cent bag of chips ... it's convenient but it's not good, but they put it there" (10) Theme: **Institutional Factors: Deceptive Marketing** • "you got to think about like a cartoon commercial ... I feel like it was a parody ... and then that's how they were trying to market it to the kids, but it's a company" (6)
Functional Health Literacy	Theme: **Individual Behaviors** • "I feel like besides going to the store and buying food or like going in the McDonald's, I feel like ... you really want to lose weight and you're concerned about what you eat then you should just like do it on your own like go walk or something. You walk or you don't have to I mean I know it's tempting, but if you really put your mind to it I feel like you could do it" (10–11)	

Table 3. *Cont.*

Dimensions of Health Literacy	Individual Health Literacy Dimensions of Individual Health Literacy (Nutbeam, 2006): Functional, Interactive, and Critical Health Literacy	Public Health Literacy Dimensions of Public Health Literacy (Freedman, 2009): Conceptual Foundations, Critical Skills, and Civic Orientation
Interactive Health Literacy	Theme: **Empowerment** • "in order to make a change within the community it has to start at a personal level. You can do community outreach things like that, but it might make a difference at that moment, but usually it doesn't make a difference for long term like all these Treyvon Martin protests, they didn't last for that long so nothing changed. Back at work, everyone's back at school so nothing changed. So I think that if you really want to make a difference within your community, you have to start with you and maybe reach out to the people closest to you, reach out to people closest to them and that makes a chain reaction" (16–17) Theme: **Liberation** • "I think that you should just say, 'It's hard to do but you still got to do it'" (9)	
Critical Skills	Theme: **Liberation** • "once you listen to what he was saying, it was the facts. It made me not even want to mess none of that, growth hormone meat. None of that how fructose corn syrup" (8) Theme: **Built Environment** • "for me living where I live, the closest healthy store is Trader Joe's, but that's across the bridge – that means I have to spend money to get there, I have to spend money when I get there so it's hard to just be healthy. It's not that easy" (9)	Theme: **Entrapment** • "Even if people wanted to be healthy they don't have the opportunity to go about it like financially or physically because they have nowhere to go" (9) Theme: **Entrapment** • "after watching the videos, I think that to an extent, it's a social justice issue for the reasons that Anonymous Number Two was saying ... that the restaurants are strategically put together like for example, Hagen Burger, the shopping center by Wal-Mart, there's "Wing Stop," "In and Out," "Candy Express," "Chipotle," "All-in-One," and none of those are healthy at all. Yes, and then like Jamba Juice, they're all together like there's not one place there and then there's a McDonald's in Wal-Mart" (9)
Civic Orientation		Theme: **Empowerment** • "Start a garden in your community. The center we have we have fresh produce in our garden. I mean we have in our garden, fresh produce I'd say that's what I can think of like community-wise" (10) Theme: **Financial Barriers and Competing Demands** • "so it's like all these places put in one place and that area is not a place where rich people live. So it's like - it's kind of scandalous in a way" (9)

4. Discussion

In clinical settings, limited health literacy contributes to health disparities, especially among older adults, immigrants, racial/ethnic minorities, and low-income individuals [15]. Improving individual health literacy, therefore, is a promising strategy to improve population health, particularly in the management of Type 2 diabetes [16]. However, encouraging at-risk youth to prevent diabetes through traditional health education is often ineffective. Furthermore, such individual-level interventions do not support broader health promotion and health policy efforts to achieve public health goals.

The Bigger Picture (TBP) is an innovative communication campaign that both features at-risk youth as creators and performers of novel public health content as well as targets at-risk youth. This model is relevant for conditions such as Type 2 diabetes, where exposures are determined by behavioral patterns solidified during adolescence. TBP model is unique in how it nurtures and supports the talent, authenticity and creativity of new health messengers: youth whose lived experience can be expressed in powerful ways. Never aiming to solely improve individual health literacy or direct individuals to change health behaviors, TBP attempts to harness core values of social justice and defiance against authority to improve youth public health literacy and foment action around social, environmental and policy change. While we are not aware of any research to shed light on the question as to whether defiance and social justice are more compelling for certain adolescent sub-groups, TBP campaign has yielded promising results in shifting low-income adolescent social norms [8]. We carried out this study to explore whether scaling up this model holds promise for low income and minority youth; determine whether the socio-ecological perspective, a complex and multilevel construct, can be integrated by youth exposed to TBP messages; and determine the extent to which facilitated discussions and reflective learning are needed to improve youth public health literacy.

Our research found that TBP PSAs elicited responses that aligned with the broad constructs of both individual health literacy and public health literacy, and their respective dimensions. Individual responses after viewing PSAs revealed a fairly even distribution of statements representing individual and public health literacy. Immediately after viewing the PSAs, in the context of an open-ended questionnaire, some participants perceived TBP messages as conveying diabetes primarily as an individual concern; these participants reflected on intended personal changes such as eating "less sugar or processed foods" and "exercising more". Other participants articulated a greater understanding of the broader social and environmental forces that shape individual behavior and can determine Type 2 diabetes risk, such as the lack of "affordable food, healthy food in poverty communities" and "how (companies) advertise the food, behind the scenes of the product". These participants, moreover, proposed changes in their community through education and health promotion that suggest increases in public health literacy.

In contrast, responses derived from the facilitated group discussions more heavily emphasized the roles of social, structural and environmental determinants, articulating a need to address diabetes through communal and civic engagement, demonstrating a more consistent paradigm shift toward public health literacy. In the setting of a group discussion, the PSAs served as vehicles for more extensive critical thinking, reflecting a more comprehensive public health literacy framework with a greater focus on socio-ecological constructs. This shift suggests that not only can a group setting amplify the messages to improve public health literacy in at-risk youth, but also supports the notion that TBP PSAs can align with youth values (defiance and social justice) to motivate social action and influence social norms.

The most striking themes that emerged in response to PSAs involved the tensions that these minority and low-income youth experience, expressed as sociopolitical themes such as entrapment vs. liberation. This speaks both to the structural barriers and behavioral complexities inherent to reducing diabetes risk in vulnerable communities, as well as the unique ability of the spoken word medium to make these challenges visible. Naming and reflecting on such tensions represent critical skills that raise communal consciousness and can promote civic engagement, fundamental dimensions of public health literacy.

Our study has a number of limitations. First, the sample was based on the number of individuals involved in the Youth Radio internship. Due to limited funding and the size of the youth group that our partner, Youth Radio, had enrolled in its program, we were unable to carry out additional focus groups. As we now have created 27 video-poems, we are attempting to obtain funding for more youth focus groups. However, we are currently carrying out a randomized trial on Facebook to determine which framing messages most engage youth to view the video PSAs. Second, while ethnically diverse and of low income, the sample was likely not fully representative, as participants had self-selected to enroll in a media literacy program. However, we carried out this work at the beginning of their internship, making it less likely that exposure to the internship influenced their responses. Third, we cannot determine whether our comparisons of the impact of TBP messages across different communication settings (individual questionnaire responses vs. group responses) were a result of the setting and format, or the order in which we elicited responses. There certainly could be bias introduced by virtue of the order in which the videos were presented and the two ways in which the videos were discussed: (a) the first wave was after individuals viewed each one and responded as individuals; and

(b) the second wave was in the context of discussing them in a focus group. Recall bias may favor the initial viewing; the focus group reflections reflect the aggregate impact of all videos. Relatedly, we cannot determine whether the shift to a more socio-ecologically oriented conceptualization in the group setting was a result of communication dynamics, or a result of participants integrating aggregate meta-messages across all nine PSAs. Fourth, participants viewed only 9 of the 27 current TBP PSAs, so we were not able to comprehensively evaluate all campaign messages. However, we selected the nine videos based on thematic, artistic and genre-related representativeness. Finally, no qualitative report can fully capture participants' perspectives. For example, some participants revealed that they did not realize that TBP youth performers and their messages reflected authentic, first person narratives, assuming some were performed by youth actors reading from a script written by adults. Had our PSAs consistently made clear that low income and minority youth were delivering their own artistic interpretations of their lived experience, it is likely that PSAs' impacts would have been even more robust.

This report suggests that TBP provides a promising artistic platform to communicate important factual and socio-political content related to the diabetes epidemic to low income and minority youth, one that appears to foster both individual and public health literacy. For some, the PSAs encouraged viewers to plan personal behavior changes and feel empowered to engage in community initiatives to prevent Type 2 diabetes. For others, the PSAs also revealed the structural and social barriers they face when trying to prevent diabetes—a revelation that was frustrating for some but activating for others. Our findings support the need for TBP—a campaign that focuses on the multilevel causes of diabetes—to be accompanied by interactive and action-oriented pedagogy if it is to achieve optimal impact. This interactive reflection could be facilitated via digital platforms or live group settings, and augmented by advocacy and action toolkits. We have recently expanded TBP's digital reach, modernized the website and are curating a new TBP Facebook group that will allow for more interactivity. In addition, we have received seed funding to institute TBP programming in a more longitudinal fashion in public high schools, potentially enhancing public health literacy, enabling culture changes with respect to social norms, and promoting civic engagement. TBP process and content have also been harnessed by the local county health department to support public health action—specifically, the installation of fresh water stations in low-income neighborhoods that have the highest rates of consumption of sugar-sweetened beverages in the county. Finally, several community pediatric practices have reported using TBP content to motivate adolescents and families enrolled in their obesity or pre-diabetes clinics. These activities suggest that the model may have broad implications for public health, specifically related to an important social determinant of health: health literacy.

5. Conclusions

TBP represents an innovative health communication and counter-marketing campaign that harnesses the talent and lived experience of minority youth poets who serve as messengers of novel and authentic first person content whose intent is to catalyze social action and influence social norms by aligning with adolescent values of defiance and social justice [5]. The key messages contained within TBP PSAs appear to often (but not always) hit home, frequently generating activating responses from youth for whom the messages are intended, both at an individual and communal level. TBP holds particular potential to promote diabetes-related public health literacy, thus building capacity among youth to both change behavioral norms as well as confront the social, economic and structural factors that largely determine these behaviors. It is likely that the TBP model is generalizable to other health conditions, and may appeal to youth stakeholders, not only to youth [6].

Author Contributions: Dean Schillinger directed all of the functions. Jessica Tran contributed to analysis and writing for this proposal. Sarah Fine contributed to conceiving and designing the qualitative study, performing the experiment as well as analysis and writing.

Acknowledgments: Ms. Tran was supported by NIH-NIDDK grant 5T32DK00741835. Schillinger and Fine were supported by NIH grant P60MD006902. Schillinger was also supported by NIH grant P30DK092924.

Conflicts of Interest: The authors declare no conflict of interest. The manuscript has not been published, but tables and figures were previously presented as part of a poster seminar at the 2017 NIH-NIDDK Medical Student Summer Research Conference.

References

1. Menke, A.; Casagrande, S.; Geiss, L.; Cowie, C.C. Prevalence of and Trends in Diabetes among Adults in the United States, 1988-2012. *JAMA* **2015**, *314*, 1021–1029. [CrossRef] [PubMed]
2. Dabelea, D.; Mayer-Davis, E.J.; Saydah, S.; Imperatore, G.; Linder, B.; Divers, J.; Hamman, R.F. Prevalence of Type 1 and Type 2 Diabetes Among Children and Adolescents From 2001 to 2009. *JAMA* **2014**, *311*, 1778–1786. [CrossRef] [PubMed]
3. Giuseppina, I.; Boyle, J.P.; Thompson, T.J.; Case, D.; Dabelea, D.; Standiford, D. Projections of Type 1 and Type 2 Diabetes Burden in the U.S. Population Aged <20 Years Through 2050. *Diabetes Care* **2012**, *35*, 2515–2520.
4. Bryan, C.J.; Yeager, D.S.; Hinojosa, C.P.; Chabot, A.; Bergen, H.; Kawamura, M.; Steubing, F. Harnessing adolescent values to motivate healthier eating. *Proc. Natl. Acad. Sci. USA* **2016**, *113*, 10830–10835. [CrossRef] [PubMed]
5. Schillinger, D.; Huey, N. Messengers of Truth and Health—Young Artists of Color Raise Their Voices to Prevent Diabetes. *JAMA* **2018**, *319*, 1076–1078. [CrossRef] [PubMed]
6. Schillinger, D.; Ling, P.; Fine, S.; Boyer, C.; Rogers, E.; Vargas, RA.; Bibbins-Domingo, K.; Chou, W.S. Reducing Cancer and Cancer Disparities: Lessons from a Youth-Generated Diabetes Prevention Campaign. *Am. J. Prev. Med.* **2017**, *53*, S103–S113. [CrossRef] [PubMed]
7. Gollust, S.E.; Lantz, P.M. Communicating population health: Print news media coverage of type 2 diabetes. *Social Sci. Med.* **2009**, *69*, 1091–1098. [CrossRef] [PubMed]
8. Rogers, E.; Fine, S.; Handley, M.A.; Davis, H.; Kass, J.; Schillinger, D. Development and Early Implementation of The Bigger Picture, a Youth-Targeted Public Health Literacy Campaign to Prevent Type 2 Diabetes. *J. Health Commun.* **2014**, *19*, 144–160. [CrossRef] [PubMed]
9. Rogers, E.A.; Fine, S.C.; Handley, M.A.; Davis, H.B.; Kass, J.; Schillinger, D. Engaging Minority Youth in Diabetes Prevention Efforts Through a Participatory, Spoken-Word Social Marketing Campaign. *Am. J. Health Promot.* **2017**, *31*, 336–339. [CrossRef] [PubMed]
10. Nutbeam, D. Health literacy as a public health goal: A challenge for contemporary health education and communication strategies into the 21st century. *Health Promot Int.* **2000**, *15*, 259–269. [CrossRef]
11. Freedman, D.A.; Bess, K.D.; Tucker, H.A.; Boyd, D.L.; Tuchman, A.M.; Wallston, K.A. Public Health Literacy Defined. *Am. J. Prev Med.* **2009**, *36*, 446–451. [CrossRef] [PubMed]
12. Hsieh, H.-F.; Shannon, S.E. Three approaches to qualitative content analysis. *Qual Health Res.* **2005**, *15*, 1277–1288. [CrossRef] [PubMed]
13. Silverman, D.; Marvasti, A. *Doing Qualitative Research: A Comprehensive Guide*; SAGE Publications: Thousand Oaks, CA, USA, 2008.
14. Booth, K.M.; Pinkston, M.M.; Poston, W.S.C. Obesity and the built environment. *J. Am. Dietetic. Assoc.* **2005**, *105*, 110–117. [CrossRef] [PubMed]
15. Benjamin, R.M. Improving Health by Improving Health Literacy. *Public Health Rep.* **2010**, *125*, 784–785. [CrossRef] [PubMed]
16. Schillinger, D.; Grumbach, K.; Piette, J.; Wang, F.; Osmond, D.; Daher, C.; Bindman, A.B. Association of health literacy with diabetes outcomes. *JAMA* **2002**, *288*, 475–482. [CrossRef] [PubMed]

© 2018 by the authors. Licensee MDPI, Basel, Switzerland. This article is an open access article distributed under the terms and conditions of the Creative Commons Attribution (CC BY) license (http://creativecommons.org/licenses/by/4.0/).

Commentary

The Health Literacy of U.S. Immigrant Adolescents: A Neglected Research Priority in a Changing World

Maricel G. Santos [1,*], Anu L. Gorukanti [2], Lina M. Jurkunas [3] and Margaret A. Handley [4,5]

1   Department of English, San Francisco State University, San Francisco, CA 94132, USA
2   Department of Pediatrics, Stanford University, Stanford, CA 94305, USA; agorukan@stanford.edu
3   American Language Institute, San Francisco State University, San Francisco, CA 94132, USA; ljurkuna@mail.sfsu.edu
4   Department of Epidemiology & Biostatistics, University of California, San Francisco, CA 94158, USA; Margaret.Handley@ucsf.edu
5   Department of Medicine Division of General Internal Medicine, Zuckerberg San Francisco General Hospital, San Francisco, CA 94110, USA
*   Correspondence: mgsantos@sfsu.edu; Tel.: +1-415-338-7445

Received: 13 July 2018; Accepted: 18 September 2018; Published: 25 September 2018

Abstract: Immigrant adolescents are the fastest-growing sector among U.S. youth, but they receive little attention in health literacy research. Immigrant adolescents are a diverse population tasked with mastering new literacies while also navigating new social systems. Many immigrant adolescents serve as important linguistic and cultural resources in their families and local communities, and yet their contributions (and struggles) as new navigators of our health care system remain invisible. In this commentary article, we argue that health literacy researchers need to devote more attention to immigrant adolescents and the pathways by which they learn new language and literacy skills while also developing their own health habits and behaviors. We contend that the study of immigrant adolescents provides a critical window into health literacy as a socially and historically situated practice, specifically how immigrant adolescents' transnational experiences shape their learning of new health literacy practices. With a coordinated interdisciplinary research agenda on immigrant adolescents, the health literacy field will expand its empirical base for what becoming "health literate" looks like in today's globalizing world.

Keywords: immigrant adolescents; health literacy; immigrant identity; adaptation

1. Introduction: Becoming "Health Literate" in a Globalizing World

Over the past decade, the number of U.S. children with at least one immigrant parent has been on the rise, increasing from 19% to 26% of all children in the U.S. [1]. The large concentration of English language learners who entered U.S. schools in preschool or elementary school earlier this decade are now moving into higher grades, generating marked increases in immigrant youth in U.S. secondary schools [2]. Currently, nearly three-quarters of immigrant youth of ages 12 to 17 are U.S.-born [3]. The recent "diaspora of teenagers" makes up two-fifths of first-generation children entering the U.S. [4]. The socioeconomic opportunities available to immigrant adolescents are also shifting in today's information-driven economy, a trend that does not bode well for the 52% (3.1 million) of immigrant adolescents living in low-income households [5]. For convenience and ease of expression, we use the term "immigrant adolescent" to refer to an adolescent from an immigrant family, i.e., lives in a home with at least one immigrant parent, regardless of country of birth, including adolescents in refugee families. However, in this paper, we address experiences that may distinguish foreign-born from U.S.-born youth, and highlight unique health literacy opportunities of children in refugee families.

Despite the fact that immigrant adolescents are the fastest-growing sector of the U.S. immigrant population [3], they remain invisible [6] in health literacy research. With rare exceptions, there has been insufficient attention to the health literacy capacities of adolescents, much less that of immigrant adolescents [7–10]. This research chasm is especially troubling since the efficacy of many health care programs and services may depend on how this cohort of immigrant adolescents fares as a whole, with lasting effects into adulthood.

Despite widespread consensus that health literacy occurs in a social context, the field has yet to fully examine the social and historical circumstances that are dynamically shaping the development of new health literacy skills and practices in immigrant communities. Today's immigrant adolescents are coming of age in a rapidly changing world: unprecedented migratory, technological, and institutional forces are structuring their childhoods, while at the same time, their demography, experiences, and choices are altering the immigration narrative.

In response to this empirical gap, our commentary focuses on how the lived, everyday transnational experiences of U.S. immigrant adolescents provide a meaningful context for the emergence of health literacy competence. To what extent do immigrant adolescents encounter opportunities to develop their health literacy in their everyday lives? What sources of information and literacy tools are immigrant adolescents motivated to use, and what are the consequences of these navigational practices for their health literacy development? Drawing on the terminology in Donald Nutbeam's health literacy framework [11], we must ask, to what extent are these everyday interactions and choices laying the groundwork for the acquisition of functional, communicative, and critical levels of health literacy in the immigrant adolescent population? Answers to these questions require a coordinated, interdisciplinary research agenda. This basic claim will be repeated throughout our commentary, as we discuss several distinct areas of research on the immigrant adolescent world where this claim could be explored.

This commentary has three goals: (1) to make a case for such a research agenda on immigrant adolescent health literacy; (2) to highlight the kinds of research questions on immigrant adolescent health literacy that productively build on existing theories and research on literacy as a social practice, adolescent literacy, and immigrant adolescent identity; and (3) to underscore the need for interdisciplinary collaboration in support of improved health literacy outcomes among immigrant adolescents. The focus of this commentary is on U.S. immigrant adolescents, but we anticipate that our call for research will resonate with practitioners in other parts of the world who already recognize the need to pay more attention to the needs of immigrant adolescent populations.

For this commentary, we undertook a targeted multidisciplinary approach to explore promising areas of research on immigrant adolescent health literacy. As literacy educators, we were compelled to revisit a seminal review paper "Re-Framing Adolescent Literacy Research for New Times: Studying Youth as a Resource" by Elizabeth Moje in which the author asserts that the "lack of attention to youth literacy… points to unstated assumptions among theorists and policy-makers alike that nothing occurs in the literacy development of youth, that no learning about literacy occurs as youth make use of literacy tools to navigate, resist, construct, and reconstruct popular, academic, and work cultures" [12] (p. 211), an assertion that may also partly explain why relatively little attention has been paid to adolescent health literacy in the health literacy field. Building on Moje's insights into adolescent literacy, youth culture, and youth literacies, we used JSTOR and Linguistics & Language Behavior Abstracts to look for qualitative studies (largely ethnographic case studies) that provide rich descriptions of immigrant adolescents' everyday literacy practices. We focused on case studies published after the 2010 U.S. Census as we wanted studies that reflected recent U.S. demographic and diasporic trends in the immigrant adolescent population, although we indicate when we draw on relevant literature published in other countries. This exploration enabled us to imagine the range of literacy experiences, resources, and interactions that could be investigated with an immigrant adolescent health literacy agenda. We also explored the health literacy literature via PubMed using the following search terms: adolescent (youth) health, health literacy, immigrant/refugee, and United

States. Because of our interest in health literacy as a situated practice, we also specifically targeted articles that did not adhere to strictly functional views on health literacy.

While the relationship between health literacy and health outcomes has been productively modeled [8,13–15], these models have yet to be fully explored with respect to adolescent health literacy (with Manganello [7] an important exception) or immigrant adolescent health literacy specifically. Thus, for this commentary, we have drawn upon several review titles in public health that expressly aimed to advance "adolescent health literacy" as a unique phenomenon [7–10]. Perry [8] conducted an integrative review of the health literacy literature, with a special focus on children with chronic illness, concluding that there remains a scarcity of literature focusing on health literacy instruments and intervention in adolescents. A comprehensive review conducted by Sanders et al. [8] emphasized the significant impact of poor literacy on poor health literacy, arguing for new measures of childhood literacy that take into account the developmental context of child health. The work of Manganello [7] and Higgins et al. [10] were particularly helpful because the authors applied socio-ecological models to explore how adolescent health literacy is linked to various social and environmental factors (peer networks, family characteristics, media, schools, and the health care system). Also significant is Fairbrother, Curtis, and Goyder's study of child health literacy in the U.K., which embraced the social practices view in ways that most directly align with our own assumptions, but focused on younger (pre-adolescent) children ages 9–10 [16]. Our hope in this commentary is that, with more research on the social contexts in which immigrant adolescents are developing their health literacy competence, our field will be better poised to empirically validate the pathways that link immigrant adolescent health literacy to immigrant adolescent health outcomes.

The following section explores reasons why immigrant adolescents have not received greater attention in the health literacy field. We then sketch some possible starting points for research as part of this proposed agenda on immigrant adolescent health literacy.

2. Explaining the Neglect of Immigrant Adolescents in Health Literacy Research

We suggest that the neglect of immigrant adolescents in health literacy research may stem from two enduring limitations in the conceptualization and study of health literacy. First, past health literacy research has focused nearly exclusively on adult populations. Research shows that many immigrant adolescents are able to acculturate more readily to life in the U.S. and gain proficiency in English ahead of their parents. Although the immigration literature abundantly supports the idea that the acculturation process is a function of a child's development stage [17], this insight seems to have barely influenced thinking about the development of health literacy among immigrant populations across the life span.

Second, the health literacy field's adherence to conceptualizations of health literacy as an individual's ability to read and write in English likely perpetuates deficit perspectives on immigrant adolescents who are still learning English. The bias towards health literacy as a competence linked to one's proficiency in English discounts the possibility that health literacy competence for immigrant adolescents may involve moving across languages and cultures—a translingual, transcultural capacity, which is regarded as a normative aspect of the migration and adaptation process [18,19]. We are not aware of any health literacy framework that fully accounts for this sociolinguistic reality in immigrant communities.

3. Understanding Immigrant Adolescent Health Literacy as a Socially Situated Practice

A functional view of health literacy, one that emphasizes an individual's individual capacity to read, comprehend, and use health information, is pervasive in health literacy research, as widely promoted by the Institute of Medicine [20]. We prefer to think of health literacy as a socially situated practice, in alignment with researchers whose scholarship is rooted in paradigmatic shifts associated with New Literacy Studies in literacy scholarship [21–23] and the "social turn" in applied linguistics [24]. To understand health literacy as a socially situated practice, the reader needs to consider what literacy is. A well-rooted convention in literacy teaching and research is the idea that literacy is a discrete set of skills that can be learned in a step-by-step fashion: learners must learn foundational skills, such as phonics (i.e., linking sounds with their correct letter combinations), or spelling, as well as higher-order information-processing skills for understanding a text's purpose, audience, and message. The skills view tends to focus on literacy as an individual achievement, reflected in the learner's ability to put autonomous skills to use in different contexts.

The *literacy as social practice* view recognizes a focus on skill-building is essential but not sufficient if we want to fully understand "the variety of literacy-related activities that individuals and communities engage with in their everyday lives or the range of meanings literacy has, depending on its social and cultural context of use" [25] (p. 24). The social practice view provides health literacy researchers with a framework for understanding how health literacy skills are shaped by the social contexts, purposes, and relationships within which reading, writing, math, or speaking skills are put to use.

Consider, for example, the context in which the basic task of making a doctor's appointment takes place. An appointment could be scheduled for oneself or behalf of someone else. The physical act of making the appointment, and the resources required (e.g., access to the Internet, a phone, or a directory) vary depending on how the appointment is made (in person, by phone or online, or with or without language assistance). The kind of information required to make the appointment may vary based on whether the person is a new or established patient, and the kind of health information to be exchanged at the appointment (is it an acute health care issue, wellness checkup, or consultation?). The social view of health literacy is concerned with these local particularities as well as with any "standards" that dictate what one is "supposed" to do to complete health care tasks. For these reasons, the social view uses the term "literacy practices" to refer to both what people do with their language and literacy skills and how people understand, feel, and value those skills and behaviors.

Despite significant efforts to reconceptualize health literacy as a social phenomenon [11,26,27], the field has yet to shake its emphasis on health literacy "skills", a bias that tends to reify the belief that health literacy outcomes should improve as people improve their language, literacy, and numeracy skills. Similarly, Pleasant has argued that the health literacy field, particularly in the development of health literacy measures, is struggling to differentiate health literacy as "the use of literacy skills in a health context" [28] (p. 1492) (the functional view) from health literacy as "a unique social construct that shares attributes with literacy" (p. 1491) (the social view). As we argue in this paper, we believe that a focus on immigrant adolescent health literacy provides an excellent platform for puzzling through these distinctions.

To further clarify our thinking about immigrant adolescent health literacy as a socially situated practice, we use a bike-riding metaphor (Figure 1), which takes inspiration from health literacy models described by the Institute of Medicine [20], Manganello [7], and Purcell-Gates [29]. Bike-riding requires the coordination of many working parts (gears, brakes, handle bars, and pedals). Each part has a unique purpose, but their contributions have little meaning apart from the whole. Similarly, we view an immigrant adolescents' process of becoming "health literate" as an evolving coordination of many working parts (e.g., reading skills, math skills, form-filling skills, linguistic choices, digital tools, or interactions that involve any of these skills and tools). The significance of these parts cannot be accurately understood when apart from the social, cultural, and historical context in which immigrant children are growing up.

From a social perspective, the question—what is immigrant adolescent health literacy?—is tantamount to grappling with a more fundamental question, what does being "health literate" mean in a globalizing world with new opportunities for connectivity and communication? The terrains where adolescents end up riding their bikes represent the varied social, cultural, and institutional contexts—schools, our health care system, this period in immigration history, the political climate, and the neighborhoods where children grow up—that are dynamically shaping their early encounters with the health care system and creating new motivations or unique barriers.

Figure 1. Understanding immigrant adolescent health literacy as socially situated practice: A bike-riding metaphor.

As shown in Figure 1, the pedals represent "everyday literacy tasks". Pedals set a bike in motion. Similarly, everyday tasks—such as interpreting a document for one's parents or opting for water over a soft drink—may incentivize the application and perfecting of "little skills", which may contribute to improvements in valued health literacy practices, such as effectively communicating with a health care professional or making good nutritional choices for oneself. The social practice view also holds promising implications for health literacy interventions, as we contemplate the kinds of everyday literacy tasks we could promote in the lives of immigrant adolescents, in and out of school, and across all levels of functional, interactive, and critical health literacy [11].

Just as learning to ride requires an ongoing "reading" of the road, learning to be "health literate" involves constant negotiation of one's own skills and motivations in response to the demands of a particular environment. A social practice view on health literacy is fascinated by the kinds of adjustments people make (the tools they use, the people they seek out, the decisions they make, and the curiosities they act on) as they carry out health care tasks. A social practice view is not so preoccupied with evaluating whether immigrant adolescents make a "good" or "bad" adjustment but rather on richly describing what the coordination of "little" adjustments can look like.

Figure 1 depicts two children riding together, illustrating that the communal experience (bike-riding with friends) is often what gives lasting meaning to the experience of bike-riding for many children. Similarly, the social practice view privileges ways that immigrant adolescent health literacy cannot be understood apart from the child's membership in social networks, her real and desired connections with other people who are also endeavoring to make sense of what it means to be healthy. In this regard, the social view is consonant with views on health literacy as an attribute of social systems, as articulated by Papen [27], Nutbeam [11], and the Calgary Charter on Health Literacy [30].

This emphasis on the socially interdependent nature of health literacy allows for the possibility that immigrant adolescent health literacy is a function of the child's competence and practices of those around them (global and local peers, teachers/coaches, parents, health professionals, and other adults charged with their care and supervision).

Lastly, Figure 1 depicts the adolescents wearing helmets, required safety gear for reducing the risk of serious or fatal head injuries. To extend our bike-riding metaphor, gaining health literacy competence as an adolescent requires learning to recognize the link between risk-preventive behaviors and positive health outcomes. At the same time, the fact that over 87% of U.S. adolescents ages 13 to 18 years old report rarely or never wearing a helmet [31] is a sobering reminder that many adolescents may engage in behaviors that place them at higher health risk. The social view on immigrant adolescent health literacy is keenly interested in richly describing the adolescents' interactions with health risk messages and understanding how these interactions shape or do not impinge on their risk perceptions and health behaviors; in other words, from the social view, risk comprehension, for many immigrant adolescents, should be viewed as a process of meaning-making, an active grappling with perceptions of risk and risk messages.

We suggest that a research agenda on immigrant adolescent health literacy requires that we examine immigrant adolescents' health care experiences from the perspective of the adolescents themselves, allowing them to articulate their own stories and understandings, and not rely only on adult-informed perspectives to operationalize what health literacy competence should look like. In this commentary, we aim to highlight several promising research domains where it would be beneficial to explore decision-making processes undergirding health care practices, including the risky ones that immigrant adolescents engage in. We are excited about new lines of health literacy research as we anticipate that immigrant adolescents have a lot to teach us about how all of us learn complex health literacy processes over time and diverse contexts.

4. Promising Research Directions on Immigrant Adolescent Health Literacy

This section addresses several promising areas of research on immigrant adolescent health literacy, with an emphasis on socially situated views on health literacy. Readers are encouraged to view these research directions as starting points for interdisciplinary deliberation and partnership-formation, rather than a comprehensive research agenda on immigrant adolescent health literacy. As suggested with our bike-riding metaphor, we are particularly interested in exploring everyday opportunities in the lives of immigrant adolescents that motivate "pedaling forward", in other words, that set in motion the learning of health literacy practices.

4.1. How Do Linguistic Brokering Experiences Create the Conditions for Learning New Health Literacy Practices?

Research has shown that immigrant children play an active role in their family's adaptation and integration processes [32]. Immigrant adolescents, whose English proficiency readily starts to surpass that of other adults in their household, often experience "role-reversal" when they must take on adult-responsibilities, as translators, interpreters, and mediators in institutional settings on behalf their family [33]. Studies have shown that, for many immigrant adolescents, linguistic brokering (the term used to describe these acts of translation and interpreting in immigrant families) is not viewed as a burden but normative, even a source of pride and a means to "protect" parents' dignity in social contexts; parents often describe these encounters as opportunities to reinforce their children's bicultural identity [34,35]. We acknowledge the serious legal and ethical concerns, as well as the potential health risks, when immigrant adolescents are asked to take on adult responsibilities in health care (e.g., violations of a family member's confidentiality, mistranslations, and emotional stress on the child) [36]. At the same time, a social practices perspective provides a valuable point of entry for exploring what is often viewed as "taboo discursive terrain" [36] (p. 386). By examining how immigrant adolescents make sense of spoken and written health information, and navigate gaps in communication, across languages, and lines of authority, we are likely to gain insight into the conditions which foster the development of interactive and critical health literacy.

Faustich Orellana et al. provide compelling evidence that linguistic brokering activates a range of linguistic and pragmatic skills that arguably correspond to functional, interactive, and critical levels of health literacy. For example, Faustich Orellana et al. highlight the experiences of "Sammy", a 15-year old Latino adolescent, who "took charge for himself and his mother during his own hand surgery, including researching information about the surgery on the Internet beforehand" [34] (p. 517). Faustich Orellana et al. also report on the case of "Lucila" who exhibited a keen awareness of the sociopolitical complexities of having to translate for her mother when composing a formal letter of complaint against the family's caseworker:

> I remember that day and I remember the tension I felt as I listened to my mom angrily complain about the lady, and the pressure I felt to translate "properly". I didn't know what to say. I wanted the complaint to sound like it came from a grown-up, my mother, but I also wanted to stress how rude (the lady) was, writing that she was very impatient with our situation and that my mom felt very uncomfortable with her and that it was really hard for her to express herself and to understand the lady. [34] (p. 519)

Faustich Orellana et al. credit Lucila for her "willingness to step into the 'adult' role" [34] (p. 519) and her persistence in finding the right language to convey her mother's complaint in English. These examples suggest that immigrant adolescents' experiences as linguistic brokers may reveal an emerging critical health literacy [37], particularly evident in the case of Lucila whose literacy practices (translating from oral colloquial Spanish to written formal English, composing a complaint letter in English) were motivated by a desire to assert her own voice and claim a sense of authority on behalf of her mother (by the way, after submitting Lucila's complaint letter, her mother was assigned a new case worker). In a study of children's linguistic brokering in the context of health insurance, Martinez et al. [38] found that immigrant children were able to figure out how various aspects of the health insurance system by "watching and supporting" their families as part of enrollment and management processes, even if the children were not included in any insurance-related decisions. For example, by assisting their parents to figure out the requisite "papers" or "cards" to present, or even which "line" to stand in at social service offices, the children seemed to gain important insight into the complexities of health insurance options based on family immigration status.

Linguistic brokering provides compelling insight into the ways that immigrant adolescents' opportunities to develop health literacy may be uniquely tied to the sociolinguistic realities of transnational family life. While there is rich ethnographic data on linguistic brokering in education, sociology, and applied linguistics [33–35,38,39], we have yet to systematically study how linguistic brokering relates to the growth of immigrant adolescent health literacy. More detailed explorations of how immigrant adolescents learn to recognize and interpret the complex power dynamics of brokering encounters in health care and adjust their messaging, using available languages, modalities (spoken, written), and registers, seems vital if we want to understand how to effectively promote interactive and critical health literacy.

4.2. What Is the Relationship between Health Literacy and Identity Development among Immigrant Adolescents?

Identity development is widely recognized as the adolescent's central task of cognitive, social, and psychological development [40]. The social practice view similarly argues that literacy development is a function of changes in an adolescents' social roles and evolving sense of identity. As Dávila argues, "Attitudes toward reading, how often, how much, and what students read have much to do with their self and positional identities, as well as their aspirations in and beyond school" [4] (p. 642).

As applied linguists, we find Bonny Norton's [41] concept of investment particularly useful for the study how immigrant adolescent identity may be related to changes in health literacy practices.

Investment is defined as the degree to which a language learner ascribes social, cultural, and political value to the enterprise of learning new skills and competencies [42]. As Norton explains, learners invest in learning new literacy practices and trying out new literacy tools, "with the understanding that they will acquire a wider range of symbolic and material resources, which will in turn increase the value of their cultural capital. As the value of their cultural capital increases, so learners' sense of themselves, their identities, and their opportunities for the future are re-evaluated" [42] (p. 87). An immigrant adolescent's desire to learn English may reflect their investment in various social identities—as a high school student, child of immigrant parents, daughter, representative of the Latina culture, friend, and so forth. Ambivalence towards a language or literacy task, accordingly, may mark an immigrant adolescent's struggle to communicate and be understood, and thus, a struggle to be recognized as a "good student" or a "helpful daughter".

Identity research already suggests ways that immigrant adolescents may be invested in health literacy practices. As reflected in the previous section, research on linguistic brokering has found that immigrant adolescents are motivated, out of a desire to be helpful, to participate in a range of health care activities on their families' behalf, such as translating and interpreting, making appointments by phone, filling prescriptions, completing medical documents, and researching treatment options on the Internet [34]. Participation as a linguistic broker may reflect an immigrant adolescent's positive response to being given opportunities to showcase their skills across languages, as evident in the case of Lucila.

Dávila's research [4] profiles a young Somali immigrant woman who exhibited strong investment in passing a driver's education course: she needed to drive because she was tasked with the grocery shopping and preparation of home-cooked Somali meals for the family, a task that is clearly tied to her family's health. This study points to possible gendered dimensions that propel health literacy development for immigrant female youth differently than for their male counterparts.

Rubinstein-Ávila [43] profiles a Dominican female teenager whose linguistic brokering for her mother during doctor's appointments revealed a level of English proficiency that was largely invisible to her school teachers who regarded her as a "reticent" language learner. Children's personal health experiences may motivate health literacy learning, as shown in Moje et al.'s study of a 15-year old boy whose prior personal history with childhood asthma and air pollution in Mexico City motivated him to study air-quality concepts in his U.S. high school science class and even investigate ecology as a career [44]. Moje et al. indicate that the boy's teachers were unaware of the source of his personal investment in the environmental ecology unit.

Longitudinal studies of immigrant adolescents' investment in health literacy practices would be able to investigate changes in health literacy competence are tied to their transnational identities as they transition from adolescence young adulthood and assume greater independence in their health care decisions. Investment research in the health literacy field also stands to make an important contribution to our understanding of the intersection of emotions (desire to learn) and literacy growth that guide adolescent immigrants' self-regulation and decision-making in early health care experiences.

4.3. To What Extent Do Immigrant Adolescents Use Their Digital Skills and Online Networks for Learning New Health Literacy Practices?

Studies on adolescent health literacy and digital environment tend to rely on a functional view of health literacy with an emphasis on knowledge or skill acquisition, such as the honing of effective information seeking skills in online environments [45–47]. In the adolescent literacy field, while there have been numerous studies of their digital literacy practices [48,49], we need more research that systematically documents the communication skills, the social networks, the array of informational resources, and the motivations/attitudes that mediate immigrant adolescents' early encounters with public health messages or the health care system.

We can draw upon a growing body of literacy studies that recognize access to the Internet as a major driver of immigrant adolescents' social and cultural adaptation to life in a new country at a pivotal time of identify formation. Elias and Lemish contend that the digital lives of immigrant adolescents should not be simply viewed as "a playground" for adventures, pleasurable experimentation, and risk-taking but a critical, "safe ground" [50] (p. 548) where immigrant adolescents are motivated to seek out resources (e.g., online news about current events in the home country; local youth activities) and explore social networks that reinforce their sense of belonging to the home country and the new country.

Earlier in our commentary, we cited the case of "Sammy" who searched the Internet to find medical information for himself and his mother about an upcoming surgery on his hand [34]. Similarly, Lam [51] has showed that immigrant youth routinely seek out online news resources in the U.S. and home country, a literacy practice, in the context of health care, would likely lead adolescents to a broader array of choices, with respect to language, content, and perspective, on a health care topic. This example suggests important research lines: In what ways do immigrant adolescents enable their families to "leapfrog" (Christina Zarcadoolas's term) from the traditional world of print (where public health information in languages other than English may be limited) to the world of digital technologies and a dizzying amount of health information online? In what languages do immigrant adolescents search for health information, and to what extent does their knowledge of multiple languages prompt them to seek out information from a broader array of health information?

While this kind of seeking and sharing of online information seems ubiquitous in today's digital world, how these digital literacy practices contribute to improvements in health literacy practices merits closer empirical investigation. As Manderino and Castek observe, "learners' ability to use the Internet's networking and knowledge-building resources is only as good as their skills in disciplinary inquiry: asking questions, constructing meaning from data, generating creative solutions, and reflecting on how to improve these solutions for different contexts" [52] (p. 79). "Disciplinary inquiry skills" here refers to the literacy practices that experts value when learning and problem-solving in their disciplines. This observation raises interesting conceptual and empirical questions regarding the relationship between digital literacies and immigrant adolescent health literacies. What exactly do "expert" digital literacy practices look like in health care contexts, and to what extent do immigrant adolescents' digital literacy practices approximate those "expert" practices?

Existing research also suggests that immigrant adolescents may cope with acculturative stress through participation in the digital world. For example, Gilhooly and Lee [53] examined the digital literacy practices of three Karen teenage brothers whose family left Burma and lived for several years in a Thai refugee camp before moving to the U.S. The teenagers learned to use a computer after arriving in the U.S. and, like Sammy in Faustich Orellana's study [34], frequently used the Internet to find and share information, such as school immunization requirements. Perhaps more poignantly, the teenagers used their digital tools to create original music videos, short autobiographical films, and photo montages that communicated their political views on the political conflict in Burma, their experience in a Thai refugee camp, and their pride in Karen cultural symbols and traditions. The authors assert that these digital literacy practices were critical to the teenagers' adaptive resilience: through their social media platforms, the boys were able to experience a sense of solidarity with distant Karen communities as well as forge new friendships with peers in the local Karen community. The boys were able to use their digital practices to forge what McLean [54] calls a "space for home" in the digital environment. As this example suggests, the significance of digital literacies for transnational adolescents seems to lie at the intersection of the adolescents' desire for self-expression and connectivity with others, their access to digital tools and digital networks, and their response to immigration stress and adaptation.

The study of immigrant adolescent digital practices can reveal how literacy learning is motivated by children's transnational knowledge and migration experiences. An example of adolescents' creative expressions of their health concerns in the digital world is evident in The Bigger Picture Project [55], a collaboration between university researchers, medical practitioners, and community-based youth organizers, this initiative engages low-income and minority adolescents as youth poets in the production of video-based public service announcements (PSAs) (composed in the spoken-word genre) that are shared among youth via multiple social media platforms. Several of the videos highlight the adolescents' hopes and fears about staying healthy in the face of broader social and environmental factors, including racism, poverty, and food insecurity. For example, in the public service announcement video entitled "Un sabor de casa" (translation: "A taste of home", https://www.youtube.com/watch?v=yuhhxTj5od0), youth poet Monica Mendoza ties the pervasive consumption of soda among her peers and family to conflicts in her cultural identity: a nostalgia for home competing with feelings of resentment towards harmful TV advertising, as captured in this stanza:

> Our heartbeats beat at the rhythm of cumbia, as mom cooks her sopes and enchiladas
>
> It just doesn't feel like a meal without that coke bottle
>
> Without the gas bubbles drowning our noses and mouths
>
> That gargling feeling that takes over our throats
>
> Coke in glass bottles from Mexico
>
> That gives us that taste and sensation of home
>
> We think this possibly can't hurt us without realizing we can't even read the ingredients on the label

On the one hand, we could argue that youth-driven digital literacy practices are exploratory rehearsals for future navigation in online environments in health care. On the other hand, as literacy researchers, we see great value in appreciating the adolescents' bilingual/bicultural digital practices as serious literacy achievements in their own right. In fact, by studying the digital literacy practices of immigrant adolescents, we may end up expanding our thinking about the kinds of inquiry skills we should focus on if we want to understand what "expert" digital practices look like when members of immigrant communities navigate the health care system.

4.4. What Unique Health Literacy Challenges and Sources of Resilience Are Experienced by Immigrant Adolescents Who Are Simultaneously Navigating the World of School, the World of English, and the World of Print Literacy

Many immigrant adolescents face a daunting task as English language learners: they must quickly develop proficiency in English while managing the complex demands of reading and writing in a variety of content areas (e.g., science, literature, and history) in a relatively short period of time. Learning is thus viewed as "double the work" for immigrant adolescents compared to native English speaking peers [56]. At particularly high risk for academic struggle are those adolescents referred to as Students with Limited or Interrupted Formal Education (SLIFE), also sometimes referred to as "unschooled youth" or "newcomers" [57–59]. These adolescents have experienced interruptions in their schooling in their home countries for a variety of reasons: poverty, civil wars, geographic isolation, legally sanctioned restrictions to schooling, resettlement processes that require families to move in order to verify their eligibility for assistance, and natural disasters [60].

The U.S. public school system serves an increasing number of SLIFE children, but their exact numbers are indeterminate, a function of the inconsistent approaches to assessing, classifying, and tracking this group of English language learners [59,61]. In 2007, Gunderson [62] reported that an alarming 75% of high school refugee students (who often fit the typical SLIFE profile) dropped out or disappeared from the public school system. Recent increases in SLIFE children also reflect the wave of over 175,000 unaccompanied minors who entered the U.S. from Central America from 2014 to 2017 [63].

A pervasive theme in the educational literature on SLIFE are the challenges of educating learners with serious emotional needs stemming from traumatic life experiences (e.g., war) and separation from family members. Of particular urgent concern is the adaptation struggles of unaccompanied adolescents placed into foster care who must navigate the transition into adulthood relatively quickly, and under incredibly stressful circumstances [63]. The unique socio-emotional and learning needs of SLIFE can easily get lost in the shuffle of school placement processes that inconsistently place based on age or completed years of schooling. In response, DeCapua, Smathers, and Tang [64] developed an extensive school-based interview protocol that aims to provide a safe zone for SLIFE to talk about their family circumstances, such as these excerpts:

> We had to leave our home because of the war. We live in camp, my mother, my sisters, but we don't know nothing about my father and brothers and we have nothing and we wait to come here with my uncles.

> I come with my brother but my mother and other brothers stay home. I living with my father and sister and brother, but I miss my mother so much [64] (p. 13)

Fortunately, in the public health world, there have already been numerous calls for improvements in counseling and mental health services (e.g., related to post-traumatic stress and sleep disruptions) for immigrant and refugee youth [65–68], a need recently punctuated by continued separation of refugee children from their families at the U.S.–Mexico border. However, more interdisciplinary research on the implications for immigrant adolescent health literacy is needed. As practitioners who have worked in schools, we are compelled to explore the range of health literacy tasks immigrant adolescents encounter in the context of mental health support and services provided by teachers and school counselors. More descriptive studies about the way SLIFE use their language and literacy tools to cope with stress and emotional trauma (as shown in the earlier example of the three Karen brothers) will provide additional evidence for ways that migration histories are tied to health literacy learning. Longitudinal studies will also be critical to assess changes in health literacy practices over time and the relationship to long-term adaptation outcomes.

Clearly, working with SLIFE learners presents a unique and challenging set of circumstances for teachers and school counselors; too often these professionals lack the training, time, and resources to adequately support SLIFE in schools. We do not know of any studies that have examined the communication and navigation practices of the school-based practitioners who are responsible for SLIFE well-being. Research on what works for SLIFE may improve the ways teachers, counselors, social workers, and other school staff work with SLIFE and their families.

Another pervasive theme in the educational literature on SLIFE learners is that they learn differently from children who have print skills in their first language [69]. For example, their prior schooling experiences are anchored in spoken language which makes the transition to learning from printed texts challenging [70]. Additionally, children who have attended school in refugee camps may have been taught in different languages, depending on whether the local policy stipulated instruction in the first-language or the host-county language, further complicating the mastery of academic skills in English. Many SLIFE children need to figure out what it means to "do school" [46], which creates additional pedagogical challenges, as described by this Australian high school teacher:

> ... I have some Sudanese students who have had a lot of schooling who came to Australia with a very good background of English so learning is quite easy, not just the learning side of it but the rituals of school. As well I have students who have lived in refugees camps for ten years and have no background in schooling, not just the learning again, but the rituals of school, how to cope with the day to day, the system of bells and requirements ... those extremes are very wide. [71] (pp. 26–27)

This example makes us curious about the ways that SLIFE, as part of their migration and adaptive experiences, are similarly figuring out how to "do health". More descriptive studies in the context of SLIFE's early interactions with the U.S. health care system will give immigrant adolescents the opportunity to describe, in their own words, what learning to "do health" means when reliance on printed texts is not a productive pathway for accessing health information.

We have argued that SLIFE, a growing sector in the immigrant adolescent population, deserves more attention as a population of study in health literacy research. With more scholarship on SLIFE in literacy education in the past decade, educational researchers and teachers have had to critically examine their discourse about "illiterate" learners and question their assumptions about the role of schooling and print knowledge in literacy learning. We anticipate that research on immigrant adolescent health literacy will require a similar reckoning of assumptions about literacy that have prevailed in the health literacy field.

4.5. How Do the Goals of Health Literacy Learning Differ or Overlap with Health Education Curricular Goals in Secondary School Settings?

A research agenda on immigrant adolescent health literacy needs to be able to clarify the relationship between health literacy and health education, which already has a long-established history in the U.S. public schools as a vehicle for promoting healthy outcomes among adolescents. Although a comprehensive review of U.S. health education policy and programming is beyond the scope of this paper, we caution against assuming that health literacy and health education are equivalent efforts, or that health literacy should be treated as a "school subject" in the same way that health education has been institutionalized in U.S. public schools.

The Calgary Charter acknowledges that individuals must have "some basic knowledge of science and health" and "an understanding of the health system"; however, there is no explicit recommendation as to which content areas comprise this "basic knowledge" and "understanding". Similarly, the National Health Education Standards (NHES), most recently revised in 2007, also emphasizes the teaching of transferable skills in U.S. health education programming, partly in recognition that there was simply not enough time in the academic school year to cover potentially relevant themes at each grade level [72]. However, states still specify content areas through which schools can address these standards. For example, California specifies six content areas through which the NHES are addressed: Nutrition and Physical Activity; Growth, Development, and Sexual Health; Injury Prevention and Safety; Alcohol, Tobacco, and Other Drugs; Mental, Emotional, and Social Health; and Personal and Community Health [73]. More research is needed to specify the health literacy competencies that might be effectively reinforced in schools for immigrant adolescents at various grades, or levels of English proficiency. Such alignment would bring greater visibility to the sources of resilience and "everyday wisdom" that immigrant adolescents cultivate as health care navigators, offsetting perceptions of adolescents as at-risk youth in need of health education.

The focus on the development of an individual learner's skill set is prominent throughout the NHES, which contrasts with the Calgary Charter's emphasis on health literacy as an attribute of individuals and systems. The NHES framework expects the high school learner to be able to analyze the influence of family, peers, community, media, and culture on health outcomes (Performance Indicators 2.12.1–2.12.6), but it remains unclear on how to account for the influence of those social factors on the learners' competence. From a social perspective, however, this influence is viewed as a given. The immigrant adolescent's health literacy and her social networks are mutually constitutive: social interactions shape health literacy, and health literacy shapes social interaction. We caution against treating health literacy learning and health education as equivalent ventures which may end up reifying assumptions that health literacy is a discrete skill set or to be treated as a "school subject" taught in schools.

As mentioned earlier, Higgins et al. makes a notable contribution, in the Canadian context, using a socio-ecological model to examine conceptual differences across health literacy, health education, and health promotion in the adolescent population [10]. Higgins et al. invites validation of their model in multilingual settings, among other contexts, which, if realized, would provide the basis for exciting partnerships between health literacy researchers and adolescent literacy practitioners in the U.S. and Canada.

5. Conclusions

To recap, our goal in this section is not to provide a definitive list of research directions on immigrant adolescent health literacy. Rather, we wanted to suggest some of the conceptual and practical motivations and potential benefits of doing this work (see Appendix A for a compilation of possible research directions). We already have evidence regarding the cognitive and social achievements that adolescent immigrants make as readers, writers, and thinkers exhibit in a variety of nonschool-related literacy activities, such as translating for family members or information-seeking across multiple media platforms. For those of us working in literacy education and applied linguists, we are optimistic that studies on immigrant adolescent health literacy will reveal pathways for literacy growth that may differ from what has been taken to be normative in schools. This work will affirm the significance of research on out-of-school literacies in its own right, not merely as a counter-response to research on in-school literacies. Moreover, research on immigrant adolescent health literacy will hopefully guide our pedagogical decisions as we try to help learners who may demonstrate impressive health literacy practices out of school but struggle to transfer these competencies to learning in school.

For the health literacy field to respond meaningfully to the diverse learning needs and migration trajectories of immigrant adolescents, it must more fully reject the premise that immigrant adolescent health literacy can be reduced to a functional set of reading skills. Simply put, the health literacy field must undergo its own "social turn". This paradigmatic shift will enable us to regard immigrant adolescent health literacy as one of many literacies adolescents learn to master, and part of a broader, evolving repertoire of communicative choices, tools for inquiry, and relationships. From the literacy as social practice perspective, we prefer to envision immigrant adolescent health literacy as a domain of social activity and adaptive change, not merely as a collection of skills and abilities.

As an interdisciplinary research team, we know firsthand that increased collaboration between our fields of immigrant literacy and public health has reinvigorated our own health literacy research directions and sparked new thinking about how to promote health literacy among immigrant adolescents in and out of schools. We hope our commentary inspires more interdisciplinary collaborations in pursuit of empirical clarity concerning the relationship between transnationalism and the development of health literacy in the immigrant adolescent population. One concrete outcome of our own interdisciplinary collaborative efforts is a shared vocabulary, understanding, and conceptualization of how we can best support the health literacy competence of immigrant adolescents. Concepts, such as investment, give us a new vocabulary for describing the social dimensions of health literacy learning, and identify new approaches for harnessing social contexts in the design of developmentally appropriate health literacy interventions and health messaging for immigrant youth.

With serious investment of time and funding, an interdisciplinary research agenda promises to reveal the ways immigrant adolescents learn what it means to navigate our health care system as they deploy multiple languages across a spectrum of modalities (print, oral, visual, and digital), participate in diverse social networks that include local and global peers, and make use of cultural resources in the U.S. and the home country.

In this regard, research on immigrant adolescents can provide fresh evidence in support of health literacy as a contextualized and embedded capacity, an evolving mastery of health literacy practices as the adolescent interacts with her environment (not a discrete set of reading and writing skills learned step by step). Greater understanding of what health literacy competence looks like for this diverse population could ultimately strengthen our knowledge about more general ways that social context influences the health literacy development of all children and adults.

Author Contributions: Conceptualization M.G.S., A.L.G., L.M.J., M.A.H.; Methodology M.G.S., A.L.G., L.M.J.; Draft preparation M.G.S., A.L.G., L.M.J., M.A.H.; Writing-Review & Editing M.G.S.

Funding: This project was funded by a subcontract award to San Francisco State University, through the Center for Health and Risk in Minority Youth and Adults (CHARM) from the National Institute on Minority Health and Health Disparities (NIMHD) grant number P60MD006902. The APC was funded by the University of California, San Francisco Library.

Acknowledgments: We would like to thank the anonymous peer-reviewers for their helpful comments, particularly regarding the discussion of our bike-riding metaphor. We also wish to thank Kerri Santos, graphic designer, for her editing work on the bike-riding graphic (Figure 1).

Conflicts of Interest: The authors declare no conflicts of interest.

Appendix A. Researching Immigrant Adolescent Health Literacy as a Socially Situated Practice: Some Exploratory Questions

Appendix A.1. Multilingual Dimensions of Immigrant Adolescent Health Literacy

1. How does the immigrant adolescents' knowledge of other languages, beyond English, manifest in their health literacy competence?
2. How does knowledge of other languages open or close-down routes to participation in health care encounters?
3. What is the role of oral language use in the development of immigrant adolescents' health literacy practices?
4. To what extent do linguistic brokering encounters provide immigrant adolescents with opportunities to develop health literacy practices across functional, communicative, and critical levels?

Appendix A.2. The Relationship between Immigrant Adolescent Health Literacy and Schooled (Academic) Literacies

1. In what ways do changes in health literacy competence reflect (or contrast with) their academic literacy competencies?
2. What skills and practices transfer across health care and school contexts?
3. How does the relationship between immigrant adolescent health literacy and schooled (academic) literacies vary for learners based on differences in print knowledge and metalinguistic awareness?

Appendix A.3. The Link between Immigrant Adolescent Health Literacy and Digital Literacies

1. To what extent is technology enabling immigrant adolescents, despite minimal English communication skills, to "leapfrog" (Dr. Christina Zarcadoolas, personal communication, 21 March 2016) over communication barriers in health care, and expanding their ability to participate more fully in health literacy activities?
2. To what extent are the immigrant adolescent health literacy activities transnational in scope, as they use technology to interact with social groups and diverse informational resources that span geographical borders?
3. How does a focus on immigrant adolescent health literacy provide examples of immigrant adolescents' ability to move across multiple media platforms, languages, and social contexts? How can these examples inform health literacy intervention efforts?

Appendix A.4. The Role of Social Contexts

1. What is the range and variation of health literacy activities in which immigrant adolescents participate? How does this participation vary based on the immigrant adolescents' family structure, level of generation, or documentation status?
2. To what extent do immigrant adolescents demonstrate an understanding of the social and institutional expectations that govern interactions in health care contexts?
3. To what extent do U.S. immigrant adolescents, as a result of their childhood experiences in health navigation and advocacy, demonstrated increased agency over their own health care choices (e.g., contraceptive use) or increased involvement in advocacy movements, such as reforms in health insurance or Deferred Action for Childhood Arrivals (DACA) policy?

Appendix A.5. The Role of Social Networks

1. How does immigrant adolescent's evolving health literacy competence influence their social relationships in the context of family, school, and community?
2. To what degree do their health literacy encounters reflect shifting power dynamics in their relationships to authority (parents, teachers, doctors) in their everyday lives?
3. What are strategies for harnessing immigrant adolescents' social ties (global and local) as resources for tackling problems in health care navigation?

References

1. Zong, J.; Batalova, J. Frequently Requested Statistics on Immigrants and Immigration in the United States. migrationpolicy.org, 2 February 2018. Available online: https://www.migrationpolicy.org/article/frequently-requested-statistics-immigrants-and-immigration-united-states (accessed on 20 September 2018).
2. Batalova, J.; Fix, M.; Murray, J. *Measures of Change: The Demography and Literacy of Adolescent English Learners—A Report to Carnegie Corporation of New York*; Migration Policy Institute: Washington, DC, USA, 2007.
3. Passel, J.S. Demography of Immigrant Youth: Past, Present, and Future. *Future Child.* **2011**, *21*, 19–41. [CrossRef] [PubMed]
4. Dávila, L.T. Diaspora Literacies. *J. Adolesc. Adult Lit.* **2015**, *58*, 641–649. [CrossRef]
5. Jiang, Y.; Ekono, M.M.; Skinner, C. Curtis, Basic Facts about Low-Income Children: Children 12 through 17 Years, 2014. Available online: http://www.nccp.org/publications/pub_1145.html (accessed on 13 July 2018).
6. Montero-Sieburth, M.; Villaruel, F. *Making Invisible Latino Adolescents Visible: A Critical Approach to Latino Diversity*; Routledge: New York, NY, USA, 2003.
7. Manganello, J.A. Health Literacy and Adolescents: A Framework and Agenda for Future Research. *Health Educ. Res.* **2008**, *23*, 840–847. [CrossRef] [PubMed]
8. Perry, E.L. Health Literacy in Adolescents: An Integrative Review. *J. Spec. Pediatr. Nurs.* **2014**, *19*, 210–218. [CrossRef] [PubMed]
9. Sanders, L.M.; Federico, S.; Klass, P.; Abrams, M.A.; Dreyer, B. Literacy and Child Health: A Systematic Review. *Arch. Pediatr. Adolesc. Med.* **2009**, *163*, 131–140. [CrossRef] [PubMed]
10. Higgins, J.W.; Begoray, D.; MacDonald, M. A Social Ecological Conceptual Framework for Understanding Adolescent Health Literacy in the Health Education Classroom. *Am. J. Community Psychol.* **2009**, *44*, 350–362. [CrossRef]
11. Nutbeam, D. The Evolving Concept of Health Literacy. *Soc. Sci. Med.* **2008**, *67*, 2072–2078. [CrossRef]
12. Moje, E.B. Re-Framing Adolescent Literacy Research for New Times: Studying Youth as Resource. *Read. Res. Instr.* **2002**, *41*, 211–228. [CrossRef]
13. Nutbeam, D. Health Literacy as a Public Health Goal: A Challenge for Contemporary Health Education and Communication Strategies into the 21st Century. *Health Promot. Int.* **2000**, *15*, 259–267. [CrossRef]
14. Paasche-Orlow, M.K.; Wolf, M.S. The Causal Pathways Linking Health Literacy to Health Outcomes. *Am. J. Health Behav.* **2007**, *31*, S19–S26. [CrossRef]
15. Sørensen, K.; Van den Broucke, S.; Fullam, J.; Doyle, G.; Pelikan, J.; Slonska, Z.; Brand, H. Health Literacy and Public Health: A Systematic Review and Integration of Definitions and Models. *BMC Public Health* **2012**, *12*, 80. [CrossRef] [PubMed]
16. Fairbrother, H.; Curtis, P.; Goyder, E. Making Health Information Meaningful: Children's Health Literacy Practices. *SSM-Popul. Health* **2016**, *2*, 476–484. [CrossRef] [PubMed]
17. Suárez-Orozco, C.; Gaytán, F.X.; Bang, H.J.; Pakes, J.; O'Connor, E.; Rhodes, J. Academic Trajectories of Newcomer Immigrant Youth. *Dev. Psychol.* **2010**, *46*, 602–618. [CrossRef] [PubMed]
18. Santos, M.G.; McClelland, J.; Handley, M.A. Language Lessons on Immigrant Identity, Food Culture, and the Search for Home. *TESOL J.* **2011**, *2*, 203–228. [CrossRef]
19. Garcia, O.; Wei, L. *Translanguaging: Language, Bilingualism and Education*; Springer: New York, NY, USA, 2013.
20. Institute of Medicine. 2004. Health Literacy: A Prescription to End Confusion. Available online: https://www.nap.edu/catalog/10883/health-literacy-a-prescription-to-end-confusion (accessed on 20 September 2018).
21. Street, B.V.; Street, B.B. *Literacy in Theory and Practice*; Cambridge University Press: Cambridge, UK, 1984.

22. Hamilton, M.; Barton, D. Literacy Practices. In *Situated Literacies: Reading and Writing in Context*; Routledge: London, UK, 1999; pp. 7–15.
23. Purcell-Gates, V. *Cultural Practices of Literacy: Case Studies of Language, Literacy, Social Practice, and Power*; Lawrence Erlbaum Associates Publishers: Mahwah, NJ, USA, 2007.
24. Block, D. *The Social Turn in Second Language Acquisition*; Edinburgh University Press: Edinburgh, UK, 2003.
25. Papen, U. *Adult Literacy as Social Practice: More Than Skills*; Routledge: New York, NY, USA, 2005.
26. Rudd, R.E. Needed Action in Health Literacy. *J. Health Psychol.* **2013**, *18*, 1004–1010. [CrossRef] [PubMed]
27. Papen, U. Literacy, Learning and Health—A Social Practices View of Health Literacy. *Lit. Numeracy Stud.* **2009**, *16–17*, 19–34. [CrossRef]
28. Pleasant, A. Advancing Health Literacy Measurement: A Pathway to Better Health and Health System Performance. *J. Health Commun.* **2014**, *19*, 1481–1496. [CrossRef]
29. Purcell-Gates, V.; Perry, K.H.; Briseño, A. Analyzing Literacy Practice: Grounded Theory to Model. *Res. Teach. Engl.* **2011**, *45*, 439–458.
30. Coleman, C.; Kurtz-Rossi, S.; McKinney, J.; Pleasant, A.; Rootman, I.; Shohet, L. *Calgary Charter on Health Literacy: Rationale and Core Principles for the Development of Health Literacy Curricula*; The Centre for Literacy of Quebec: Montreal, QC, Canada, 2011.
31. Eaton, D.K.; Kann, L.; Kinchen, S.; Shanklin, S.; Ross, J.; Hawkins, J.; Harris, W.A.; Lowry, R.; McManus, T.; Chyen, D.; et al. Youth Risk Behavior Surveillance—United States, 2009. *MMWR Surveill. Summ.* **2010**, *59*, 1–142.
32. Portes, A.; Rivas, A. The Adaptation of Migrant Children. *Future Child.* **2011**, *21*, 219–246. [CrossRef]
33. Chuang, S.S.; Costigan, C.L. *Parental Roles and Relationships in Immigrant Families: An International Approach*; Springer: Berlin, Germany, 2018.
34. Orellana, M.F.; Dorner, L.; Pulido, L. Accessing Assets: Immigrant Youth's Work as Family Translators or 'Para-Phrasers'. *Soc. Probl.* **2003**, *50*, 505–524. [CrossRef]
35. Weisskirch, R.S. *Language Brokering in Immigrant Families: Theories and Contexts*; Routledge: London, UK, 2017.
36. Orellana, M.F. The Work Kids Do: Mexican and Central American Immigrant Children's Contributions to Household. *Harv. Educ. Rev.* **2001**, *71*, 366–389. [CrossRef]
37. Chinn, D. Critical Health Literacy: A Review and Critical Analysis. *Soc. Sci. Med.* **2011**, *73*, 60–67. [CrossRef] [PubMed]
38. Martinez, K.; Orellana, M.F.; Murillo, M.A.; Rodriguez, M.A. Health Insurance, from a Child Language Broker's Perspective. *Int. Migr.* **2017**, *55*, 31–43. [CrossRef]
39. Katz, V. Children as Brokers of Their Immigrant Families' Health-Care Connections. *Soc. Probl.* **2014**, *61*, 194–215. [CrossRef]
40. Steinberg, L.; Morris, A.S. Adolescent Development. *Ann. Rev. Psychol.* **2001**, *52*, 83–110. [CrossRef] [PubMed]
41. Norton, B. *Identity and Language Learning: Extending the Conversation*; Multilingual Matters: Bristol, UK, 2013.
42. Norton, B. Identity, Literacy, and English Language Learning. *Iran. J. Lang. Teach. Res.* **2013**, *1*, 85–98.
43. Rubinstein-Ávila, E. From the Dominican Republic to Drew High: What Counts as Literacy for Yanira Lara? *Read. Res. Q.* **2007**, *42*, 568–589. [CrossRef]
44. Moje, E.B.; Ciechanowski, K.M.; Kramer, K.; Ellis, L.; Carrillo, R.; Collazo, T. Working toward Third Space in Content Area Literacy: An Examination of Everyday Funds of Knowledge and Discourse. *Read. Res. Q.* **2004**, *39*, 38–70. [CrossRef]
45. Gray, N.J.; Klein, J.D.; Noyce, P.R.; Sesselberg, T.S.; Cantrill, J.A. The Internet: A Window on Adolescent Health Literacy. *J. Adolesc. Health* **2005**, *37*, 243. [CrossRef]
46. Ghaddar, S.F.; Valerio, M.A.; Garcia, C.M.; Hansen, L. Adolescent Health Literacy: The Importance of Credible Sources for Online Health Information. *J. Sch. Health* **2012**, *82*, 28–36. [CrossRef]
47. Jain, A.V.; Bickham, D. Adolescent Health Literacy and the Internet: Challenges and Opportunities. *Curr. Opin. Pediatr.* **2014**, *26*, 435–439. [CrossRef] [PubMed]
48. Lam, W.S.E.; Warriner, D.S. Transnationalism and Literacy: Investigating the Mobility of People, Languages, Texts, and Practices in Contexts of Migration. *Read. Res. Q.* **2012**, *47*, 191–215. [CrossRef]
49. O'Mara, B.; Harris, A. Intercultural Crossings in a Digital Age: ICT Pathways with Migrant and Refugee-Background Youth. *Race Ethn. Educ.* **2016**, *19*, 639–658. [CrossRef]
50. Elias, N.; Lemish, D. Spinning the Web of Identity: The Roles of the Internet in the Lives of Immigrant Adolescents. *New Media Soc.* **2009**, *11*, 533–551. [CrossRef]

51. Lam, W.S.E. Literacy and Capital in Immigrant Youths' Online Networks across Countries. *Learn. Media Technol.* **2014**, *39*, 488–506. [CrossRef]
52. Manderino, M.; Castek, J. Digital Literacies for Disciplinary Learning: A Call to Action. *J. Adolesc. Adult Lit.* **2016**, *60*, 79–81. [CrossRef]
53. Gilhooly, D.; Lee, E. The Role of Digital Literacy Practices on Refugee Resettlement: The case of three Karen Brothers. *J. Adolesc. Adult Lit.* **2014**, *57*, 387–396. [CrossRef]
54. McLean, C.A. A Space Called Home: An Immigrant Adolescent's Digital Literacy Practices. *J. Adolesc. Adult Lit.* **2011**, *54*, 13–22. [CrossRef]
55. Rogers, E.A.; Fine, S.; Handley, M.A.; Davis, H.; Kass, J.; Schillinger, D. Development and Early Implementation of The Bigger Picture, a Youth-Targeted Public Health Literacy Campaign to Prevent Type 2 Diabetes. *J. Health Commun.* **2014**, *19*, 144–160. [CrossRef]
56. Short, D.; Fitzsimmons, S. *Double the Work: Challenges and Solutions to Acquiring Language and Academic Literacy for Adolescent English Language Learners; A Report Commissioned by the Carnegie Corporation of New York*; Alliance for Excellent Education: Washington, DC, USA, 2007; Available online: http://www.carnegie.org/literacy/pdf/DoubletheWork.pdf (accessed on 22 April 2018).
57. King, K.A.; Bigelow, M.; Hirsi, A. New to School and New to Print: Everyday Peer Interaction among Adolescent High School Newcomers. *Int. Multiling. Res. J.* **2017**, *11*, 137–151. [CrossRef]
58. DeCapua, A.; Marshall, H.W. Marshall, Reaching ELLs at Risk: Instruction for Students with Limited or Interrupted Formal Education. *Prev. Sch. Fail.* **2011**, *55*, 35–41. [CrossRef]
59. Browder, C.T. *English Learners with Limited or Interrupted Formal Education: Risk and Resilience in Educational Outcomes*; University of Maryland: Baltimore, MD, USA, 2014.
60. Shapiro, S.; Curry, M.J.; Farrelly, R. *Educating Refugee-Background Students: Critical Issues and Dynamic Contexts*; Multilingual Matters: Bristol, UK, 2018.
61. Sugarman, J. *Meeting the Education Needs of Rising Numbers of Newly Arrived Migrant Students in Europe and the United States*; Migration Policy Institute: Washington, DC, USA, 2015.
62. Gunderson, L. *English-Only Instruction and Immigrant Students in Secondary Schools: A Critical Examination*; Lawrence Erlbaum Associates: Mahwah, NJ, USA, 2007.
63. Pierce, S. Unaccompanied Child Migrants in U.S. Communities, Immigration Court, and Schools. migrationpolicy.org, October 14, 2015. Available online: https://www.migrationpolicy.org/research/unaccompanied-child-migrants-us-communities-immigration-court-and-schools (accessed on 20 September 2018).
64. DeCapua, A.; Smathers, W.; Tang, L.F. *Meeting the Needs of Students with Limited or Interrupted Schooling: A Guide for Educators*; University of Michigan Press: Ann Arbor, MI, USA, 2009.
65. Betancourt, T.S.; Newnham, E.A.; Layne, C.M.; Kim, S.; Steinberg, A.M.; Ellis, H.; Birman, D. Trauma History and Psychopathology in War-Affected Refugee Children Referred for Trauma-Related Mental Health Services in the United States. *J. Trauma. Stress* **2012**, *25*, 682–690. [CrossRef] [PubMed]
66. Ellis, B.H.; Miller, A.B.; Baldwin, H.; Abdi, S. New Directions in Refugee Youth Mental Health Services: Overcoming Barriers to Engagement. *J. Child Adolesc. Trauma* **2011**, *4*, 69–85. [CrossRef]
67. Burns, J.R.; Rapee, R.M. Adolescent Mental Health Literacy: Young People's Knowledge of Depression and Help Seeking. *J. Adolesc.* **2006**, *29*, 225–239. [CrossRef] [PubMed]
68. Merrill Weine, S.; Ware, N.; Hakizimana, L.; Tugenberg, T.; Currie, M.; Dahnweih, G.; Wagner, M.; Polutnik, C.; Wulu, J. Fostering Resilience: Protective Agents, Resources, and Mechanisms for Adolescent Refugees' Psychosocial Well-Being. *Adolesc. Psychiatry* **2014**, *4*, 164–176. [CrossRef] [PubMed]
69. Custodio, B.; O'Loughlin, J.B. *Students with Interrupted Formal Education: Bridging Where They Are and What They Need*; Corwin Press: Thousand Oaks, CA, USA, 2017.
70. Bigelow, M.; Tarone, E. The Role of Literacy Level in Second Language Acquisition: Doesn't Who We Study Determine What We Know? *TESOL Q.* **2004**, *38*, 689–700. [CrossRef]
71. Miller, J.; Mitchell, J.; Brown, J. African Refugees with Interrupted Schooling in the High School Mainstream: Dilemmas for Teachers. *Prospect* **2005**, *20*, 19–33.

72. Nobiling, B.D.; Lyde, A.R. From the School Health Education Study to the National Health Education Standards: Concepts Endure. *J. Sch. Health* **2015**, *85*, 309–317. [CrossRef]
73. California Department of Education. *Health Education Content Standards for California Public School, Kindergarten through Grade 12*; California Department of Education: Sacramento, CA, USA, 2009. Available online: http://www.cde.ca.gov/be/st/ss/documents/healthstandmar08.pdf (accessed on 22 April 2018).

© 2018 by the authors. Licensee MDPI, Basel, Switzerland. This article is an open access article distributed under the terms and conditions of the Creative Commons Attribution (CC BY) license (http://creativecommons.org/licenses/by/4.0/).

Article

The Measurements and an Elaborated Understanding of Chinese eHealth Literacy (C-eHEALS) in Chronic Patients in China

Angela Chang [1,2,*] and Peter J. Schulz [2]

1. Department of Communication, University of Macau, E21, Avenida da Universidade, Taipa, Macau, China
2. Institute of Communication and Health, Lugano University, Switzerland, Ex Laboratorio, Via Buffi 13, 6904 Lugano, Switzerland; peter.schulz@usi.ch
* Correspondence: wychang@umac.mo; Tel.: +853-8822-8991

Received: 26 June 2018; Accepted: 19 July 2018; Published: 23 July 2018

Abstract: The rapid rise of Internet-based technologies to disseminate health information and services has been shown to enhance online health information acquisition. A Chinese version of the electronic health literacy scale (C-eHEALS) was developed to measure patients' combined knowledge and perceived skills at finding and applying electronic health information to health problems. A valid sample of 352 interviewees responded to the online questionnaire, and their responses were analyzed. The C-eHEALS, by showing high internal consistency and predictive validity, is an effective screening tool for detecting levels of health literacy in clinical settings. Individuals' sociodemographic status, perceived health status, and level of health literacy were identified for describing technology users' characteristics. A strong association between eHealth literacy level, media information use, and computer literacy was found. The emphasis of face-to-face inquiry for obtaining health information was important in the low eHealth literacy group while Internet-based technologies crucially affected decision-making skills in the high eHealth literacy group. This information is timely because it implies that health care providers can use the C-eHEALS to screen eHealth literacy skills and empower patients with chronic diseases with online resources.

Keywords: literacy knowledge; health promotion; health status; Internet; mobile use

1. Introduction

Health literacy has received much attention as a causal agent of health outcomes. For example, low health literacy has been associated with obesity [1,2], low adoption of health behaviours [3–5], poor use of health care services [6,7] and poor access to electronic health (eHealth) resources [5]. The rapid rise of Internet-based technologies that disseminate health information and services enhances the acquisition of online health information [8–10]. Therefore, eHealth literacy has drawn the attention of researchers as a condition for utilising such information and services [8,11,12].

The present study represents the 1.37 billion people in mainland China who are (as is the rest of the world) undergoing a drastic media communication revolution. Among them, 688 million were Internet users (users) by the end of 2015; of these, a majority of more than two-thirds uses mobile phones [13]. China represents an important case that can reflect how systemic and institutional factors influence and facilitate health communication in the context of rapid media and technological development. Additionally, considering the country's recent rapid and extraordinary economic growth, it is inevitable that China will eventually encounter the public health problems that developed countries currently experience. Therefore, examination of the relationship between the health status of users and their eHealth literacy is crucial for developing efficient health communication strategies in the future.

eHealth Literacy

Oh and others [14] analysed 51 unique definitions of eHealth with varying degrees of emphasis on health and computer technology use. The term 'eHealth' has been widely used to encompass a set of disparate concepts such as online health management [15] and information searching [16].

Norman and Skinner [17] developed the eHealth literacy scale (eHEALS) based on young users' (aged < 25 years) eHealth literacy, which was defined as the ability to read, use computers, search for information, understand health information, and put it into context. They understand eHealth literacy as being dependent on basic reading and writing skills. eHEALS is currently the only instrument that aims to measure an individual's confidence in their ability to locate and evaluate online health information [17,18]. There are six eHealth core skills or areas of literacy comprised in the original Lily model of eHEALS, namely traditional literacy, health literacy, information literacy, scientific literacy, media literacy and computer literacy, the latter measuring working knowledge of computers [17–19], in addition to basic understanding of science and appreciation of the social context.

The theoretical grounding and measurement of eHealth literacy has been challenged partially due to the development of social media and users' increasingly versatile approach to information-finding and problem-solving [20]. Researchers have urged closer examination of the health-related behaviour interventions of adult patients [21–23]. Moreover, Macker, et al. [19] reviewed the methodology of eHealth studies and found that a majority of studies tended to employ domain-specific health literacy measures, and concluded that exploratory data collection techniques would improve the quality of research. Another example is in Petrič, et al. [24], who used a revised and extended eHEALS in Slovenia to analyse how patients in online health communities managed their health. To increase the accuracy of eHEALS predictions, Chan and Kaufman [25] proposed a more rigorous theoretical and methodological eHealth framework for characterizing the complexity of eHealth tasks. It could be used to diagnose and describe literacy barriers encountered by participants in performing the tasks.

eHealth literacy is a foundational skill, and eHealth information is a critical predictor of preventive health measures. Chan and others [26] supported the idea that using a problem-based approach to search for reliable health information is effective for increasing the competency level of Chinese university students in Hong Kong. Mackert and colleagues [19] proposed that respondents with high eHealth literacy tended to be younger and more educated than their less eHealth-literate counterparts. A number of other studies confirmed their finding [18,27–30]. The eHEALS has mainly been administered to young people, who are heavy users, and the participants in studies that use the eHEALS in different countries were also quite health-literate [18,19,31,32]. Reviewing the literature, we concluded that there is a need to recruit adult patients, an overlooked and vulnerable group in online health communication and eHealth research [9,10,33].

The established eHEALS model is a theoretically informed concept with an eight-item baseline for assessing a person's ability to use eHealth resources [14,15,31,34]. Several studies have criticized the eHEALS model as adopting a unidimensional approach and performing insufficiently in psychometric evaluation [24,35–38]. However, others have concluded that eHEALS was a valid measurement for predicting health outcomes, and, furthermore, that it improved users' health communication and the benefit they derive for health care services. For example, Chung and Nahm [39] validated the eHEALS test in English, supporting eHealth interventions to engage older adults in health care and to help them manage their own health. Moreover, Paige and others [33] concluded that eHEALS was a valid and reliable measure of self-reported eHealth literacy among patients with chronic disease in the U.S. Their research supported the use of the eHEALS as part of a screening instrument to help identify patients' eHealth literacy skills and as a diagnostic tool to define patients who are in need of improving their health literacy.

Several eHEALS are available in a range of languages other than English, including Spanish [31], German [34], Japanese [35], Dutch [36], Italian [37], Portuguese [40] and traditional Chinese [32,41]. The eHEALS measures the use of online health resources and content while considering cultural sensitivities in health information and online communication. However, the considerable body of research on the validity and reliability of eHEALS has been largely limited to the developed Western countries [33,38,39,42]; they have not been examined systematically in simplified Chinese for users in China. Considering China's recent rapid and extraordinary economic growth, it is inevitable that it will encounter the public health problems currently experienced by the developed countries.

Our study gave us the opportunity to replicate earlier analyses and generalize findings from other societies and cultures. Therefore, the dual objectives of the present study are first to compare the Chinese eHEALS (C-eHEALS) with other eHEALS findings to determine whether C-eHEALS model provided reliability evidence with chronic disease patients in China. In addition, previous studies have concluded that patients' access to online health information was affected by their low computer skills and low level of health literacy [33,38]. Thus, the second objective is to examine and compare how the large patient segments access eHealth resources to find and apply eHealth information to their health problems in China.

2. Materials and Methods

2.1. Measures and Development of the C-eHEALS

The C-eHEALS expands on previous eHEALS studies of the Chinese in mainland China by including: (1) an eight-item questionnaire baseline for acquiring information from the Internet; (2) a 10-item scale measuring media and computer literacy; and (3) a nine-item literacy scale pertaining to the use of information [14,19,20,33]. The structured questionnaires use a five-point Likert scale (strongly disagree = 1; strongly agree = 5); a higher score indicates a higher eHealth literacy level.

Additionally, we included six questions on socioeconomics and four questions on perceived health status [14,32,33]. The socioeconomics questions were on sex (male or female), age ($\geq$18 years), highest level of education (primary and secondary school, junior high, high school, college or bachelor, master's degree or higher), residency (Guangdong or others), occupation (business owner, student, self-employed, public servant, clinician or others) and monthly income (<RMB1000, 1000–3000, 3001–5000, 5001–7000, $\geq$7001). The questions on health status included the frequency of visiting doctors, cost of visiting doctors, and the perceived health condition. Additionally, participants were presented with a list of chronic diseases and required to select all conditions they had, including: cardiovascular disease, metabolic disease, cancer, allergy and other chronic diseases. For the eHealth investigation, online questionnaires were circulated for access via exploratory data collection techniques.

We followed a strict protocol for the translation to ensure that this version was linguistically, technologically and psychometrically robust. The eHEALS was first translated into simplified Chinese to measure respondents' combined knowledge and perceived skills at finding and applying eHealth information to health problems. The simplified C-eHEALS was then back-translated by a native English-speaker. This did not change any words and all words had equivalent translations. However, two top search tools—an instant messaging app (i.e., Tencent's Quick Question (QQ)) and a search engine forum (i.e., Baidu) [8]—in the nine-item scale on media and information channel use were specified to allow the questionnaire to be more applicable for the acquisition of health information in China.

2.2. Data Collection

The first author and the research team performed the study at a public hospital in Shenzhen, Guangdong, mainland China. The hospital is a major and comprehensive Grade 2A hospital with approximately 2000 employees and 1200 hospital beds. Randomized clinical studies are usually based on convenient sampling [33,38]. In this study, trained interviewers approached patients awaiting admittance at an outpatient department at the hospital. The outpatients were consecutively selected according to their convenient accessibility during the night clinic on every Wednesday and Saturday from October 2015 to June 2016. The C-eHEALS was administered as an online survey via mobile phone, tablet or laptop computer provided by the interviewers or interviewees. The study protocol was approved by the Ethics Committee of the University of Macau (MYRG2015-0123-FSS).

Participants were recruited based on the following inclusion criteria: aged ≥ 18 years, Mandarin-speaking, and a member of the ethnic majority (Han). Respondents were required to select the appropriate answer regarding their comprehension of a series of statements pertaining to the six key eHealth skills. All respondents read an information sheet explaining the purpose of the study before deciding to participate; they provided verbal informed consent for inclusion before their participation in the study began. The C-eHEALS study was tested using a sample of 352 respondents.

2.3. Data Analysis

The Statistical Package for the Social Sciences and Analysis of Moment Structures (AMOS) version 24 (IBM Corp., Armonk, NY, USA) were used in this study. Descriptive analyses and factor analysis were used for an analytical model. For dimensionality reduction from a multidimensional dataset, a pre-determined number of three clusters within the properties of the data was implemented by the K-means algorithm. Cluster analysis of the K-means was used to contrast two groups of low- and high-eHealth literacy. Moreover, a Pearson product–moment correlation coefficient was computed to assess and predict the relationship between the C-eHEALS score and media usage. A chi-square test of independence was performed to examine the relationship between the C-eHEALS scores and users' demographic information and their reported literacy.

3. Results

3.1. Identifying C-eHEALS Items

A Kaiser–Meyer–Olkin test (KMO) was used to measure the sample adequacy and conclude the worthiness of factor analysis. The KMO showed a value of 0.928, and the Bartlett test of sphericity was significant (x^2 = 2814.70, degree of freedom [df] = 28, $p < 0.001$). KMO values > 0.9 are superb, while values between 0.7 and 0.8 are good; KMO values between 0.5 and 0.7 are mediocre [43]. The calculated Cronbach's α coefficient was 0.954, and the Guttman split-half coefficient was 0.92, indicating good internal consistency for the scale [35,42,43]. Table 1 shows the high internal reliability and validity tests via Pearson's correlation between the known predictors and the C-eHEALS.

Table 1. Results of reliability and validity tests.

Reliability		Validity				
Cronbach's alpha	Split-half	Media & Computer literacy	Computer skills	Information literacy	Health status	Education attainment
0.95 ***	0.92 ***	0.13 *	0.44 ***	0.12 *	0.08	0.11 **

*** $p < 0.001$, ** $p < 0.01$, * $p < 0.05$.

Validity was assessed using factor analysis, which yielded a single-factor solution (eigenvalue = 4.85, 75.81% of the variance explained). The eight items of the baseline C-eHEALS showed high item–total correlation ranging from 0.622 to 0.831, which demonstrates a more valid indication of eHealth literacy skills. Table A1 displays the factor analysis of the C-eHEALS with factor loading and item–total correlation results (Appendix A).

The inter-item correlation matrix assessed the strength of the eight-item C-eHEALS as well as the direction of the relationship between the two variables for reliability. We found high and positive correlation values, indicating that the items measure the same characteristic. Several factor loadings exceeding 0.7 were indicative of a well-defined structure (e.g., items 2 and 3, and items 4 and 5). Variables with correlation values in the range of 0.3 to 0.4 meet the minimum level for interpretation of structure, values > 0.5 are considered practically significant, and values of 0.7 are considered highly correlated [34,43,44]. Overall, eight factor loadings were classified as excellent (between 0.6 and 0.8). Table 2 shows the baseline eight-item inter-item correlation of the C-eHEALS ($p < 0.001$).

Table 2. Inter-item correlation of the C-eHEALS.

Item	1	2	3	4	5	6	7	8
1. I know what health resources are available on the Internet	1							
2. I know where to find helpful health resources on the Internet	0.839	1						
3. I know how to find helpful resources on the Internet	0.780	0.869	1					
4. I know how to use the Internet to answer my questions about health	0.708	0.764	0.777	1				
5. I know how to use the health information I find on the Internet to help me	0.703	0.760	0.754	0.852	1			
6. I have the skills I need to evaluate the health resources I find on the Internet	0.698	0.721	0.722	0.709	0.73	1		
7. I can tell high quality health resources from low quality health resources on the Internet	0.635	0.660	0.668	0.635	0.656	0.725	1	
8. I feel confident in using information from the Internet to make health decisions	0.638	0.671	0.688	0.669	0.706	0.769	0.73	1

Note: Significant at the $p < 0.001$ probability level for all cells (two-tailed test).

3.2. The C-eHEALS Model

Principal components analysis produced a single-factor solution, and confirmatory factor analysis (CFA) for the baseline eight-item model fit demonstrated high indices (goodness of fit index [GFI] = 0.989, comparative fit index [CFI] = 0.999, root mean square error of approximation [RMSEA] = 0.022, Akaike information criterion [AIC] = 61.292) [43]. Consistent with prior research (e.g., [17,35]) the CFA of the extended C-eHEALS showed a better model fit compared to the original model (GFI = 0.830, CFI = 917, RMSEA = 0.182, AIC = 63.904). Figure 1 depicts the revised conceptual model for the C-eHEALS by AMOS.

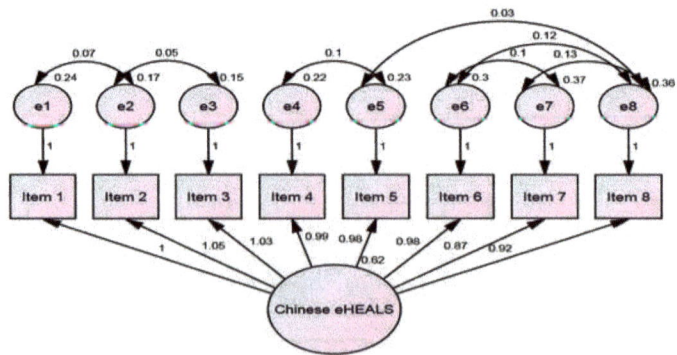

Figure 1. Conceptual model for the relationship between the baseline 8-item of C-eHEALS.

3.3. Sample Characteristics

The respondents were aged 18–75 years (mean = 28.98 years; SD = 15.53), predominantly male (53.1%; $n = 187$), from the non-Guangdong area (63.2%; $n = 223$) and college-educated (67.6%; $n = 238$).

The participants all had chronic conditions. However, the perceived health status was reported as good or very good (41.25%, n = 148). In addition, 33 respondents reported that their perceived health status was poor or not good (9.38%). Specifically, 31 respondents reported allergies (8.81%), followed by high blood sugar/pressure (8.24%, n = 29), other chronic diseases not listed (6.82%, n = 24) and cardiovascular, metabolic diseases or cancer (2.84%, n = 10).

From the baseline eight-item C-eHEALS, the group comprising participants aged ≥ 55 years had higher scores (mean = 30.80, SD = 7.04) than the other age groups. A higher mean score was also recorded from male respondents (mean = 29.19, SD = 6.63), post-graduates (mean = 29.43, SD = 5.77) and student respondents (mean = 30.60, SD = 5.50). Table 3 shows the socioeconomic characteristics of the sample and the eight-item C-eHEALS results.

Table 3. Socioeconomic analysis and level of eHealth literacy in China.

Variables		n (%)	8-Item Score
		352 (100)	Mean ± SD
Sex	Male	187 (53.1)	29.19 ± 6.63
	Female	165 (46.9)	28.75 ± 6.27
Age	18–25	124 (35.2)	29.84 ± 6.79
	26–35	137 (38.9)	28.64 ± 6.26
	36–45	56 (15.9)	28.39 ± 6.16
	46–55	30 (8.5)	27.80 ± 6.27
	Over 55	5 (1.4)	30.80 ± 7.04
Education	Primary & secondary school	2 (0.6)	20.00 ± 5.66
	Junior high	9 (2.6)	28.67 ± 3.64
	High school	22 (6.3)	25.73 ± 7.67
	College or bachelor	238 (67.6)	29.22 ± 6.55
	Master degree or above	81 (23.0)	29.43 ± 5.77
Resident ***	Guangdong	129 (36.6)	28.63 ± 6.60
	Others	223 (63.2)	29.46 ± 6.48
Occupation	Business	180 (51.5)	28.74 ± 6.54
	Student	63 (17.9)	30.60 ± 5.50
	Self-employed	34 (9.7)	29.60 ± 6.45
	Public servant	29 (8.2)	29.96 ± 4.82
	Clinicians	27 (7.7)	26.25 ± 5.33
	Others	19 (5.4)	24.95 ± 9.36
Income (RMB)	less than 1000	55 (15.6)	29.35 ± 5.55
	1000–3000	50 (14.2)	29.32 ± 6.69
	3001–5000	85 (24.1)	28.61 ± 6.94
	5001–7000	75 (21.3)	28.59 ± 6.49
	7001 & above	87 (24.7)	29.26 ± 6.44

Note: *** significant at the $p < 0.001$ probability level.

3.4. Cluster Analysis of eHealth Literacy

The K-means cluster analysis showed that the high eHealth literacy group had the most frequent agreement regarding the function of sending and receiving emails (61.9%, n = 218), while the low–eHealth literacy group had the capability to attach files in email (66.8%, n = 235). There were significant differences in the computer skill items between the low- and high-eHealth literacy groups (x^2 = 615.59, df = 9, $p < 0.001$). Compared to the low-eHealth literacy group, a relatively higher percentage of the high eHealth literacy group worried about computer viruses (61.1%, n = 215), were capable of using the Internet to search for information (56.0%, n = 197) and could find information online (52.6%, n = 185). Table 4 lists a comparison of working knowledge of computer skills and technology literacy categorized in terms of low- and high-eHealth literacy groups ($p < 0.001$).

Table 4. Reported computer and technology skills of the C-eHEALS by groups of low and high eHealth literacy.

Item	Low eHealth n	%	High eHealth n	%
1. Able to attach files in email	235	66.8	71	20.2
2. I worry about computer virus	62	17.6	215	61.1
3. My computer skills are better than my peers	43	12.2	73	20.7
4. Have knowledge about intellectual property	33	9.4	98	27.8
5. Can use a computer to do my work	25	7.1	159	45.2
6. Know how to use a word processor	24	6.8	160	45.5
7. Can send and receive email	20	5.7	218	61.9
8. Can use the Web to search for information	19	5.4	197	56.0
9. Can find the file on my computer after downloading	19	5.4	174	49.4
10. Can find information on the Web	12	3.4	185	52.6

Compared to the low-eHealth literacy group, the high eHealth literacy group used many eHealth resources to access a greater variety of eHealth content. The reported use of media and information channels related to the C-eHEALS between the low- and high-eHealth literacy groups was significantly different ($x^2 = 703.87$, df = 8, $p < 0.001$). To repeat with pre-determined numbers of three clusters within the properties of the data, the K-mean cluster analysis showed that the most frequent use of resources was online encyclopaedias (high-eHealth literacy group: 67.3%, n = 237) and face-to-face inquiry (low-eHealth literacy group: 50.9%, n = 218). In addition, social media such as QQ were important to the high eHealth literacy group (66.5%, n = 234), while the low-eHealth literacy group used mobile phone apps frequently. Table 5 shows a comparison of C-eHEALS media and information channels categorized in terms of low- and high-eHealth literacy groups ($p < 0.001$).

Table 5. Reported media and information channels of the C-eHEALS by groups of low and high eHealth literacy.

Item	Low eHealth n	%	High eHealth n	%
1. Face-to-face inquiry	179	50.9	73	20.7
2. Mobile phone apps	72	48.9	19	5.4
3. Specific health websites	167	47.4	28	8.0
4. Hospital website	160	45.5	27	7.7
5. Online forum	125	35.5	37	10.5
6. Websites with instant feedback	77	21.9	205	58.2
7. Social media (e.g., QQ)	65	18.5	234	66.5
8. Online Encyclopedia	45	12.8	237	67.3
9. Search engine (e.g., Baidu)	19	5.4	155	44.0

A Pearson product–moment correlation coefficient was computed to assess the relationship between C-eHEALS score and media use. The correlation coefficient for eHealth literacy and computer skill scores was 0.44 ($p < 0.001$). There was a significant association between the C-eHEALS score and personal computer use ($r = 0.14$, $p < 0.01$) and between the C-eHEALS score and mobile phone use ($r = 0.22$, $p < 0.001$). In addition, the amount of time spent online correlated significantly with the respondents' eHealth literacy scores ($r = 0.38$, $p < 0.01$). Respondents who used the Internet for more than 3.1–5 h per day had the highest eHealth literacy scores.

A chi-square test of independence was performed to examine the relationship between the C-eHEALS scores and online behaviour, taking into consideration information, media and technological literacy. The most significant difference was in the C-eHEALS score and using a mobile phone for online surfing (x^2 = 370.47, df = 284, p < 0.001). A higher frequency of mobile phone use for going online was correlated with a higher level of eHealth literacy. There was a significant relationship between the C-eHEALS score and time spent on social media (x^2 = 459.90, df = 284, p < 0.001). More time spent on social media was correlated with a higher eHealth literacy score. However, there was no significant difference in C-eHEALS scores and use of a personal computer to go online (x^2 = 289.61, df = 284, p = 0.40).

Previous eHEALS studies have examined the association between sociodemographic variables and the use of electronic devices on eHealth literacy levels (e.g., [32,39,42,45]). The present C-eHEALS findings provide further evidence for the idea that eHealth literacy levels are associated with demographic variables such as age and education level. A statistically significant difference was found between eHealth literacy score and age (x^2 = 326.80, df = 284, p < 0.05) and between eHealth literacy score and education (x^2 = 455.00, df = 284, p < 0.001). However, sex, occupation, income, health status and residency were not predictive of the respondents' eHealth literacy scores. These results could be subject to bias because of the non-representative nature of the respondents.

4. Discussion

The C-eHEALS uses the concept of eHealth to assess patients' comfort and skill in using information technology for health purposes. One of the results supports the idea that the use of computer skills increases health information. To be consistent with previous studies (e.g., [34,35,37,42]), the C-eHEALS is a foundational skill set, a critical predictor of preventive health measures and a validated determinant of various health information-searching behaviours.

The C-eHEALS results also provide an analytical measurement of health literacy by encouraging closer attention to patient age. In line with previous studies (e.g., [17,34,40,45]), the one-factor structure of the C-eHEALS is reliable and internally consistent, with predictive validity among patients in China. The C-eHEALS emerges as an effective screening tool for examining and predicting eHealth use and literacy in clinical settings.

4.1. Low and High eHealth Literacy

Developed in China, the C-eHEALS is comparable to the eHEALS in terms of psychometric properties and predictive ability for patients. In the present study, men, respondents aged > 55 years, respondents with low incomes and respondents who frequently search the Internet had higher C-eHEALS scores. The eHealth user profiles were very different from those in previous studies in developed countries (e.g., [17,37]). However, similarities were also found among the high-health literacy group in the present study as compared to those in previous studies (e.g., [19,33]). The possible explanations are that patients with high C-eHEALS scores tended to use more search strategies to access all types of information online while scrutinizing information more carefully than the respondents with low C-eHEALS scores. The extensive use of the Internet for obtaining health information has highlighted the existence of a high-eHealth literacy group that demonstrates that technologies crucially affect its computer skills. In comparison, we observed that low eHealth literacy levels are potentially associated with poor skills in using a word processor, downloading files, finding health information online, and experiencing difficulty in receiving help from online sources. In summary, high eHealth literacy levels are positively associated with success in using computer skills to find health information and services online.

We found that two items of media and information study (i.e., face-to-face inquiry and websites that provide instant messaging features) were equally important for both the low- and high-eHealth literacy groups. The online resource primarily involved texting, posting, and instant messaging with chat acronyms. To some extent, this could rebut the argument that there is an association between high eHealth literacy and low health literacy in China [45]. The justification relies on the fact that respondents, regardless of eHealth literacy level, considered both face-to-face communication and communication over websites important. In summary, eHealth literacy allows people to acquire the necessary online and offline skills to make informed health decisions.

Those with low eHealth literacy had a high self-perceived interest in face-to-face inquiry, mobile phone app usage, and browsing specific health websites. In comparison, those with high eHealth literacy reported a high use of online encyclopaedias, social media (QQ) and websites with instant messaging communication capabilities. However, the manner in which the low and high eHealth-literate adults perceive the trustworthiness of health information from online health communication channels and information sources is beyond the scope of the present study.

4.2. Limitations

Several limitations of this study should be addressed. First, a variety of health-related information and services in China may be found on popular social media sites such as WeChat, Sina Weibo, or Tudou Youku, or on specific health-related platforms (e.g., Keep) [8]. Comprehensive analysis of the current diversity of online media to address hybrid social media issues was not performed. Second, the current eHealth resources are considered merely a means for enhancing human activities or as a substitute in a resource-poor health care environment. Nonetheless, the potentially negative influence and impact of digital media sources and content on users should also be examined [8,18]. Third, we evaluated the properties and the development of the C-eHEALS in a patient population in a selected focus hospital. The cross-sectional design of our study should obtain more sufficient information from patients in a more diverse population from other provincial-level administrative units of mainland China to validate the reliability and validity of the scale. Additional investigations will be required to provide empirical evidence of the generalizability of the scale to other Chinese population samples.

5. Conclusions

C-eHEALS is a valid and reliable measure of self-reported eHealth literacy among chronic disease patients in China. This information is timely because it implies that health care providers can use the C-eHEALS to screen eHealth literacy skills and empower patients with chronic diseases with online resources. Moreover, a strong association between eHealth literacy level, media information use, and computer literacy was found. To be specific, Internet-based technologies crucially affected decision-making skills in the high eHealth literacy group while the emphasis of face-to-face inquiry for obtaining health information was important in the low eHealth literacy group. Although Internet and other digital technologies mediate eHealth communication and health promotion efforts, extensive research is required to determine whether the technical advantages of eHealth communication can be effective within the social reality of the diverse means by which people communicate and perceive reliable health content. An improved follow-up implementation using controlled intervention for evaluating web based eHealth programs in a specific clinical environment should also be considered Increased eHealth literacy should be examined as an important determinant of a range of health-related behaviours and an important predictor in the utilization of preventative health measures.

Chinese patients frequently access health information via social media, online encyclopaedias and websites that provide instant messaging features. The present study reflects the influence and features of the aforementioned online resources that facilitate health information acquisition. One of the practical implications is that health care providers must be aware of their patients' eHealth literacy levels to maximize the benefits of eHealth technologies in the digital era. Furthermore, the knowledge and skillsets required for eHealth literacy must be increased by improving certain levels of computer competency.

Author Contributions: P.J.S. conceived and designed the research; A.C. compiled, analyzed the data, and wrote the original draft preparation. P.J.S. and A.C. both revised and approved the final manuscript.

Funding: This research was funded by University of Macau grant MYRG2015-0123-FSS.

Acknowledgments: The author would like to thank the participants for their response, and anonymous reviewers and journal editors for their valuable comments.

Conflicts of Interest: The authors declare no conflict of interest. The founding sponsor had no role in the design of the study; in the collection, analyses, or interpretation of data; in the writing of the manuscript, and in the decision to publish the results.

Appendix A

Table A1. Factor analysis of the C-eHEALS with factor loading and item–total correlation results.

Item	Factor Loading	Communalities	Item-Total Correlation	α, If Item Deleted
1. I know what health resources are available on the Internet	1	0.744	0.730	0.949
2. I know where to find helpful health resources on the Internet	0.839	0.819	0.831	0.945
3. I know how to find helpful resources on the Internet	0.780	0.812	0.798	0.946
4. I know how to use the Internet to answer my questions about health	0.708	0.773	0.772	0.947
5. I know how to use the health information I find on the Internet to help me	0.703	0.785	0.777	0.947
6. I have the skills I need to evaluate the health resources I find on the Internet	0.698	0.759	0.713	0.948
7. I can tell high quality health resources from low quality health resources on the Internet	0.635	0.665	0.622	0.952
8. I feel confident in using information from the Internet to make health decisions	0.638	0.707	0.681	0.950

Note: eigenvalue = 4.85; cumulative variance explained 75.81%.

References

1. Chari, R.; Warsh, J.; Ketterer, T.; Hossain, J.; Sharif, I. Association between health literacy and child and adolescent obesity. *Patient Educ. Couns.* **2014**, *94*, 61–66. [CrossRef] [PubMed]
2. Nelson, M.C.; Story, M.; Larson, N.I.; Neumark-Sztainer, D.; Lytle, L.A. Emerging adulthood and college-aged youth: An overlooked age for weight-related behavior change. *Obesity* **2008**, *16*, 2205–2211. [CrossRef] [PubMed]
3. Frisch, A.L.; Camerini, L.; Diviani, N.; Schulz, P.J. Defining and measuring health literacy: How can we profit from other literacy domains? *Health Promot. Int.* **2012**, *27*, 117–126. [CrossRef] [PubMed]
4. Ishikawa, H.; Takeuchi, T.; Yano, E. Measuring functional, communicative, and critical health literacy among diabetic patients. *Diabetes Care* **2008**, *31*, 874–879. [CrossRef] [PubMed]
5. Liu, Y.B.; Liu, L.; Li, Y.F.; Chen, Y.L. Relationship between health literacy, health-related behaviors and health status: A survey of elderly Chinese. *Int. J. Environ. Res. Public Health* **2015**, *12*, 9714–9725. [CrossRef] [PubMed]
6. Berkman, N.D.; Davis, T.C.; McCormack, L. Health literacy: What is it? *J. Health Commun.* **2010**, *15*, 9–19. [CrossRef] [PubMed]
7. Howard, D.H.; Gazmararian, J.; Parker, R.M. The impact of low health literacy on the medical costs of medicare managed care enrollees. *Am. J. Med.* **2005**, *118*, 371–377. [CrossRef] [PubMed]
8. Zhang, X.T.; Wen, D.; Liang, J.; Lei, J.B. How the public uses social media wechat to obtain health information in China: A survey study. *BMC Med. Inform. Decis. Mak.* **2017**, *17*, 71–100. [CrossRef] [PubMed]
9. Tennant, B.; Stellefson, M.; Dodd, V.; Chaney, B.; Chaney, D.; Paige, S.; Alber, J. Ehealth literacy and web 2.0 health information seeking behaviors among baby boomers and older adults. *J. Med. Internet Res.* **2015**, *17*, e70.
10. Tse, M.M.; Choi, K.C.; Leung, R.S. E-health for older people: The use of technology in health promotion. *CyberPsychol. Behav.* **2008**, *11*, 475–479. [PubMed]
11. Bodie, G.D.; Dutta, M.J. Understanding health literacy for strategic health marketing: Ehealth literacy, health disparities, and the digital divide. *Health Mark. Q.* **2008**, *25*, 175–203. [CrossRef] [PubMed]

12. Cline, R.J.; Haynes, K.M. Consumer health information seeking on the internet: The state of the art. *Health Educ. Res.* **2001**, *16*, 671–692. [CrossRef] [PubMed]
13. Lee, M. China's Nearly 700 Million Internet Users Are Hot for Online Finance. Forbes. Available online: https://www.forbes.com/sites/melanieleest/2016/01/25/chinas-nearly-700-million-internet-users-are-hot-for-online-finance/ (accessed on 26 January 2016).
14. Oh, H.; Rizo, C.; Enkin, M.; Jadad, A.; Powell, J.; Pagliari, C. What is ehealth: A systematic review of published definitions. *J. Med. Internet Res.* **2005**, *7*, e1. [CrossRef] [PubMed]
15. Ghaddar, S.F.; Valerio, M.A.; Garcia, C.M.; Hansen, L. Adolescent health literacy: The importance of credible sources for online health information. *J. Sch. Health* **2012**, *82*, 28–36. [CrossRef] [PubMed]
16. Neter, E.; Brainin, E. Ehealth literacy: Extending the digital divide to the realm of health information. *J. Med. Internet Res.* **2012**, *14*, e19. [CrossRef] [PubMed]
17. Norman, C.D.; Skinner, H.A. eHEALS: The ehealth literacy scale. *J. Med. Internet Res.* **2006**, *8*, 3–31. [CrossRef] [PubMed]
18. Norman, C.D.; Skinner, H.A.; Ronson, B.; Simms, M. Ehealth literacy: Essential skills for consumer health in a networked world. *J. Med. Internet Res.* **2006**, *8*, e9. [CrossRef] [PubMed]
19. Mackert, M.; Champlin, S.E.; Holton, A.; Muñoz, I.I.; Damásio, M.J. Ehealth and health literacy: A research methodology review. *J. Comput.-Mediat. Commun.* **2014**, *19*, 516–528. [CrossRef]
20. Norman, C. Ehealth literacy 2.0: Problems and opportunities with an evolving concept. *J. Med. Internet Res.* **2011**, *13*, e125.
21. Manganello, J.A. Health literacy and adolescents: A framework and agenda for future research. *Health Educ. Res.* **2008**, *23*, 840–847. [CrossRef] [PubMed]
22. Pan, F.C.; Su, C.L.; Chen, C.H. Development of a health literacy scale for Chinese-speaking adults in Taiwan. *Int. J. Biol. Sci.* **2010**, *6*, 150–156.
23. Pleasant, A.; McKinney, J.; Rikard, R.V. Health literacy measurement: A proposed research agenda. *J. Health Commun.* **2011**, *16*, 11–21. [CrossRef] [PubMed]
24. Petrič, G.; Atanasova, S.; Kamin, T. Ill literates or illiterates? Investigating the ehealth literacy of users of online health communities. *J. Med. Internet Res.* **2017**, *19*, e331. [PubMed]
25. Chan, C.V.; Kaufman, D.R. A framework for characterizing ehealth literacy demands and barriers. *J. Med. Internet Res.* **2011**, *3*, e94. [CrossRef] [PubMed]
26. Chan, J.; Leung, A.; Chiang, V.C.; Li, H.C.; Wong, E.M.; Liu, A.N.; Chan, S.S. A pilot project to build e-health literacy among university students in Hong Kong. In Proceedings of the Positioning the Profession: The Tenth International Congress on Medical Librarianship, Brisbane, Australia, 31 August–4 September 2009; pp. 1–15.
27. Hove, T.; Paek, H.-J.; Isaacson, T. Using adolescent ehealth literacy to weigh trust in commercial web sites. *J. Advert. Res.* **2011**, *51*, 524–537. [CrossRef]
28. Paek, H.J.; Hove, T. Social cognitive factors and perceived social influences that improve adolescent ehealth literacy. *Health Commun.* **2012**, *27*, 727–737. [CrossRef] [PubMed]
29. Percheski, C.; Hargittai, E. Health information-seeking in the digital age. *J. Am. Coll. Health* **2011**, *59*, 379–386. [CrossRef] [PubMed]
30. Skinner, H.; Biscope, S.; Poland, B.; Goldberg, E.; Gray, N.; Richardson, C. How adolescents use technology for health information: Implications for health professionals from focus group studies. *J. Med. Internet Res.* **2003**, *5*, e32. [CrossRef] [PubMed]
31. Paramio Perez, G.; Almagro, B.J.; Hernando Gomez, A.; Aguaded Gomez, J.I. Validation of the ehealth literacy scale (eHEALS) in Spanish university students. *Rev. Esp. Salud Publ.* **2015**, *89*, 329–338. [CrossRef] [PubMed]
32. Koo, M.; Norman, C.D.; Chang, H.M. Psychometric evaluation of a Chinese version of the ehealth literacy scale (eHEALS) in school age children. *Int. Electron. J. Health Educ.* **2012**, *15*, 29–36.
33. Paige, S.R.; Krieger, J.L.; Stellefson, M.; Alber, J.M. Ehealth literacy in chronic disease patients: An item response theory analysis of the ehealth literacy scale (eHEALS). *Patient Educ. Couns.* **2017**, *100*, 320–326. [CrossRef] [PubMed]
34. Soellner, R.; Huber, S.; Reder, M. The concept of ehealth literacy and its measurement: German translation of the eHEALS. *J. Media Psychol. Theor. Methods Appl.* **2014**, *26*, 29–38. [CrossRef]
35. Mitsutake, S.; Shibata, A.; Ishii, K.; Okazaki, K.; Oka, K. Developing Japanese version of the ehealth literacy scale (eHEALS). *[Nihon koshu eisei zasshi] Jpn. J. Public Health* **2011**, *58*, 361–371.

36. Van der Vaart, R.; van Deursen, A.J.; Drossaert, C.H.; Taal, E.; van Dijk, J.A.; van de Laar, M.A. Does the ehealth literacy scale (eHEALS) measure what it intends to measure? Validation of a Dutch version of the eHEALS in two adult populations. *J. Med. Internet Res.* **2011**, *13*, e86. [PubMed]
37. Diviani, N.; Dima, A.L.; Schulz, P.J. A psychometric analysis of the Italian version of the ehealth literacy scale using item response and classical test theory methods. *J. Med. Internet Res.* **2017**, *19*, e114. [CrossRef] [PubMed]
38. Hyde, L.L.; Boyes, A.W.; Evans, T.J.; Mackenzie, L.J.; Sanson-Fisher, R. Three-factor structure of the ehealth literacy scale among magnetic resonance imaging and computed tomography outpatients: A confirmatory factor analysis. *JMIR Hum. Factors* **2018**, *5*, e6. [CrossRef] [PubMed]
39. Chung, S.Y.; Nahm, E.S. Testing reliability and validity of the ehealth literacy scale (eHEALS) for older adults recruited online. *CIN Comput. Inform. Nurs.* **2015**, *33*, 150–156. [CrossRef] [PubMed]
40. Tomás, C.C.; Queirós, P.J.P.; Ferreira, T.D.J.R. Analysis of the psychometric properties of the Portuguese version of an ehealth literacy assessment tool. *Rev. Enferm. Ref.* **2014**, *4*, 19–28. [CrossRef]
41. Karnoe, A.; Kayser, L. How is eHealth literacy measured and what do the measurements tell us? A systematic review. *Knowl. Manag. E-Learn. Int. J.* **2015**, *7*, 576–600.
42. Nguyen, J.; Moorhouse, M.; Curbow, B.; Christie, J.; Walsh-Childers, K.; Islam, S. Construct validity of the ehealth literacy scale (eHEALS) among two adult populations: A rasch analysis. *JMIR Public Health Surveill.* **2016**, *2*, e24. [CrossRef] [PubMed]
43. Hutcheson, G.D.; Sofroniou, N. *The Multivariate Social Scientist: Introductory Statistics Using Generalized Linear Models*; Sage: Newcastle upon Tyne, UK, 1999.
44. Tsai, T.I.; Lee, S.Y.D.; Tsai, Y.W.; Kuo, K.N. Methodology and validation of health literacy scale development in Taiwan. *J. Health Commun.* **2011**, *16*, 50–61. [CrossRef] [PubMed]
45. Wu, Y.; Wang, L.; Cai, Z.; Bao, L.; Ai, P.; Ai, Z. Prevalence and risk factors of low health literacy: A community-based study in Shanghai, China. *Int. J. Environ. Res. Public Health* **2017**, *14*, 628–638. [CrossRef] [PubMed]

© 2018 by the authors. Licensee MDPI, Basel, Switzerland. This article is an open access article distributed under the terms and conditions of the Creative Commons Attribution (CC BY) license (http://creativecommons.org/licenses/by/4.0/).

Article

Mental Health Literacy in Young Adults: Adaptation and Psychometric Properties of the Mental Health Literacy Questionnaire

Pedro Dias [1,2], Luísa Campos [1,2,*], Helena Almeida [3] and Filipa Palha [1,2,4]

1. Faculty of Education and Psychology, Universidade Católica Portuguesa, Rua Diogo Botelho, 1327, 4169-005 Porto, Portugal; pdias@porto.ucp.pt (P.D.); fpalha@porto.ucp.pt (F.P.)
2. Research Center for Human Development, Rua Diogo Botelho, 1327, 4169-005 Porto, Portugal
3. Faculty of Education and Psychology, Universidade Católica Portuguesa, Rua Diogo Botelho, 1327, 4169-005 Porto, Portugal; helenamfalmeida@hotmail.com
4. ENCONTRAR+SE—Association for the Promotion of Mental Health, Rua Professor Melo Adrião 106, 4100-340 Porto, Portugal
* Correspondence: mcampos@porto.ucp.pt

Received: 30 April 2018; Accepted: 18 June 2018; Published: 23 June 2018

Abstract: Mental health literacy (MHL) is considered a prerequisite for early recognition and intervention in mental disorders, and for this reason, it has become a focus of research over the past few decades. Assessing this construct is relevant for identifying knowledge gaps and erroneous beliefs concerning mental health issues, to inform the development of interventions aimed at promoting mental health literacy as well as the evaluation of these interventions. Recently, we developed a new self-reporting measure (MHLq) for assessing mental health literacy in young people (12–14 years-old), meeting the need to assess MHL from a comprehensive perspective of the construct instead of focusing on a restricted number of mental disorders or specific dimensions (e.g., knowledge concerning specific disorders; stigma). The present study aimed to adapt the MHLq for the young adult population and to examine its psychometric properties, according to the following steps: (1) item adaptation, using a think aloud procedure (n = 5); (2) data collection (n = 356, aged between 18 and 25 years old; and (3) psychometric analyses (exploratory factor analysis and internal consistency analysis). The final version of the questionnaire included 29 items (total scale α = 0.84), organized by four dimensions: (1) knowledge of mental health problems (α = 0.74); (2) erroneous beliefs/stereotypes (α = 0.72); (3) help-seeking and first aid skills (α = 0.71); and (4) self-help strategies (α = 0.60). The results suggest that the MHLq-adult form is a practical, valid, and reliable screening tool for identifying gaps in knowledge, beliefs, and behavioral intentions related to mental health and mental disorders, planning promotion programs, and evaluating intervention effectiveness.

Keywords: mental health literacy questionnaire; psychometric properties; young adults

1. Introduction

Mental health literacy, a concept introduced by Jorm and colleagues [1], was first defined as "knowledge and beliefs about mental disorders which aid their recognition, management or prevention" (p. 182). A recent update on this concept included the ability to provide support to someone presenting with a mental health problem, that is, first aid skills [2]. Accordingly, mental health literacy is not limited to having knowledge as knowledge is linked to beliefs that together determine attitudes (e.g., resistance to seek professional help).

The assessment of knowledge and beliefs related to mental health problems allows for the identification of stigma associated to those problems, which is considered to be one of the main barriers to early recognition and intervention [3]. Furthermore, assessing the knowledge gaps and erroneous beliefs concerning mental health issues enables the development of interventions aimed at promoting mental health literacy [4,5] as well as the evaluation of these interventions.

Several instruments have been developed to assess mental health literacy, the stigma associated with mental health problems, and the related constructs, e.g., the interview used for the Australian national survey of youth and parents [6]; the questionnaire used to evaluate the program, "Crazy? So what!" [4]; the instrument developed under the scope of the Mind Matters project [7]; the Attribution Questionnaire [8]; The Attitudes to Mental Illness Questionnaire [9]; and the Mental Health Knowledge Schedule, MAKS [10]. As we have pointed out in a previous article [11], most of the available instruments either assess specific dimensions of mental health literacy (e.g., knowledge; stigmatizing perceptions) or specific mental health problems or diagnoses (e.g., schizophrenia; depression). Taking into account the updated construct of MHL, and the abovementioned limitations of previous measures, there is a need for new instruments to provide a more up-to-date assessment of this construct.

Recently, we developed a new self-reporting measure (MHLq) for assessing mental health literacy in young people (12–14 years-old), meeting the need to assess it from a comprehensive perspective of the construct instead of focusing on a restricted number of mental disorders or specific dimensions. The questionnaire includes 33 items, organized in three subscales: first aid skills and help seeking; knowledge/stereotypes; and self-help strategies. The MHLq showed good internal consistency and excellent test-retest reliability. It is a practical, valid, and reliable tool for identifying gaps in knowledge, beliefs, and behavioral intentions in large samples, allowing the development and evaluation of interventions aimed at promoting mental health in young people [11].

This article presents the process of adapting the MHLq for young adults and the study of its psychometric properties through two studies. Study 1 looked at the adaptation of the MHLq for the young adult population, and Study 2 looked at the psychometric properties of the MHLq-young adult form. Figure 1 presents a flowchart of the study design.

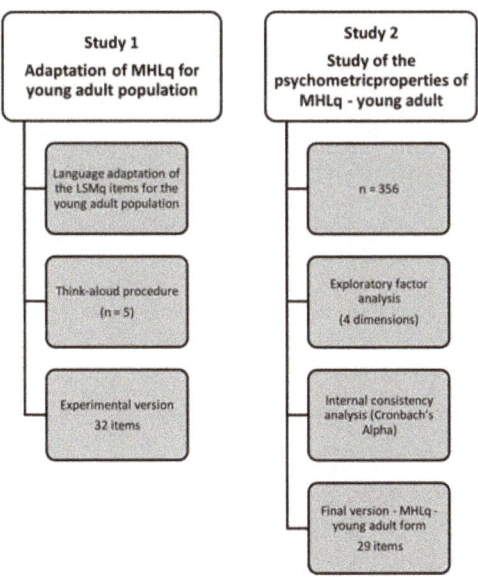

Figure 1. Development of adaptation and study of psychometric properties of the mental health literacy questionnaire (MHLq)-young adult.

2. Study 1: Adaptation of MHLq-Young Adult Population

Study 1 followed two stages: (1) language adaptation of the MHLq [11] items to the young adult population; and (2) the think-aloud procedure.

2.1. Language Adaptation of the MHLq Items to the Young Adult Population

The research team revised the phrasing of both the socio-demographic form and the MHLq items (since the questionnaire was developed for a target population of young people) by replacing it by more formal speech (e.g., in the sociodemographic form, the question "Are you a girl?" in the MHLq was changed to "Gender" in the MHLq-young adults form), and other questions were also added (e.g., marital status, academic qualifications, and profession/occupation).

2.2. Think-Aloud Procedure

The second stage of the adaptation of the MHLq was a think-aloud procedure with a group of five participants aged between 22 and 35 years old; two females and three males; four postgraduate students and one professional technician in the area of multimedia. Informed consent was given by all participants. All of the 32 items were presented individually to this group, and participants were asked to comment on the items based on item interpretation and suggested rephrasing for increasing their suitability for the target age group. All comments and suggestions made by the participants were registered by the research team.

2.3. Results

Based on the team's revision and the think-aloud procedure, 15 items were rephrased, two items were removed from the questionnaire because their content was redundant when compared to another item, and two items were added to the young adult form, replacing one item in the original form. Table 1 presents the changes from the MHLq to the experimental version of the MHLq-young adult form.

Table 1. MHLq items, MHLq-young adult version Portuguese and English version.

Mhlq	Mhlq-Young Adult (Original Version in Portuguese)	Mhlq-Young Adult (English Version)
If a friend of mine developed a mental disorder, I would offer her/him support.	Se uma pessoa próxima de mim estivesse com uma perturbação mental, oferecia-me para ajudar.	If someone close to me had a mental disorder, I would offer him/her help.
Physical exercise helps to improve mental health.	A prática de exercício físico contribui para uma boa saúde mental.	Physical exercise contributes to good mental health.
A person with depression feels very miserable.	Uma pessoa com depressão sente-se muito infeliz.	A person with depression feels very miserable (unchanged item).
People with schizophrenia usually have delusions (e.g., they may believe they are constantly being followed and observed).	Em casos de esquizofrenia, é comum as pessoas terem ideias delirantes (p. ex., podem acreditar que estão a ser constantemente seguidas e observadas).	People with schizophrenia usually have delusions (e.g., they may believe they are constantly being followed and observed) (unchanged item).
If I had a mental disorder I would seek my family's help.	Se eu estivesse com uma perturbação mental, procuraria ajuda de pessoas da minha família.	If I had a mental disorder I would seek my relatives' help.
If a friend of mine developed a mental disorder, I would encourage her/him to look for a psychologist.	Se uma pessoa próxima de mim estivesse com uma perturbação mental, eu encorajava-a a procurar um psicólogo.	If someone close to me had a mental disorder, I would encourage her/him to look for a psychologist.
Mental disorders don't affect people's behaviors.	Uma perturbação mental não afeta o comportamento.	Mental disorders don't affect people's behaviors (unchanged item).
If a friend of mine developed a mental disorder, I would talk to her/his parents.	-	Removed
Good sleep helps to improve mental health.	Dormir bem contribui para uma boa saúde mental.	Sleeping well contributes to good mental health.
If I had a mental disorder I would seek professional help (psychologist and /or psychiatrist.	Se eu estivesse com uma perturbação mental, procuraria a ajuda de um psicólogo. Se eu estivesse com uma perturbação mental, procuraria a ajuda de um médico psiquiatra.	If I had a mental disorder I would seek a psychologist's help (new item). If I had a mental disorder I would seek a psychiatrist's help (new item).
A person with anxiety disorder may panic in situations that she/he fears.	Uma pessoa com perturbação de ansiedade pode entrar em pânico perante situações de que tenha medo.	A person with anxiety disorder may panic in situations that she/he fears (unchanged item).
People with mental disorders come from families with little money.	As pessoas com perturbação mental são de famílias com baixos recursos económicos.	People with mental disorders belong to low-income families.
If a friend of mine developed a mental disorder, I would listen to her/him without judging or criticizing.	Se uma pessoa próxima de mim estivesse com uma perturbação mental, eu ouvia-a sem julgar ou criticar.	If someone close to me had a mental disorder, I would listen to her/him without judging or criticizing.
Alcohol use may cause mental disorders.	O consumo de álcool pode causar perturbações mentais.	Alcohol use may cause mental disorders (unchanged item).
Mental disorders don't affect people's feelings.	Uma perturbação mental não afeta os sentimentos.	Mental disorders don't affect people's feelings (unchanged item).
The sooner mental disorders are identified and treated, the better.	Quanto mais cedo forem identificadas e tratacas as perturbações mentais, melhor.	The sooner mental disorders are identified and treated, the better (unchanged item).
Only adults have mental disorders.	Só os adultos têm perturbações mentais.	Only adults have mental disorders (unchanged item).

Table 1. Cont.

Mhlq	Mhlq-Young Adult (Original Version in Portuguese)	Mhlq-Young Adult (English Version)
Only adults have mental disorders.	Só os adultos têm perturbações mentais.	Only adults have mental disorders (unchanged item).
Brain malfunctioning may cause the development of mental disorders.	Alterações no funcionamento cerebral podem levar ao aparecimento de perturbações mentais.	Changes in brain function may lead to the onset of mental disorders.
If a friend of mine developed a mental disorder, I would encourage her/him to get medical support.	Se uma pessoa próxima de mim estivesse com uma perturbação mental, eu encorajava-a a procurar um médico psiquiatra.	If someone close to me had a mental disorder, I would encourage her/him to see a psychiatrist.
If I had a mental disorder I would seek my friends' help	Se eu estivesse com uma perturbação mental procuraria a ajuda de amigos.	If I had a mental disorder I would seek friends' help.
Having a balanced diet helps to improve mental health.	Uma alimentação equilibrada contribui para uma boa saúde mental.	A balanced diet contributes to good mental health.
One of the symptoms of depression is the loss of interest or pleasure in most things.	Um dos sintomas da depressão é a falta de interesse ou prazer pela maioria das coisas.	One of the symptoms of depression is the loss of interest or pleasure in most things (unchanged item).
A person with anxiety disorder avoids situations that may cause her/him distress.	-	Removed
If a friend of mine developed a mental disorder, I wouldn't be able to help her/him.	Se uma pessoa próxima de mim estivesse com uma perturbação mental, eu não poderia fazer nada para a ajudar.	If someone close to me had a mental disorder, I could not be of any assistance.
The symptom's length is one of the important aspects to determine whether a person has or does not have a mental disorder.	A duração dos sintomas é um dos critérios importantes para o diagnóstico de uma perturbação mental.	The symptom's length is one of the important criteria for the diagnosis of a mental disorder.
Depression is not a true mental disorder.	A depressão não é uma verdadeira perturbação mental.	Depression is not a true mental disorder (unchanged item).
Drug addiction may cause mental disorders.	O consumo de drogas pode causar perturbações mentais.	Drug addiction may cause mental disorders (unchanged item).
Mental disorders affect people's thoughts.	Uma perturbação mental afeta os pensamentos.	Mental disorders affect people's thoughts (unchanged item).
If a friend of mine developed a mental disorder, I would talk to the form teacher or other teacher.	-	Removed.
Doing something enjoyable helps to improve mental health.	Fazer algo que dê prazer contribui para uma boa saúde mental.	Doing something enjoyable contributes to a good mental health.
A person with schizophrenia may see and hear things that nobody else sees and hears.	Uma pessoa com esquizofrenia pode ver e ouvir coisas que mais ninguém vê e ouve.	A person with schizophrenia may see and hear things that nobody else sees and hears (unchanged item).
Talking over problems with someone helps to improve mental health.	Falar sobre os problemas pessoais com alguém próximo contribui para uma boa saúde mental.	Talking over problems with someone close to me contributes to a good mental health.
Highly stressful situations may cause mental disorders.	Situações de grande stress podem causar perturbações mentais.	Highly stressful situations may cause mental disorders (unchanged item).

3. Study 2: Study of the Properties of MHLq-Young Adults Form

3.1. Materials and Methods

3.1.1. Participants

The experimental version of the MHLq-young adults form was administered to a group of 356 participants aged between 18 and 25 years old (M = 21.13; SD = 3.69). Of the young adults, 47% were male, 97.5% were single, and 97.2% were Portuguese. Most participants (88.6%) were students, attending college (n = 214) and other adult training programs in professional schools (n = 89). The non-students participants' (n = 35) educational attainment was predominantly secondary education (n = 30) (see Table 2).

Table 2. Sociodemographic characteristics of the sample.

Sociodemographic Variables	n	Valid %
Gender		
Female	186	53
Male	165	47
Mean age (SD)	21.13	(3.69)
Occupation		
Studying in college/university	214	63.3
Studying in adult training programs	89	26.3
Working	35	10.4
Marital Status		
Single	346	97.5
Married	9	2.5
Nationality		
Portuguese	345	97.2
Other	10	2.8
Working	35	10.4

A total of 159 participants (44.7%) reported knowing someone who had a mental health problem, 160 students (44.9%) stated they did not know anyone with these problems, and 37 (4%) were not aware of anyone with these problems. Regarding the degree of proximity, it was mentioned most often as being friends (n = 48; 30.2%).

3.1.2. Measures

The experimental version of the questionnaire resulting from Study 1 included: (1) a socio-demographic form comprised of questions related to the participants' gender, age, marital status, nationality, residence, academic qualifications, profession/occupation (if they were a student, they indicated the school grade), proximity to people with mental health problems including the nature of the relationship; and (2) 32 items, organized in a 5-point Likert response scale (1 = strongly disagree; 2 = disagree; 3 = neither agree nor disagree; 4 = agree; and 5 = strongly agree).

3.2. Procedures

3.2.1. Data Collection

Data collection followed ethical guidelines with all participants signing an informed consent form. The sociodemographic form and the experimental version of the MHLq-young adults form were self-administered to participants in their educational or work environments. In order to increase the number of non-students, a snowball sampling procedure was implemented.

3.2.2. Analytic Plan

Psychometric properties, i.e., the construct validity and internal consistency of the MHLq-young adults form were evaluated using exploratory factor analysis (principal components analysis, with Varimax rotation) and Cronbach's Alpha. Both analyses were used as complementary procedures for determining the final structure of the instrument [12]. The criteria used for the factor analysis were: (a) item loadings larger or equal to 0.20; and (b) the content of items loading in factors should be compatible with the underlying theoretical content.

Descriptive statistics were used to characterize the participants' mental health literacy levels, and the overall scores (sum of the values of all the items) and scores by factors (sum of the values of the dimension items). Higher values in all dimensions and the total MHLq score corresponded to higher levels of mental health literacy. For that reason, six items had to be reverse-coded.

The relationship between mental health literacy levels and sociodemographic variables (gender and proximity to mental health problems) was also explored, using t-tests for independent samples.

In all hypothesis tests a level of significance of $\alpha = 5\%$ was considered.

The analysis was performed using the statistical analysis program IBM SPSS Statistics® v.22.0 (IBM Inc., Armonk, NY, USA).

3.3. Results

The first exploratory factor analysis, retaining all factors with an eigenvalue higher than 1.0 failed to meet the conceptual organization of the instrument.

Therefore, new exploratory factor analyses, using a fixed number of factor extraction procedures (three factors based on the original version of the MHLq, and four factors based on the conceptual option) were conducted. The four-factor structure was the best solution in terms of explained variance and conceptual item loading.

The final factor structure included: (1) items related to knowledge of mental health problems; (2) items related to erroneous beliefs/stereotypes; (3) items related to first aid skills and help seeking behavior; and (4) items related to self-help strategies. This solution was responsible for 36.99% of the variance. Three items were removed from the questionnaire: one did not load in any of the factors and two did not load in the corresponding conceptual dimension.

Table 3 presents the factorial structure of the MHLq-young adult form including the 29 items that were maintained.

Table 3. Exploratory factor analysis of the MHLq-young adult form item description and factor loadings (final version, 29 items).

MHLq-Young Adult Form Items	Factor 1 Knowledge of Mental Health Problems	Factor 2 Erroneous Beliefs/Stereotypes	Factor 3 First Aid Skills and Help Seeking Behaviour	Factor 4 Self-Help Strategies
25. Mental disorders affect people's thoughts.	0.587			
27. A person with schizophrenia may see and hear things that nobody else sees and hears.	0.580			
24. Drug addiction may cause mental disorders.	0.561			
16. Changes in brain function may lead to the onset of mental disorders.	0.552			0.294
28. Highly stressful situations may cause mental disorders.	0.552			
3. People with schizophrenia usually have delusions (e.g., they may believe they are constantly being followed and observed).	0.516			
12. Alcohol use may cause mental disorders.	0.482			
22. The symptom's length is one of the important criteria for the diagnosis of a mental disorder.	0.464	0.299		
26. Doing something enjoyable contributes to a good mental health.	0.428			0.347
20. One of the symptoms of depression is the loss of interest or pleasure in most things.	0.424	0.308		
23. Depression is not a true mental disorder.	−0.285	−0.274		
10. People with mental disorders belong to low-income families.		−0.707		
15. Only adults have mental disorders.		−0.658		
6. Mental disorders don't affect people's behaviors.		−0.607		
14. The sooner mental disorders are identified and treated, the better.		0.574	0.213	0.248
13. Mental disorders don't affect people's feelings.	−0.232	−0.568		
9. A person with anxiety disorder may panic in situations that she/he fears.	0.349	0.507	0.204	
11. If someone close to me had a mental disorder, I would listen to her/him without judging or criticizing.		0.391		0.350
29. If I had a mental disorder I would seek a psychiatrist's help.			0.745	
17. If someone close to me had a mental disorder, I would encourage her/him to see a psychiatrist.			0.710	
8. If I had a mental disorder I would seek a psychologist's help.			0.661	
4. If I had a mental disorder I would seek my relatives' help.			0.630	

Table 3. Cont.

MHLq-Young Adult Form Items	Factor 1 Knowledge of Mental Health Problems	Factor 2 Erroneous Beliefs/Stereotypes	Factor 3 First Aid Skills and Help Seeking Behaviour	Factor 4 Self-Help Strategies
5. If someone close to me had a mental disorder, I would encourage her/him to look for a psychologist.		0.511	0.516	
2. A person with depression feels very miserable.	**0.227**		0.291	
19. A balanced diet contributes to good mental health.	0.308			**0.634**
1. Physical exercise contributes to good mental health.	0.204			**0.563**
7. Sleeping well contributes to good mental health.	0.203	0.260		**0.541**
21. If someone close to me had a mental disorder, I could not be of any assistance.		−0.220		**−0.488**
18. If I had a mental disorder I would seek friends' help.			0.403	**0.453**
R^2 (%)	10.86	10.32	8.59	7.22

Note: loadings in bold represent items retained for each factor.

Cronbach's Alpha values were good for the total score, ranging from acceptable to questionable for the subscales: Total Score (29 items) α = 0.84; Factor 1, knowledge of mental health problems (11 items) α = 0.74; Factor 2, erroneous beliefs/stereotypes (eight items) α = 0.72; Factor 3, first aid skills and help seeking behavior (six items) α = 0.71; Factor 4, self-help strategies (four items) α = 0.60. Factor 4, which presented the lowest Alpha value, includes only four items. Therefore, the item-total correlation for this subscale was analyzed. Results ranged between 0.29 and 0.49, and the removal of any of the subscale items would result in a decrease in Alpha value.

The total score for the 29 items of the MHLq-young adults form ranged between 29 and 145 (M = 105.27; SD = 7.05). The knowledge of mental health problems factor scores ranged between 11 and 55 (M = 44.50; SD = 4.45). Erroneous beliefs/stereotypes factor scores—six of the eight items were reverse-scored (items 6, 10, 13, 15, 23, and 27)—ranged between 8 and 40 (M = 19.75; SD = 2.92). The first aid skills and help seeking behavior factor ranged between 6 and 30 (M = 24.13; SD = 3.33). The self-help strategies factor scores ranged between 4 and 20 (M = 16.90; SD = 1.90).

Socio-demographic variables (gender and proximity with people presenting with mental disorders) are related to differences in MHLq scores (see Tables 4 and 5). Regarding gender differences, females showed higher scores than males on the MHLq global score and in all dimensions, except for Erroneous beliefs/stereotypes, in which no significant differences were found. Participants who indicated knowing someone with a mental health problem showed higher scores than participants who did not know anyone presenting such problems, on the MHLq total score, knowledge of mental health problems, self-help strategies, and low erroneous beliefs/stereotypes dimension.

Table 4. Gender differences in mental health literacy (MHLq global score and dimensions).

	Gender		
	Male	Female	
Mental health literacy (global score)	(n = 153) Mean (sd)	(n = 174) Mean (sd)	t(325)
	103.93 (7.10)	106.37 (6.89)	−3.15 **
Knowledge of mental health problems	(n = 158) Mean (sd)	(n = 181) Mean (sd)	t(337)
	43.71 (4.44)	45.16 (4.37)	−3.03 **
Erroneous beliefs/stereotypes	(n = 159) Mean (sd)	(n = 181) Mean (sd)	t(338)
	20.03 (3.07)	19.45 (2.75)	1.85
First aid skills and help seeking behavior	(n = 163) Mean (sd)	(n = 182) Mean (sd)	t(343)
	23.63 (3.46)	24.53 (3.20)	−2.52 *
Self-help strategies	(n = 163) Mean (sd)	(n = 182) Mean (sd)	t(343)
	23.63 (3.46)	24.53 (3.20)	−2.52 *

* $p < 0.05$; ** $p < 0.01$.

Table 5. Differences in mental health literacy (MHLq global score and dimensions) based on proximity to people with mental health problems.

	Proximity to People with Mental Health Problems		
	Yes	No	
Mental health literacy (global score)	(n = 149) Mean (sd)	(n = 152) Mean (sd)	t(299)
	106.62 (7.04)	104.34 (6.62)	−2.90 **
Knowledge of mental health problems	(n = 156) Mean (sd)	(n = 155) Mean (sd)	t(309)
	45.81 (4.48)	43.48 (3.98)	−4.85 ***
Erroneous beliefs/stereotypes	(n = 157) Mean (sd)	(n = 152) Mean (sd)	t(307)
	19.99 (2.71)	19.22 (2.80)	−2.46 *
First aid skills and help seeking behavior	(n = 156) Mean (sd)	(n = 158) Mean (sd)	t(312)
	24.17 (3.64)	24.31 (2.95)	0.38
Self-help strategies	(n = 159) Mean (sd)	(n = 160) Mean (sd)	t(317)
	17.28 (1.75)	16.66 (1.97)	−2.98 **

* $p < 0.05$; ** $p < 0.01$; *** $p < 0.001$.

4. Discussion

The likelihood of most individuals developing a mental health problem is high, as demonstrated by the significant increase in the prevalence of mental health problems throughout the lifespan [3,13]. Increasing levels of mental health literacy contributes to the promotion of mental health and may play an important role in early identification and intervention when a psychological/mental health problem develops [2,13].

The present study aimed to adapt and examine the psychometric properties of a brief self-report questionnaire designed to assess mental health literacy in young adults, based on a previous measure developed for young people [11].

The experimental version of the MHLq-young adult form was applied to a sample of 356 participants. Construct validity, assessed by exploratory factor analysis, revealed a four-dimension factorial structure of the MHLq-young adult form, consistent with the multidimensional perspective of the construct of mental health literacy [2]. Internal consistency, assessed with Cronbach's Alpha, showed acceptable to good reliability scores for three of the questionnaire's dimensions and global score. The lower alpha of the Self-help strategies subscale (α = 0.60) could be explained by the scale's low number of items (c.f. [14]). Nevertheless, the item-total correlation of its four items, as well as the fact that item deletion procedures would not result in higher internal consistency scores, supported the decision to keep this subscale in this first version of the instrument. Future research should reassess internal consistency scores of this subscale and, if scores remain low, its revision should be considered.

This study explored the impact of sociodemographic variables on the levels of mental health literacy. Differences were found regarding gender and proximity with someone with a mental health problem. In general, females and participants who reported knowing someone with a mental health problem showed higher levels of mental health literacy, in line with previous research [8,11,15–19].

Future research should expand the study of the psychometric properties of the MHLq-adults form with larger and representative samples of the adult population. The sample of the present study included, mostly, university level students, with a high degree of familiarity with education and elaborated language. The use of a more heterogeneous sample would allow testing the items language appropriateness with lower-educated individuals, as well as to examine Mental Health Literacy levels in the adult population. Furthermore, other analyses should include more sophisticated psychometric analyses, based on Structural Equation Modelling procedures, such as confirmatory factor analysis, and convergent and discriminant validity procedures. The evolution of the Mental Health Literacy construct, already displayed in this instrument through the inclusion of items related to self-help strategies may also be subject to new studies, focusing on the positive MHL, as suggested by recent works (e.g., [20]).

5. Conclusions

The Mental Health Literacy questionnaire-young adults form overcomes several limitations of other MHL assessment instruments, which include an exclusive focus on specific MHL dimensions and/or a restricted number of mental disorders and time-consumption. It does this by providing a short, valid and reliable self-report assessment, based on a comprehensive approach to this construct, including knowledge about mental health problems, erroneous beliefs/stereotypes, first-aid skills and help seeking behavior, and self-help strategies.

Mental health professionals and researchers may use this measure for designing and evaluating mental health literacy promotion programs, and as a screening tool for the identification of intervention needs in the young adult population in different settings, for example in the work environment and in higher education organizations. Since this instrument was developed in the Portuguese language, the use of MHLq-young adult form in other languages should be preceded by its translation, back translation and validation to local culture, and psychometric study.

Author Contributions: P.D. contributed to the design of the experiments, analysis and interpretation of the data, reviewed the literature and wrote the manuscript. L.C. contributed to the conception and design of the research, the design of the experiments, supervised the data collection and interpretation of the data, reviewed the literature and wrote the manuscript. H.A. contributed to data collection and analysis, reviewed the literature, and revised the manuscript. F.P. contributed to the conception and design of the research, reviewed the literature, and revised the manuscript. All authors approved the final version of the document.

Funding: This research was funded by Fundação para a Ciência e a Tecnologia grant number UID/CED /4872/2016.

Acknowledgments: The authors would like to thank the support from Ana Isabel Duarte, Natália Costa, and the participants of the study.

Conflicts of Interest: The authors declare no conflict of interest.

References

1. Jorm, A.; Korten, A.; Jacomb, P.; Christensen, H.; Rodgers, B.; Pollitt, P. "Mental health literacy": A survey of the public's ability to recognise mental disorders and their beliefs about the effectiveness of treatment. *Med. J. Aust.* **1997**, *166*, 182–186. [PubMed]
2. Jorm, A. Mental Health Literacy: Empowering the community to take action for action for better mental health. *Am. Psychol.* **2012**, *67*, 231–243. [CrossRef] [PubMed]
3. World Health Organization. Social Cohesion for Mental Well-Being among Adolescents. Available online: http://www.euro.who.int/__data/assets/pdf_file/0005/84623/E91921.pdf (accessed on 1 March 2018).
4. Schulze, B.; Richter-Werling, M.; Matschinger, H.; Angermeyer, M. Crazy? So what? Effects of a school project on student's attitudes towards people with schizophrenia. *Acta Psychiatr. Scand.* **2003**, *107*, 142–150. [CrossRef] [PubMed]
5. Link, B.; Yang, L.; Phelan, J.; Collin, P. Measuring Mental Illness Stigma. *Schizophrenia Bull* **2004**, *30*, 511–541. [CrossRef]
6. Jorm, A.; Wright, A.; Morgan, A. Beliefs about appropriate first aid for young people with mental disorders: Findings from an Australian national survey of youth and parents. *Early Interv. Psychiatr* **2007**, *1*, 61–70. [CrossRef] [PubMed]
7. Wyn, J.; Cahill, H.; Holdsworth, R.; Rowling, L.; Carson, S. MindMatters, a whole-school approach promoting mental health and wellbeing. *Aust. N. Z. J. Psychiatry* **2000**, *34*, 594–601. [CrossRef] [PubMed]

8. Corrigan, P.; Green, A.; Lundin, R.; Kubiak, M.; Penn, D. Familiarity with and social distance from people who have serious mental illness. *Psychiatr. Serv.* **2001**, *52*, 953–958. [CrossRef] [PubMed]
9. Luty, J.; Fekadu, D.; Umoh, O.; Gallagher, J. Validation of a short instrument to measure stigmatized attitudes towards mental illness. *Psychiatr. Bull* **2006**, *30*, 257–260. [CrossRef]
10. Evans-Lacko, S.; Little, K.; Meltzer, H.; Rose, D.; Rhydderch, D.; Henderson, C.; Thornicroft, G. Development and psychometric properties of the mental health knowledge Schedule. *Can. J. Psychiatry* **2010**, *55*, 440–448. [CrossRef] [PubMed]
11. Campos, L.; Dias, P.; Palha, F.; Duarte, A.; Veiga, E. Development and psychometric properties of a new questionnaire for assessing Mental Health Literacy in young people. *Univ. Psychol.* **2016**, *15*, 61–72. [CrossRef]
12. Janda, L. *Psychological Testing: Theory and Applications*, 1st ed.; Pearson: Massachusetts, MA, USA, 1998; ISBN 0205194346.
13. Jorm, A. Mental health literacy: Public knowledge and beliefs about mental disorders. *Br. J. Psychiatry* **2000**, *177*, 396–401. [CrossRef] [PubMed]
14. Cortina, J. What is Coefficient Alpha? An Examination of Theory and Applications. *J. Appl. Psychol.* **1993**, *78*, 98–104. [CrossRef]
15. Angermeyer, M.; Matschinger, H.; Corrigan, P. Familiarity with mental illness and social distance from people with schizophrenia and major depression: Testing a model using data from a representative population survey. *Schizophr. Res.* **2004**, *69*, 175–182. [CrossRef]
16. Cotton, S.; Wright, A.; Harris, M.; Jorm, A.; McGorry, P. Influence of gender on mental health literacy in young Australians. *Aust. N. Z. J. Psychiatry* **2006**, *40*, 790–796. [CrossRef] [PubMed]
17. Lauber, C.; Ajdacic-Gross, V.; Fritschi, N.; Stulz, N.; Rössler, W. Mental health literacy in an educational elite—An online survey among university students. *BMC Public Health* **2005**, *5*, 1–9. [CrossRef] [PubMed]
18. Mackenzie, C.; Gekoski, W.; Knox, V. Age, gender, and the underutilization of mental health services: The influence of help-seeking attitudes. *Aging Ment. Health* **2006**, *10*, 574–582. [CrossRef] [PubMed]
19. Martínez-Zambrano, F.; García-Morales, E.; García-Franco, M.; Miguel, J.; Villellas, R.; Pascual, G.; Arenas, O.; Ochoa, S. Intervention for reducing stigma: Assessing the influence of gender and knowledge. *World J. Psychiatr.* **2013**, *3*, 18–24. [CrossRef] [PubMed]
20. Bjørnsen, H.; Eilertsen, M.; Ringdal, R.; Espnes, G.; Moksnes, K. Positive mental health literacy: Development and validation of a measure among Norwegian adolescents. *BMC Public Health* **2017**, *17*. [CrossRef] [PubMed]

© 2018 by the authors. Licensee MDPI, Basel, Switzerland. This article is an open access article distributed under the terms and conditions of the Creative Commons Attribution (CC BY) license (http://creativecommons.org/licenses/by/4.0/).

MDPI
St. Alban-Anlage 66
4052 Basel
Switzerland
Tel. +41 61 683 77 34
Fax +41 61 302 89 18
www.mdpi.com

International Journal of Environmental Research and Public Health Editorial Office
E-mail: ijerph@mdpi.com
www.mdpi.com/journal/ijerph

www.ingramcontent.com/pod-product-compliance
Lightning Source LLC
LaVergne TN
LVHW071942080526
838202LV00064B/6655